IT Project Health Checks

IT Project Health Checks

Driving Successful Implementation and Multiples of Business Value

Sanjiv Purba

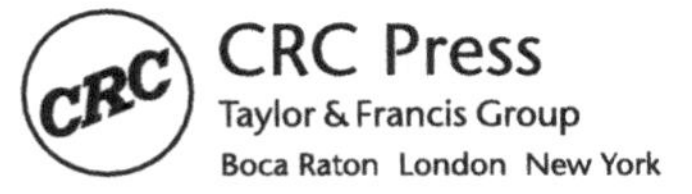

CRC Press is an imprint of the
Taylor & Francis Group, an **informa** business
AN AUERBACH BOOK

First edition published 2022
by CRC Press
6000 Broken Sound Parkway NW, Suite 300, Boca Raton, FL 33487-2742

and by CRC Press
4 Park Square, Milton Park, Abingdon, Oxon, OX14 4RN

CRC Press is an imprint of Taylor & Francis Group, LLC

ISBN: 978-0-367-34288-3 (hbk)
ISBN: 978-1-032-21730-7 (pbk)
ISBN: 978-1-003-26978-6 (ebk)

DOI: 10.1201/9781003269786

Typeset in Garamond
by SPi Technologies India Pvt Ltd (Straive)

For my wife Kulwinder and children Naveen, Neil, Nikhita,
and my mother Inderjit.

Contents

Preface

Project or program health checks provide tremendous value to businesses and pay for themselves by multiples of magnitude in terms of business value. No matter how well a project or program is performing, there are always activities that can provide better value, reduce costs, or introduce more innovation. IT Project or Program Health Checks can help organizations reach their stretch goals and dramatically improve Return on Investment (ROI).

IT Health Checks Pay for Themselves

The value IT Health Checks bring to organizations easily pay for their costs and the efforts of project teams to participate in them. Well executed IT Health Checks can be completed in a timeframe measured in weeks or at most a few months and can be structured to minimize impacts to the initiatives being reviewed. In fact, any involvement of team members can be structured to add value to the initiative itself. An architect should have a documented solution architecture, a BA should have documented business requirements, and a Project Manager should have a documented project plan. A lack of any of these would be a business risk. It's a big red warning flag if too much time is being taken to collect these and other deliverables as they should already be in place. If complaints of distraction rise when these are requested, it might be worth taking a deeper look at what's actually being included on project status reports and what's really happening on the project or program.

As shown in Figure P.1, there are key high-level benefits that make a strong case for having an independent health check performed on an initiative. Chief among these is to drive business value through a careful process of identifying business benefits, building to optimize them, to measure them, monitor them, and to continually improve them.

Organizations can be proactive in driving the following benefits by commissioning an independent project or program health check:

- Multiply Business Value: Find opportunities to drive multiples of business value during Visioning, discovery, development, implementation, and the sustainment phases.

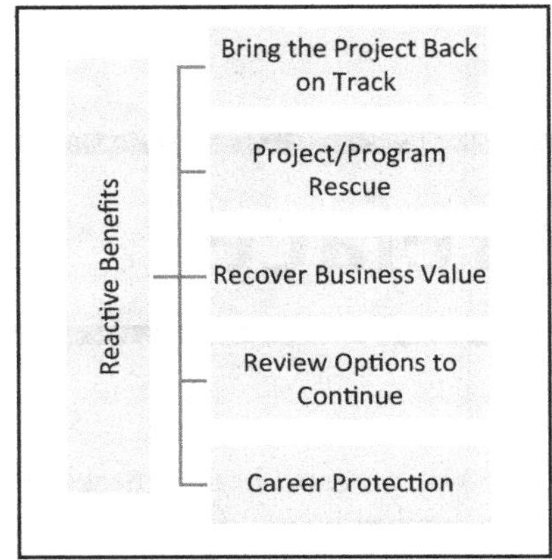

Figure P.1 Proactive and reactive health check benefits.

- Exceed Project Success Metrics: Exceed on the traditional project success metrics of on time, on budget, and full functionality.
- Exceed Expectations: Reach stretch goals in terms of business value that is driven by the initiative, e.g. access to more customers at a cheaper price.
- Career Advancement: Reducing the chances that an initiative is going to fail on any metric while driving higher multiples of business value will drive personal career Measurement. Also, identifying and dealing with issues upfront removes the surprise that shocks members of Steering Committees, Executive Management, and the Board of Directors, and keeps them from having to make the tough people decisions when information is given to them too late in the project process.
- Independent Risk and Quality Assessment: An independent review of the initiative to examine risks and mitigation strategies for each of them, and an examination of the quality of the deliverables.

From a reactive perspective, organizations can use health checks to recover projects from a negative trajectory, explain options for incremental improvement and adjustment, and recover or rescue projects entirely, as follows:

- Bring the Project Back on Track: Independent, experienced-, and fact-based recommendations to bring a project on track for successful delivery before the problems became too acute.
- Project/Program Rescue: Completely rescue a project based on proven project rescue methodologies. Recast the project with metrics that are acceptable to executive management and optimize the ability to deliver on those successfully.
- Recover the Business Value: In addition to delivering the project, focus on the critical Key Performance Indicators (KPIs) and Critical Success Factors (CSFs) that translate into business performance and increased Return on Investment in a measurable way.

- Review Options to Continue: Receive fact- and experienced-based options on how to continue a project that is experiencing challenges and may be on the verge of cancellation.
- Career Protection: Independent advice in a timely manner provides another opinion and opportunity to position facts in front of Executive Management before they are forced to act on a project that is running overbudget, late, missing functionality, and losing business focus. Get in front of the question they will ultimately ask when they hear about problems on the project: "Why didn't we hear about this sooner?"

Defining Project or Program Success

Project or Program success is traditionally thought of as crossing a finish line. The outcome is viewed as binary: the project was successful or the project failed. Even project status is reported in the colors of green, yellow, or red throughout the project lifecycle to show whether the project is moving towards one or the other direction. Sometimes orange pops up when the team does not want to admit the project is in red status. Dark red is sometimes introduced to really impress on the corporate steering committee that a project is not only red but well past it—hurtling toward a terrible outcome.

In reality, project success is not so binary. The outcome is about meeting a list of objectives, the majority of those being related to driving business value. There is an underserved opportunity to multiply business value exponentially by going deeper into how a project or program is performing. This approach extends the traditional view of project governance and management. This moves the business case that often sits in the background during a project delivery lifecycle and puts the business parameters front and center.

IT Project Health Checks drive a renewed emphasis on NOT only driving project success in the traditional sense but also ensuring that specific business drivers are always front and center and not lost in the usual tradeoffs that are done when prioritizing change requests and defects. Defining success for an IT Project or program requires consideration of many factors. Collectively these offer an opportunity to substantially multiply business value related to a program or project—which should be the ultimate objective of every IT investment or expenditure.

Picking an IT Health Check Team

IT Health check teams can be sourced from a variety of places. Each type of source offers pros and cons that are discussed in this book. Figure P.2 shows four sources, as follows:

- Independent External Team: Sourced from an independent experienced vendor or consultant with proven references and a solid track record of completing meaningful project or program health checks.

Figure P.2 Finding the health check team.

- Members of the Project Management Team: A subset of the existing team tasked with applying a heath check methodology from time to time and issuing a health check assessment report. Rules of engagement around transparency and objectivity would need to be established for this group. They will need to feel they can be open about their findings.
- Another Part of the Organization: e.g. PMO or a dedicated group: Another part of the organization tasked with assessing projects that exceed a certain size and complexity.
- Audit Group: A special request to the audit group to review the project or program.

Purpose of This Book

This book offers a proven approach for evaluating IT Projects or Programs in order to determine how they are performing and how the eventual outcome of a project or program initiative is currently trending. The Project or Program Health Checks provide a set of techniques that produce a set of actionable recommendations that can be applied for any combination of the following outcomes:

1. Drive more business and technical value from a program.
2. Set a project or program back on track for successful implementation as defined by executive management.
3. Rescue a program that is heading toward failure.
4. Act as additional assurance or insurance for initiatives that are too important to fail.

A project or program health-check can be completed as a one-time event, before major gates on projects, or on a recurring basis (e.g. monthly). Organizations have benefited from any of these cadences and found that the health check provides actionable information for the project stakeholders and core team members to act.

This book shows how a review can quickly identify whether a project or program needs to be rescued even when the project team is not aware that it is hurtling toward failure. It also provides techniques for driving business value even when a project team believes it's been stretched as much as possible. Here are some other outcomes described in this book:

- Objectively develop a project Health-Check Scorecard that establishes how well a project is doing and the direction it is headed
- Demonstrate how to drive business value from an IT program regardless of how well or badly it is tracking
- Understand a methodology or framework to rescue an IT program that is troubled and heading toward failure
- Provide surgical advice to improve a project's outcome
- Use the many templates and sample deliverables to get a quick start on your own project or program health check

Intended Audience

This book is designed to provide significant value to any member of a project team, program team, stakeholders, sponsors, business users, system integrators, trainers, and IT professionals. The ideas in this book can be used by a subset of a project team to assess their own initiative and build a set of recommendations their team can implement. Departmental leaders can do the same. Another part of an organization can be called to do a quasi-independent health check for another part of the organization. Consulting organizations, both small and large, can use this book to conduct independent health checks for projects and programs in any industry.

Some of the key titles that can benefit from reading and using this book include the following:

- Project Managers
- Program Managers/Directors
- Team Leads
- Quality Assurance (QA) Testers
- Project Advisors

- Consultants
- Systems Analysts
- Change Management Experts
- User Trainer
- Technical Writers
- Data Modelers
- AI Specialists
- Organization Change Management Experts
- Process Mapping Specialists
- VP IT
- CIO
- CDO
- CMO
- COO
- CEO
- CFO
- VP HR
- CHRO
- Business Owners
- Business Stakeholders
- Business Leaders
- Business Analysts

Organization of the Book

This book has four (4) major sections and appendices as shown in Figure P.3. Readers should read the chapters in sequence, unless they are looking for specific templates or other information to quickly analyze what they are observing on initiatives being evaluated.

The project or program health check assessment provides a view into how a project is performing. If things are going well, there may be an opportunity to improve on one of the levers – cost, timeline, quality, more requirements or provide more business value. If assessments are pointing to a difficult situation, then it must be determined whether to make small incremental adjustments to bring the project back on track or to undertake a full project rescue intervention.

Business value is the ultimate goal of any program. There are several standard areas that can drive business value and these can be planned from the start, monitored in requirements gathering, development, and testing activities and then optimized in post-implementation or sustainment phases.

The four sections of this book describe opportunities to drive project success and increase business value by a multiple factor of magnitude. They are described in more detail below.

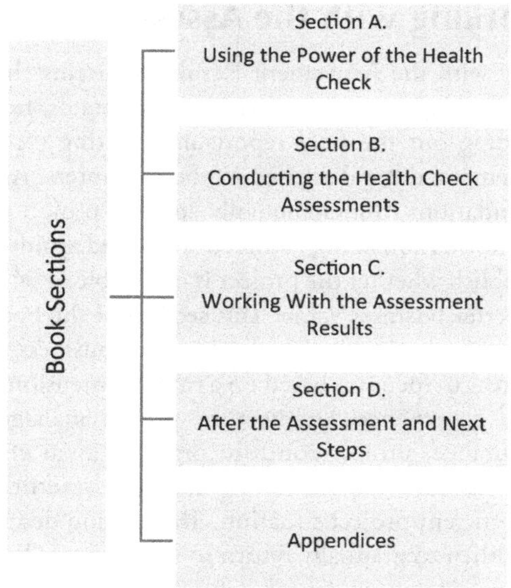

Figure P.3 Book breakdown by sections.

Section A: Using the Power of the Health Check

"Section A: Using the Power of the Health Check" contains chapters that describe a Health Check Methodology and the tools and templates needed to do a comprehensive health check on a project or program. The process that organizations use to select a team to conduct a health check is discussed in this section, along with how to develop a Health Check Project Charter with a clear scope and mandate based on asking the right questions from the start. Recognizing project warning signs are included in these chapters. There are several approaches to conducting project health checks. This section defines each type of health check and provides parameters on when and how to use each of them.

Section B: Conducting the Health Check Assessments

"Section B: Conducting the Health Check Assessments" contains chapters that describe how to complete the discovery activities to extract information from deliverables, documentation, and through user interviews. This involves understanding the business case, project charter, deadlines, funding, and the organization's culture. The expectations of stakeholders are gathered in interviews using questionnaires that are customized for the initiative. Their answers are compared to the documentation and expectations of the implementation team. The book provides step-by-step information on where to look and how to summarize key information.

Section C: Working with the Assessment Results

"Section C: Working with the Assessment Results" contains chapters to build and socialize the health check assessment report in several states, from interim to final. Techniques for building out the final report and crafting recommendations that are likely to be implemented are discussed in these chapters. Also covered are how to provide recommendations to incrementally adjust a project or to conduct a full project rescue. The information being gathered is assessed against a list of criteria the book provides to establish whether the project is in trouble or where there are opportunities to provide better business value. This section of the book describes how to mount a successful project rescue or how to improve business value. This involves identifying the key areas to focus on based on a multi-dimensional evaluation matrix that includes project governance, architecture, project management tools, methodology, quality assurance, project controls, organizational change management, security, and other areas. Each dimension is described in terms of core values that can be matched to a current project situation. This section describes how to mount the intervention and then to gradually return to a continual "happy" project state.

Section D: After the Assessment and Next Steps

"Section D: After the Assessment and Next Steps" contains chapters to bring all the information presented in the book together in one place. There are also selected case studies of projects and programs that commissioned health checks and how these helped their outcomes. Recommendations for driving business value in the sustainment phase after a project is implemented are also included in this section.

Acknowledgements (in Alphabetical Order)

I would like to acknowledge the support or encouragement I've received over the years from the following accomplished individuals (in Alphabetical Order) in my career. There are also others, too numerous to list:

Abhishek Sinha
Alex Taub
Alf Cowling
Alice Chan
Andrew Hilton
Andi Woolman
Atanu Basu
Atul Gera
Bailey Lafarga
Benjie Thomas
Cathy Tait
Charlie Atkinson
Chris Woodill
Claudette Taylor
Credit Mills Family
David Evans
David Mahr
David Shapendonk
Debbie (Gillis) Lewis
Debbie Manchur
Doug Woolridge
Duke Butler
Elizabeth Mahr
Estrella Frias
Francis Hartman
Gayemarie Brown
George Colwell
Glen Pleshko
Gord Shields
Graham Smith
Harpal Singh
Helga AuYeung
Hervans Kaur
Ian Tait
Imad Jawadi
Irene Zaguskin
Joe Evers
Jeff Rosin
Jeff Watts
Johannes Tekle
John Leggett
John Macdonald
John Wyzalek
Judy Dinn
Kapil Goyal
Kate Hill
Kathleen Brown
Kerris Hougardy
Kim Chernecki
Lumina Purandare
Lynn Reynolds
Mandeep Dhillon

Maria Churchill
Mario Perez
Mary Parniak
Michael Klubal
Michelle Patel
Mihai Strusievici
Mike Boyd
Mike Flynn
Morgan Storie
Nabarun Chaudhuri
Narinder Dhillon
Natalie Mohammed
Naveen Kumar
Norman Angus
Pamela Bourne-Chase
Paul Saunders
Peter Baxter
Peter Mastromarini
Prashanth Fernando
Rani Turna
Raj Joshi
Richard A. O'Hanley
Rick Doull
Richard Gelfond
Rob Rowe
Robert Lei
Robin McNeil
Rodney Evely
Ruth Tan
Samprati Vishal
Shawn Rivers
Sarah Hitchcock
Selim El Raheb
Silvy Picianno
Sridhar Kotari
Srinivas Padmanabharao
Stephanie Terrill
Stephen Taylor
Brad Scrivner
Sue Banting
Susan Certoma
Tarun Gulati
Tina Manthorne Ramsden
Tom Beckerman
Tomer Meldung
Tony Small
Yvon Audette

Interviewed for Questionnaire

Steve Litwin
Charlie Wade
Dr. Domenico Lepore
Karnan Ariaratnam
Ludmila Pirogova
Mary Whittle
Marc-André Renaud
Robert Wong
Stephen Worrall
Veronica Noronha
Debbie (Gillis) Lewis

Author

Sanjiv Purba is an award winning, hands-on transformational Executive and board member with over 25 years of progressive Technology and Business experience within Industry and Consulting Organizations. He has built a long list of enthusiastic client references by delivering large complex business transformational projects as a CIO, Interim CIO, COO, or as a senior advisor. Several large programs he has managed have won client awards and have been identified as examples of best practices by SAP, IBM, and Oracle.

Sanjiv works with C-Suite & Corporate Boards of mid-to-large sized companies who want to digitally transform their business and surgically leverage IT solutions such as ERP, CRM, HRIS & Data Analytics to maximize share price through effective implementation and ongoing operations. A key aspect of this has been to conduct health checks to identify opportunities to make improvements from the current state of their programs by dramatically increasing business value. In other instances, project rescues or other project management interventions were successfully applied to bring programs back on track towards successful implementation.

The author has held senior roles at a variety of organizations including Deloitte, KPMG, IBM, Microsoft, and IMAX. In his most recent position, Sanjiv runs the digital transformation consulting practices at Prodigy Labs, a division of Prodigy Ventures Inc., based in Toronto, Ontario, Canada.

Sanjiv has written more than 19 books and hundreds of articles for such publications as *The Toronto Star* and *The Globe & Mail.*

USING THE POWER OF THE HEALTH CHECK

Chapter 1

Drive Business Value Through Project Health Checks

Are you worried about your business or IT projects or programs? Actually, you should be. This feeling would not be unique to you at all. In fact, business and technical stakeholders across all industries have asked this question, at least to themselves or to a small group of colleagues, at many points during a project lifecycle. Too often, there is no answer until someone puts a dark red status on a project management report and starts warning of outright project failure.

In other cases, a CFO is asked two years after a project goes live if the investment was driving business value and by how much. The latter question stumps many executives. Some Boards and CEOs will even ask if more business value could have been drawn from the investment and why it was not. At a minimum they are asking for clear accounting on how much actual business value the project or program delivered. Some questions that come up:

- Are we getting the most value from our IT investments?
- Is the project going to be implemented successfully?
- Is the organization ready for the implementation?
- Could we be doing anything better?
- Can you just give us an independent opinion on how we are doing, what we should do better, and whether we are going to be successful?
- What specific business value are we going to get? How can we measure it?

DOI: 10.1201/9781003269786-2

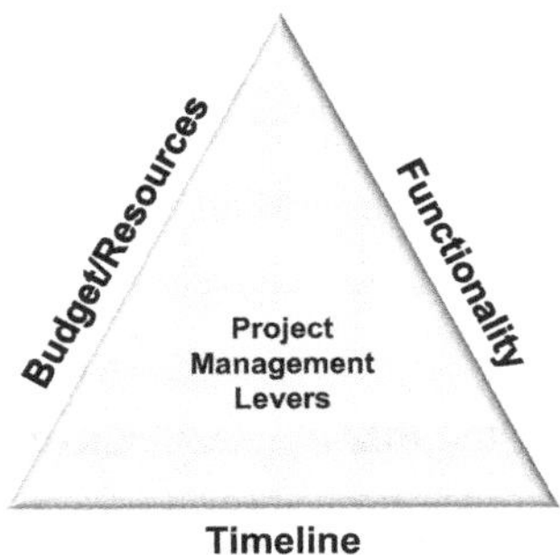

Figure 1.1 Project management levers triangle.

An IT project or program health check is a proven tool for answering these questions, and generally provides a multiple of business value from its findings. They are a valuable tool that offers program or project advice that can be independent and value-added to significantly enhance the benefits coming out of an initiative. The value from a one-month health check can pay for itself by 10x or more within the first quarter after an initiative goes live into production.

Multiple studies from organizations like IBM, Accenture, KPMG, and The Gartner Group show that IT projects and programs have a high likelihood of failure. This can be measured in terms of missing functionality, implementing later than planned, or going over budget. Figure 1.1 shows the classic project management levers that can be used to manage project outcomes.

Common Reasons for Project or Program Failure

A common theme among surveys that are completed year after year shows a majority of projects fail to meet at least one of these metrics. Here are some conclusions drawn from analyzing easy to find current surveys on the state of project delivery that can be located through a quick search of the web:

- A KPMG survey revealed that 70% of all organizations have suffered at least one **initiative failure** in the prior 12 months. This is consistent across industries and different core technologies
- Only **a third** of all initiatives were successfully completed on time and on budget in a given year.
- An IBM survey of executives reported **only 40%** of initiatives met schedule, budget, and quality goals.

Beyond project failure, a horrible outcome in itself, the very existence of an organization can sometimes be put at risk. This could be due to the cost of the

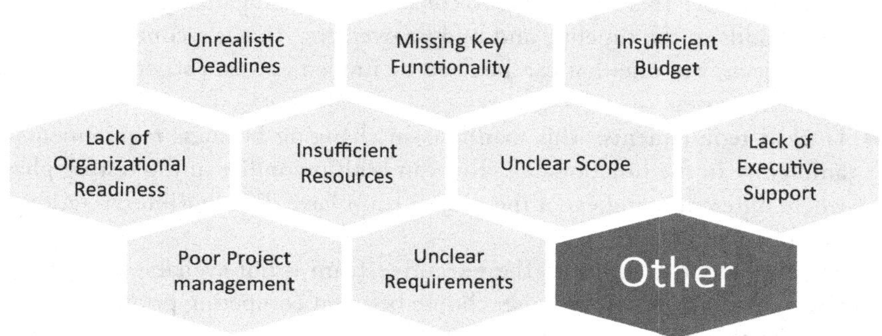

Figure 1.2 Common reasons for project failure.

initiative that needs to be written off in the periods specified by accounting principles. For public companies, this hits the bottom line and can have massive implications on stock price. Imagine showing a $15 million write-down in a single quarter. Not only was the money lost, but the write down could bring management abilities into question in public view. In other cases, the project failure means the company cannot deal with competitors, meet regulatory requirements, or replace the systems that drove the need for the project in the first place.

Best practices, surveys, and project experience reveal some of the more common reasons for project failure as shown in Figure 1.2 and explained further here. This is not an exhaustive list but it brings out some of the more common items that become very easy to spot in a health check review of a project.

- Unrealistic Deadlines: If the deadlines are impossible to meet, regardless of the resources or compromises made by the business, the initiative's success Is an impossibility. In such a situation the morale of the team will make failure a self-fulfilling event.
- Missing functionality: Some of the core functionality from the "must-have" list identified by the business is missing in the final product, or not behaving as required.
- Insufficient Resources: This can be due to a lack of qualified stakeholders, subject matter expects, or technical resources. Key resources could also be split between day jobs and working on the project initiative.
- Insufficient Budget: Some organizations take a budget that is recommended for an initiative and only approve a subset of it for any number of reasons. In other cases, estimates used to build the budget were flawed to begin with, or there was not enough contingency to deal with unexpected changes or events. An example of this could be a project where more testing was required than orginally planned, requiring more defect fix and retest cycles than originally planned as well.

- Unclear scope: This contributes to constantly changing business requirements which adds to the timeline and budget overages. This is a common problem on projects, but one that can be fixed by implementing a strict change management process.
- Unclear requirements: This manifests in changing business requirements or ambiguity in the functionality. This can lead to conflict in the testing phases where different members of the project team have different interpretations of the functionality.
- Lack of executive support: The Executive Team is not available or willing to make the difficult compromise, choose between competing priorities, or allocate the resources the initiative requires to succeed.
- Poor project management: Lack of following project management best practices, such as applying the project delivery methodology properly.
- Lack of organizational readiness: The organization is not ready or trained to work on the new system, even if it met specifications.
- Other: There are many other potential reasons for project failure, such as corporate culture, destructive project politices, regulatory changes, and others that will be examined in later chapters of this book in the context of identifying red/warning flags and ultimately making meaningful recommendations during a project health check.

Driving Business Value

Driving business value is a key objective of most, arguably all, IT-based projects and programs. The challenge is that between project initiation and implementation, there is usually so much complexity that some important factors do not remain in the forefront. On many corporate-wide projects, the goal starts out with a lot of business benefits in mind and then eventually becomes a tactical exercise that involves just getting the solutions implemented into production in any shape or form that looks half decent. This tends to be true regardless of the project delivery methodology (e.g. waterfall, agile, pure agile, hybrid) that is being used. At some point a large budget was identified and an approval was initiated to justify some level of expenditure based on benefits and perceived value. Over a period of time, and with comprises needed to meet the Project Management Triangle shown in Figure 1.1. A simplified project delivery lifecycle is shown in Figure 1.3. This combines elements of agile and waterfall approaches and is not atypical of real-world examples.

Figure 1.3 shows that identification of opportunities to increase shareholder and business value is included in a business case and or project charter. These are translated into business requirements and then ultimately test scenarios and test use cases

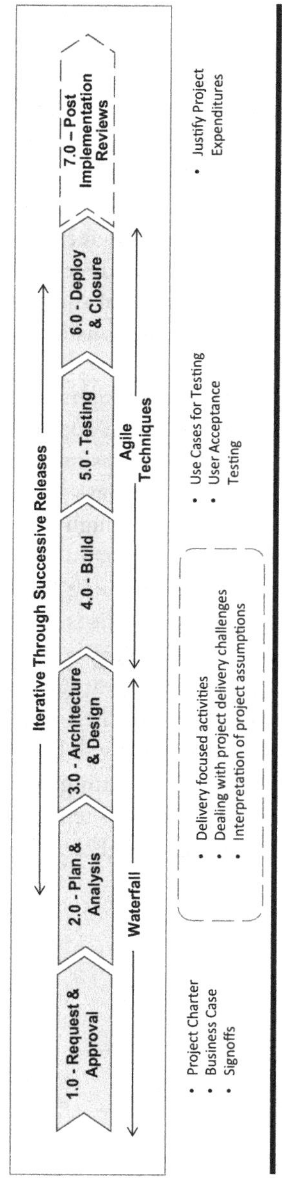

Figure 1.3 Business & shareholder value analysis.

that are executed in the User Acceptance Testing phase. The challenge is that in many real-world projects, the direct tie to the business value defined in the Project Charter begins to get muddled in the "Design" and "Build" phases. This omission is not purposeful—it happens through what can be described as a "thousand" little cuts or changes. For example, when selecting a technology architecture, the selection criteria may not cover every business value lever and so compromises are made. Later in the lifecycle, when the solution is being tested, defects are raised and classified with different types of urgency: generally, critical, high, medium, and low. Some of these may not be completed before going live because the cost of continuing the project might be unsustainable. Say the project is burning around $1,000,000 a month in costs, and the functionality delivered from a defect provides $1,000 of profit in a month. At some point, the decision will be made to go live to save project development costs, but at the expense of some pieces of the original business case. Each of these decisions begins to modify the original business case and how value can be measured.

IT projects and programs, because of their alignment with business outcomes are complex to structure, manage, and deliver. What appears to be a good direction early in the project can have unforeseen implications as more information is uncovered. In fact, a major warning flag is when a team is always feeling confident that everything is under control without at least once going through a feeling of panic. This overconfidence suggests the team does not fully understand the complexity of the initiative. This will be revisited in the "Red or other warning flags" chapter. Figure 1.4 shows the general tendency between the optimism at the start of the initiative and the focus between business value and getting the technology solution working.

At the start of an initiative, no scope will appear too small and the project team will be focused on delivering tremendous value to the business and enabling substantial functionality. The numbers in the business case will back it up, and expenditures will generally have an optimistic viewpoint. The contingency is generally calculated on a best case scenario as well, however, most observers tend to cut that in half, for example, at the start of a project, which makes it even tighter. They are feeling very optimistic

Figure 1.4 Subset of focus areas over time.

at that point. A board member once remarked: "I've never seen a three year business case that I didn't like!". The original business case is generally approved using these optimistic and highly business focused metrics. As time proceeds, the focus shifts to getting the technology and configurations working properly. The inevitable defects that arise in software development and API integration will pull resources away from building new functionality. This is where the tradeoffs of project timeline, resources, and functionality then come into play, and the emphasis shifts to getting something of value implemented. If this is done incorrectly, business value is traded off inefficiently for something that is simply working in production without providing optimal business value (e.g. requiring too many manual checkpoints). A proper assessment would be to follow a critical path that provides maximum value, while limiting expenditures or having expenditures that decrease over time. A lack of a defined critical path is also a major warning flag in assessing a project or program.

Other project phases and events will only add to these emerging tradeoffs. Testing is then generally allocated tight timeframes to make up for other slippages in the project plan. While testing should not be a contingency bucket, in practice, the pressures of going live will, despite people's best intentions, put pressure on the System Integration Testing (SIT) and User Acceptance Testing (UAT) work effort. This forces the team to make compromises and often allocate priorities to defects and issues that push deadlines out into a future phase. At this point in time, the focus generally becomes going live with minimal user training and working. Minimal is not reasonable and is usually a mistake. Reviewing the project plan, it's important to ask to see "contingency" at various points of possible resource contention to avoid the situation of going minimalistic in terms of functionality or even below that threshold.

Sometimes after going live, and after the new systems are running in production for a period of time, the question of return on investment (ROI) for the initiative's expenditures will start to be revisited by the executive team. The stakeholders and Chief Financial Officer (CFO) level officials will be asked questions similar to the following:

- What value did we get from our IT initiative?
- Did we drive as much business value as we could?
- Specifically, how much business value and where did we get this?
- What business value can we expect into the future?
- Why are so many change requests still coming through, even though the project is live?

About two years after going live appears to be a sweet spot for these questions to arise.

Independent health checks can objectively provide an ongoing assessment of whether the project is adhering to the original principles of the business value it was intended to deliver and how to make adjustments to make this happen.

Defining Project Success

Projects are often evaluated in Boolean terms, on whether they were delivered successfully or not? Did the project fail? The reality of the answer is more complex than this simple question would suggest. Follow-up questions would be: How successful was the project? Did the team reach high enough? Were business benefits delivered? How effective was the ROI? How do we measure the business benefits?

Success and failure are opposites in meaning and a continuum of states. A failed project is not a successful project. It follows then that a successful project should not be a failed project. However, defining project success is more complex and specific to the organization and what is acceptable to management.

Figure 1.5 shows a number of outcomes that could be considered successful if management agrees. Example 1 in the figure shows a defined timeline, resources ($ and people), and a set scope/functionality. In this project, all three metrics were met or exceeded, as follows:

- The project was delivered at budget or under;
- The project was implemented on or earlier than the defined implementation date;
- The project was delivered or exceeded the desired scope and functionality. This also assumes that any additional functionality was approved by the Steering Committee.

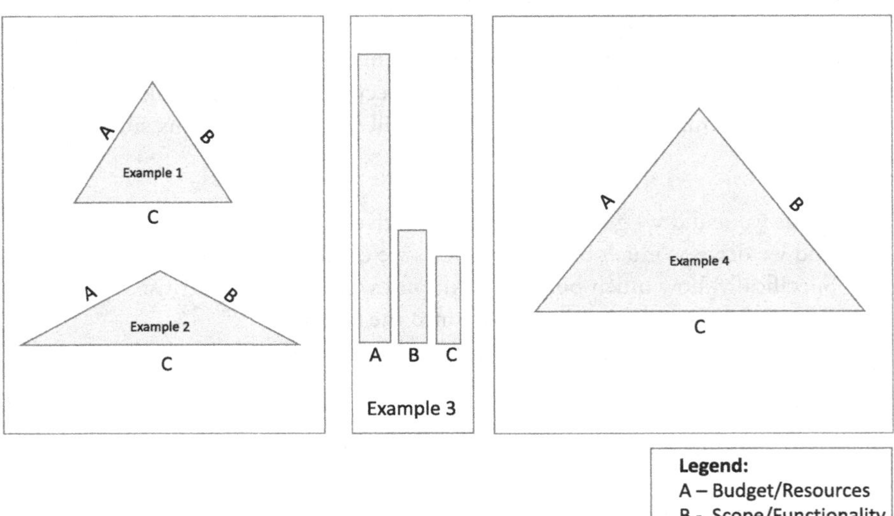

Figure 1.5 Project outcomes.

Example 2 shows what could very well be a real-world example. Based on the original specifications for budget/resources-scope-timeline, the project management team and the Steering Committee needed to make tradeoffs and made adjustments that were acceptable to them, as follows:

- The project's budget and timeline were increased to deliver a scope that was mandatory
- Additional resources were added to the project team to meet the scope
- The additional budget and timeline were acceptable to project governance to meet the desired functionality.

In Example 3 in Figure 1.5, we see that the project definition clearly missed some mandatory requirements. The project needed to be implemented in a much tighter timeline. This meant that the project budget needed to be increased dramatically, while the scope needed to be reduced to a minimum viable product level (MVP) to meet the desired timeline. An example of this might be a regulatory requirement that must be met for business to continue. This situation, while not ideal might be acceptable to the Steering Committee. In fact, this could be considered wildly successful if the project was able to meet regulatory requirements that could impact the business—even though a reduced set of business functionality (perhaps some manual processes remain) was implemented.

In Example 4, we see that the project definition was understated on all three dimensions. The project needed a higher budget, more time, and a bigger scope to be viable. This project would only be acceptance if the Steering Committee approved the changes.

Example 1 in Figure 1.5 is the ideal situation and the one we think of when talking about project success most of the time. A Project Charter and business case were approved that set aside a budget, timeline and scope. Delivery met all the criteria, so was generally deemed successful (more on this later in this book because this may not be true). The other examples could be considered wildly unsuccessful or failures, or project successes depending on the approvals and expectations of the Steering Committee, Executive Management, and the Board of Directors.

Independent IT project or program health checks are particularly useful in helping organizations define project success and understand the nature of reasonable project outcomes. Examples 2, 3, 4, and other variations of these will have a very different management response if they come as a total surprise out of the blue. In fact, the closer we get to the implementation date, the higher the probability that the project will be deemed unsuccessful if there are any deviances to the project requirements. Consider the common scenario of having the Project Manager (PM) going to the steerco a month before the project was scheduled to launch and informing them that the project is going to be well over budget, not deliver what was initially scoped, and/or that the delivery timeline is shifting again. Without better justification, more lead time to evaluate and select a course of action acceptable to the

Steering Committee, abrupt messaging like this will usually not be well received and can result in project cancellation. This situation can also result in dramatic career impacts. Many executives have been let go from their positions due to late identification of problems on important IT initiatives.

Driving Multiples of Business Value

Getting 10x or some other multiple of business benefits and value is an admirable objective. One of the ways to accomplish this in the confines of IT programs and projects is to aggressively drive business value which in turn drives shareholder value. Figure 1.6 enhances the traditional view of what a successful project is measured by—namely, timeline-budget-scope—and adds several very important factors that should be considered and evaluated when determining if a project is successful. As the figure shows, while the usual discussion is around project success or failure, we need to get more precise and drive the business or shareholder value. These include more levers than the traditional view, and to be met, must be in consideration throughout the project lifecycle—from the initiation phases to post implementation support. Figure 1.6 components are discussed in more detail in the following sections.

Successful Implementation

This is really table-stakes in terms of a desired project outcome. This is typically defined as being: on or before the approved timeline, on or below budget (with approved contingency), and with the approved scope.

Figure 1.6 Driving business and shareholder value phases.

Sustainability

In terms of Return on Investment (ROI) and potential cost over-runs, this phase is one of the most significant. It's commonly believed that the project delivery activities are the most expensive. But consider the situation in terms of timeline. The project lifecycle is measured in months or years and the project team size is a subset of the organization. After implementation, the systems are going to be used for ten or more years. This could even be for many decades. The system may also be integrated with other systems and even in situations where the organization is moving to a new platform, the system will still be used for conversion purposes. Instead of impacting a subset of the organization, in the post implementation period, the system will impact the organization as a whole, and even third parties that work with the organization (e.g. supply chain vendors). Additional change requests, data requests, reporting, defect fixes, and user training are all ongoing. And key to our discussion, the sustainability phase is where the organization begins to receive business benefits.

Business Process and Organizational Improvements

Digital transformation drives improvements in business process to improve service to customers and stakeholders. The health check should inspect how the program deliverables are going to improve both of these areas. Business processes should trend toward more "happy path" scenarios that have greater automation and less exception handling or manual workarounds. They should also demonstrate greater service to the end client, be they internal or external. Organizational changes should demonstrate increased productivity, higher learning, more capabilities and a robust environment to support changing worker needs. Future needs are trending toward a workforce that can be inhouse or remote. Remote workers can increasingly mean working from anywhere in the world. This adds complexity to maintaining workplace standards, culture, and enforcement that will need to be addressed by most organizations going forward.

Return On Investment (ROI) Improvements

Ongoing, independent health checks can be used to review status of the project and ensure that the business and shareholder value considerations are not being de-emphasized or forgotten by the project team and steering committee (s) over time. Return on Investment (ROI) is a good method for evaluating the benefits of an IT expenditure. This should include both direct benefits and costs as well as indirect ones. The health check should look for how ROI is going to be measured, how the information is going to be captured, how it is interpreted, and how it is reported.

A challenge in working with ROI is to establish a baseline for measurements. This considers what the situation would be without the impact of the IT program or project. Another challenge is to establish specifically what to measure. An absence of these, or an insufficient identification of these should be escalated to a Steering Committee for immediate resolution.

Critical Success Factors (CSFs) and Key Performance Indictors (KPIs)

Critical Success Factors and Key Performance Indicators can be used as part of a health check to establish how well a project is doing in terms of successful delivery. They are a good approach to abstract the complexity into a manageable bucket of items that are easier to communicate and track. Based on experience, there is an optimum range of specific CSFs and KPIs, that tend to be between 8 and 12 for each group, which should be identified as part of the Project Initiation activities to explain why a project is being proposed. As shown in Figure 1.7, the same set of CSF and KPI details should be revisited at each of the phases shown in the figure.

It may seem that more CSFs and KPIs would be better at driving business value. In fact, too many of either group become impossible to manage. The idea is that the program cannot go live without meeting the CSF's and the KPI baseline. If the health check cannot identify these during the review, an escalation on this item needs to be done to the Steering Committee.

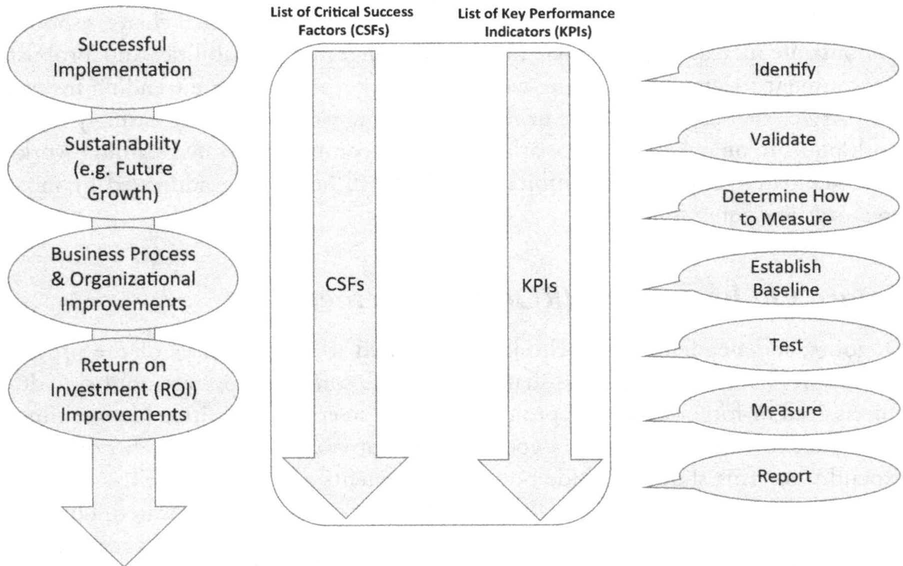

Figure 1.7 Critical success factors (s) and key performance indicators (s).

What Is a Project or Program Health Check?

So we go back to the basic question that was posed at the start of the chapter. How well is your project doing? Maybe the project is part of a larger program with different deadlines and impacting different parts of the business. Members of the project team are saying one thing, vendors are saying another, and the governance team yet another. There are multiple methodologies and technologies incorporated in the solution, and adherence to standards is not consistent due to all the different team members and potentially vendors involved in the core team. Questions are being asked of the core project team and project management which usually boil down to some variation of the following:

- Is the budget being spent delivering the functionality equivalent to the spend?
- Are we on track for successful implementation?
- Do we have a definition of success by the Steering Committee Level?
- When is the solution going to be implemented so that we can train the users on time?
- When will the solution be ready for testing? For Implementation?
- Did we make the right choices along the way?
- Are we getting good value for the investment?
- How are we tracking against best practices in terms of project deliverables?
- How good are the project deliverables?
- Will we be able to pass an independent project audit?
- What are the project risks? Are they mitigated?
- How is the project team going to deal with any items that are being postponed?

This is where project health checks can be instrumental in helping projects be successful and meet management's definition of that term. Health Checks offer an independent viewpoint from the core project team to objectively evaluate how a project or program is performing and what can be done to improve the opportunity for successful implementation. Some other benefits of health checks include the following:

- Optimize value from an initiative
- Independent viewpoint with actionable recommendations
- Cooperative and collaborate—not a report card
- The health check success is based on the success of the project
- Protect executive and other careers

Health Check Process

At a high level, there are five key phases in a Heath Check Process, as shown in Figure 1.8. These can be modified for a specific project, and aligned to an organization's standard project review activities.

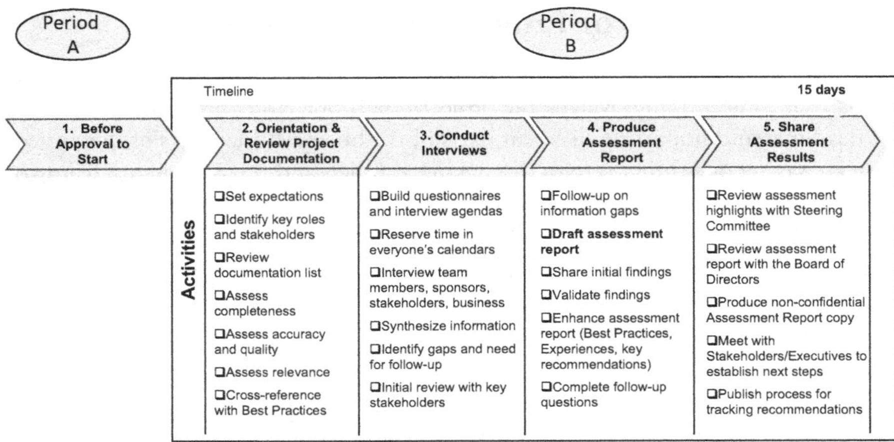

Figure 1.8 Health check phases and activities (high Level).

These five phases are described below:

- Before Approval to Proceed: These are the activities leading up to signing an agreement to do the health check. This generally involves some business/technology sponsors from the initiative, and members of the IT Health Check team. These activities occur in Period A. Period B covers all the specific health check activities once a written agreement has been reached. A Period C will be introduced later in this book and discussed at length within the "Roles & Responsibilities Needed for an Effective Assessment" chapter.
- Orientation and Review Project Documentation: Activities in this phase involve bringing the Health Check team together with the project/program stakeholders and executive management to establish common expectations, identify resources that are involved in the health check to provide information and to answer questions. Documentation is categorized and reviewed by the Health Check Team. Figure 1.9 shows an example of a list of objectives that should be confirmed with this core team to ensure that they understand why their time is being used in this initiative. The output of this phase is an updated project schedule.
- Conduct Interviews: Detailed interview questionnaires are created using best practices and the results of the documentation review. The project executive should communicate to all the project stakeholders that their involvement in upcoming interviews is mandatory. The interviews are conducted and findings are documented. The output of this phase consists of detailed minutes of interviews and correlation with best practices.
- Produce Assessment Report: Initial reports are created and reviewed with stakeholders and iteratively enhanced. Best practices are also incorporated into the report to ensure that recommendations are produced that are both specific to the

Specific Objectives of the Health Check Review for Company SmartCorp

1. Determine the status of the ERP and CRM project using a Health Check evaluation framework;
2. Determine the feasibility of an April 30, 20xx implementation deadline;
3. Provide recommendations to meet the stated project KPIs;
4. Provide recommendations to meet the stated corporate CSFs;

Figure 1.9 Health check specific objectives.

organization, but validated by mainstream activities. The output from this phase includes a draft assessment report and a list of actionable recommendations.

- Share Assessment Results: A full report and executive summary is created and shared with the Steering Committee. Depending on the size and impact of the organization, the health check team may also present findings to the Board of Directors. The output from this phase includes the final report, executive summary, and a confidential report.

Sample of an Executive Level Dashboard

Figure 1.10 shows a sample Executive Level dashboard of a health Check review. This board shows the result of a health check that focused on specific dimensions as shown in the figure. The intent of the presentation is to show at a glance the status of the project. Notice that this version does not rely on the colors of red, yellow, or

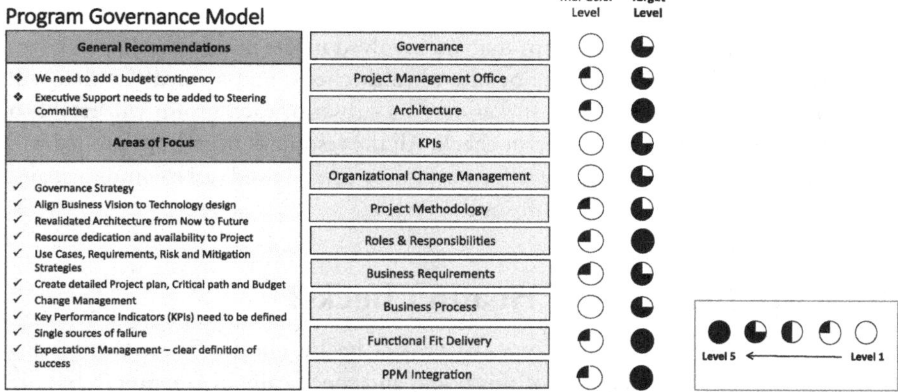

Figure 1.10 Sample health check dashboard.

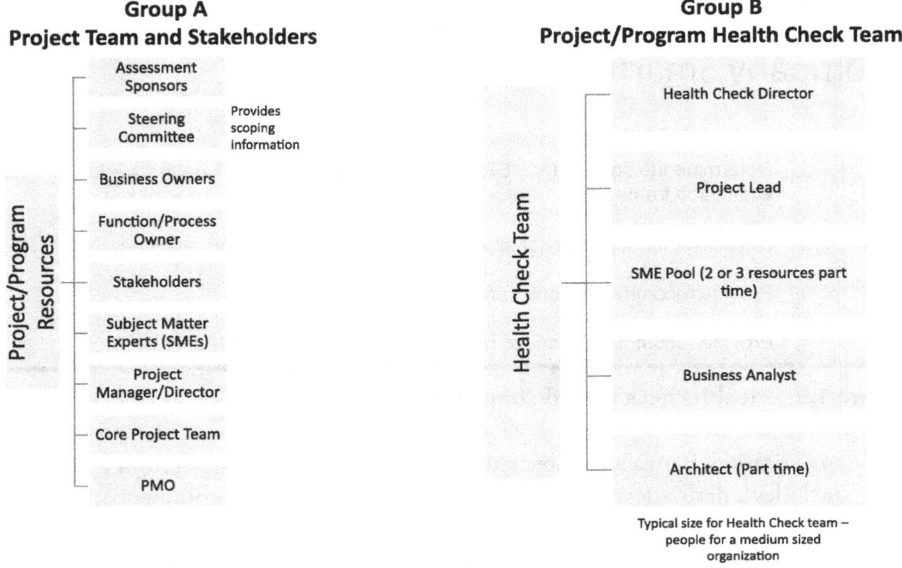

Figure 1.11 Health check participants.

green. This is deliberate as the intention is to focus the audience, usually the Steering Committee or executive stakeholders about specific dimensions. Also notice that there are two columns in the assessment. The first column is current state. The second column is the desired state.

The circles allow the information to be communicated readily. An empty circle means there is a really big issue in the initiative that requires remediation immediately. Completely filled in circles mean things are going well in that dimension.

Who Conducts the Health Check Process?

Figure 1.11 shows two main groups that are involved in the health check. As shown previously, there are two main periods in a health check, and a third (C) that will be introduced later in this book. In Period A, a subset of each group will establish the scope and objectives of the health check. All the resources from both groups will be involved in Period B to supply information, be interviewed, assess findings, and implement the recommendations from the review.

What Are the Types of Health Checks?

Figure 1.12 shows the common types of project health checks. These will be discussed at length in later chapters of this book, and specifically in Chapter 2, but are introduced below:

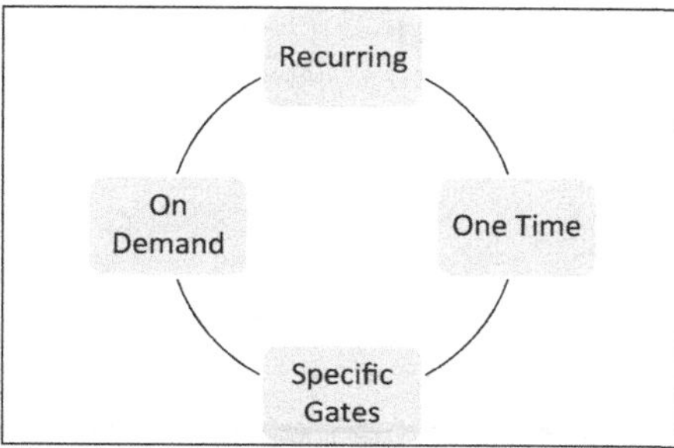

Figure 1.12 Types of project health checks.

One Time

Health checks can be commissioned to run once for any of the following reasons:

- The Executive Team does not know how the project is performing
- The Executive Team wants another opinion
- The Executive Team feels that adjustments need to be made to get the project back on track
- The initiative (s) are too important to fail
- Too many metrics are being missed—the project may be in trouble
- Need a Project Rescue

Specific Gates

The project health check can be commissioned to run at critical gates. They can be viewed as a final gate keeper to ensure that key metrics and deliverables are being met. Some of the key dates to consider are the following:

- Focus on phase entry/exit criteria
- Phase gate report is generated at the end of the review
- Work program is refreshed after each progress deliverable depending on previous period observations.

On Demand

A project executive team might keep a health check team on standby and have them complete a health check on demand. An example of this is to do a business readiness review prior to signing off on a Go/No Go decision in conjunction with an implementation. A health check may also be requested by a Board of Directors to help them get an independent perspective on the status of an important initiative.

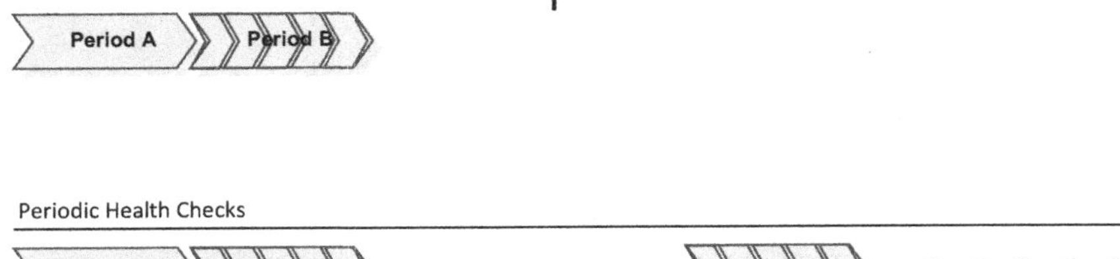

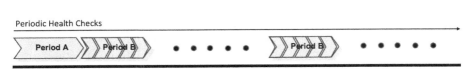

Figure 1.13 Recurring health checks.

Recurring

Some organizations commission recurring independent health checks to drive specific benefits. These can be monthly, bimonthly, and sometimes quarterly. Figure 1.12 shows that in a recurring health check, the initial effort of setting up pays dividends in subsequent sessions (Figure 1.13).

Closing Perspective

Despite attempts at implementing different types of project delivery and management methodologies, the complexity of IT programs makes project failure a too common experience for too many organizations. Furthermore, emerging technologies are always impacting and modifying best practices. Figure 1.14 shows a variety

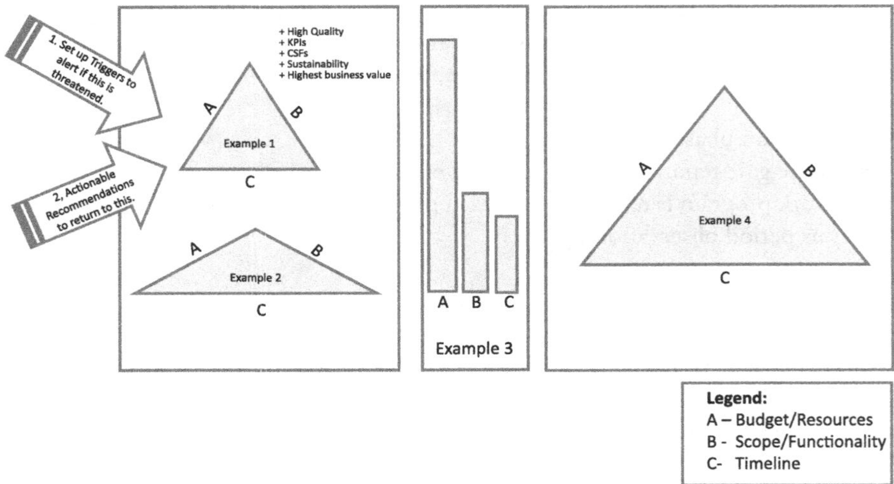

Figure 1.14 Keep focused and alert.

Collaborative

1. Maximize Business Value from an initiative
2. Provide an independent, collaborative viewpoint and identify gaps that may have been missed
3. Set up triggers based on red flags and warnings to keep a project on track
4. Find iterative adjustments to bring a project back on track before major issues emerge
5. Rescue a project that is on a track to fail
6. Early involvement of a health check team has been found to protect careers as there is a sharp reduction of surprises for the Steering Committee

Figure 1.15 Health check benefits keep the team focused and alert.

of project outcomes. Independent project health checks provide an opportunity to detect red warning flags before the situation moves off Example 1 in Figure 1.14. Furthermore, health checks provide an opportunity to keep business interests front and center and to minimize surprises

Independent project health checks are a proven vehicle for driving magnitudes of business value. They almost always pay for themselves many times over, and reduce overall project costs and timeline. They can be used to setup triggers or flags whenever a project team moves off Example 1 in Figure 1.14. In such circumstances, health check initiatives provide actionable recommendations to get the project back to the state shown in Example 1.

Project or Program IT health checks should be considered mandatory for all non-trivial projects that are needed to maximum business value. Figure 1.15 summarizes some of the key benefits of these initiatives. These are discussed in more detail in Chapter 2.

Chapter 2

Health Check Prerequisites, Types of Health Checks, and Success Strategies

A single type of project health check does not precisely fit all possible project situations. In many instances, health checks are only commissioned when problems begin to emerge on a project and people start talking about the project failing. Take the following case as an example. A project had spent $20 million and missed four major deadlines. A review of the functionality revealed that many key transactions were actually a step backward for the business users. Estimates to project completion could not be reasonably finalized because many discovery activities were still remaining. This could be anywhere from 1 year to 3 years or more. It was a very bad, public situation. That's when the leadership team decided to ask for an independent health check assessment like the ones described in this book. The project had been in red status for over a year and there were talks of canceling it. The COO, CEO, HR Leadership, and the Chairman all felt that canceling it would be a disaster for the company. Not only would the budget spent have to be written down as an expense item in one quarter, causing a net profit impact, and consequently a bottom-line impact, but the original reasons for the initiative would be left unaddressed.

A one-time project review of a total 6-week duration–3 weeks to do the work and 3 weeks to share and communicate the results—was commissioned by management. The health check shared the items that were going well and the items that needed improvement. There were specific recommendations to bring the project back on

DOI: 10.1201/9781003269786-3

track in key areas using the dashboard formats that will be discussed in Chapter 3. This resulted in recovery of the program and meeting all the success parameters of the program once it was reset. This example will be discussed further in the Case Study chapters as there were important lessons to be gained from its resolution.

Reasons Health Checks Are Commissioned

IT Health Checks are generally commissioned by a senior executive based on advice or information they are getting from members of the team. There can be proactive or reactive reasons for the request, as shown in Figure 2.1. These reasons will be discussed in more detail in Chapter 7, but essentially there are three categories of health check drivers for consideration that are discussed in more detail in the following sections.

Insurance

Like an insurance policy, the senior executive (e.g. CEO, CFO, COO, CIO, CRO, VP HR, other VP level resources, or other Director level resources) is looking to invest a small amount of money to insure the project against future issues or problems. Health Checks are a smart investment and are like insurance policies that actually pay back many multiples more than the premium invested. While ensuring that the initiative stays on track, the health check team will find opportunities to be more efficient. A monthly recurring health check is an example of this type of insurance.

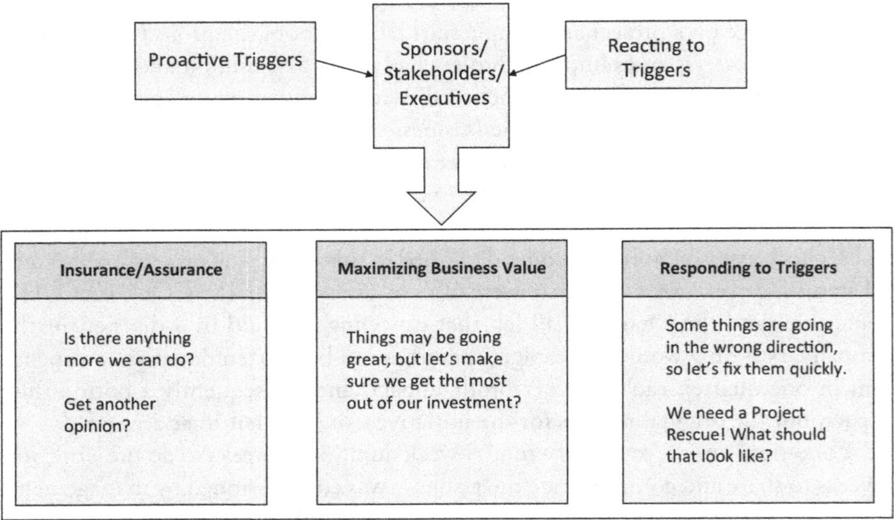

Figure 2.1 Commissioning health checks.

Maximizing Business Value

Some sponsors may be proactive and want to drive multiples of business value. Their ask from the health check team could be to come in and examine the Key Performance Indicators and business value levers identified by the project team to determine if the variables and values have been fully defined, included in the architecture, included in test scenarios, and if there is a sustainment plan to measure and optimize the business value after the project is implemented. Furthermore, they could want the assessment to contrast the proposed functionality to industry best practices, examine what the industry is doing versus what is being proposed, and look for any missed opportunities. They may also want to confirm whether the project team is aiming high enough.

Responding to Triggers

The sponsors could also be responding to triggers such as hearing that the project is not doing well, hearing of general problems such as missed deadlines, being concerned about the ability of some key members of the team or some other collection of concerns. Here are some other common triggers that might entice some executives to sponsor an independent Health Check:

- Missing multiple project deadlines or deliverables
- Very poor morale where team members feel they are on a project hurtling toward failure
- Make adjustments to get the project back on track because some incremental misses are being reported
- Feed the need for a Project Rescue to avert a pending project disaster

Making Health Checks Successful

Chapter 1 introduced the different types of health checks that can be invoked for projects or programs. This book uses the word initiative to refer to either projects or programs. Health checks can apply to either since programs or even portfolios consist of different projects or subprojects. Regardless of the type of health check being applied, there are some key consistent considerations to make them successful. These will be discussed at length in this chapter and in other parts of this book.

Human Emotions

An important element to consider in order to make IT project health checks successful is to understand the human emotions that come into play and be prepared to

Team Reactions to a Health Check

12. Part of the Course
1. Resentment
2. Confusion
3. Denial
4. Fear
5. Passive Aggressive
6. Aggressive
7. Political Survival
8. Desperation
9. Show me
10. Optimism
11. Hope

Figure 2.2 Reactions to a health check.

respond to them in a positive manner to move forward with maximizing value for an initiative. Figure 2.2 shows reactions from different members of the team that will manifest as soon as they hear that a health check is going to take place. The circular nature of the image reflects that some emotional states are transitory. Individuals could keep cycling through a range of these in short periods of time.

Some emotions will clearly be destructive to the health check process, and certainly also to the project or program, and so a strategy needs to be developed to deal with those when they are encountered. While getting 100% support from members of the project team would be ideal, it is not always possible to do that. In that case, that, of course, would be part of the assessment findings and a major warning or risk to the project.

To be clear, getting support from members of the project team will create an environment where the reviewers will get access to information, get clear answers, and buy-in for the recommendations coming out of the health check. However, it may be difficult to get 100% support, in which case the health team should focus on the key influencers, decision-makers, and where they are getting meaningful cooperation from members of the project team. The project sponsors and executives should be at the top of this list.

Here are some of the emotions that will emerge on the project team and some considerations on how to deal with them. They range from negative to positive in terms of project team member's anticipation of the health check. It is not necessary to get everyone to a positive emotional state for the health check to be successful, but it is important to build enough momentum for the recommendations to be formulated with supporting facts and to ultimately be supported by enough members of the project team to be implemented. It's also important to understand how best to get data from the team members and to reduce negative emotions permeating throughout the team. It's not helpful if team members are attacking the integrity of the health check itself. Again, if this happens, this becomes a major review finding and a risk element that is included in the final report.

Figure 2.3 labels the emotional states as negative and positive to the health check effort and ultimately the project or program. There is not always an absolute right or wrong here, just facts around emotions team members legitimately feel and how the health check team can deal with those feelings. The emotional states are described below, along with suggestions on how to deal with them. Remember that all the

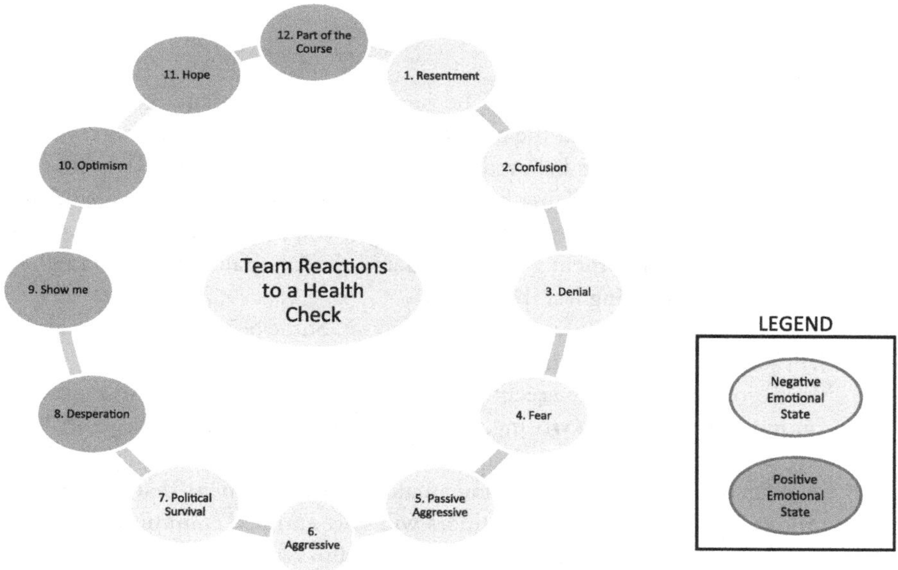

Figure 2.3 Defining reactions to a health check.

mitigation strategies must be truthful, fact-based, and transparent with the best interests of the project in mind.

1. Resentment
   State: Negative
   Description: Some members of the project team will harbor resentment towards an outside group being brought into what they may be perceiving as having someone looking over their work to find small issues. They may feel micromanaged. They may also feel that their hard work is not being appreciated by management and the executive team.
   Impact: This includes creating a very negative environment, challenging the legitimacy of the health check, and potentially other actions that might suppress key information from being shared. It also casts doubt on the recommendations coming out of the report.
   Mitigation Strategy: The assessment team should stress the value of the work that has been done to date, talk about past successes on similar types of projects, and talk about the nature of the upcoming recommendations in general terms. If possible, a preamble to every interaction with the team members who feel this way, stressing the assessment team's collaborative approach, with examples, is helpful. Also mentioning access to best practices and other information that the core team would not have access to can also sometimes soften their resentment by giving them a reason why the assessment team could have been called in without blaming anyone.
2. Confusion
   State: Negative
   Description: The core team may be totally un-nerved, afraid, or concerned. They may not understand the objectives of the review or why it was commissioned. They may have believed that things were going well. They may be afraid for their role, or being blamed for problems on the project. Suddenly they are aware that another group is coming in and they believe that the group is going to be giving them a report card and they're afraid of getting a failing grade or even anything less than an "A".
   Impact: This could manifest as a lack of buy-in. Some people may worry about their jobs or think of finding a new one.
   Mitigation Strategy: The executives commissioning the health check need to communicate clearly, in writing, the reason for the review, the mandate, how long it's going to last, and the parameters. If no one's job is at risk, this should be alluded to in some way without making a commitment that could limit options in the future. But the rumors will start and this communication will be the fact-based explanation people will need to read.
   Mitigation Strategy: The health check team should refer to the messaging from the executive team. That will speak louder than anything the reviewer is going to say.

3. Denial
   State: Negative
   Description: The core team may go into a state of denial that anything could possibly be wrong with the project they have been working on with all their energy and passion.
   Impact: Time will need to be invested to listen to the denials before getting substantive information from them. There may be multiple segueways into unrelated topics.
   Mitigation Strategy: Follow a detailed agenda for each interaction so that the denial statements do not distract from the core mission. Explain that the health check does not have to even identify that something is wrong as the focus could be to raise business value and to point out the positives.
4. Fear
   State: Negative
   Description: Some team members are afraid for their career, afraid they will be blamed, and generally in a state of panic that an external party is examining their collective work.
   Impact: They will be reserved in the conversation, not open, and probably not helpful.
   Mitigation Strategy: At the start of the conversations, explain the parameters of the review and try to put them at ease. The reviewers need to highlight what's in it for them, before sharing anything too grandiose. This is a 1–1 conversation. Discuss past health check initiatives and how they helped the individuals on the projects.
5. Passive Aggressive
   State: Negative
   Description: This can be challenging behavior that is difficult to deal with in an interview. Team members are almost playing games. Being open, then coy, then distant, and all sorts of other emotions.
   Impact: This makes information received from them suspect.
   Mitigation Strategy: Stick to a written agenda. Confirm information received with other sources.
6. Aggressive
   State: Negative
   Description: Team members are aggressive in tone, mannerisms, and speech. This can be unnerving for the assessment team and difficult to navigate to get information.
   Impact: Can be very destructive in terms of even getting through an agenda.
   Mitigation Strategy: It might be a good idea to pair up with a colleague for the interviews. Turn the 1–1 meeting into a 1–1–1. If the resource is too aggressive, they should be dropped from the interview list temporarily after a few questions do not provide reassurance. Do not take any chances with personal physical safety. Speak to management about next steps.

7. Political Survival
   State: Negative
   Description: Team members are being highly political and starting to lay blame at other people's doorstep. They are basically covering their tracks (there are other less polite words to say this), making excuses, and being coy.
   Impact: This does not lead to a balanced understanding of the project. Information being corrected would also be highly suspect.
   Mitigation Strategy: The health check team will need to double check the information that is received through other sources. This would be a general audit finding as well (e.g. "lots of destructive politics seen in the team culture").
8. Desperation
   State: Negative trending Positive
   Description: If the team members are getting desperate for a solution, they may be searching for an answer to their problems.
   Impact: They may be very forthcoming during the interview.
   Mitigation Strategy: The assessment team should try to put them at ease by discussing past successes and the plan to deal with the current initiative. Be open, transparent, and create a relationship based on a mutual desire to do what's best for the project.
9. Show me
   State: Positive with some Negative
   Description: This state is rated just a tad higher than the last one because while it may be challenging, the team will be open to investigate new ideas. However, there is a risk of unhealthy competition.
   Impact: There may be hesitation in sharing too much information, as they want to see what the assessment team can do.
   Mitigation Strategy: Work on removing the competition through a preamble at the start of individual discussions that focuses on examples of past collaborative successes.
10. Optimism
    State: Positive
    Description: Team members are open and optimistic that help is on the way.
    Impact: Open sharing of information
    Mitigation Strategy: Be collaborative and open. Use an agenda to cover all the details and other points. Create a relationship that goes beyond the meeting and tee up how recommendations will be adopted in the future.
11. Hope
    State: Positive
    Description: Team members understand that assessments like the one being conducted have helped organizations in other cases.
    Impact: Open sharing of information
    Mitigation Strategy: Be transparent and balanced in responding to messages that "you will solve all their problems". Provide examples of what is and what

is not possible. Set expectations that are realistic, otherwise there may be disappointment and resentment later on when the reports are being reviewed.

12. Part of the Course:
    State: Positive
    Description: Members of the project team understand that they are involved in a complex initiative. They understand that independent help might be required from time to time and welcome the expertise the assessment team brings to the initiative.
    Impact: The Project Team shares the information that the assessment team is requesting without emotion, negativity, or obstacles.
    Mitigation Strategy: Work collaboratively on the assessment and spend energy on solutions and recommendations. This is arguably the best emotional state as expectations could be realistic.

Past experience shows how resources definitely shift emotions from state to state in short spans of time. In one example, which was a recurring health check, a senior member went from "hopeful" having incredible expectations in the first review, to very 'aggressive' by the second one because some findings related to improvements required in his team. By the third review, the emotions had cycled through "fear", "passive aggressive", and then "aggressive again". The reviewer had determined the emotional states of the individual in the first month or two and was expecting to spend time dealing with this. Calling a 1–1 meeting, the reviewer stressed independence from the company, reiterated that the health check team had no motives other than getting the project implemented so that they could reference it in the future, and stressing that the executive's team was vital to a successful conclusion. After some discussion, this approach allowed the executive's emotional state to return back to "Part of the Course". It stayed that way until the very high-profile project—which involved over 2,000 users in the company—was successfully implemented six months later.

Health Check Prerequisites

Figure 2.4 shows some of the standard prerequisites that need to be in place to drive a successful Project Health Check assessment. Each of these are described in more detail in this section.

Executive Level Support

This is the primary driver for success on a project, but also for the health check assessment to be effective. A clear mandate from the executive team, e.g. CEO, CFO, CIO, COO, or some other executive or group of executives needs to be highly visible to the team.

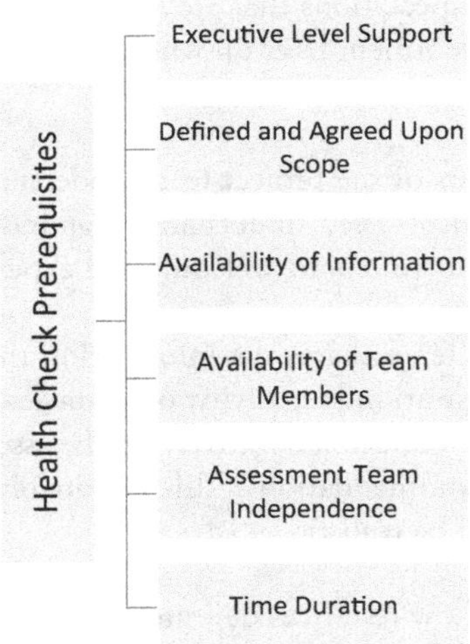

Figure 2.4 Health check prerequisites.

Defined and Agreed Upon Scope

This must be done between the executive sponsors and the assessment team in writing in the form of a Health Check Project Charter or an engagement letter. Any changes to the scope must be approved by both parties or deferred to a future health check.

Availability of Information

The health check team must be given full access to the project repositories that include all the deliverables and even artifacts of previous attempts at the project. This access must be given to all the members of the assessment team before the health check officially begins. Included in the list of deliverables should be all status reports, meeting schedules, and communications to the board of directors. There should also be a process for the assessment team to request access to information they may not have but might require. For example, in the assessment, the team may need information from other projects that have a relationship to the one being assessed.

Availability of Key Team Members

Team members must be available to participate in the health check. This involves three time periods as shown in Figure 2.5 and described below:

- Before the health check, team members may need to provide information and documentation;
- During the health check, team members will be required to clarify the information they have provided, sit down for a 1–1 interview lasting an average of

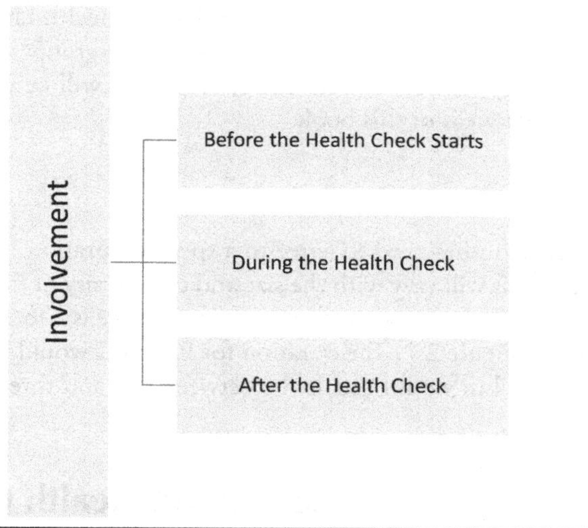

Figure 2.5 Periods of involvement.

one hour, and be available with reasonable notice for follow-up questions. The assessment team would also need access to team member calendars or help from someone who does to set up the interview and other touchpoints.

- After the health check, the team members may need to support specific recommendations that impact their groups.

Assessment Team Independence

The assessment team regardless of where they are sourced must have the independence to do a thorough review and present recommendations without fear of reprisal. Figure 2.6 shows some groups that could be used to staff a health check team.

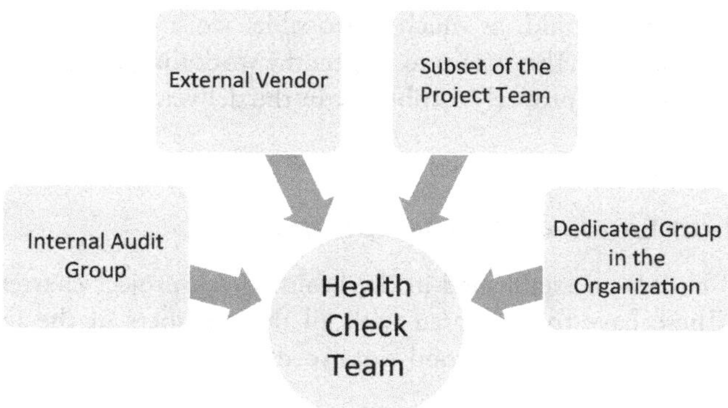

Figure 2.6 Sourcing the health check team.

External vendors that are experienced in conducting health checks would potentially be the highest level of independence. The other groups can be made to be more independent by written executive support. These will be discussed further in Chapter 7 and other areas of this book.

Time Duration

The health check sponsors need to agree to a specific duration for the health check to be conducted. This will vary with the size and complexity of the initiative. A good starting point based on best practices and past experience is 3 to 9 weeks to complete Periods A and B in Figure 2.7. The duration for Period C would be determined with the project sponsors but would usually be between one and three months.

Setting the Stage for a Meaningful Health Check

The prerequisites discussed in the last section primarily focused on what the commissioning organization needs to do to better position the organization for success prior to the start of a health check. As shown in Figure 2.8, this section identifies some additional conditions that the health check team needs to directly drive themselves or work through the assessment sponsors to ensure that the conditions are present throughout the time period of the assessment.

Be Transparent

This characteristic will need to be exhibited throughout the health check assessment. Team members must see that the assessment team has no other motives but to ensure the successful implementation of the initiative.

Be Collaborative

The assessment team should, as much as possible, work collaboratively with the project or program team. This means to respect the work that has already been done, and to include portions, properly attributed, in the deliverables of the health check assessment.

Set Common Goals and Expectations

These should have been established in the health check project charter or engagement letter. These have to be shared with all the members of the team directly involved in the health check. A good time to do this is in the preamble of each

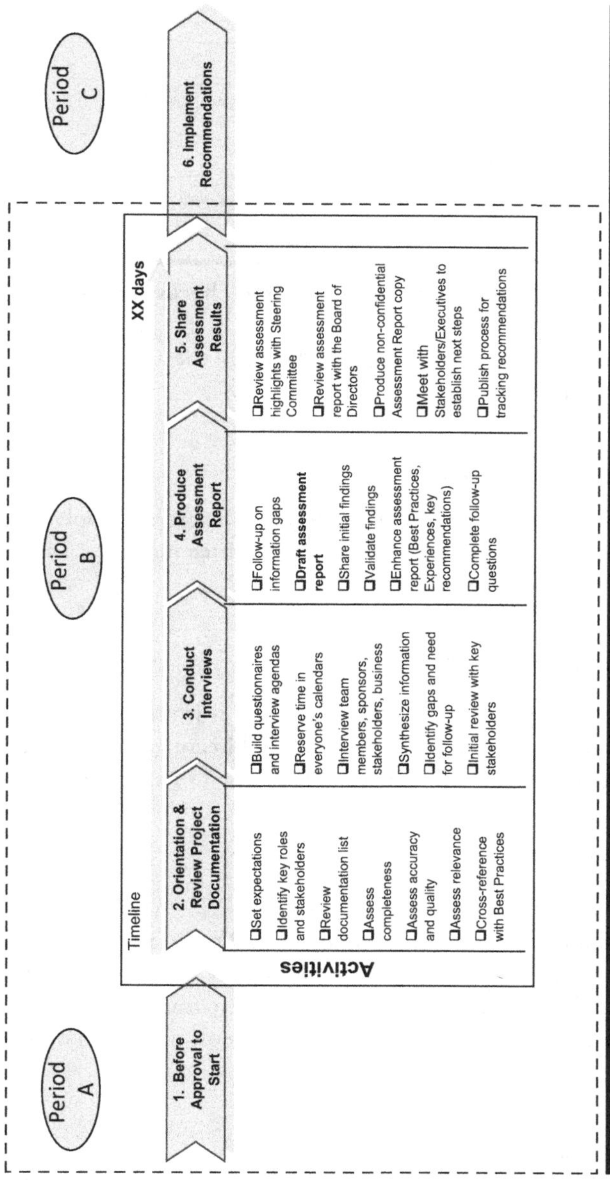

Figure 2.7 Health check time duration.

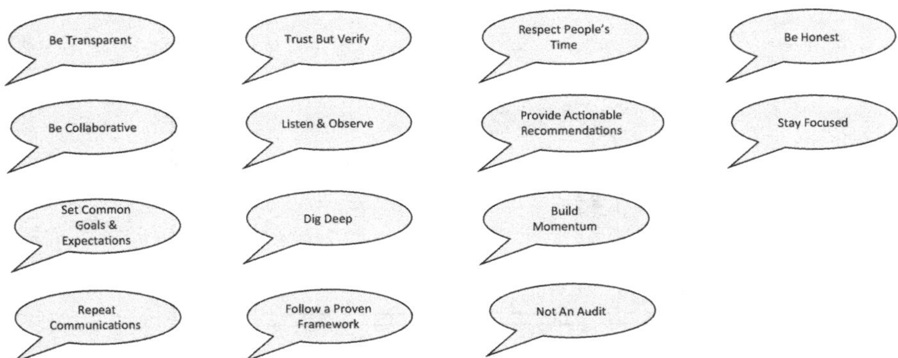

Figure 2.8 Key considerations for making health checks successful.

1–1 interview. It should also be included in the email the assessment sponsors circulate to socialize the initiative.

Repeat Communication

Reiterate the common messages and themes to all the groups involved in the health check. This includes 1–1 meetings, steering committee meetings, and the final recommendations meetings as well.

Trust but Verify

Trust the information you are receiving, but verify it from a variety of sources. For example, if person A states that the solution architecture is complete, there is no need to challenge it. Look for the deliverable yourself or speak to another architect on the team.

Listen and Observe

A lot of the assessment team's time should be used to listen to the individual team members and what they have to say. Questionnaires should be designed to let the interviewees do a lot of the talking. The assessment team should also observe the interactions between team members and even sit in on status and other meetings.

Dig Deep

The analysis should be thorough, detailed, and cross-referenced. The generic staffing model for a health check team is shown in Figure 2.9. While this will be discussed in greater detail in Chapter 5, notice that there are roles to provide specific expertise in Figure 2.9. These should be leveraged to go as deep as possible in the analysis.

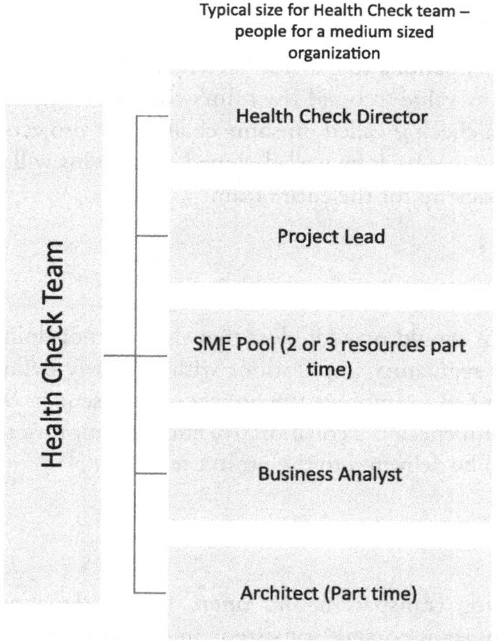

Figure 2.9 Generic health check team.

Follow a Proven Framework

The health check team should use a health check assessment methodology for their work. An example of this was shown in Figure 2.7. This methodology has three time periods that span pre-assessment to post-assessment activities. It would also be included in the project charter for the health check.

Respect People's Time

The assessment team should be mindful that the project is continuing while they are conducting their assessment. It is important to be well prepared and precise for any time requests and to use them efficiently. Do not take people's time for granted.

Provide Actionable Recommendations

Recommendations that are specific, time-boxed, and resourced with defined outcomes are more likely to be prioritized and adopted by management, more so than generic ones.

Build Momentum

Design the recommendations to provide incremental success and to go after low-hanging fruit to show value to build the team's confidence again. Not surprisingly, by the time a health check is called on some challenging projects, the team has lost confidence. Building this back by well-designed quick wins will begin to drive collective confidence back up for the entire team.

Not an Audit

The assessment team should make it clear that they are not doing an official audit. An audit may have regulatory implications with narrowly defined objectives. The health check is designed to improve the project or to rescue it. While the audit is a report card, the health check is a collaborative effort to improve results. This is a key message that should be delivered to the project team.

Be Honest

In addition to being transparent and open, be honest about intentions and objectives. It's important to stay consistent in messaging. The assessment team should hold back on answering questions until they can be consistent, open, and honest.

Stay Focused

Keep the objectives defined at the start of the assessment in focus. It's important not be distracted, even if the team is ahead of schedule, by trying to fit other deliverables into the initiative.

Types of Health Checks

Chapter 1 introduced the different types of health checks that can be invoked by an organization. Since prevention is preferred to a more expensive and invasive cure, it is preferable to bake independent health checks directly into a project or program from the beginning. In fact, a common observation from stakeholders after a health check is completed is to offer that they should have been started sooner or at the start of the initiative. Figure 2.10 shows the different types of Project or Program Health Checks that are commissioned by stakeholders, executives, business sponsors, or IT sponsors. The four basic types of health checks are as follows: 1). One Time; 2). Specific Gates; 3). On Demand; 4). Recurring. These are each explained below in further detail.

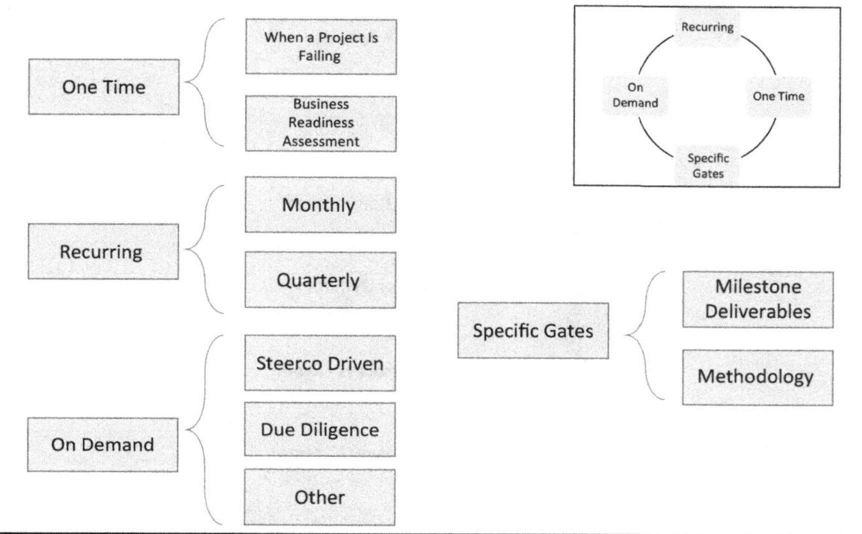

Figure 2.10 Types of project health checks.

One Time

A one-time health check is generally a response to a trigger that was shown in Figure 2.1, or it could be a form of insurance or assurance. Other examples include when a project is failing, conducting a business readiness check, or finding ways to drive additional business value for the organization.

Recurring

A recurring health check is generally a proactive approach by management to commission a health check that runs concurrently with the project or program. The intent is to confirm progress, look for areas of improvement in driving business value, and ensure that there are no surprises. These approaches work well when all teams are working collaboratively. A cadence is usually monthly, bimonthly or quarterly.

On Demand

These types of health checks are generally commissioned by one of the stakeholders shown in Figure 2.11 who are driven by a specific trigger. This could include situations where the project ownership is changing, i.e. a new director is being hired and wants to get a transparent understanding of what they are walking into. Other examples include a steering committee or board of directors member's request to ensure that all statutory requirements are being met.

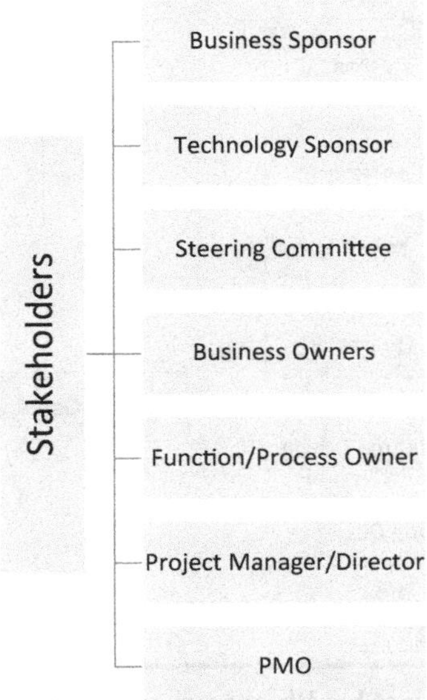

Figure 2.11 Stakeholders who generally commission health checks.

Specific Gates

Some organizations want to confirm that a project has completed all the requirements required to complete one gate before starting the next one. For example, an organization wants to ensure that the business requirements have been fully gathered either for a phase or for a sprint and development can only start when that is confirmed by an independent team. A methodology can be used to identify these gates in advance and to retain a health check assessment team aligned to that timing.

Closing Perspective

This chapter examined specific prerequisites that are required to position a health check assessment to be meaningful and effective. Coupled with this were examples of emotional states that are commonly observed among project team members and how to understand and work with them.

Figure 2.12 shows examples of some of the common types of health checks that are commissioned by organizations and how these could be positioned throughout a calendar year. Four basic types of health checks were discussed in this chapter, namely the following:

1. One Time Health Check: An executive may commission this because several deadlines have been missed.

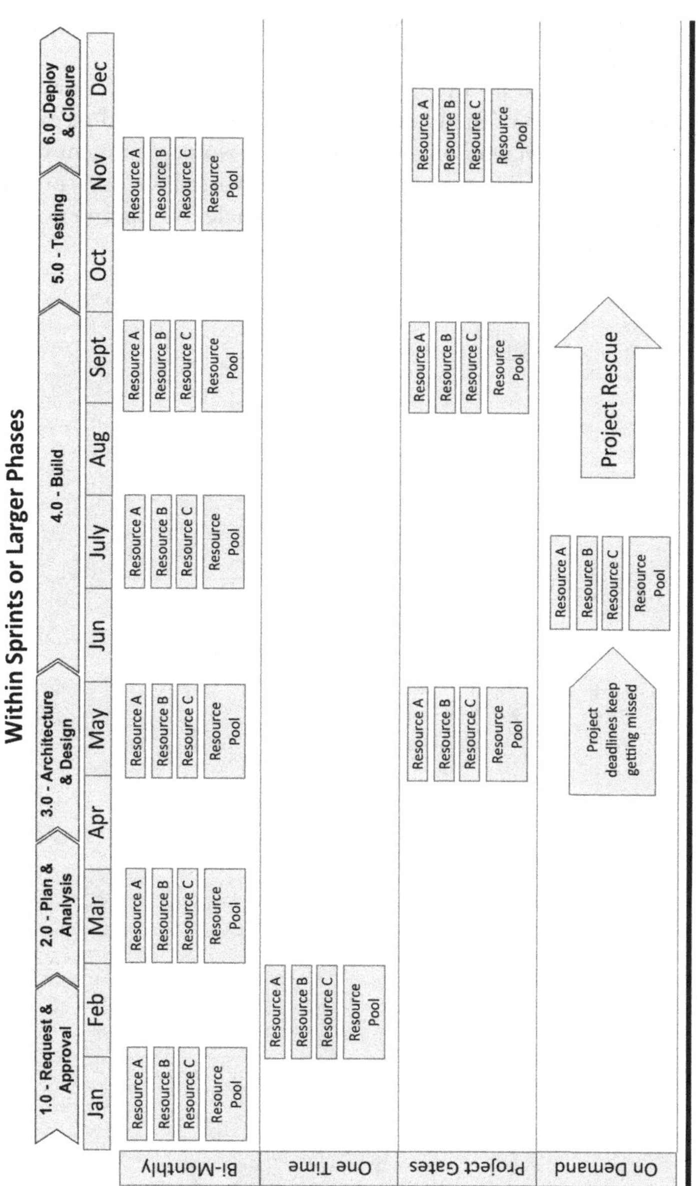

Figure 2.12 Health check resource distribution.

2. Specific Gates: An organization may commission this to be done at every milestone gate in a project lifecycle methodology.
3. On Demand: An organization may commission this at the request of a new director taking over a project so they have a baseline for what they are getting themselves into.
4. Recurring: This could be a proactive monthly health check on a large ERP/CRM implementation. The intent would be that at the end of each month, the health check team would issue a report that would comment on the state of the project, identify risks, specify how to deal with those risks, provide short term recommendations, and make any other relevant commentary for the project's executive team.

Chapter 3

Health Check Evaluation Framework

Once a health check is requested by a project sponsor, a framework for the evaluation needs to be customized for the specific initiative and team in question. This chapter examines the basic evaluation frameworks that can serve as a baseline and which can be customized to suit the specific requirements of the initiative being assessed. Descriptions and key considerations are provided with each evaluation dimension discussed in this chapter to enable a health check team to build customized checklists to evaluate and catalog the results of their discovery activities.

Evaluation of People–Process–Technology Dimensions

We can start with the basic dimensions that are almost always going to be in scope for a project assessment as shown in Figure 3.1. People, process, and technology are the essential tenants of the Project or Programs that would be the focus of almost any Health Check. The assessment team must get an understanding of how these dimensions are set up on the initiative being reviewed. They are the core dimensions driving the more rigorous evaluation framework that is the subject of this chapter. These three dimensions are discussed in more detail in the sections below.

People

The capabilities, responsibilities, and commitment of the people involved in the initiative being assessed are evaluated in this dimension. This would be in the context of the project's objectives. The key roles in consideration would be the executive

DOI: 10.1201/9781003269786-4

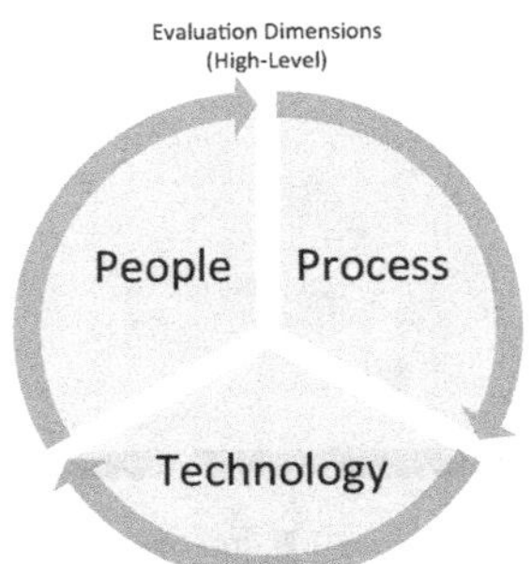

Figure 3.1 High-level dimensions to include in a health assessment.

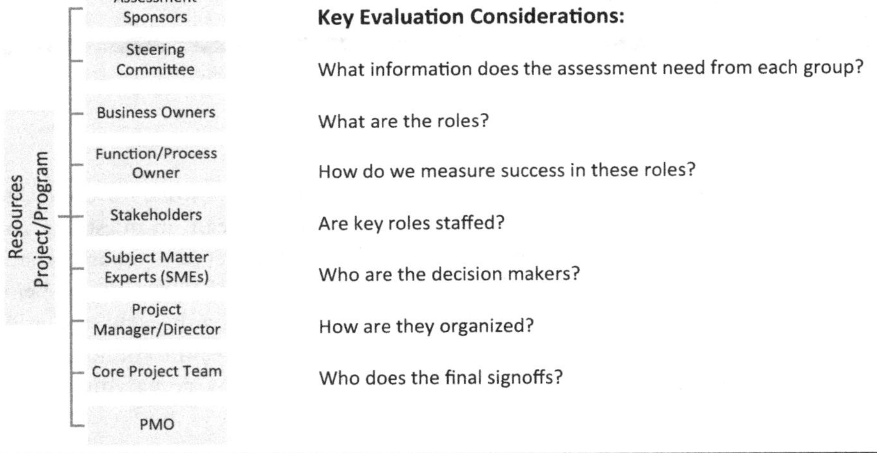

Figure 3.2 Project/program resources involved in the health check.

sponsors, stakeholders, subject matter experts (SMEs), project managers, architects, business analysts, testers, and business users as shown in Figure 3.2. Roles and responsibilities will be discussed in further detail in Chapter 5 of this book. For the purpose of the evaluation framework, the people section is key to get alignment, set expectations, and communication across relevant parts of the organization for the health check. The assessment team will need to understand both "as-is" and "to be" roles. For the assessment evaluation, we will need to understand their involvement and expectations.

Some questions relating to the key evaluation considerations are also shown in Figure 3.2. The evaluation criteria must include these types of questions in the assessment to fully understand how the people dimension has been performing on the project or program being assessed compared to the level that needed to be met as part of the project plan. Furthermore, it will be the same group of resources that will ultimately own the recommendations coming out of the review. Their capabilities will make or break the project delivery.

Process

Processes are a key dimension to include in the evaluation in the health check. These can be categorized as shown in Figure 3.3. This figure shows some of the key process areas that will be in the scope of most assessments. Notice that there are two variations, namely the "As Is" version of the processes which are current state in the first column. The section column shows the "To Be" versions of some of the processes for the post-implementation world. Some of the "As Is" processes should still be evaluated, but they do not need to be migrated to a new state as they are specific to the project development lifecycle e.g. data conversion. The assessment will examine the completeness of the process table of contents in both variations and then try to understand how the project or program will migrate to the "To Be" version. Both "As Is" and "To Be" versions should be included in the evaluation.

Here are examples of some of the subdimensions that the team should be evaluating in the process dimension:

- Are key business processes documented?
- Are the key processes shared and accessible to those who require them?
- Is there any evidence that the processes have been signed off by management?
- Is it clear which roles are involved in the processes?

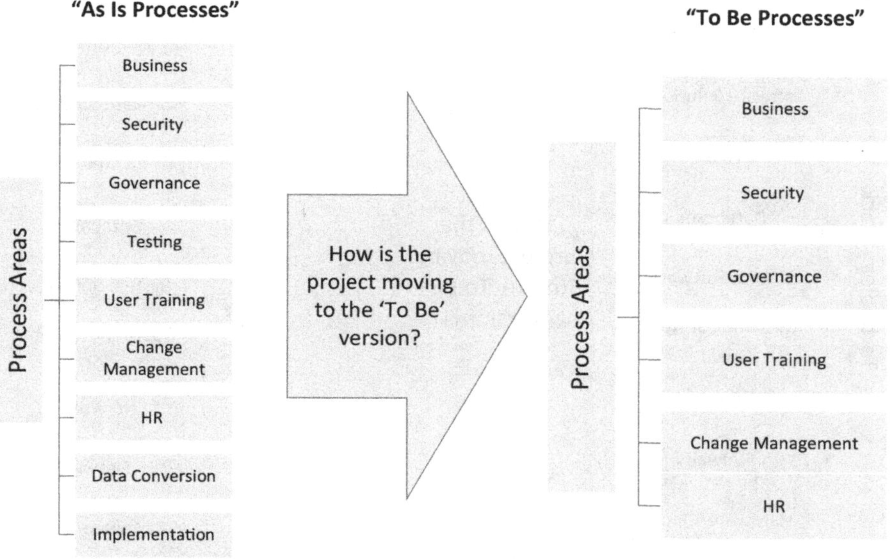

Figure 3.3 Process areas for evaluation.

- What are the processes based on?
- Are they as efficient as they could be?

Technology

Technology is the third high-level dimension to include in the evaluation. There is a lot to unpack in the technology dimension and how technology is driven and managed in the project. The evaluation team needs to look at both the "As Is" and the "To Be" versions of the technology solution. The components can be categorized in a technology stack as shown in Figure 3.4. The organization should have a view of the technology at various levels for the solution, business, and technology architectures and design. Since these are related it is helpful to ensure that they are logistically consistent. Here are some views to look for:

- Conceptual: an abstracted view of the technology architectures.
- Logical: One step above the conceptual architecture, but without specific product information.
- Physical: A fully detailed view with product components and low-level solutions shown.

Figure 3.5 shows a recommended "To Be" Reporting and BI Technology example showing technology tools and some processes in the same physical view of the

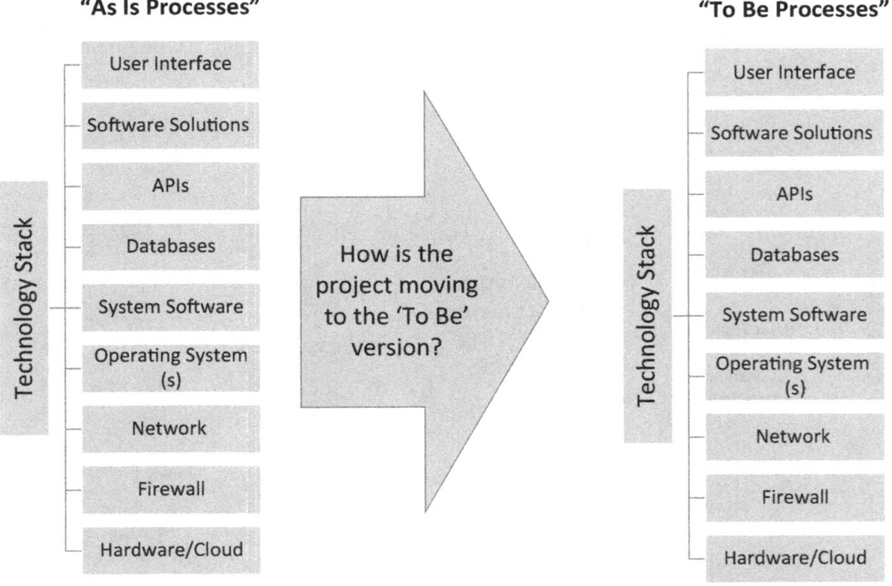

Figure 3.4 Simplified view of a technology stack.

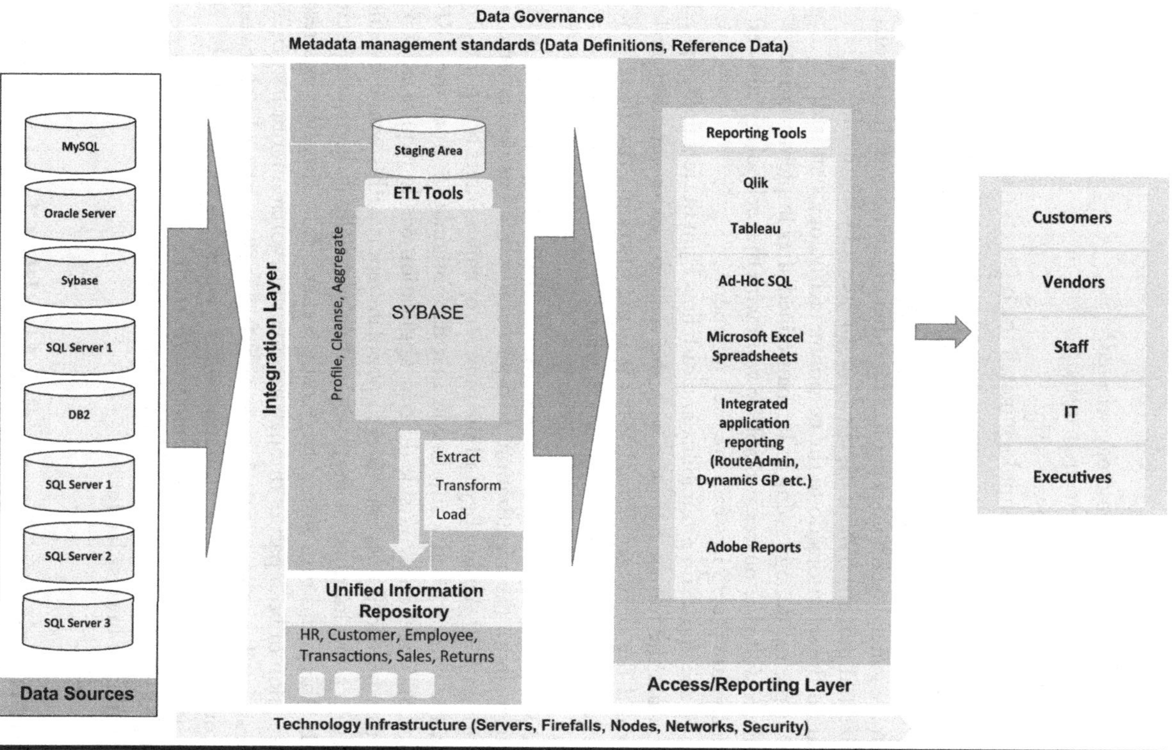

Figure 3.5 Reporting and BI technology example.

diagram. These can be mapped to the "As Is" view to determine a migration path between the two versions of architecture.

Some examples of questions that the evaluation team will need to consider for Technology are as follows:

- How was the "To be" technology selected?
- Have the components been stress tested?
- What is the total cost of ownership?
- How does the selected technology match the business requirements?
- How does the selected technology match the nonfunctional requirements?
- Were other technology choices considered?
- Why were the other technology choices dropped?
- What are general technology choices for other organizations that are of a similar size and industry? What explains our differences with them?
- What do the selections do to the corporate technology standard?
- How is the technology going to be maintained after implementation?
- Are there skilled resources available to work with the technology choices? How expensive are they? How easy are they to retain?
- What is the impact on profitability and cash flow from the technology purchase?
- Where are the formal contracts with the vendors? How were they reviewed? How did the price get vetted? What was the discount? Are there any risky terms and conditions in the signed contracts?

Technology contracts have to be reviewed rigorously with the legal group either internally or externally to the organization. In a past example, a business entered into a contract with an ERP vendor. Beyond the number of named users being the primary cost factor, the contract had a stipulation that data originating from the ERP and loaded into data warehouses outside the core application would require extra named licenses if that offloaded data was used to populate reports. This would expand the user base from a few hundred to many thousands, especially if the reports were put on the web. This could turn into a very costly scenario. The situation was resolved to the satisfaction of both parties through good faith negotiation, but it's prudent to finalize these details in the negotiation phase upfront. The relationship between the vendor account team and the organization was very positive so it was a good result. Had there been more contention, it could have been drawn out and costly.

The almost always complex, but interesting, technology dimension is discussed in more detail later in this chapter.

Evaluation Criteria Across the Health Check Lifecycle

The health check evaluation criteria are used to establish a clear, unambiguous scope for an assessment. After confirmation of scope and negotiation with the health check sponsors, it is placed into the scoping document which forms part of the statement of work, project charter, or the engagement letter. As shown in Figure 3.6, these

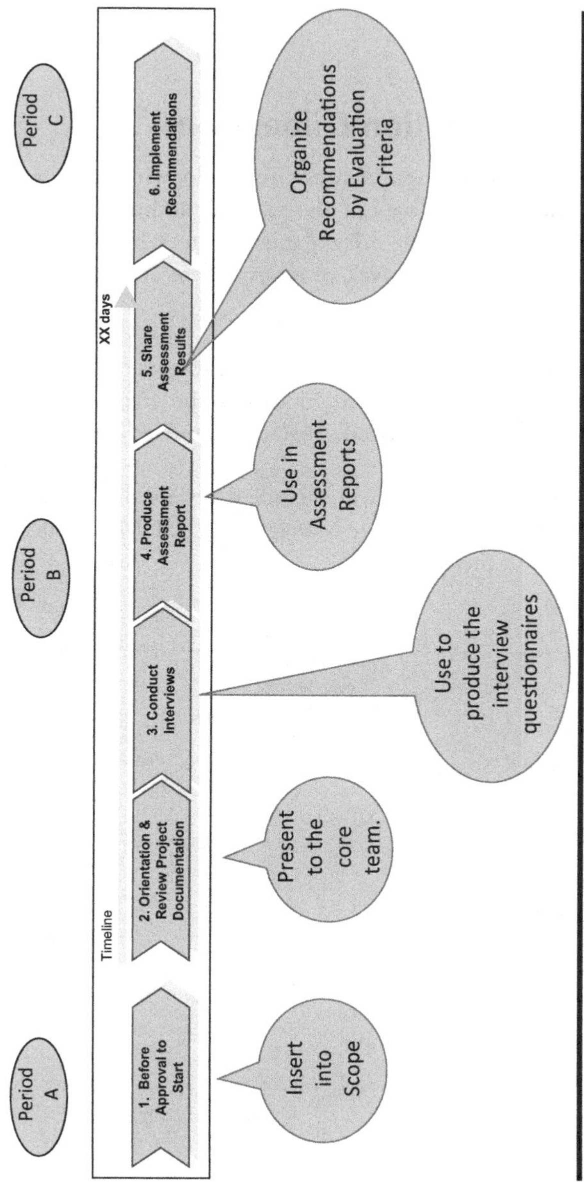

Figure 3.6 Evaluation criteria across the health check lifecycle.

approved evaluation criteria are used throughout the health check lifecycle. It is a checklist for the documentation review. It is the basis for building the questionnaires for the 1–1 team interviews. It is used to organize observations and feedback. The recommendations are also organized by the evaluation criteria.

Expanding the Evaluation Dimensions

Based on the combination of People, Process, Technology in the context of the project or program in consideration, we can also consider additional evaluation areas to include in the health check. Figure 3.7 expands Figure 3.1 with additional dimensions that would impact an initiative's progress. These additional dimensions are described in more detail below:

- Governance: This will include a review of the governance processes, organization, and mandate. Included in this is the steering committee mandate, how decisions are escalated, obstacles removed, and upward feedback mechanisms.
- People: As stated earlier, this will include a review of all the people-related activities. Organizational Change Management (OCM) and user training will also be included in this dimension.

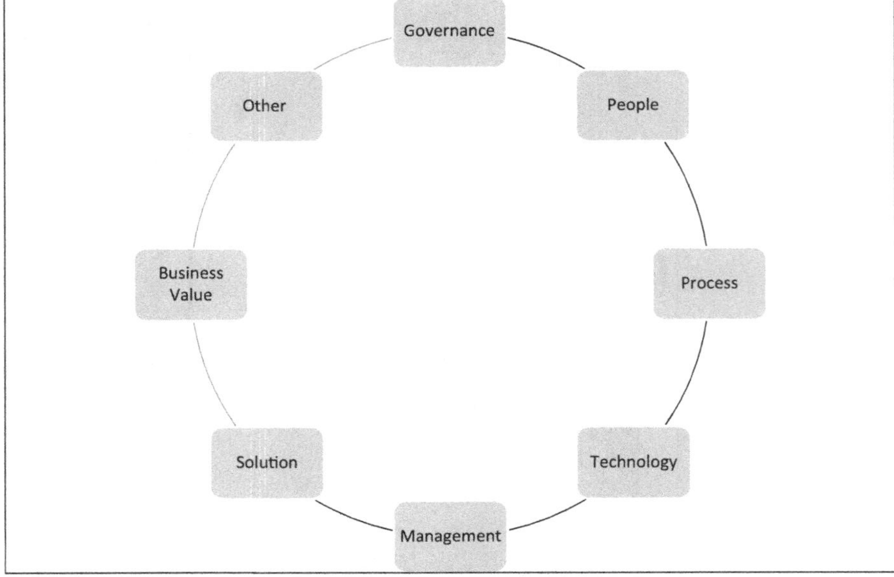

Figure 3.7 An expanded view of areas to consider in the health assessment.

- Process: As Discussed earlier, this would include a review of the "As-Is" and "To-Be" variations of process flows and how the "To-Be" versions will be achieved.
- Technology: As discussed earlier, this would include a review of the "As-Is" and "To-Be" variations and how the "To-Be" versions will be achieved.
- Management: This will include a review of the management processes, resources, and practices. This will include a review of status reporting, risk management, issue management, a project management office (PMO), and roles and responsibilities.
- Solution: This will be a review of the solution architecture and design based on the detailed business requirements. There should be extensive signed-off documentation to show where business value is created and measured, or a plan to build these out in the course of the project or program.
- Business Value: This will include a combination of the seven states for driving business value, as shown in Figure 3.8. These include the full end-to-end lifecycle of definition, building, testing, and actuation.
- Other: In consultation with the assessment sponsors, other areas can be included in the evaluation framework. This could include any items related to the project or programs about to be assessed, e.g. premises, legal issues. The health check team needs to be vigilant about maintaining scope control and trying to keep a realistic timeline for the health check to complete say between three weeks to three months duration.

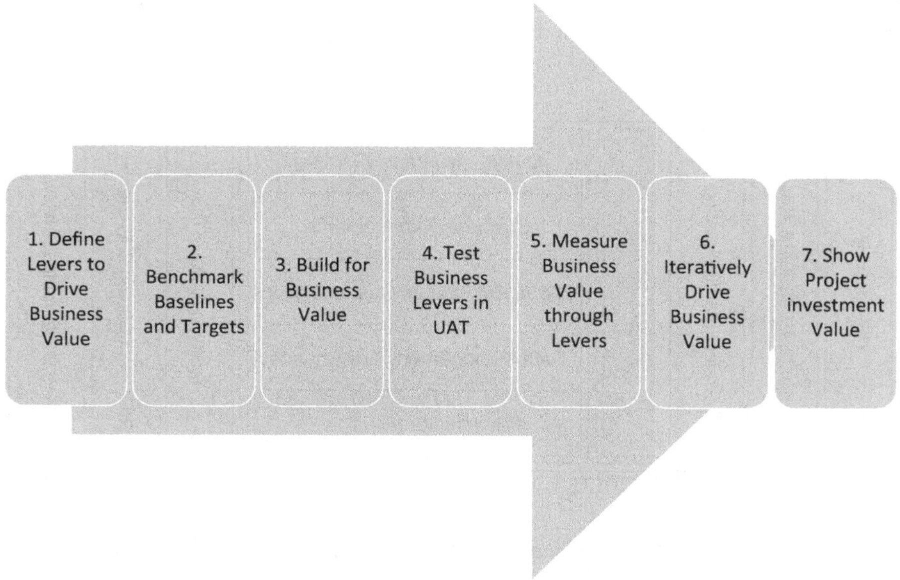

Figure 3.8 Seven (7) stages for driving business value.

Building the Evaluation Framework

We have discussed some of key considerations in building out an evaluation framework for the health check review. These can be collected into combined views and enhanced with additional dimensions that have commonly been requested by stakeholders on past health check initiatives. This is the subject of the next section.

Starting with the Baseline Framework

Figure 3.9 shows the dimensions that have served as a strong baseline on many past health check initiatives. The framework should be reviewed with the project sponsors requesting the health check to ensure that all their interests are included in it. The framework can be expanded with additional dimensions to cover any additional scope requests. It is better not to reduce too many of the suggested dimensions from a health check as the items shown in the baseline framework offer a good end-to-end perspective on most projects in diverse industries. It has served as an excellent starting point and a minimal set of dimensions to work with as well. If the dimension is not very complex, it can still be included in the review with only a small amount of time invested in discovery activities.

As already mentioned, the particular framework shown in Figure 3.9 offers a generic starting point and has been used on many dozens of client health checks in the past so it is proven and effective. The groupings shown in the figure are specific and show some collection of similar dimensions in the vertical columns on the left, the vertical columns on the right, the ones in the middle running horizontally, and the horizontal dimensions at the bottom that sweep across the entire list of project processes.

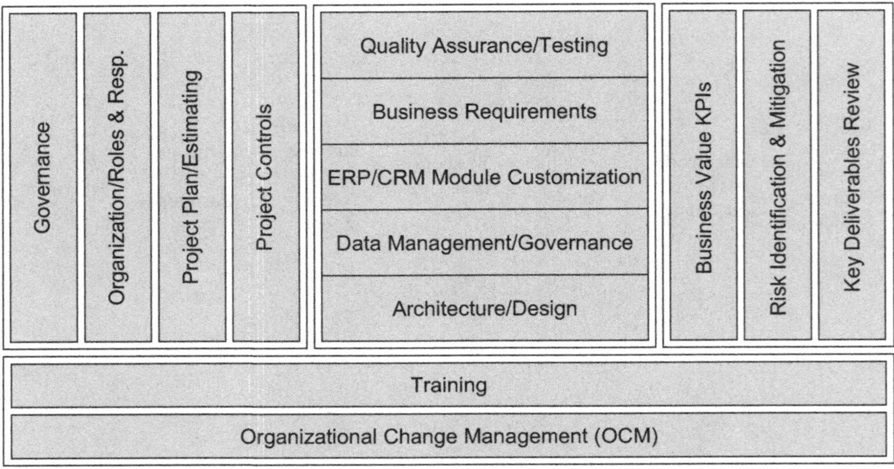

Figure 3.9 Generic baseline health check evaluation framework.

For project teams, including this figure in the presentation makes it easy to encapsulate how the review is going to work and the sequence of steps in the review. Depending on the project's specific needs, the specific dimensions can be changed to the figure shown in Figures 3.10 and 3.11.

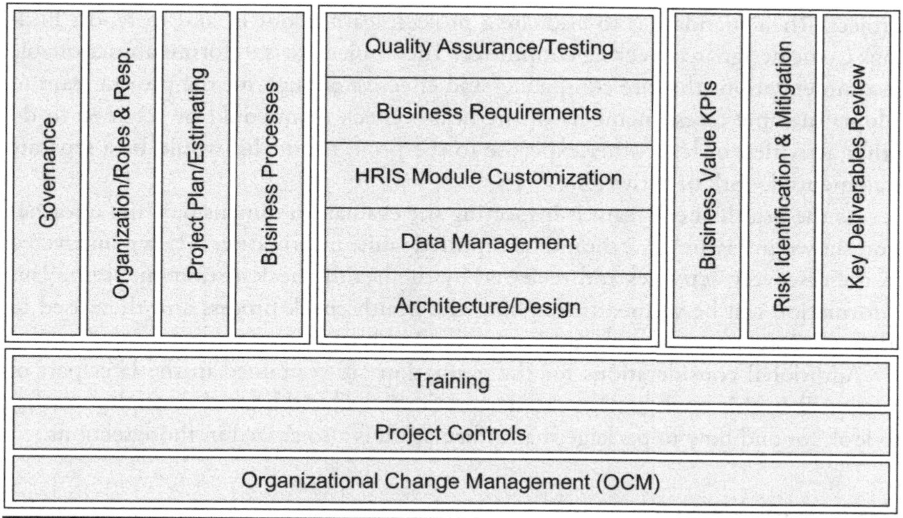

Figure 3.10 Customized health check framework.

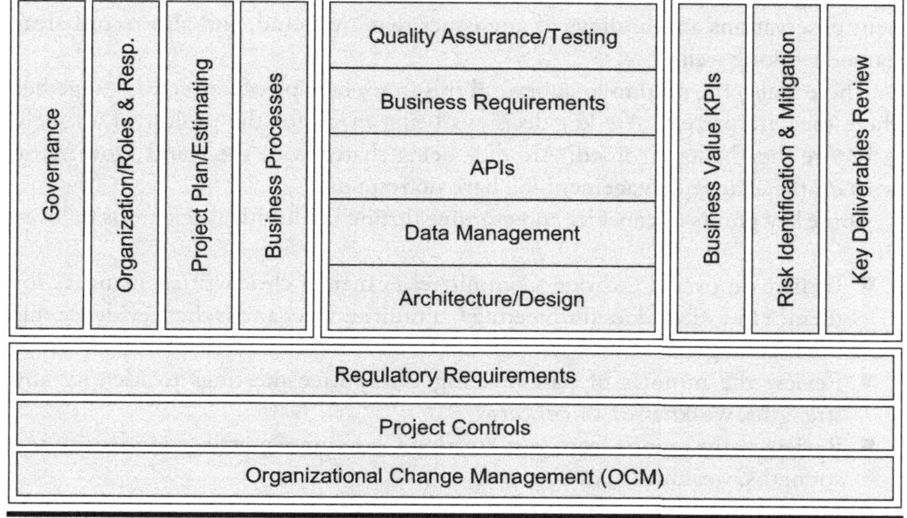

Figure 3.11 Customized health check framework.

The sections below describe key considerations for evaluating each of the dimensions shown in Figure 3.9. When the dimensions are modified due to the specific project assessment requirements, the list below can be customized by the health check team to suit the specific needs of the project in consideration.

It's important to note that from a contractual perspective, the health check assessment team should not be made responsible for resolving the issues on the project. Their mandate is to evaluate a project, learn about it, and to report findings to the designated steering committee. Their objective is to formulate actionable recommendations that are compelling and effective enough for the project team to adopt. In some cases, members of the health check team could be retained to do other activities, or lend other expertise to the project, but this would be a separate statement of work or activities.

As the health check team is inspecting the evaluation dimensions, the information shown in Figure 3.12 should be captured while information is being uncovered in the discovery activities and reviewed by the health check assessment team. This information can be verified throughout the health check process and then used to draft the Assessment Report and Executive Dashboards.

Additional considerations for the evaluation are contained in the later part of Section B in this book, and at the start of Section C. Additional examples of what to look for and how to package that information is also shared in those sections.

Governance

Overall program governance will be key to the project success. The assessment team needs to build a cross-referenced list to examine what pieces are in place and where there are gaps compared to best practices. Remember to make health check assessment observations and findings of any issues that are found, and also record areas that are working well.

There is also the need to look beyond this to see how pieces are coming together where they are present. Are key decisions being made for the project in a timely basis? Are they being recorded? Are they being shared with the team? How many items on the change management log have no response?

Some key points to consider and examine during the health check are as follows:

- Is there an overall Steering Committee? Is there a clear written mandate for them? How often does the Steering Committee meet and is there evidence this is happening?
- Review the minutes of past Steering Committee meetings to identify any strengths, weaknesses, or concerns.
- Review status reports from past Steering Committee meetings to identify any strengths, weaknesses, or concerns.
- Has the Steering Committee reported status to the Board of Directors?
- Do any members of the Steering Committee sit on the Board of Directors?

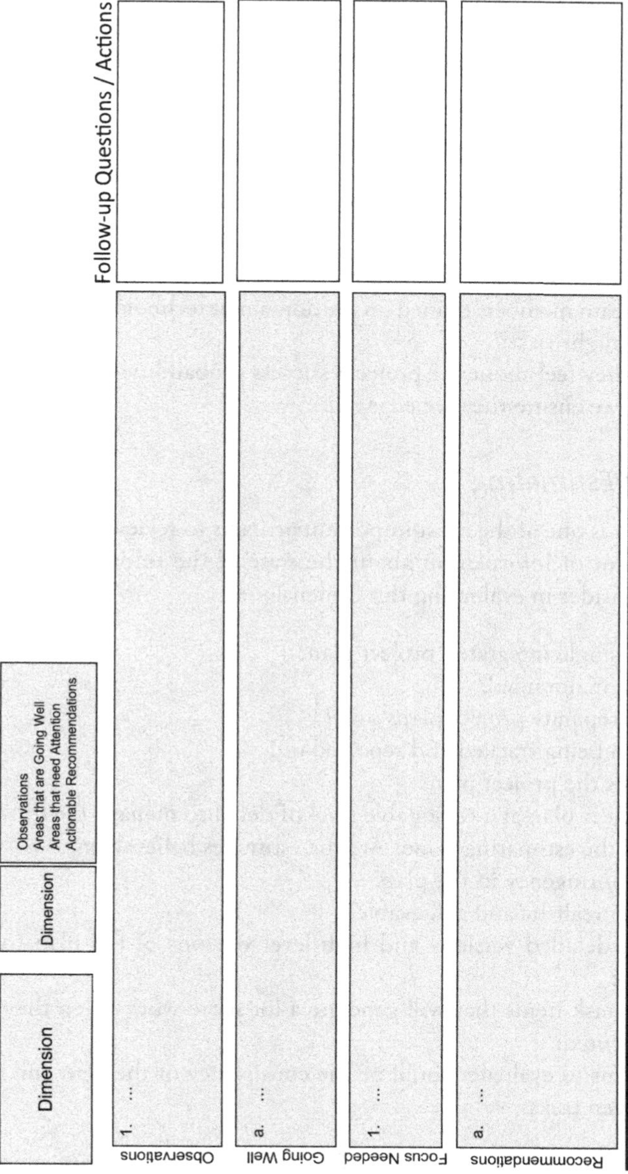

Figure 3.12 Recording notes.

Organization/Roles and Responsibilities

The roles and responsibilities should be documented and key roles need to be filled in a timeframe suitable for the project being reviewed. The Project Plan should identify workload and specific resources throughout the project lifecycle. Chapter 5 will review the roles and responsibilities in detail. Some key considerations to consider are as follows:

- Are key resources dedicated to the project or are they multi-tasking with other positions in the organization?
- What is the team morale?
- What is the level of politics on the project or program?
- How are team members selected?
- How are team members trained on the domain or technology skills they require?
- Are there flight risks?
- How do they feel about the project's success probability?
- How can we ensure they are engaged?

Project Plan/Estimating

The project plan is one of the most important artifacts to review in the health check. It can reveal a lot of information about the state of the initiative. Here are some questions to consider in evaluating this dimension:

- Is there a single integrated project plan?
- Is it being maintained?
- Are there separate project plans only?
- Is the plan being tracked and reported on?
- Who owns the project plan?
- Is the project plan at a reasonable level of detail to manage the initiative?
- How was the estimating done? Are the estimates believable?
- Is there contingency in the plan?
- Is the plan realistic and achievable?
- Are there detailed versions and high-level versions of the plan for different audiences?
- Are there task items that will generate a lot more work when they are themselves executed?
- Other items to evaluate would be the consistency of the plan and dependencies between tasks.

On one HRIS implementation using Oracle technology, an integrated project plan was built to an incredibly complex low level of detail. The plan showed tasks and subtasks. Every subtask had resources with their percentage time allocation to the initiative. There were detailed dependencies throughout the plan. It was over 100 pages long and growing. After the project started, the project managers and coordinator discovered it was too time-consuming to maintain and decided to cut it down to about 20 pages of detail. This turned out to be manageable with an appropriate level of detail to manage the project.

Project Controls

Look for evidence that the project has strong controls around budgets, security, managing risk, estimating costs, managing the cost, managing scope, and controlling the deliverable versions. Examine how resources are onboarded and how their security profiles are built. Ensure there are procedures that remove resources from the security pool when they are no longer on the project.

Quality Assurance/Testing

There should be a quality assurance plan that was produced early in the lifecycle. There should be evidence that testing is a core stream of activity that is starting early in the project lifecycle. There should be evidence of the following testing types being done:

- Unit Testing: Performed by the development/configuration team.
- System Integration Testing: There could be several levels of SIT testing. Examine how testers are assigned, onboarded, and trained. Examine how test scripts are built and whether they are signed off. How are defects prioritized?
- Stress Testing: The health check assessment team will need to ensure that key transactions and non-functional requirements are stress tested.
- Regression Testing: This would greatly speed up testing. This would be an assessment finding and recommendation if it is not being done.
- Functional Testing: Specific functionality, such as payroll, will require additional levels of cycle testing to test for paycheck-to-paycheck processing.
- User Acceptance Testing: This is very close to going live so the assessment team needs to examine which test cases are in scope, how business value is being tested, how testers are assigned, onboarded, trained, and managed. There should also be a process for prioritizing defects, fixing them, and retesting them.

Check on whether there is clear criteria to enter and exit a testing gate.

Business Requirements

This is an important pinning to the entire program. Are the business requirements being documented, reviewed, and formerly signed off? Are they aligned to the solution architecture and the testing scripts? How are they being used to create test scenarios and test scripts. Are the business requirements aligned to the project objectives? Beware the situation where project team members declare that the requirements are to replace the previous system, but only better. Their business requirements must be formally documented and signed off.

ERP/CRM Module Customization

There should be controls around the level of customization done to the software system, as well as a process for determining and approving what is customized versus what is configured. Look for guidelines and standards on how much customization is acceptable and if these are being followed.

Data Management/Governance

A data governance lifecycle should be developed in the project deliverables. There should be inclusion of specific data requirements and user stories, along with the following:

- Define an initial baseline for A Data Governance Framework that includes the following:
  - Data ownership and management
  - Data quality
  - Data council
- Identification of current data and source systems aligned to the functional and nonfunctional requirements
- Proposed Data Architecture future state
- A detailed data governance roadmap

Figure 3.13 shows a list of data governance deliverables that can be reviewed by the assessment team. If they are not yet built, the plan should be reviewed on when they will be available and whether the timing is consistent with the scope of the review.

Architecture/Design

There should be a clear mapping of functional requirements and nonfunctional requirements to the proposed architecture. It will be important to understand how it was selected and the capabilities of the organization to maintain it into the future.

Data Governance Components	Description
Business Requirements & Requests	Report, dashboard, and process requests identification.
Business Request Prioritization	Update and prioritise request list.
"As Is" Data Architecture	"As Is" list of data sources, processes, and technology.
"To Be" Data Architecture	Define a "To Be" conceptual Data Architecture .
Data Governance Council	Must consist of the following: Data map, Data Dictionary, Data Ownership and management, Data update processes, Roles and responsibilities, Data Governance processes.
Organization Chart	To support the detailed BI Roadmap and to support a post-production environment.
Detailed BI Roadmap	A detailed roadmap to show delivery of the prioritized report, technical architecture evolution, data architecture evolution, and resourcing needs.
Road Map and Project Plan	A detailed project plan to move from "As Is" to the 'To Be" data architecture in an iterative manner.

Figure 3.13 Data governance deliverables.

Business Value/KPIs

The business KPIs, as discussed previously, are important to identify and drive business value. There should be a logical transition between their identification, requirements gathering business rules, and alignment with the architecture. The assessment team should review that the KPIs are carried across the end-to-end project lifecycle and tracked post-implementation.

Risk Identification and Mitigation

Risk management is a key project management and governance function. The evaluation team should review the risk log and check that there is evidence that it is being maintained. Some questions to consider:

- Is the risk log reviewed with the team?
- Is the risk log actively maintained?
- Are there mitigation strategies for each defined risk?
- Is the Steering Committee aware of the critical risks?

Risk management is discussed at length in Chapter 12.

Key Deliverables Review

Conduct an overall review of all the project deliverables versus when they are required. These are the subject of Chapter 9.

Training

Training can include core team training and End-User training can be explained by a series of 'W's as shown in Figure 3.14. These parameters define the overall success of the training function, which will be vital to the success and business value of the project.

- Who: Which specific users are being trained?
- What: What is the training material and courses they need?
- When: When will they be trained? Close to go live? How many can go after go live?
- Why: When do they need the courses that have been assigned to them? Can they be reduced to save time?
- Where: Is the training offered in a classroom, over the internet, or through some other combination?

Who ➡ What ➡ When ➡ Where ➡ Why

Figure 3.14 The W's of training.

Organizational Change Management (OCM)

OCM is arguably the most influential stream in terms of making a project successful and to drive business value. A system cannot be successful unless users know how to use it. Business value cannot be drawn if a system is not being used well or expertly. Of course, the technology and process streams have to happen otherwise there is nothing to use. In many organizations though, emphasis is placed on those to get them delivered and OCM tends to be a part time function that is started too late in the project to be as successful as it could be. The major components in OCM to review in the health check are as follows:

- Communication Plan
- Change Plan
- Training Plan
- Organization Plan
- "As Is" and "To be roles" for the users
- Alignment of new roles with security/permissions

Preparing for the Assessment

Once the evaluation criteria is confirmed with the health check sponsors and included in the scoping documentation, the assessment team can then drive each dimension in the criteria into lower levels of detail as shown in Figure 3.15. This allows the development of questionnaires in the 1-1 interviews as well as serving as a checklist for review of the documentation. The information in Figure 3.15

Evaluation Sub-Criteria

The evaluation dimensions should also be divided into sub-criteria, as follows:

- ❑ Project Plan Key Considerations
  - ❑ Approach to estimating
  - ❑ Contingency
  - ❑ Alignment with Development Methodology & Deliverables
  - ❑ Milestone hierarchy
- ❑ Organization
  - ▫ Roles and Responsibilities
  - ▫ Availability
  - ▫ % availability on the Project
- ❑ Methodology/Development Framework
  - ▫ Project Team Structure
  - ▫ Change Control
  - ▫ Standards
- ❑ Architecture/Design
  - ▫ Reusability
  - ▫ Robust & scalable Architecture
  - ▫ Performance
  - ▫ Security
  - ▫ Maintainability
  - ▫ Environments
- ❑ Overall
  - ▫ Single points of ownership

Figure 3.15 Evaluation sub-criteria.

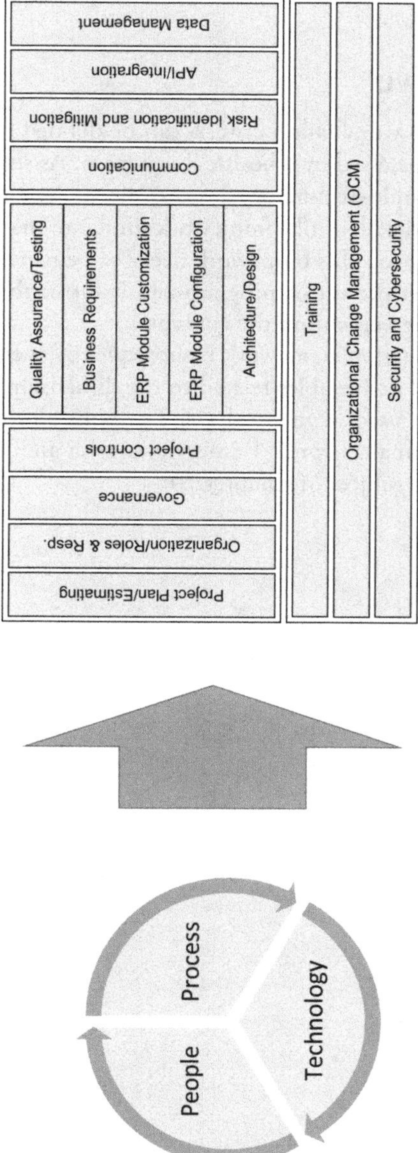

Figure 3.16 Customized health check framework.

should be included in the Final Assessment Report to explain how the health check's methodology and evaluation criteria was applied to the initiative in a customized manner.

Closing Perspective

This chapter examined how evaluation criteria can be defined for a specific project or program that is being assessed by a health check team. As shown in Figure 3.16, a starting point is the People-Technology-Process dimensions figure, then drilling down into lower levels of detail, until a framework similar to that shown on the right side of Figure 3.16 is defined. This framework needs to be reviewed with the health check sponsors for a given project or program and it forms the basic scope of the assessment once there is agreement on the contents.

The health check evaluation framework is subsequently used to build checklists to guide the evaluation of deliverables related to the dimensions in the framework. These dimensions will be used to map roles and responsibilities to the evaluation criteria to build questionnaires for 1-1 interviews with individual project team resources. This will be the subject of Chapter 10.

Chapter 4

The Health Check Report (s)

As discussed in Chapter 2, the health check assessment produces several significant outputs during the lifecycle of the assessment process. The Health Check Report is chief among these and has as at least four states during the assessment lifecycle as shown in Figure 4.1 and discussed further below:

- Interim Report State: This could include snippets or key messages that need to be shared during the interview process. The individual Interim reports generally form the foundation of the draft report and its appendices.
- Draft Report State: This report should be labeled clearly "DRAFT" in a header or footer before it is shared with anyone on the project team. This allows the assessment team an opportunity to socialize the contents and allows the project or program team members an opportunity to provide further commentary and input. This will be important to getting acceptance of the recommendations in the final report.
- Final Report State: This is the final published form of the report with the "DRAFT" label removed. This will be used in roadshows with various groups and subgroups in the initiative's team to socialize and explain the contents. The number of meetings, presentations, and audience will be determined by the Steering Committee. A general sequence of presentations can be in the following sequence: (1). core team; (2). Assessment Sponsors; (3). Steering Committee; (4). Other Closely Held Teams; (5). Wider Road Show.
- Revised Report State: There may be further information and commentary received during the roadshows. For example, a recommendation (s) may

DOI: 10.1201/9781003269786-5

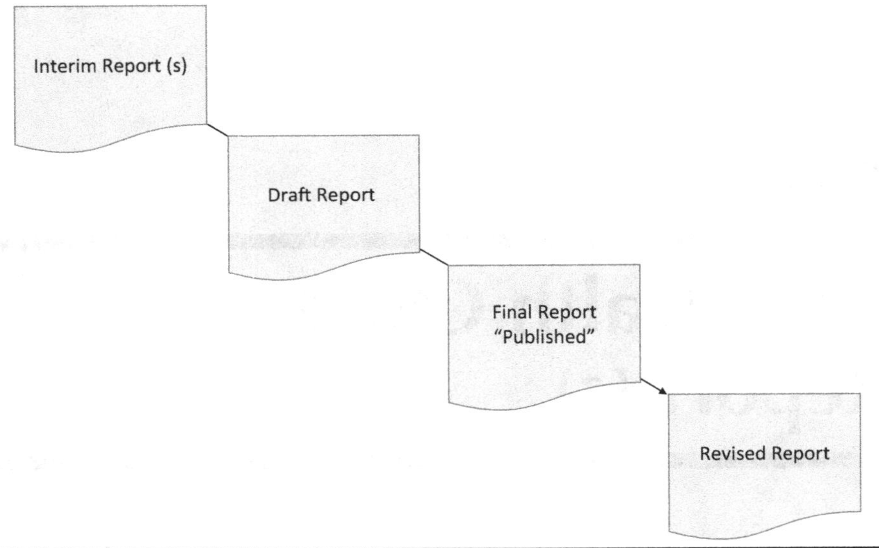

Figure 4.1 Report states.

have already been completed or certain situations could have gotten better or worse. The assessment team should resist altering the final report and instead produce a revised one with new findings in an appendix or preamble at this stage of the presentations.

The health check assessment does not produce a single report only, rather the output will be a combination of reports and dashboards. It is important to be transparent and use the same information on each report, just with different views and focus areas depending on the purpose of the document and for the audience it is intended to be used. For example, the Steering Committee may only want to review the recommendations in the Executive Summary and will feel confidence seeing that there is more detail available for other members of the project team to review in their own time.

On one past assessment, an interim report for a mid-sized business-consumer organization, was being presented to the CEO and other members of the executive team. The assessment's presenter had used a variation on a standard Health Check reporting framework table of contents, as shown in Figure 4.2:

- Executive Summary: Objectives of the review, overall executive summary slide, key messages.
- Evaluation Guidelines: The process that was followed to complete the review. The resources that were interviewed and the documentation that was reviewed.

Table of Contents

1. Executive Summary
   - ❑ Objectives
   - ❑ Assessment Methodology
   - ❑ Overall Executive Review Dashboard
   - ❑ Action Plan for the First 30 Days
2. Evaluation Guidelines
   - ❑ Critical Success Factors (CSFs) for Business & Shareholder Value
   - ❑ Evaluation Framework
   - ❑ Review Approach
   - ❑ Discovery Reference Material
3. Project Review Summary
   - ❑ Overall Review Dashboard
   - ❑ Summary of Observations & Recommendations
   - ❑ Summary of CSFs for Business & Shareholder Value
4. Assessment Review Details
5. KPIs & CSFs
6. Definition of Project Success
7. Conclusion & Next Steps
8. Appendices
   - ❑ Heat Map

Figure 4.2 Sample final report table of contents.

- Project Review Summary: Includes key recommendations and the key message.
- Project Review Details: Includes Areas that are working well, Areas that need improvement, Risk and Mitigation Items.
- KPIs: A list of the Business Key Performance Indicators (KPIs).
- CSFs: A list of the Business and Technical Critical Success Factors (CSFs).
- Definition of Success: A summary of the definition of success as agreed to with the initiative's Steering Committee.
- Conclusion: Overall summary and commentary.
- Next Steps: Activities to be performed, such as a roadshow or implementing immediate recommendations.
- Appendices: Includes other summaries such as Heat Maps showing areas of greatest concern.

When the presenter reached the third slide in the Executive Summary of the presentation, the CEO was exasperated and slammed the desk with the flat portion of his open hand and called out the report saying that the focus seemed to be only on what the project was doing wrong and embarrassing the group. He offered a direct challenge to the process and visibly showed that he was impatient—knowing the project in question was spiraling out of control in terms of cost, timeline, and scope, but not seeing value in looking at what was wrong. The fact that the project could be canceled and that he would have to write off millions of dollars and then to have to start again had been on his mind and his feelings had likely gotten more intense with every missed deadline. This was a key moment in terms of hidden politics, personal goals, and corporate goals. These will be discussed throughout this book.

The presenter recognized the importance of the moment. The next move would be critical to whether the report's recommendations would be accepted or whether the entire assessment process would lose its executive support. He was able to bring the meeting back under control by showing the context of the balance in the report. He pointed out that the negative observations were there to be clear about what needed to change. He also pointed out that there were positive observations as well so this was not an attempt at scare tactics but at being transparent and fact based. The assessor then pointed out that there was also an actionable 30-day plan, as shown in Figure 4.3.

The CEO and Executive Team wanted to immediately see this plan. By the third bullet, this view was extremely well received by the CEO, and then by other members of the Executive Team. With the CEO buyin, this was not surprising. The other pieces of the assessment process, individual interviews, and all the other activities prior to this presentation lay the groundwork and built the credibility that the reviewer understood the material. To the CEO, the crisp action-oriented recommendations with a tight timeframe provided additional reasons to trust the recommendations. He could see that these were not high-level recommendations, generic, with delivery dates six months to a year or more away. This is done too often in the business and can draw out the problems and provide no results. In essence, people end up getting paid to deliver nothing of value to the project in terms of getting it out of its predicament. The deadlines for these recommendations were only 30 days away, and then it would be very visible whether the recommendations succeeded or whether they were just boilerplate stuff. The CEO and consequently the executive

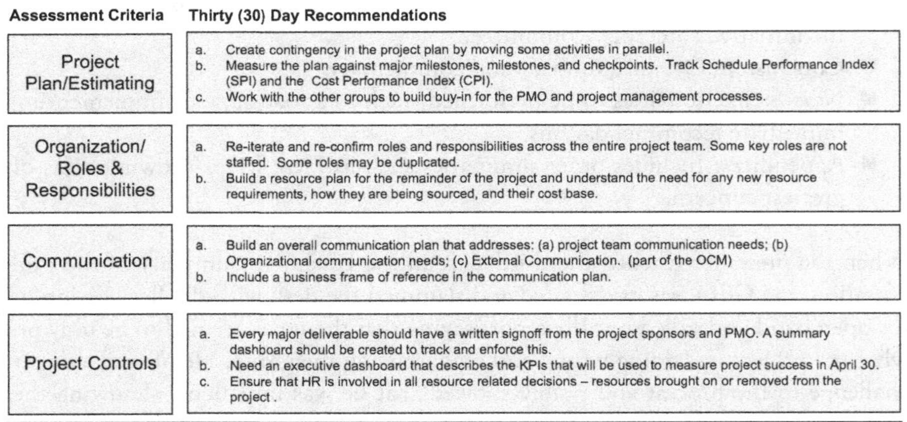

Assessment Criteria	Thirty (30) Day Recommendations
Project Plan/Estimating	a. Create contingency in the project plan by moving some activities in parallel. b. Measure the plan against major milestones, milestones, and checkpoints. Track Schedule Performance Index (SPI) and the Cost Performance Index (CPI). c. Work with the other groups to build buy-in for the PMO and project management processes.
Organization/ Roles & Responsibilities	a. Re-iterate and re-confirm roles and responsibilities across the entire project team. Some key roles are not staffed. Some roles may be duplicated. b. Build a resource plan for the remainder of the project and understand the need for any new resource requirements, how they are being sourced, and their cost base.
Communication	a. Build an overall communication plan that addresses: (a) project team communication needs; (b) Organizational communication needs; (c) External Communication. (part of the OCM) b. Include a business frame of reference in the communication plan.
Project Controls	a. Every major deliverable should have a written signoff from the project sponsors and PMO. A summary dashboard should be created to track and enforce this. b. Need an executive dashboard that describes the KPIs that will be used to measure project success in April 30. c. Ensure that HR is involved in all resource related decisions – resources brought on or removed from the project .

Figure 4.3 Snippits of the thirty (30)-day action plan.

team bought into the report and signed on for next steps. This project is discussed further in the case studies chapters in the last section of the book. There were a lot of lessons learned on it that are worth further analysis.

Generic Executive Reporting Dashboard

Many formats of the report will be discussed in this chapter, but the basic dashboard that forms the essential communication to the executive team is shown in Figure 4.4. The elements in the dashboard are customed using the Assessment Framework Dimensions discussed in Chapter 3. This format has been used to present results to Board of Directors, CEOs, CFOs, Directors, Managers, Business Analysts (BAs), Developers, Consultants, Business Owners, Subject Matter Experts (SMEs), and pretty much anyone else related to the program team on everything from Global multinationals to small family-owned companies. The feedback has been positive from executives who want to see everything on a single page to those who want to dig into the details of supporting material.

The left side of the dashboard is open-ended and intended to capture key overall messages for the executives and readers to digest. Areas of the project that are going well, general observations, and areas that need improvement are written here. Also, an overall recommendation on how well the project is performing should be included. The middle of the dashboard should be customized based on the specific dimensions that were in scope of the assessment. Sub-dimensions can be shown on additional views. The right side of the dashboard will change based on the dimensions, but can also be customized depending on the tone of the assessment and the message that the health check team wants to impart on the project team. The first of the two columns shown in Figure 4.4 represents the "As Is" state of each dimension that was assessed. The second column represents the "To Be" state of each dimension. This second column is pivotal to tone. Including it in the dashboard positions the conversation as a journey of where the project is currently and where they may want to be given the proper investments the organization is willing to make. It allows the conversation to happen with less finger pointing. Omitting this column is like shining a bright light on someone's face. A lot of empty circles or squares is glaring in what's missing. The health check team needs to understand the culture of the organization and work with the executive sponsors to position the messages. Notice that the information is the same. That should not objectively change. Positioning based on what will work with the organizational culture is a consideration that the health check assessment team should weigh.

Two generic formats to report findings that the reviewers may want to highlight to the executive team are shown in Figure 4.5 and Figure 4.7. Figure 4.5 focuses on recommendations while providing space to support the recommendations under a generic headline of "Observations". These are used to establish facts, identify strengths, or weaknesses. They are grouped under one heading to keep the emphasis

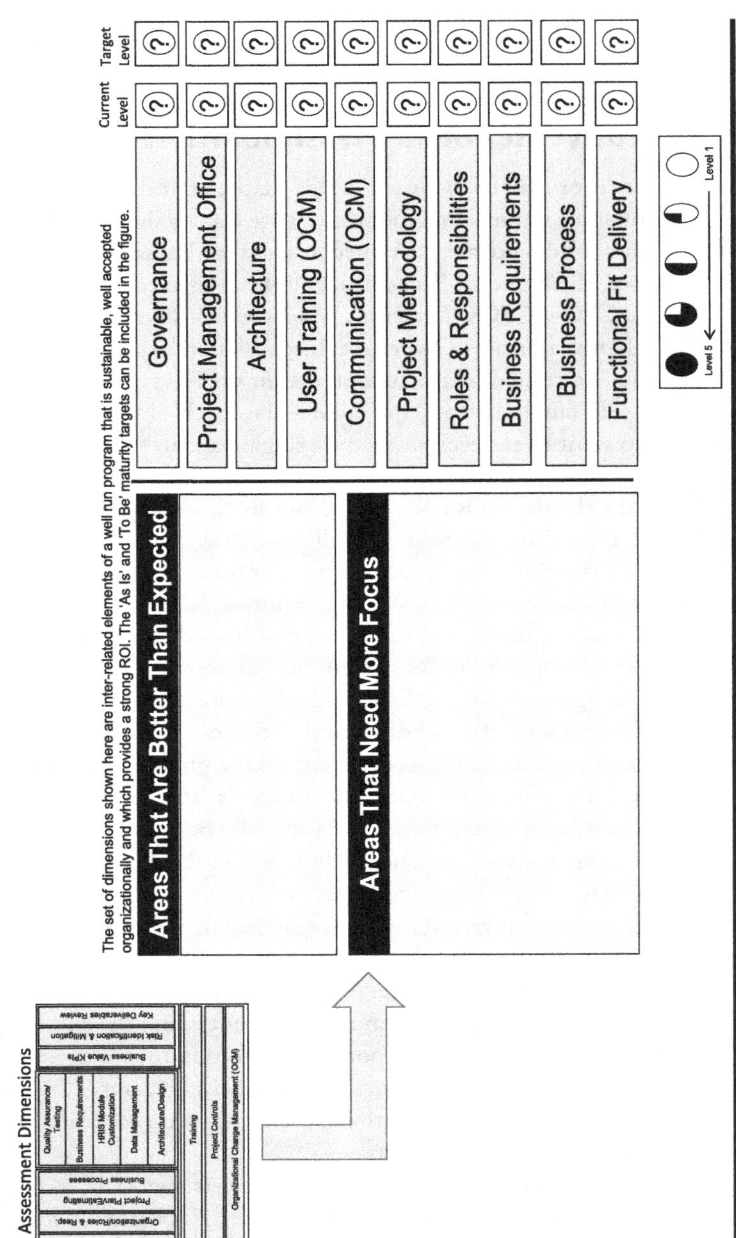

Figure 4.4 Generic executive dashboard.

Figure 4.5 Detailed findings template 1.

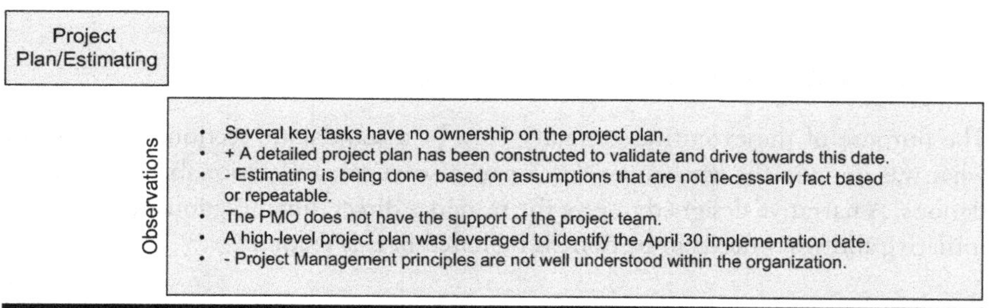

Figure 4.6 Annotating the observations.

on the recommendations. If some differentiation is required, a "+" or "–" can be used as a prefix to indicate whether the finding is a strength or weakness to the project or program, as shown in Figure 4.6. The prefixes can be grouped together as well, but there is an argument that keeping them mixed brings the attention back to the recommendations instead of getting lost in comparing the stacks of pluses and minuses.

Figure 4.7 expands the messaging in Figure 4.6 and shows the observations, and positive and negative findings separately. This generally starts a detailed discussion on the discovery activities when presenting the material in the roadshows.

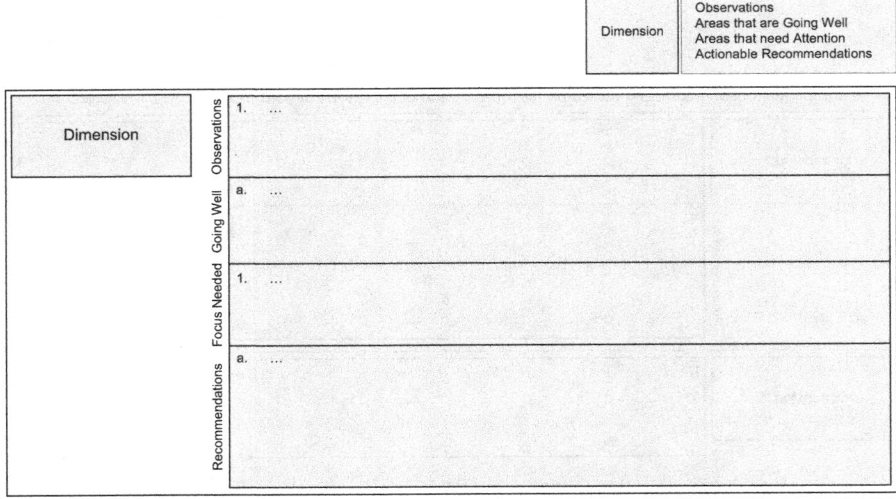

Figure 4.7 Detailed findings template 2.

Detailed Reporting Components

This section details the sections in the table of contents shown in Figure 4.2.

Executive Summary

The purpose of the executive summary is to be a standalone section that conveys what was done in the assessment, key items discovered, and actionable recommendations. A narrative designed to give the readers a direct, unambiguous status of the initiative and what needs to be done is included in this section.

Objectives

Figure 4.8 shows an example of specific objectives for a Health Check initiative. The driving objectives which should have been captured in the Project Charter are included in this section. They may have been revised or more detailed through the course of the assessment. It is important to have confirmed these in the Executive Interviews that were completed in the "Conduct Interviews" phase of the health check.

Assessment Methodology

It's important to describe how the health check assessment was conducted as part of the presentation of the report. This is done to ensure that the audience understands

1. Determine the status of the ERP, HRIS, and CRM project using a Health Check evaluation framework;
2. Determine the feasibility of an Oct 27 20xx implementation deadline;
3. Provide recommendations to meet the stated project KPIs;
4. Provide recommendations to meet the stated corporate CSFs;
5. Build a Business Readiness Check

Figure 4.8 Health check assessment specific objectives.

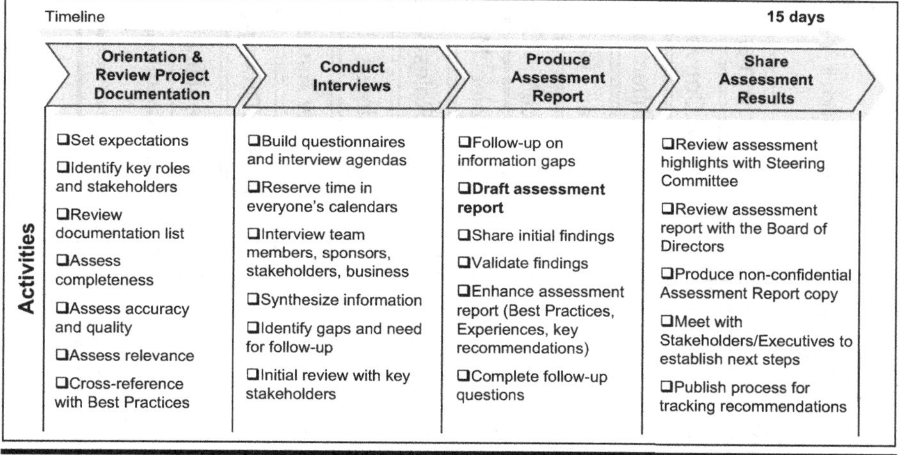

Figure 4.9 Assessment methodology.

the extent of the discovery activities and the depth of the information that was researched. Figure 4.9 shows an example of the assessment methodology that was followed for real-world health checks.

Executive Summary Dashboard

A variant of the executive summary dashboard is shown in Figure 4.10. This example shows that the project requires a lot of work for the implementation within a tight timeframe—the assessment was done six months before the Oct 27 implementation deadline. The deadline is possible, but the focus needs to be on implementing a minimum viable product. Another constraint on the project was that no additional budget was available. So when there is a specific timeline, the only other lever available to project management to manage an initiative is to micro-focus on the functionality list.

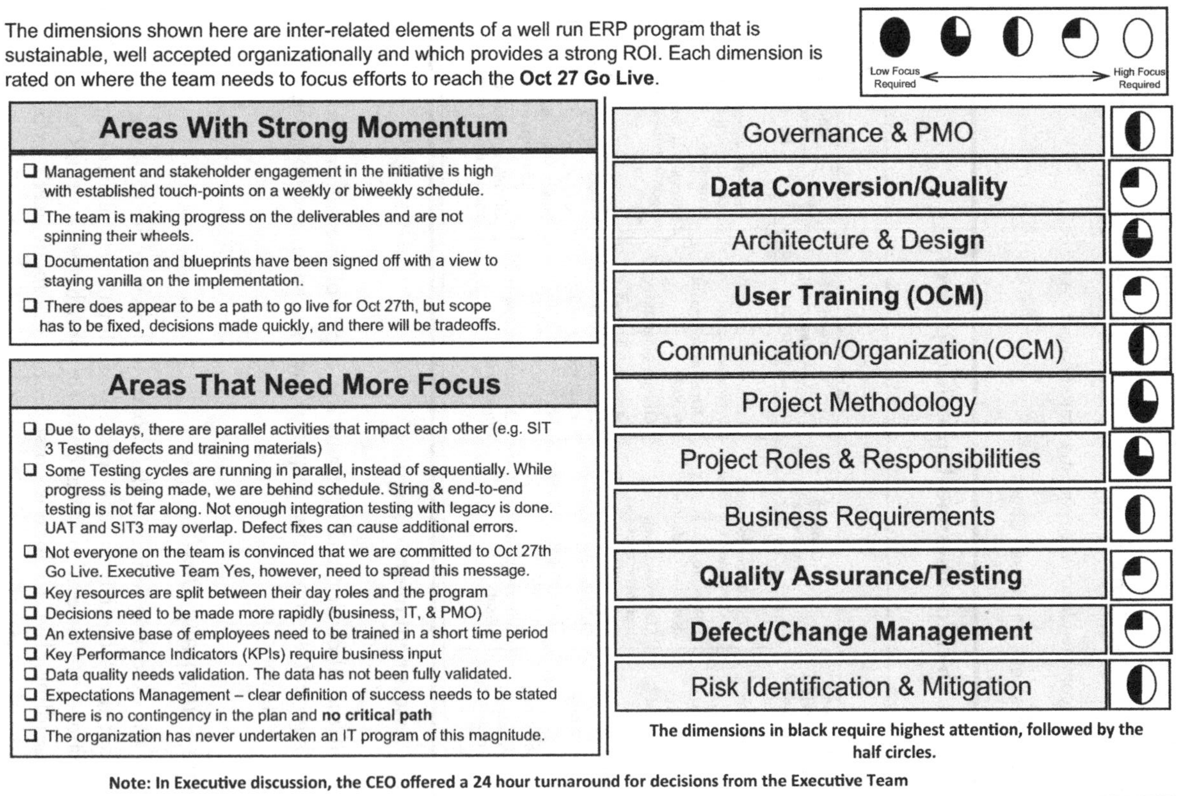

The dimensions shown here are inter-related elements of a well run ERP program that is sustainable, well accepted organizationally and which provides a strong ROI. Each dimension is rated on where the team needs to focus efforts to reach the **Oct 27 Go Live**.

Low Focus Required ⟷ High Focus Required

Areas With Strong Momentum

- ❑ Management and stakeholder engagement in the initiative is high with established touch-points on a weekly or biweekly schedule.
- ❑ The team is making progress on the deliverables and are not spinning their wheels.
- ❑ Documentation and blueprints have been signed off with a view to staying vanilla on the implementation.
- ❑ There does appear to be a path to go live for Oct 27th, but scope has to be fixed, decisions made quickly, and there will be tradeoffs.

Areas That Need More Focus

- ❑ Due to delays, there are parallel activities that impact each other (e.g. SIT 3 Testing defects and training materials)
- ❑ Some Testing cycles are running in parallel, instead of sequentially. While progress is being made, we are behind schedule. String & end-to-end testing is not far along. Not enough integration testing with legacy is done. UAT and SIT3 may overlap. Defect fixes can cause additional errors.
- ❑ Not everyone on the team is convinced that we are committed to Oct 27th Go Live. Executive Team Yes, however, need to spread this message.
- ❑ Key resources are split between their day roles and the program
- ❑ Decisions need to be made more rapidly (business, IT, & PMO)
- ❑ An extensive base of employees need to be trained in a short time period
- ❑ Key Performance Indicators (KPIs) require business input
- ❑ Data quality needs validation. The data has not been fully validated.
- ❑ Expectations Management – clear definition of success needs to be stated
- ❑ There is no contingency in the plan and **no critical path**
- ❑ The organization has never undertaken an IT program of this magnitude.

Governance & PMO

Data Conversion/Quality

Architecture & Design

User Training (OCM)

Communication/Organization(OCM)

Project Methodology

Project Roles & Responsibilities

Business Requirements

Quality Assurance/Testing

Defect/Change Management

Risk Identification & Mitigation

The dimensions in black require highest attention, followed by the half circles.

Note: In Executive discussion, the CEO offered a 24 hour turnaround for decisions from the Executive Team

Figure 4.10 Executive summary dashboard.

This section contains further information on each dimension. Observations are grouped into positive or general impact, indicated by a square or checkmark. Observations identifying negative impact to the program are indicated by a (-). Key recommendations are also provided for next steps.

	Observations	Key Recommendations (30 days)
Governance & PMO	✓ Project Management artifacts meet expected criteria ✓ There are documented roles and responsibilities throughout the project team ✓ Blueprints were signed off by the business - Some key sponsors have retired or are in the process of retiring - Decision making is by consensus on many issues	• Identify a trio of resources for each functional area to make final decisions every day (includes a business stakeholder, IT, and PMO) • Continue senior hands-on involvement in the program (e.g. CEO) • Ensure that message we are going live on Oct 27th is shared unequivocally throughout the project team and beyond. • Need to document all pending decisions and completed decisions
Data Conversion/ Quality	✓ SIT testing has been supported with masked data and generated data in conjunction with user data ✓ User data has been extracted and used for a lot of tests - Full set of user data is still being validated and so the ultimate quality is still not known	• Complete the detailed payroll data validation • Prioritize data elements to ensure their accuracy first • Re-confirm tolerance levels and ensure these are understood by the testers • Complete testing using user data only with NO data generation anywhere in the cycle
Architecture/ Design	✓ Standard ERP architecture coupled with linkage to legacy systems - There are several defects related to the ERP modules that are dependent on resolution from the vendor. - A patch will be applied in Aug after evaluation of its impact. This is a near mandatory patch and will require retesting of some test cases.	• Run an end-to-end integration test on the solution to finalize the architecture between the cloud and the legacy systems • Agree on the parameters of the workarounds or temporary/interim user processes

Figure 4.11 Action plan for the first 30 days.

Action Plan for the First 30 Days

The action plan involves a list of recommendations that must be implemented in the first 30 days. Similar tables can be included for 60-day and 90-day deliverables (Figure 4.11).While any numbers of days can be used, the first thirty generally have good traction in executive meetings.

Evaluation Guidelines

The evaluation guidelines consist of several sections in the report, as described below.

Critical Success Factors (CSFs) for Business and Shareholder Value

A confirmed list of Critical Success Factors that drives business value and which can be used as part of a "GO"/"NO GO" decision on when the solution is approved to go into production should be included here. Figure 4.12 shows some areas for which critical success factors should be identified and provides some examples for each of the areas.

Evaluation Framework

The evaluation framework confirms the project dimensions that were included in the scope of the review. As shown in Figure 4.13, these dimensions are comprehensive

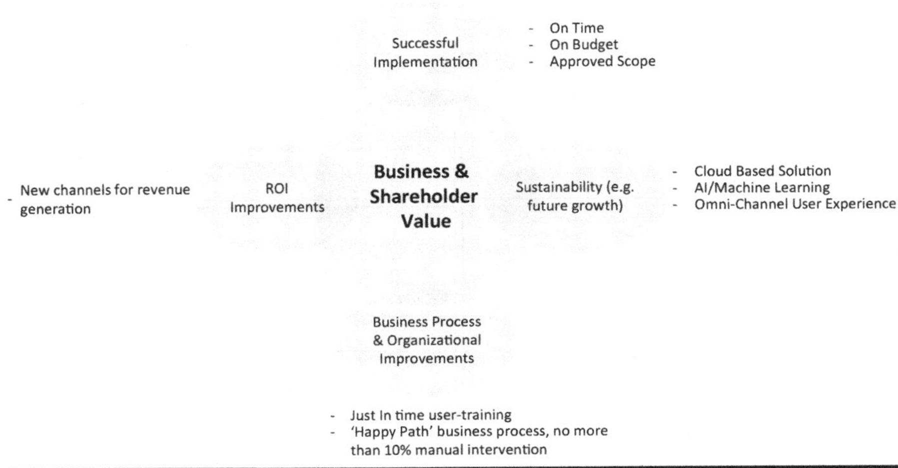

Figure 4.12 Critical success factors (CSFs) for business and shareholder value.

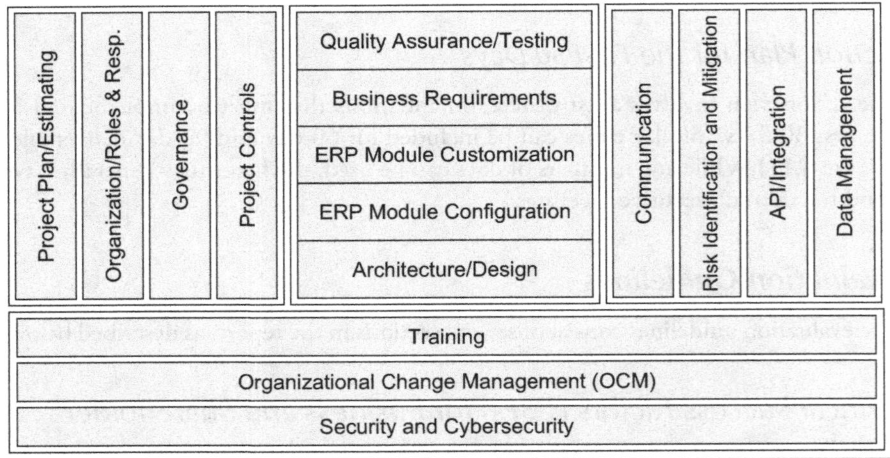

Figure 4.13 Health check framework.

in terms of breadth. They form the foundation of the agreement with the Project Sponsors on what was included in the scope of the review. This list can be customized for specific Health Check engagement.

Review Approach

This is a high-level view of how the discovery activities were done. Figure 4.14 shows the phases that are traditionally followed in a health check. There are also some

❑ The objective of this review was to assess the **ERP Program** from several key perspectives.

❑ Information was gathered from several sources including the following:
(1) Project Management team;
(2) PMO members;
(3) Documentation review;
(4) Interviews with stakeholders, architects, and other team members;
(5) Project experiences; and
(6) Best practices.

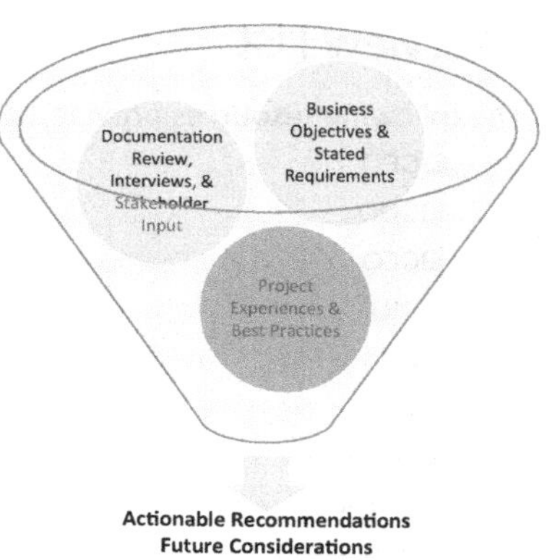

Figure 4.14 Review approach.

activities that precede the start of the process—namely to get a scope baselined and a project charter to be assigned to do the health check assessment.

Discovery Reference Materials

As shown in Figure 4.15, this section of the report contains a list and title of all the people interviewed for the discovery sessions and a detailed list of all the documents that were reviewed. This is an important section in the report showing the depth of the discovery and who was given an opportunity to provide input. Including this documentation list in the final report serves several purposes, as follows:

- The list shows the depth of the review undertaken by the Health Check team.
- The list shows the amount of work completed by the Health Check team in their discovery.
- The list allows the project team to identify any missing documents before this becomes a part of the permanent record.
- The list serves as a checklist for the health check team to ensure that they have completed a comprehensive discovery of the documents that were available. This is arguably the biggest advantage of including this list in the report.

Project Review Summary

This section of the report has more detail than the Executive Summary but still leaves the bulk of the detailed information to a later section in the report. Some of the key recommendations should be brought to the front of this section that would make an immediate positive impact on the project.

Interview List

The following resources provided background material and input into this process:

❑CEO	❑Business Owner 1	❑Test Lead
❑COO	❑Business Owner 2	❑User Training
❑CFO	❑Business Owner 3	❑OCM Lead
❑CIO	❑Process Owner 4	❑SME 1
❑VP 1	❑Process Owner 5	❑SME 2
❑VP 2	❑Auditor 1	❑SME 3
❑VP 3	❑Auditor 2	❑SME 4
❑Director 1	❑SI lead	
❑Director 2	❑Develop	
❑Developer	❑UI Designer	

Documentation List

❑Project Charter
❑Business Requirements
❑Blueprints
❑Functional Requirements
❑Non-Functional Requirements
❑Organization Chart – roles and responsibilities
❑Detailed project plan
❑Issue log
❑Change Management Register
❑Risk Assessment and Mitigation Strategy
❑Quality Strategy
❑Testing Strategy
❑Technical Architecture
❑Technical Design
❑Business Rules
❑Defect log

Figure 4.15 Discovery reference materials.

Overall Review Dashboard

An overall dashboard showing the areas that are going well and those that need improvement are included in this report. The dashboard can also highlight some key activities that need to be started right away. Figure 4.16 shows a project that is in deep trouble, as conveyed by the extensive empty review circles.

Figure 4.16 can be modified with a single column to combine recommendations with the ratings. Figure 4.17 essentially positions the project in two states. The current state shows a project in real trouble and falling off a cliff. The second column, however, positions what the circles need to be to save the project. The recommendation on the page and then in the detail sections of the report reflect how this can be done. The second column, in fact, provides the group with an opportunity to set targets for each dimension, with the assessment team's assistance, and accept these recommendations right away.

During a presentation of a summary dashboard very similar to the one shown in Figure 4.17. The executive team accepted the findings and the recommendations. The CEO's comment, as people were leaving the room, was to essentially confirm that the circles would be "more filled in" when the team would meet next. The visual

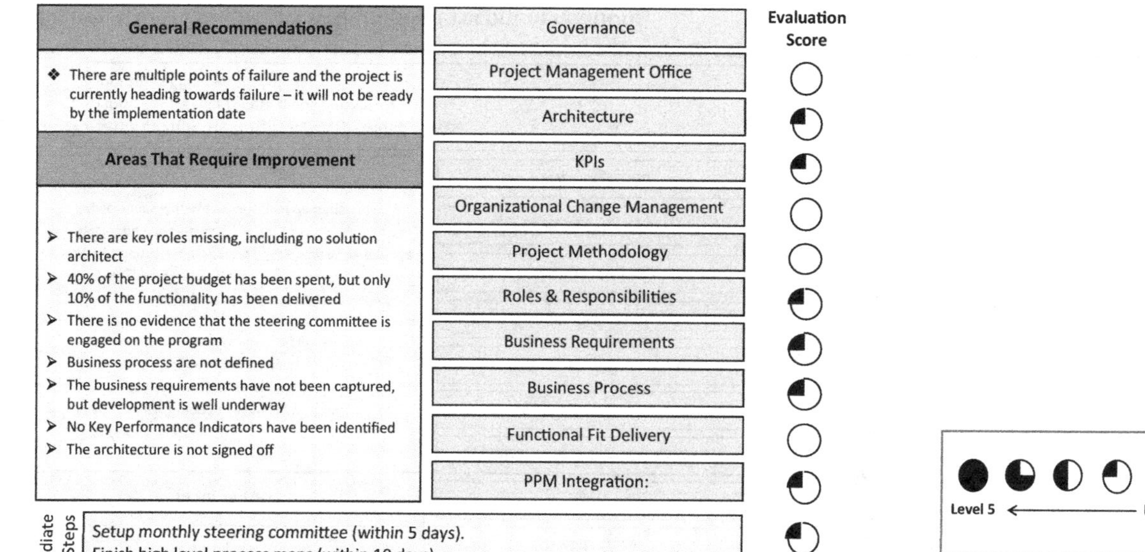

Figure 4.16 Dashboard that shows a project is in deep trouble.

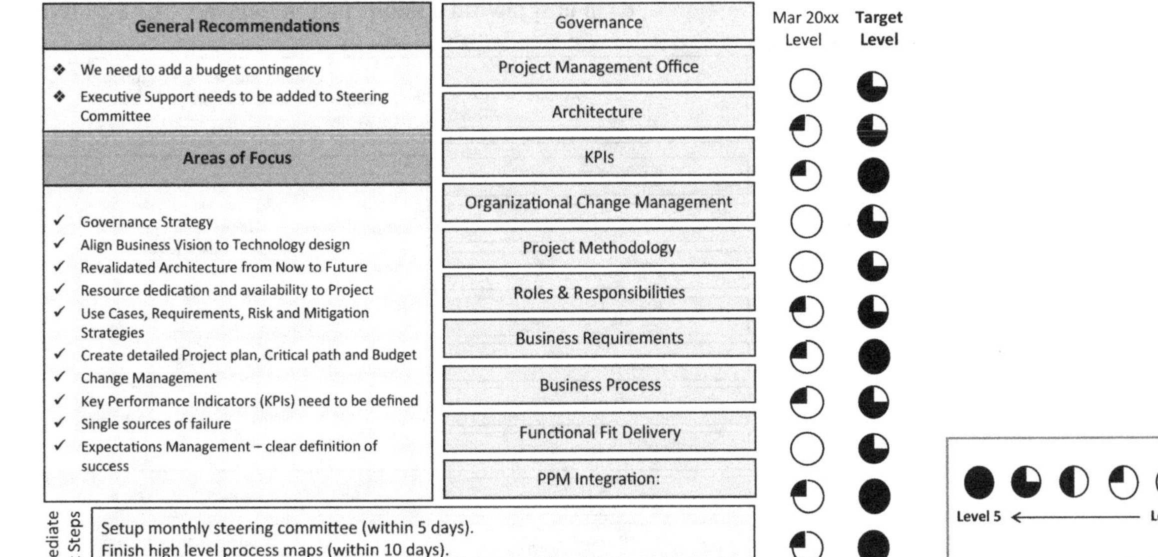

Figure 4.17 Dashboard with implicit recommendations.

was very easy to explain to a very busy group of Global Executives. This has been common feedback from Executives across a variety of projects in different industries. The distilled visual status of current status and desired future status is very easy to understand using these visual tools.

Summary of Observations and Recommendations

An overall summary of the key discovery observations and key recommendations are shown in Figure 4.18. This section can be enhanced with summary observations categorized by any of the assessment dimensions in scope of the health check.

Summary of CSFs for Business and Shareholder Value

The importance of identifying and communicating CSF's has been discussed throughout this book. On one failing project, the assessment team members were given a list of over 100 CSFs. Their interim recommendation was to bring this down to a list of the 12 most critical items to the business. After receiving some pushback, the business analysts and business owners did just that exercise and were able to complete the task. That list of 12 CSFs was used for the final "Go" decision made in writing by the Executive Stakeholders including the COO, CFS, CRO, CIO, and other executives. The project was implemented successfully and met the criteria established by management.

Assessment Review Details

There are a variety of formats this section can take. Figure 4.20 shows a tabular view of observations and recommendations. The observations sections contain both "areas that are doing well" and "areas that need improvement". The first is shown with a checkmark prefix and the latter has a "—" prefix.

Key Performance Indicators (KPIs)

Figure 4.21 shows specific KPIs for Categories and success factors. The last column on the right show specific measurements as targets. This list would be part of the set presented to the team for development, testing, and then signoff. The KPI's are critical to define priorities throughout the project lifecycle.

Critical Success Factors (CSFs)

Critical success factors should be documented for different parts of the project cycle. For example, Figure 4.2 identifies some critical success factors for the governance group. Specific expectations from that group are documented so there is clarity in

	Discovery Keys	Key Recommendations
Overall	❑ The project team is making progress on the program ❑ There is no contingency remaining in the plan so activities are beginning to overlap ❑ There are some defects that require resolution from the ERP vendor ❑ Not everyone believes that there is universal commitment to the Oct 27 date ❑ Business users are working on their day jobs while supporting the program. More time is required from them.	❑ We need to collectively focus on key dimensions to support the Oct 27th Go Live Data ❑ Re-iterate the message that WE ARE GOING LIVE on Oct 27th. Identify what are reasonable workarounds to support this – or how to get one approved rapidly. The CEO needs to send out this message through email. ❑ Dedicate the requested business resources to this project – removing their day to day responsibilities. ❑ Streamline the decision making so that the team can move faster and build a log to document each decision that is made and who supported it. ❑ Agree on the Roadmap Approach (A & B) and the sequencing approach ❑ Finalize the EXIT CRITERIA for each module ❑ Respond to this program by aligning industry best practices with the corporate culture (e.g. need to stick to Vanilla) ❑ Finalize the user training stream – schedule, delivery, materials ❑ Improve the speed of defect resolution ❑ Complete the data validation ❑ Identify a set of 10 – 12 key performance indicators to focus on the acceptance criteria

Figure 4.18 Summery of observations and recommendations.

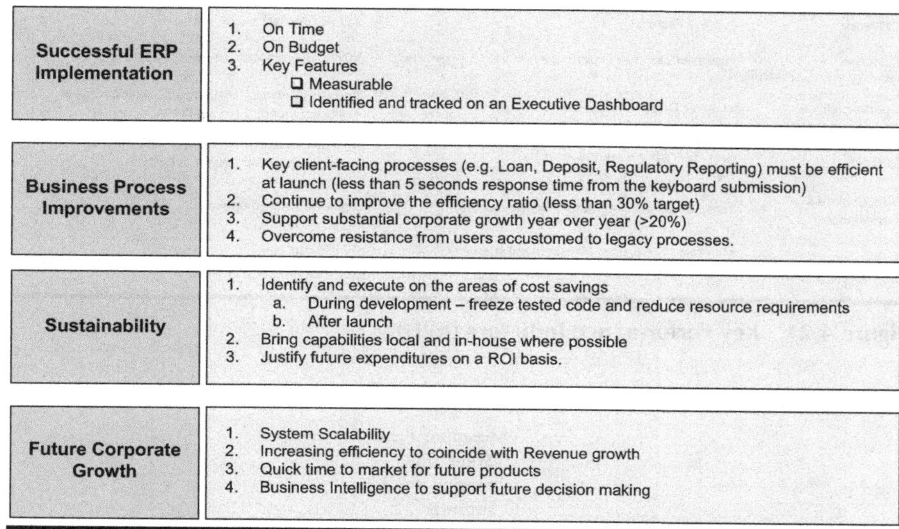

Successful ERP Implementation

1. On Time
2. On Budget
3. Key Features
   - ❑ Measurable
   - ❑ Identified and tracked on an Executive Dashboard

Business Process Improvements

1. Key client-facing processes (e.g. Loan, Deposit, Regulatory Reporting) must be efficient at launch (less than 5 seconds response time from the keyboard submission)
2. Continue to improve the efficiency ratio (less than 30% target)
3. Support substantial corporate growth year over year (>20%)
4. Overcome resistance from users accustomed to legacy processes.

Sustainability

1. Identify and execute on the areas of cost savings
   a. During development – freeze tested code and reduce resource requirements
   b. After launch
2. Bring capabilities local and in-house where possible
3. Justify future expenditures on a ROI basis.

Future Corporate Growth

1. System Scalability
2. Increasing efficiency to coincide with Revenue growth
3. Quick time to market for future products
4. Business Intelligence to support future decision making

Figure 4.19 Summary of CSFs for business and shareholder value.

	Observations	Recommendations
User Training	✓ User training materials are being built and rollout will use a combination of techniques such as in class training, elearning . - User training materials sometimes need to be reworked as defects are resolved - Training materials are still being built and the team is requesting additional resources	• Finalize plan for preparing and deploying Super Users • Agree on the minimal set of training requirements by user group and augment with productivity aides • Finalize the number of users that need to be trained by time of implementation (up to 100%) and in the post implementation period
Communication/ Organization (OCM)	✓ Strong awareness of the program exists and the team is discussing how to overcome user resistance - Messaging around Go-Live dates must be reinforced - There is an uneven sense of urgency on the project team - Inconsistent messaging among the groups	• Communication must focus on the Oct 27th Go Live and what the organization needs to do to be ready for this • Re-examine the 'To Be' Role and role mapping to the "As Is" state • Consider additional user surveys to collect and guide user participation
Project Methodology	✓ We are following the standard ASAP methodology ✓ Deliverables and Gates have been established based on this methodology	• Finalize a critical path to implementation • Identify opportunities for additional streamlining

Figure 4.20 Assessment review details.

Category	Success Factors	KPI (Examples)
Customer	Improve Customer Experience	90% positive google reviews
Operational	Improve Operating Efficiency	Reduce Operation costs by 10% year over year Reduce Finance Carrying Costs
Financial	Grow Margin / Revenue	Improve Margin / Operating Profit by 20% Reduce cost per transaction by 10%
Risk, Control & Compliance	Compliance with Regulatory Requirements	100% on time compliance
Systems	Maintain high system transactional stability/ completeness	99.99% uptime 100% uptime for help desk

Figure 4.21 Key Performance Indictors (KPIs).

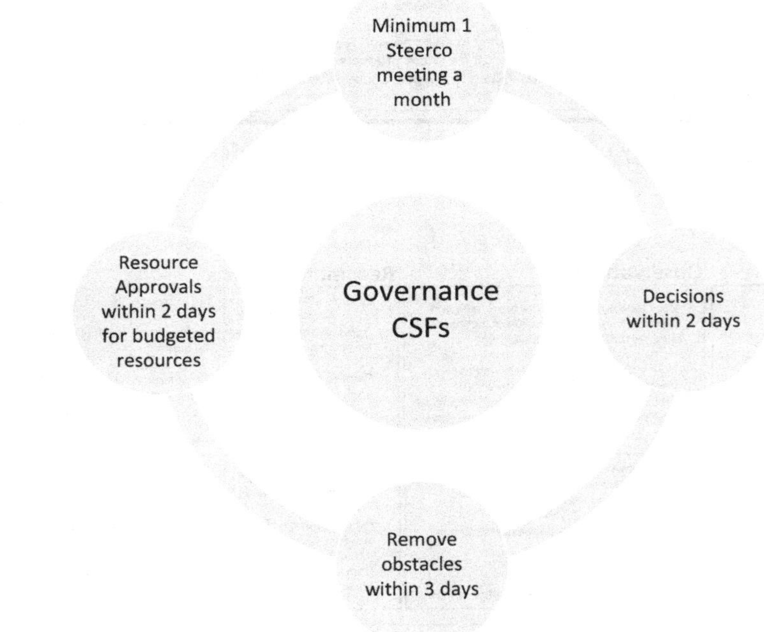

Figure 4.22 Critical Success Factors (CSFs).

how they will respond to requests. These can be modified from time to time as the project moves through the project development lifecycle.

Definition of Project Success

Figure 4.23 shows a set of definitions for project success. These go beyond the traditional on time, on budget measurement, although these are included in the list.

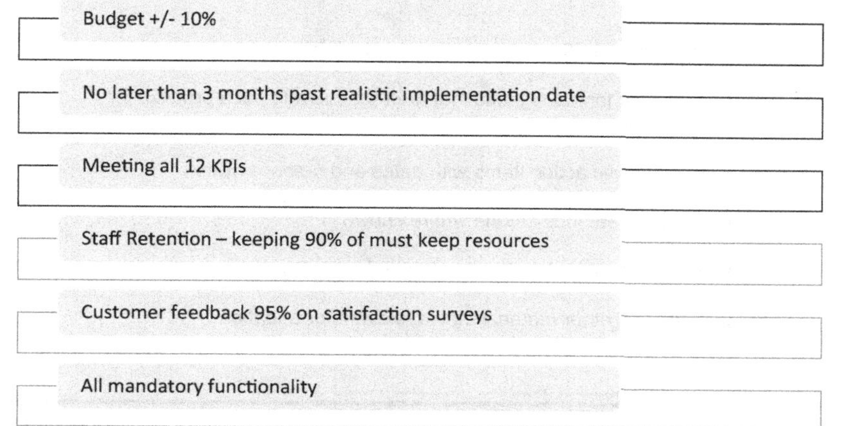

Budget +/- 10%
No later than 3 months past realistic implementation date
Meeting all 12 KPIs
Staff Retention – keeping 90% of must keep resources
Customer feedback 95% on satisfaction surveys
All mandatory functionality

Figure 4.23 Definition of project success.

There is a longer-term business focus and operational excellence focus in this partial list. These can be reiterated at every presentation so that there is a common baseline for this definition across the team and other stakeholders, including the Board of Director's when they are involved in the process.

Conclusion

The conclusion slides or material should loop back to the original objectives and show how they were addressed as shown in Figure 4.24. It is a good idea to provide a response to every objective on this slide to demonstrate what was achieved at a very detailed level.

- ❑ Determine the status of the ERP project using an evaluation framework;
  - All the dimensions in the evaluation framework show that specific risks remain in the project
- ❑ Determine the feasibility of an April 30 implementation deadline;
  - An April 30 implementation date is possible with aggressive and detailed project level risk management and implementation of the recommendations.
  - There is a significant need to AGREE on and communicate a clear definition of success (time, cost, functionality, and money)
  - Manage expectations and reinforce messaging from the top. There are several opinions of what is going to be delivered on April 30.
  - Look beyond April 30 to ensure that the proper ROI is achieved and a sustainable organization is built. The ERP program is continuing after this date.
- ❑ Provide recommendations to meet the stated project targets
  - Prioritize and address the conclusions summarized on the Evaluation Dashboard
  - Build a Roadmap that can be used to guide decisions and expectations.

Figure 4.24 Conclusion.

❑**Should be positioned as a clear call to action**

❑Identify any formal signoffs that are required and set a process for getting these

❑List of specific action items with dates and responsibilities

❑Include acceptance criteria where known

❑Identify remaining touchpoints for the Heath Check

❑Include any other material that is relevant for adoption

Figure 4.25 Next steps.

Next Steps

Figure 4.25 shows a list of action items that serve as next steps following delivery of the assessment report. These should be action oriented and include the key recommendations to bring the project or program to a better state. Members of the client team who are needed to execute these action items can also be included on this page.

What You're Trying to Convey

The assessment reports are a vital tool to impress the findings and recommendations back to the core project team. Even within the table of contents presented in this chapter, there are a lot of options, columns, graphs, and figures that can be used to present information back to the team. Other formats can also be used to stress specific messages. When trying to settle on a format, keep the following considerations in mind:

- Be Transparent: The messages should be the same to every audience in the organization. There should be no hidden motive or information held back. This does not include confidential or controversial information that should first be shared with the Executive Sponsors and managed through their direction.
- Build Trust: Use facts and figures to convey specific information as often as possible. Show the project team that the assessment team has reviewed the documentation and listened carefully during all the interviews.
- Building Confidence in the Results: Lead up to the results so that when they are presented, they are a natural outcome of all the information that precedes them.

- Portray Urgency: If the project needs immediate changes, reflect this in the report. Put the key recommendations on the first page of the Executive Summary.
- Show Collaboration: The Health Check is a collaborative tool. Show where different team members provided information, reports, and opinions. Be generous in pointing these out during presentations—without going overboard. However, place a line there because the assessment and recommendations that are yours.
- Limit Surprises: While the assessment report must be objective, try to ensure that the contents are not a complete surprise to the intended audience. Socialize it in advance.
- Show Independence: Collaboration aside, the summary report should stress the independence in the assessment and recommendations parts of the report.
- Don't Make it Personal: Never make the report adversarial or personal. There should be no attempt to highlight one group over another unless there is something important to the advancement of the project.
- Show Options Where Possible: In recommendations, provide choice where it makes sense to do so from a cost and effectiveness perspective.
- Tough Messages: Do not be shy about giving tough messages, but ensure the report has the supporting material from the discovery activities to justify them.

Closing Perspective

This chapter examined the different formats of the health check assessment report. The Executive Summary generally gets a lot of attention first. It provides key information such as the following:

- What is going well
- What needs improvement
- An overall assessment of the project or program
- Report card on key dimensions that were included in the review

Following the executive dashboard, the next section that gets a lot of attention is the list of recommendations to either drive more business value, adjust the project, or how to rescue a project that is failing. Other sections of the Assessment report flesh out the details around these sections. This includes detailed sections around the observations and assessment of the documentation and information gathered in stakeholder interviews.

The final health check report is assembled from several interim reports, as shown in Figure 4.26. These interim versions are socialized with members of the project team to ensure verification of the information collected and to give them an opportunity to clarify any information that is in the reports.

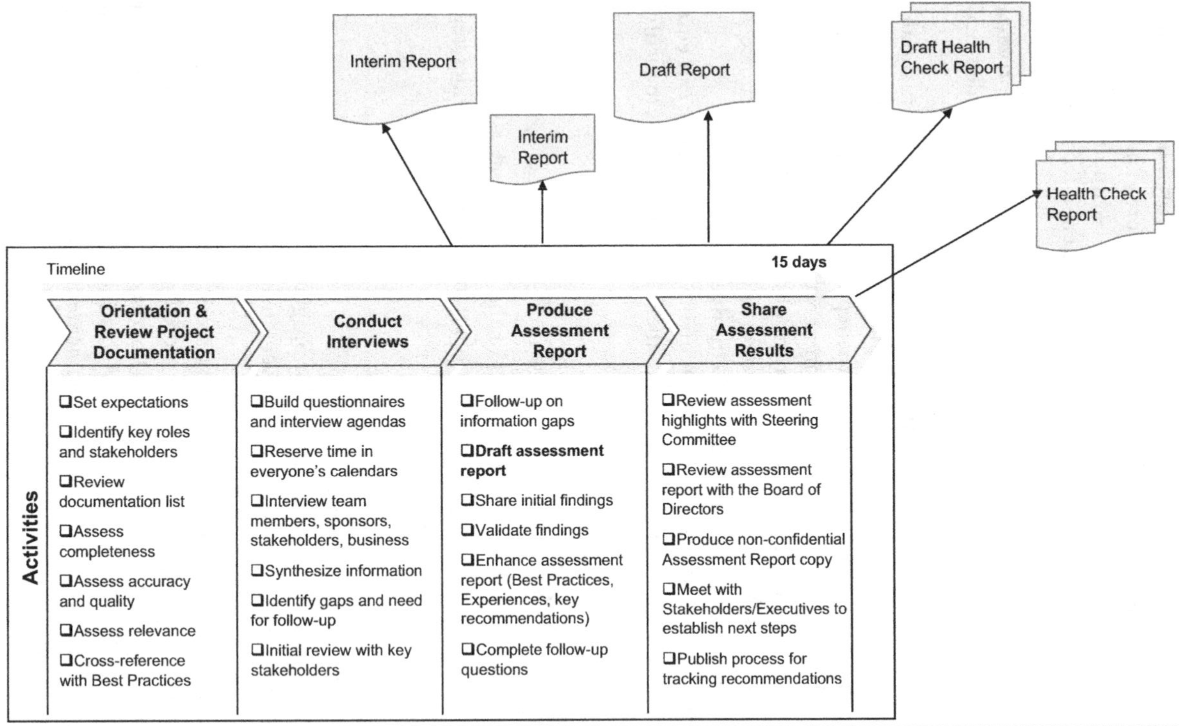

Figure 4.26 Report lifecycle.

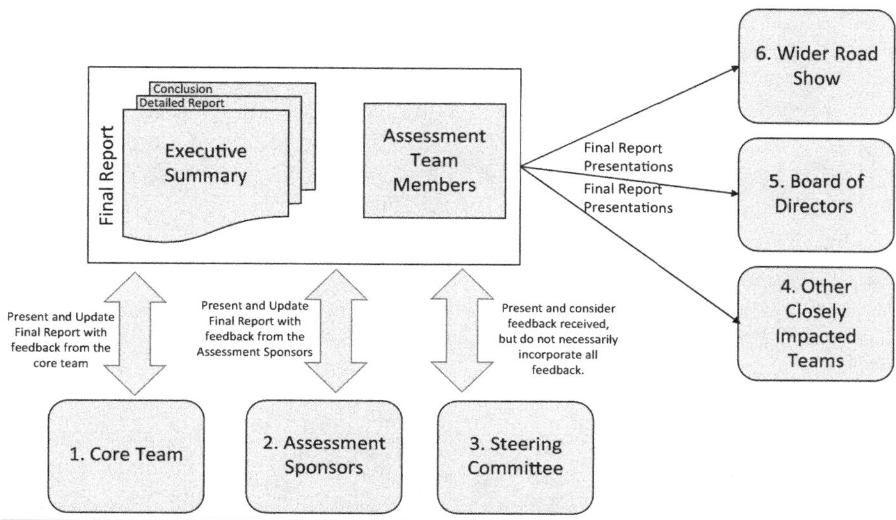

Figure 4.27 Road trip.

The final health check report is socialized through the organization via a series of meetings or workshops, as shown in Figure 4.27. The first meetings are with the core project team and the business/technology sponsors that commissioned the health check. Their feedback is incorporated in the final report where it makes sense. After this, a typical next presentation involves the Steering Committee, especially when the report addresses urgent needs around a project rescue or ways to drive higher levels of business value. It's not unusual to do a wider roadshow that can include the Board of Director's and other parts of the organization after this.

Chapter 5

Roles and Responsibilities Needed for an Effective Assessment

The health check assessment is a partnership between the assessment team, the executive (s) sponsoring the initiative, and the Steering Committee. In addition to this, other stakeholders will be involved in the decision-making process to get started and then again during the assessment. They will also be critical for implementing the recommendations coming out of the project assessment activities. Figure 5.1 shows the roles that will be directly involved in the assessment. These will be discussed in more detail in the following sections of this chapter.

There is an ongoing discussion in many organizations on whether the business owns an IT base project (e.g. an ERP implemention) or whether the Information Technology (IT) group owns it. There are pros and cons associated with each type of ownership, but perhaps the question is not just about ownership but also about involvement and responsibility. The reality is that the business is paying for the projects directly or indirectly. This makes them a key stakeholder in every project. However, IT is the enabling organization. They bring a set of skills and experiences to solve the problem, and they will be supporting the solution once it goes live. For this reason, most IT projects should be considered owned by the business or co-owned between a business sponsor and a technology sponsor. Co-ownership actually produces a better outcome because it brings business value considerations and technology considerations to the forefront. Having either of those neglected will produce a substandard outcome. With that in mind, the following section drills into

DOI: 10.1201/9781003269786-6

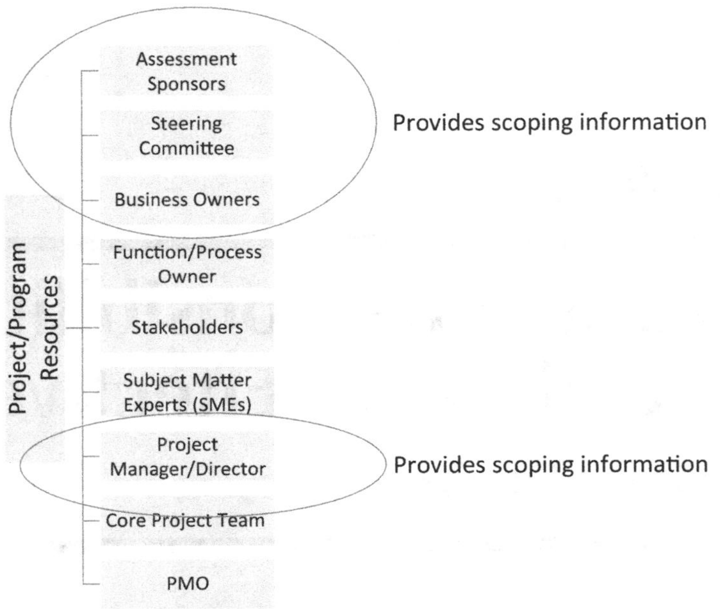

Figure 5.1 Project/program resources (high level).

the type of roles that will be involved in the pre-assessment, during the assessment, and post- assessment processes and how to best leverage these resources at various points in time.

Project/Program Resources

Generally speaking, the first contact between an assessment team is between the leader of the assessment team and an executive, perhaps the business or technology sponsor—perhaps both - from the project or program that is underway. As shown in Figure 5.2, there could be several single or compound reasons for this out-reach to an independent Health Check Assessment team as described in the sections below.

Insurance or Assurance

As part of their project, some organizations run an independent health check in parallel with the project or program. The health check assessment team reports into an executive such as the COO, CIO, CDO, CFO, CEO, CHRO, or another designate. The health check team provides a regular update to the executive team (say monthly, bimonthly) with some crisp recommendations and observations. Project Management and the Executive Team have the right to accept, modify,

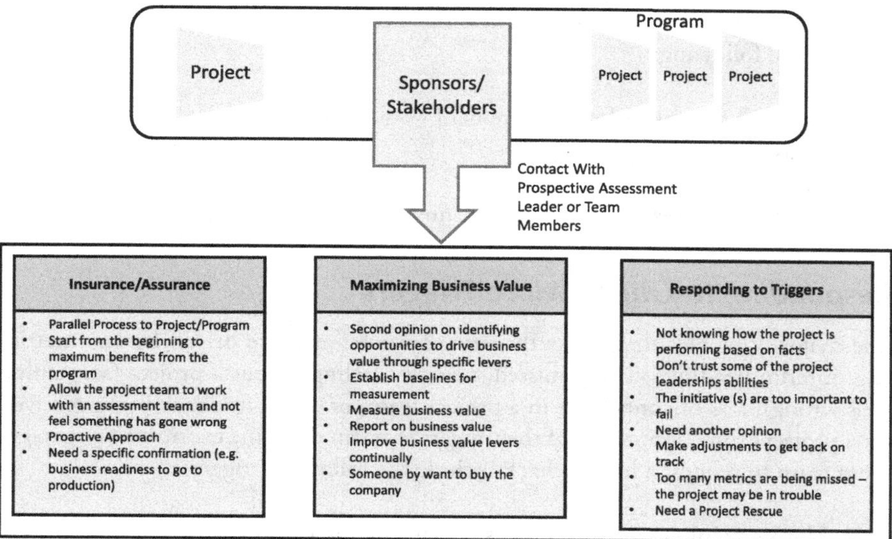

Figure 5.2 Reasons for contacts with the assessment team.

reject, or postpone any of the recommendations. The process requires them to provide an explanation for their decision so that the decision cannot be questioned at a future date.

This is a proactive approach that works best using an independent assessment team. Some of the other drivers for pursuing this approach in the mind of project sponsors or other project executives are the following:

- Start from the beginning to maximum benefits from the program
- Allow the project team to work with an assessment team and not feel something has gone wrong
- Need a specific confirmation (e.g. business readiness to go to production)
- This is a good vehicle for some career protection to minimize the risk of future issues for a very small, almost nominal, cost.

Maximizing Business Value

Another reason for a team to approach an independent team is to conduct health checks to ensure that the project or program is going to deliver measurable business value. By the time a project has progressed into a development phase, sometimes with multiple sprint outputs going into production, the business drivers start to suffer. This is especially true when a period of de-prioritization is reached where decisions are being made to reduce scope in order to implement in a specific timeframe.

An independent team may be commissioned to do a one-time health check to confirm the following:

- Establish a baseline for measurement
- Measure business value
- Report on business value
- Improve business value levers continually

Responding to One or More Triggers

The majority of Health Checks that are commissioned are driven by key metrics (e.g. interim deadlines) being missed, negative feelings about a project (something feels wrong), loss of confidence in a project team, or direct feedback being received for a project's direction. Some of the triggers that can drive the executive or management team to request a health check include the following triggers:

- Not knowing how the project is performing based on facts
- The initiative (s) are too important to fail and need reassurance about direction
- Need another opinion on what's happening on the project
- Make adjustments to get back on track because something is wrong
- Too many metrics are being missed—the project may be in trouble
- Need a Project Rescue to avert a project disaster

Project/Program Roles and Responsibilities

Figure 5.3 shows three periods of time to consider when discussing project team contacts. In Period A, someone related to the project has expressed interest in having a health check done. This group will be referred to as the Assessment Sponsors.

The assessment sponsors will reach out to someone on the health check team or someone that the health check team reports into. This will start a series of discussions to define the scope, objectives, and timeline of the project. Figure 5.4 shows the key roles that will begin to interact between the project resources and a subset of the health check team. In Period A this will likely be the Director and the Project Lead with some small support from the BA or Architect.

In Period B, the full project team resources and the full assessment team will interact in the detailed activities shown in the subprocesses within that time period. The project sponsor will need to ensure that the project team resources are available as required by the assessment team during this period—which is generally 3–6 weeks in a standard health check assessment.

In Period C, a subset of the project team will take the initiative to implement the recommendations. The involvement of the Health Check team in Period C will

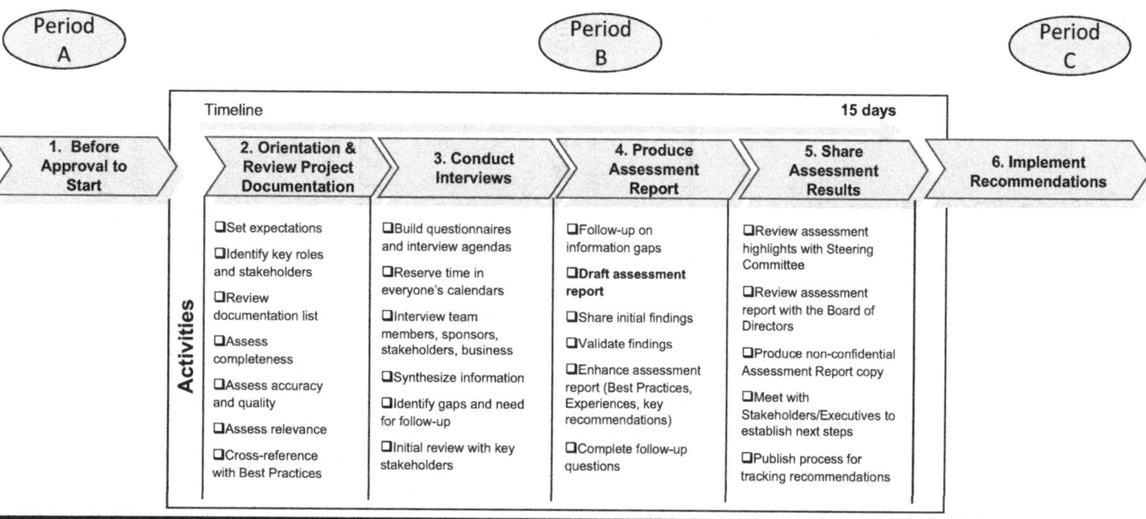

Figure 5.3 Key time periods across the health check lifecycle.

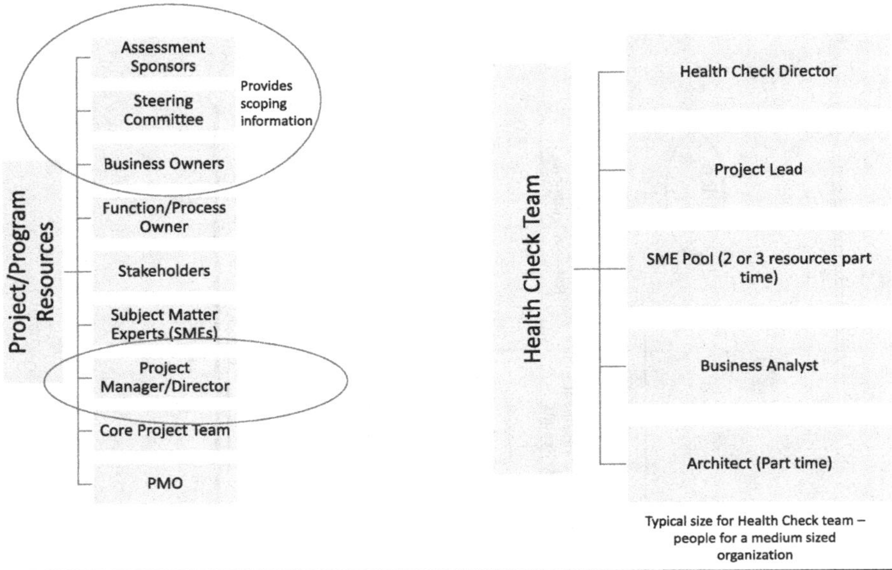

Figure 5.4 Scoping resources.

depend on the type of Health Check that was commissioned. If the periodic options were selected, Period B and Period C would repeat as shown in Figure 5.5.

The roles and responsibilities of the core project or program team groups and individual resources are described in the sections that follow:

Assessment Sponsors

The assessment sponsors will work with the Health Check leadership to establish the scope and objectives for the assessment. They will need to establish and communicate the parameters of the review with the project team and ensure they are available to the assessment team.

Steering Committee

The Steering Committee members may also contribute to scope and objectives. They will be interviewed for the assessment and will receive the report and recommendations.

Business Owners

This group will be available for the interview process and should share any concerns or experience they have on the project or program.

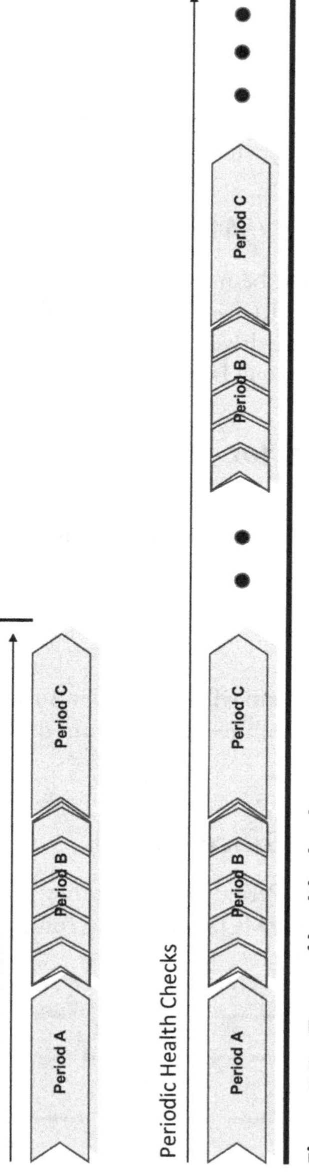

Figure 5.5 Types of health checks.

Function/Process Owners

The function/process owners will need to provide information and be available for interviews. They will be involved in implementing the recommendations as well.

Stakeholders

Stakeholders should be included in the interview list. They will be involved in the benefits identification, tracking, and reporting.

Subject Matter Experts (SMEs)

Subject Matter Experts should be included in the interview list to provide domain expertise. Some of them might have provided warnings to the Steerco if they were not seeing business value being driven in the initiative. SMEs are among those who know the business best and so will be a valuable source to interview.

Project Manager/Director

Depending on the reasons for the health check, the overall manager/director of the initiative should be involved in the scoping activities. In some instances, the individual (s) in this role may have commissioned the health check on a proactive basis.

Core Project Team

Members of the core project team will be interview subjects in Period B of the health check assessment based on recommendations from the Steering Committee and the organization charts.

Project Management Office (PMO)

The PMO can be involved in Periods A, B, C if they have involvement in the initiative. As shown in Figure 5.6, PMO's can serve a continuum of services on projects.

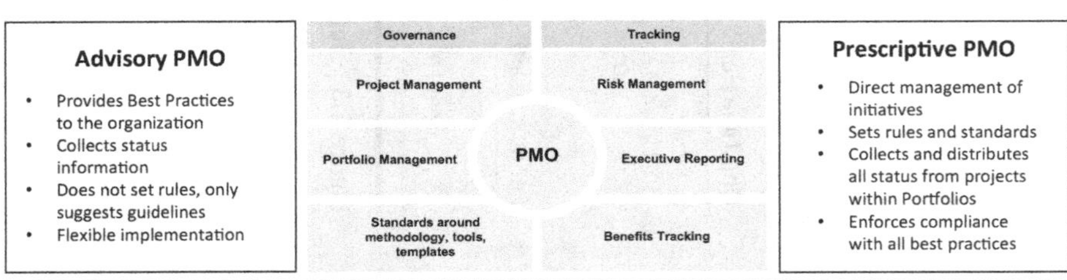

Figure 5.6 Project Management Office (PMO) structure.

They can be largely advisory, in which case they are providing recommendations and are likely not involved in the direct management of initiatives. They can be interviewed, but will not likely be involved in Period A or C.

PMOs that are more prescriptive or directly involved in the management of programs should be included in all three Time Periods.

The PMO manages all the activities required to execute on the business strategy:

- Implement a project management framework
- Manage the Initiatives/projects
- Take corrective action when necessary
- Communicate with the Executives and business Sponsors

The Assessment Team

As shown in Figure 5.7, the assessment team can be sourced from a variety of places. These include the following:

- External Vendor: The health assessment team is independent from the organization. As such they will bring a fresh perspective to the initiative and will look in places that might be neglected by the core team for any number of reasons.
- Subset of the Team: Some organizations opt to have a subset led by the project manager conduct their own health checks. This approach does have the

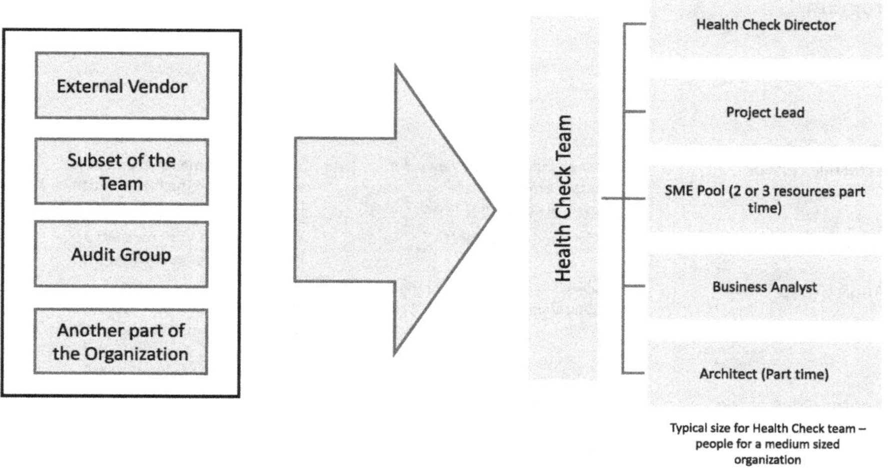

Figure 5.7 Sourcing the project health check team.

benefit of double-checking facts on the ground, but the team will not know what they don't know. They will bring a preset perspective to the health check, but can still give the team a chance to take a step back and gives them permission to speak up about problems they may have been reluctant to bring forward in their usual project role.

- Audit Group: This could be a dedicated part of the organization that is required to audit projects that meet certain criteria. While the audit report is very critical, auditors must also remain separate from the core project team (e.g. unbiaised and objective) and so will not likely be allowed to provide specific recommendations. Also, project management should not be going to audit for a health check as that is not the purpose of this otherwise important vehicle.
- Another Part of the Organization: Some organizations have departments dedicated to checking the health of projects and programs within an organization. This could be a function of a PMO, for example, or a business sponsorship group.

Figure 5.8 shows some of the common pros and cons with each approach. In general, the external group is the most independent and so can be collaborative and transparent. The other groups have more knowledge of the organization, but may have structural constraints. They also will not have true independence in the purest sense, but this can be mandated by the executive team and organizational culture may be able to drive it forward. Because Health Check initiatives generally pay for themselves many times over, cost should have a smaller consideration in the sourcing direction selected by an organization to conduct health checks.It is also possible to source different health checks from different groups over the life of a project or program.

	Pros	Cons
External Vendor	• Offer an independent Viewpoint • External experience • Experts at completing health checks	• Will require some ramp up to the organization on the first iteration of the health check.
Subset of the Team	• Understands the project	• Will not have a fresh perspective • Will not have independence
Audit Group	• Understands the culture of the organization	• Generally does not provide recommendations for improvement • Only checks compliance to specific standards • This is not a health check vehicle
Another Part of the Organization	• Understands the culture of the organization	• May be influenced by corporate culture. • Will not have best practices from other external and similar initiatives.

Figure 5.8 Table of pros and cons of the sourcing options.

Roles/Responsibilities for the Program

The list below reflects a subset of the common roles and responsibilities on different types of IT projects. These specific roles should be considered for the interview list that is being developed as part of the project health check in Time Period B. One set of deliverables that the health check team will request before their work starts, or certainly early in their activities, are the "organization chart" and the "roles & responsibilities" documentation. The organization chart package should include the corporate organization chart and a project-specific organization chart as shown in Figure 5.9.

Some of the resource roles will appear on both charts. A warning flag for the health check team to consider are the parameters that have been put in place to allow resources to work in their day jobs in the corporate structure and to support specific project initiatives at the same time. There are mechanisms for doing this that include backfills, performance bonuses, and other structural changes. The Health Check team needs to dig into these during the interview sessions to ensure that the work arrangements do not put risk on the project timeline and deliverables.

As part of the assessment, the team will need to determine how the role definitions align to similar projects in the industry and then identify any missing roles or misalignment of the role definition for further review during the interview process

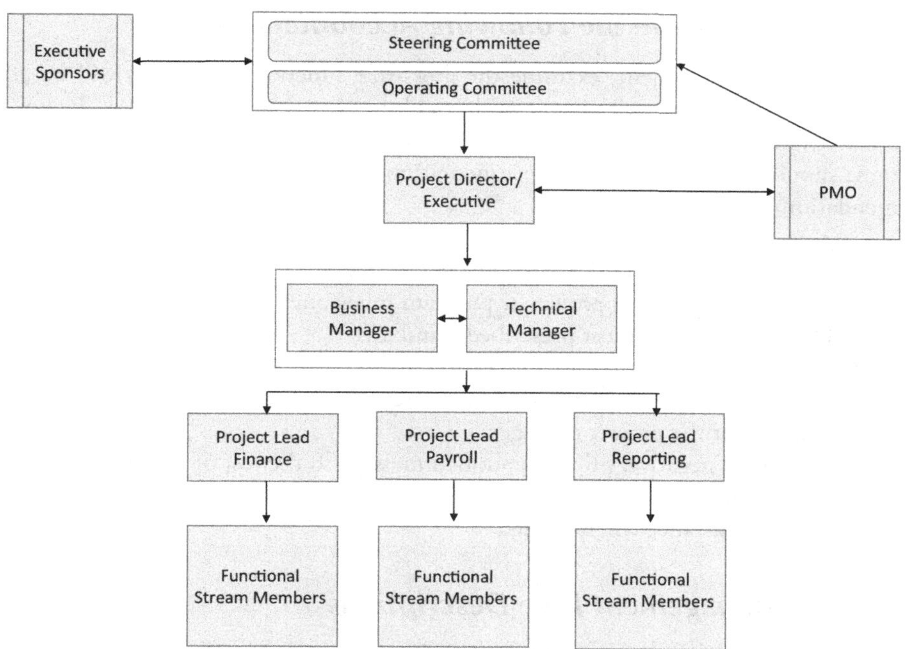

Figure 5.9 Simplified project organization chart.

activities. There are some example descriptions for consideration below-containing information that has proven to be effective on many past projects. These should be customized to meet the specific needs of the health check initiative being planned.

The assessment team should map the requirements and architecture to the organization chart and identify any gaps and register these as assessment findings. As part of the interview plan, consider the roles in the list below to determine if there are any red flags e.g. missing roles or unfilled open spots.

Common Responsibilities and Accountabilities

Ensure that members of the project team understand what their roles are in terms of accountability, responsibility, and authority. During the interview process on a past health check initiative, it was surprising to hear that certain key tasks, such as owning deadlines, had no accountability or ownership across the entire project team. In other words, project leads were working toward deliverables, but did not believe they were accountable for meeting any deadlines. It's imperative to ensure that key tasks map to roles that are staffed on the project. Another common red flag to look for is that roles may be well described, but not staffed. This leads to the same accountability problems. For example, quality is the QA Manager's responsibility—and that individual has not yet been hired.

All the Roles Have the Following Accountabilities

As part of the assessment, examine the cross-role functionalities. This will be an indication of the proactivity in the project culture that is being fostered at the governance level. Here are a sample of accountabilities that apply to each resource and these should be included in the documentation being reviewed (or create a recommendation to do so):

- Accountable to meet the dates assigned to them
- Accountable to meet project or program milestones
- Deliverables must meet prescribed standards
- Deliverables must meet quality expectations
- All resources are accountable to escalate issues and concerns to their direct manager or the project manager
- Do not be negative, provide a unified message to the rest of the team
- Raise issues and suggest solutions
- Ask for assistance when needed

Sample Management Role Descriptions

The assessment of the organization charts should begin with a review of the management roles on the project to ensure that high level principles are in place and to

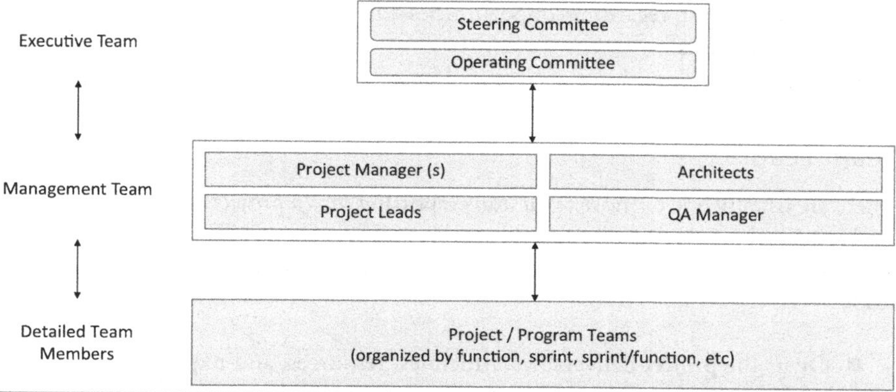

Figure 5.10 End-to-end management interaction.

look for any red flags at this layer as problems here will ripple across all levels of the project or program. The review needs to understand the management and reporting practices between the Steering committee and the working team, as shown in Figure 5.10. Members from these groups should be included in the interviews being planned in Period B of the assessment.

Project Manager/Project Director

The Project Manager has overall responsibility for delivery of the project or program. They report into the Steering Committee. Responsibilities can include the following:

- Own the project plan, scope, schedule, resources, cost estimates, budgets, Organizational change management, communication, risk and mitigation strategies, governance
- Overall accountability for the success of the project
- Overall accountability to drive and report on business benefits
- Monitor progress on the project plan against key milestones and critical dates
- Escalate key issues to the Steering Committee
- Works with the Steering Committee to remove obstacles
- Facilitate signoff of key deliverables
- Liaison with other stakeholders in the organization
- Report into the Steering Committee and the Board of Directors
- Execute project tracking against baseline schedule, manage issues and risks to deliverables
- Hold weekly status meetings with team members to gather status
- Report project status to project director and publish in a shared location for other team members to view

- Provide input regarding opportunities for continuous process/productivity improvements
- Establish/communicate new/revised process flows within the project team

Team Lead

There are usually one or more team leads reporting into a project manager. The team lead is critical for staying on top of the project. The responsibilities described below apply to anyone in a lead role on the project or program, e.g. Test Lead, technical lead.

- Owns the project deliverables, timelines, resources, and requirements for one or more business processes or functions
- Escalate recommendations, issues, concerns, risks to their direct manager
- Manages members of their sub-team and ensures they are following the development and management methodology
- Ensures the integrity of the business deliverables, including contributing content where it is missing
- Works with other project leaders to ensure cross-team sharing and collaboration
- Provides status reports to direct manager or their designate
- Keeps the Project Manager informed of ongoing activities
- Escalates risk to the project manager without delay
- Maintains their part of the budget
- Ensures that all deliverables follow standards

Solution Architect/Other Architects

Look for one or more architects to be responsible for the different types of "As-Is" and "To-Be" architectures in the solution. Some of these include Data Architecture, Reference Architecture, Technical Architecture, Business Architecture, Solution Architecture, and Process Architecture. There can also be conceptual and physical models of each. An absence of "As-Is" and "To-Be" views is a red flag that requires deeper investigation in the interview process.

- Overall ownership over the non-functional requirements
- Map Working Environments:
  - align with other teams to coordinate population of the environments at different points in the workstream
  - Ensure effective migration from one environment to another
  - Ensure effective setup of development, test, user acceptance test, training, and production environment

  - Ensure disaster recovery and contingency environments have been established and tested
- Support conducting proof of concepts to verify that non-functional requirements are being met and there are no showstoppers in the design
- Ensure cross-development teams are coordinating efforts and best practices e.g. reusing code
- Ensure that technical issues are tracked and resolved
- Research technical feasibility of different solutions
- Work closely with the other leads to ensure that solutions will work as designed
- Share established technical standards for the project
- Ensure that the final architectures will meet the requirements of the initiative
- Ensure that the final architectures are cost-effective and provide value into the future (e.g. optimize the total cost of ownership)

Quality Assurance Manager/Lead

Quality Assurance is an end-to-end function that should start early in the project lifecycle so that all the requirements and designs can be verified through testing scenarios. This role provides on the ground realistic status to management who then provides this to the Steering Committee. This process must be optimized and thorough enough to provide meaningful data so that governance processes can react. For example, if the BAs are reporting that the requirements are complete, the testing team needs to send out an immediate alert if the test scenarios being constructed from the requirements deliverables are not covering all the real-world cases. There must be meaningful accountabilities in the management layer to effectively escalate this information.

Some of the key responsibilities for this role are as follows:

- Prepare a QA and overall test plan
- Plan all the types of testing including System Integration Test (SIT), Regression Testing, Stress Testing, Functional Testing, User Acceptance Testing, and others.
- Ensure automation of the testing processes, especially over time so that testing continues to be cost-effective and rapid
- Escalate findings to Project Management and the Steering Committee
- Ensure that the testing scope is confirmed
- Ensure that the test data supports the corporate standards (e.g. masking of production data)
- Ensure there is sufficient and meaningful data to support testing
- Works with the Architects to co-ordinate physical environments for testing
- Ensure defects are retested

Other Team Member Roles

Other team roles will be specific to the type of project being assessed. Here are some of the common roles that occur on most non-trivial IT projects. The health check team should look for two types of red flags:

- Cross-reference the roles and responsibilities document and organization chart to the project plan to assess consistency, completeness, and identify missing roles.
- Assess the completeness of the roles and responsibility descriptions.

Functional Configuration Specialist

The functional configuration specialists must have domain and system knowledge of the software being implemented, e.g. ERP, CRM, HRIS, EPM, Data Analytics and others. A couple of specific responsibilities include:

- Configure the software solution being implemented
- Unit Test the configuration
- Escalate issues to the project lead
- Meet the timelines agreed to and included in the project plan

Developer or Senior Developer

Developers for custom work or integration work are usually doing a bulk of the actual activities on the project. This is usually a very extensive, time-consuming stream with the need for extensive testing at several levels (integration, stress, others). Some of their key responsibilities include the following:

- Design, develop, unit test modules or APIs
- Ensure that the business requirements are fully met
- Ensure work adheres to corporate standards and participate in code walkthroughs
- Follow the development methodology or framework
- Meet the timelines agreed to and included in the project plan

Business Analyst

The Business Analyst (BA) is the knowledgeable interface between the business and the technical teams. Their absence on projects is a red flag that deserves a deeper look to see what impacts their absence is causing to the project schedule or functionality. Some of their responsibilities include the following:

- Build the functional specification package (use case narrative, business rules, data elements, screen mockups)

- Facilitate workshops with Subject Matter Experts to gather business requirements
- Work with Process owners to build the "As Is" and "To Be" process documents—sometimes in conjunction with other groups

UI/Navigation Specialist

This role is responsible for the User interface and navigation design, including the following:

- Build UI Mockups
- Support Omni-Channel views
- Work with architect/BAs/Designers to define solutions
- Responsible for look and feel standards

OCM Leader

The organization change management lead role is crucial to the success of projects. The assessment team needs to ensure this leader is involved from early in the project, has domain expertise, and manages all the OCM streams concurrently. Some responsibilities include the following:

- Build the OCM Plan
- Work with stakeholders to build a communication strategy and corresponding documents
- Work with the training lead to build a training plan, supervise the building of training materials
- Work with HR to plan for user training
- Work with HR to finalize "to be" role descriptions in the organization

Training Lead

The Training lead is usually in the OCM stream and is responsible for ensuring that user training is done in time to support the business post-implementation activities. This can require 100% coverage of all users before system go live. Key responsibilities include the following:

- Build the training plan
- Supervise the construction of training materials
- Work with OCM Leader to finalize how training will be done and supported in the future
- Train the trainers
- Escalate any concerns to the OCM Leader
- Provide meaningful statistics and program to management

Communication Specialist

The Communication Specialist is responsible for keeping the rest of the organization, outside the core team, informed of the project, excited about the future, and bring back any issues or concerns to Project Management. This role serves as eyes and ears on the ground and can share information about the mood and motivation they are seeing in the organization. On one health check assessment, the communication team brought back the message that many users did not believe the project was going to be successful due to past failures. The management team was able to address this head on with facts and examples of how the team had incorporated past learnings to ensure the current initiative was going to be successful this time around. Some key responsibilities include the following:

- Build the communication plan
- Organize business swat team to disseminate information
- Work with business champions to organize townhalls
- Oversee the construction of newsletters and other forms of communication
- Work with project management on the type of messaging, content, and other facts to share with the organization
- Escalate any concerns that are being heard in the organization
- Supervise the construction of training materials

Data Modeler

One of the outputs from every IT initiative is the utilization of business data. This is another important role on the project, and a red flag if absent. Some of the key responsibilities of this role include the following:

- Owns the data governance and lifecycle
- Supports data mapping for data conversion purposes, reporting, analytics
- Own the logical security over the corporate data

Subject Matter Expert (SME)

The subject matter experts provide domain expertise to the BAs, testers, and others to build out the business requirements and the business rules. These resources are sometimes sequestered to the core team for the duration of the project. Some are asked to maintain some activities in their business role while supporting the project. A couple of red flags to look for is their level of time commitment to the project and if their day job has been backfilled. If not, they may be pulled away from the project during critical times. This is especially true for SMEs from the Finance group who get pulled by every month-end and for even longer periods of time on quarter ends and year-ends. Some of their key responsibilities include the following:

- The SME defines what needs to be done by the solution
- Can be involved in user acceptance testing

- Needs to ensure that the business requirements are complete and thorough
- Needs to identify how business benefits will be achieved

Business Lead

The business lead owns a function or process. They support the project by providing SMEs to the project, making business decisions for their focus area, and providing sign-off on all key deliverables. Their involvement is key to the success of projects.

- Work closely with the SMEs to provide business information to the Bas and the technical side of the project team
- Make business decisions
- Provide business signoff

Closing Perspective

As shown in Figure 5.11, there are a wide variety of roles that are involved in all the Time Periods of a health check assessment. This includes the project/program team, the assessment team, and all the other key stakeholders.

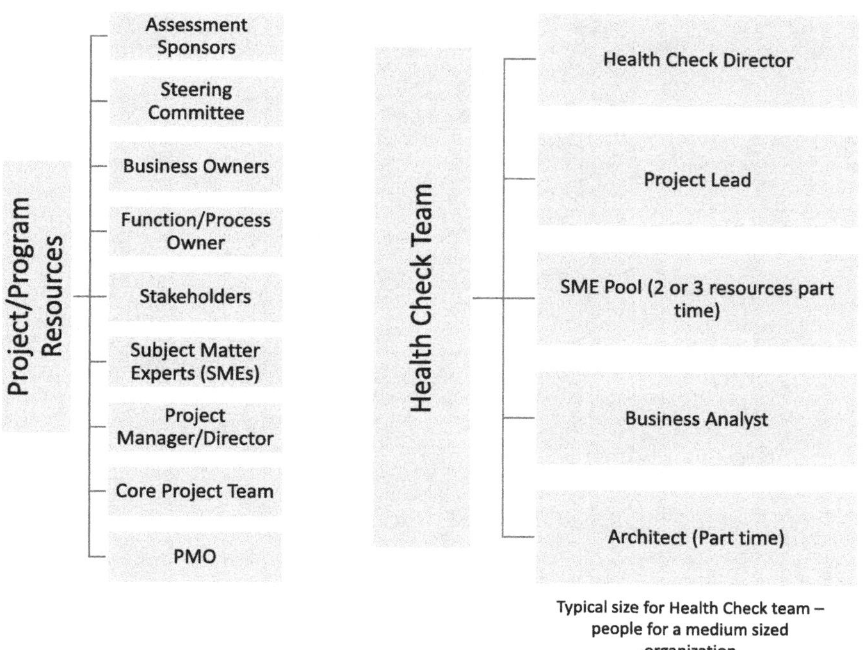

Figure 5.11 Roles involved in the health check.

It's imperative for the assessment sponsors and the assessment team to establish parameters around the engagement in terms of scope, timelines, results, and tone. The default of every health check should be collaborative and focused on providing actionable recommendations and transparent discussions. This and other roles must be established before the health check assessment begins.

There are also mandatory roles on every IT project or program. This chapter identified some of the key roles and responsibilities that must be reviewed as part of the health check and identified some situations that should be viewed as red or warning flags, thereby requiring deeper investigation by the health check assessment team.

Chapter 6

Business Value Levers

After spending $20 million for a program that was implemented on time, on budget, and supported the business, the CFO of a medium-sized distribution company was asked to explain how the organization had benefited from that ERP-CRM implementation and just how much of the bottom line since the go-live was clearly related to the program that went live. This type of questioning is not unusual. The challenge for most organizations is that the data is not available to answer this question with any degree of clarity.

Similarly, if the corporate line begins to suffer, it becomes easy to blame the program that was implemented and not some other business reasons that were inevitable or already a problem that no one noticed. In one company, a month after a software solution went live, meeting its parameters, it was discovered that 25% of the correspondence being shipped to customers was going to wrong addresses and being returned. It was a costly situation. How could the new system be so wrong? How dare the testers miss such an important scenario? After some root-cause analysis, it was discovered that the data was wrong, had always been wrong, and was not included in the scope of the initiative. With all hands-on deck, the data was cleaned up within weeks and a costly problem that had always been there was resolved. Other processes were also addressed to fix the situation that allowed this to go on for so long without being escalated to management.

It's interesting to paint a "what if" scenario for executives. What if you could identify the areas where benefits clearly would accrue after go-live? What if you received data for each of those areas after go-live to show how the business value is accruing? What if you could also get insight into where you could push for more business value? And what if you could go back to the original business case and project charter and track actuals against that want list? The answer of course is generally a resounding "would love it!". With planning and focus throughout the project lifecycle, this can be a reality.

DOI: 10.1201/9781003269786-7

Why Tracking Business Value Is Difficult

A lot of activity occurs between the time a business case is formulated and approved and much later when a system goes live. Tradeoffs and decisions need to constantly be made throughout the project development lifecycle and especially during testing/defect management. Then there is the post-implementation support period where the organization is just putting into practice all the new skills that were included in their user training. A lot of other factors can enter the equation as well, such as new regulatory requirements, market pressures to go live, and many people considerations. Figure 6.1 shows what the reality looks like. A business case feeds into a set of processes that can almost be a black box and results come out the other side, leaving executive teams to pick up the different pieces and assemble them like a puzzle to demonstrate measurable business value out of almost anecdotal and outdated information.

This becomes a very difficult question to answer years after the program goes live. This becomes an embarrassing situation for anyone involved in the project, especially the executive team and project managers.

Instead of trying to play an impossible catchup, it would be better to plan for this line of highly likely questioning from the beginning of the initiative. Even more importantly, doing this is the best way to drive up business value.

People–Process–Technology

Figure 6.2 shows the familiar figure of the three levers that impact business value, and just about everything else, inside organizations. People–Process–Technology at a high level is going to drive the business value delivered by an IT project. There is a lot of underlying complexity and dependencies in just these three components. For this discussion, consider the following information in terms of what would need to be done to drive up business value for a given organization:

- People: Well-trained, engaged, creative, skilled, and loyal to the organization. They should be incentivized by improvements to the bottom line of the organization and aligned with the business strategic plan.
- Process: Increasing support for the happy path, integrated within an end-to-end supply chain with external vendors. Minimize manual exceptions where possible. Reduce costs cross the board including taxes, distribution costs, tariffs, and costs of goods (COGS).
- Technology: Must be secure, robust, rapid, extendable, expandable, and maintainable. Total cost of ownership must be going down over time, certainly as a component of overall operating expenditures.

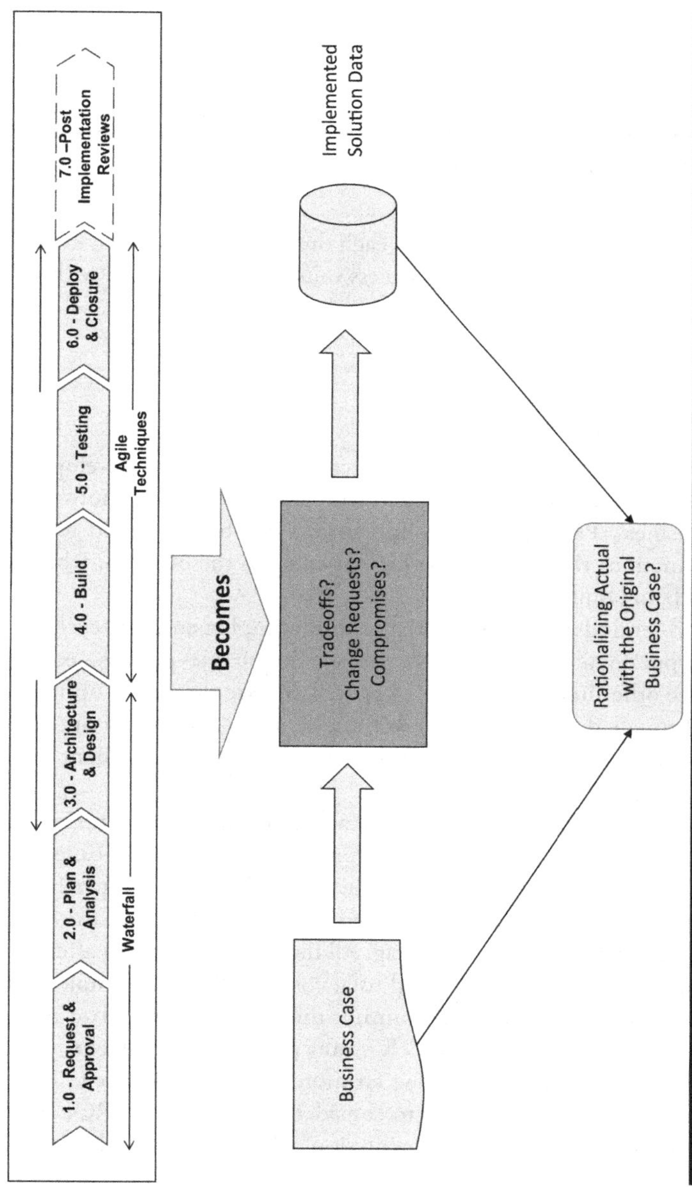

Figure 6.1 Tracking business case to actual value.

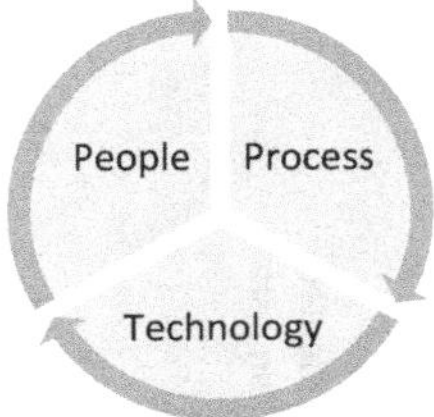

Figure 6.2 People–process–technology.

This is only one scenario. Each industry, each organization, and each executive team is unique. The approach for driving business value higher can begin with some common levers and be customized for the specific situation in play.

Business Value Lifecycle

In terms of project delivery, business value can be delivered by development cycles that are faster, cheaper, and better aligned with the release of functions that are useful to the business. Prioritization around sprints can be structured to deliver and start using functions that provide the highest value to the business, while the other ones are still being built.

Figure 6.3 reminds us that the actual solution implementation cycle is only one piece of the puzzle, albeit an important one. The people–process–technology pie extends to the other items in Figure 6.3 as well and are the key to optimizing business value through the project delivery lifecycle and through the operations time period when significantly more value is extracted from the investment made in the project.

Creating multiples of business value are achieved through optimizing each value point shown in Figure 6.3. A common misconception is that an on-time, on-budget, and full functionality implementation is the dream. While this is partly true, as we are seeing in Figure 6.3, implementation represents a small part of the overall timeline in which a system solution is running. All the activities coming after implementation have a larger impact on ROI and total cost of ownership. Implementation is an important setup and prerequisite, but not the place to stop. A bad implementation creates a hopeless foundation which means that the other benefits will never be realized. A good implementation allows far more value to be realized.

A staircase may be a better visual to consider with maximum ROI at the top of the stairs. Without a successful implementation, which represents the first few rungs of the stairs, we can never get to the operations rungs. If do not plan properly and stop with the implementation, then we never get to maximum ROI that is waiting for us at the top of the staircase (Figure 6.4).

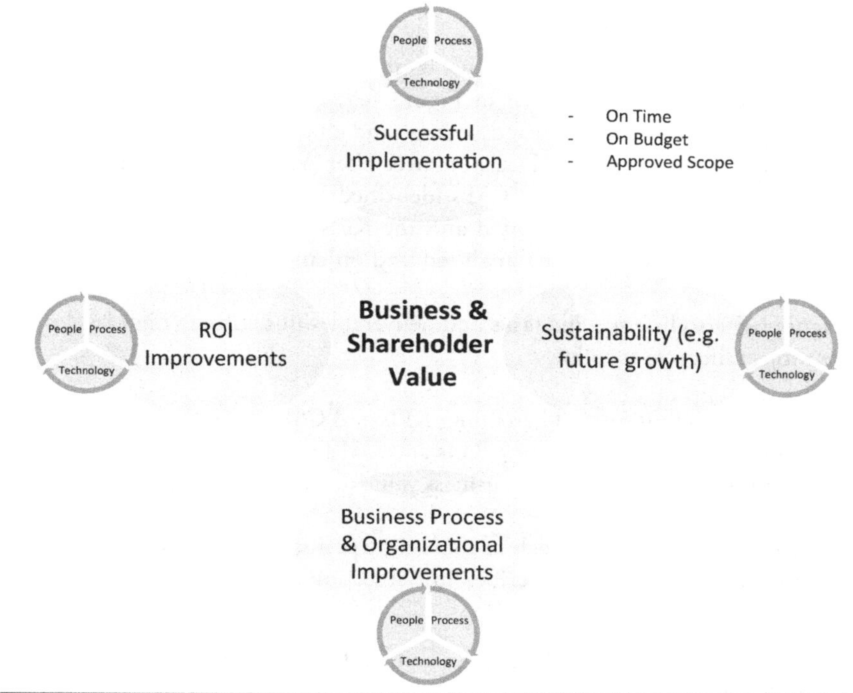

Figure 6.3 Driving end-to-end business benefits.

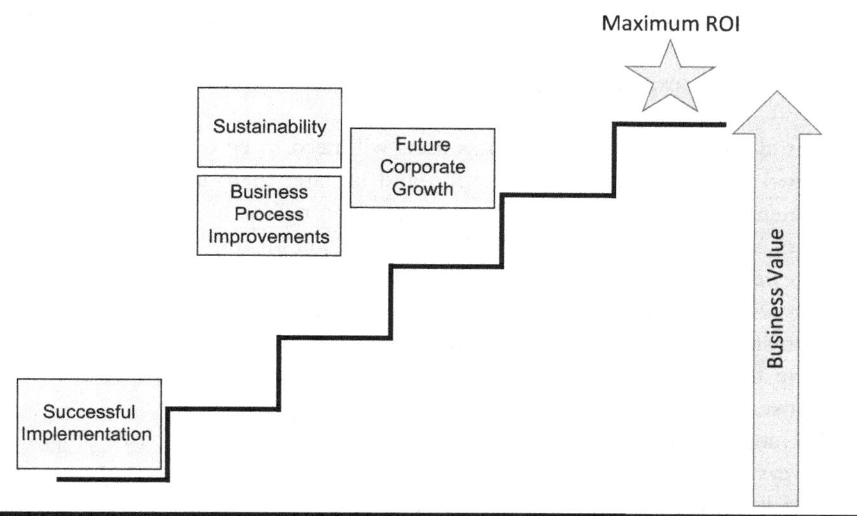

Figure 6.4 Stopping too early.

Successful Implementation

Successful project implementation must contain a set of KPIs and CSFs for driving the business value. As shown in Figure 6.5, this process begins before the project is launched in the business case stage and continues into development and testing. A key metric for a Go Decision after User Acceptance Testing should be the realization of those KPIs and CSFs identified in the business case. With this approval, the system is implemented and the KPIs and CSFs are tracked during operations. They should also be analyzed and enhanced to continually improve business value.

Figure 6.5 also lists specific tasks and deliverables under three high level phases of the project lifecycle as follows:

- Period 1: Definition and baselining KPIs and CSFs
- Period 2: Building and testing KPIs and CSFs
- Period 3: Measurement and business value realization and optimization

The tasks and deliverables for each of these time periods in the project delivery lifecycle shown in Figure 6.5 are described in the section below.

Define Critical Success Factors (5–12 measures recommended)

We are beginning with a definition around CSFs before the KPIs. Although the two concepts are related, KPIs can be more specific baselines and targets than CSFs. Between 5 and 12 CSF criteria are recommended, if possible. Any more than this makes the list unwieldly. Any less and they may be too abstract to measure. CSFs identify key activities or circumstances to ensure corporate success and optimal business value. Some examples could be the following:

- End-User Training: All business users will need to be trained no earlier than two months from implementation and no later than one week from implementation. Considering the amount of planning and logistics to get this done for say 1,000 employees, it's clear why having an implementation date and realistically sticking with it is very important.
- Sales Order Entry: Order entry must be omnichannel. Users should be able to start their order online and walk into a storefront and have the clerk call up the same order. The user experience should be equivalent and no data lost.
- Google reviews (or some equivalent) drive business volume based on past surveys, so the scores must be optimized. All customer-facing resources must be training on customer service. Processes must be designed for each customer interaction.

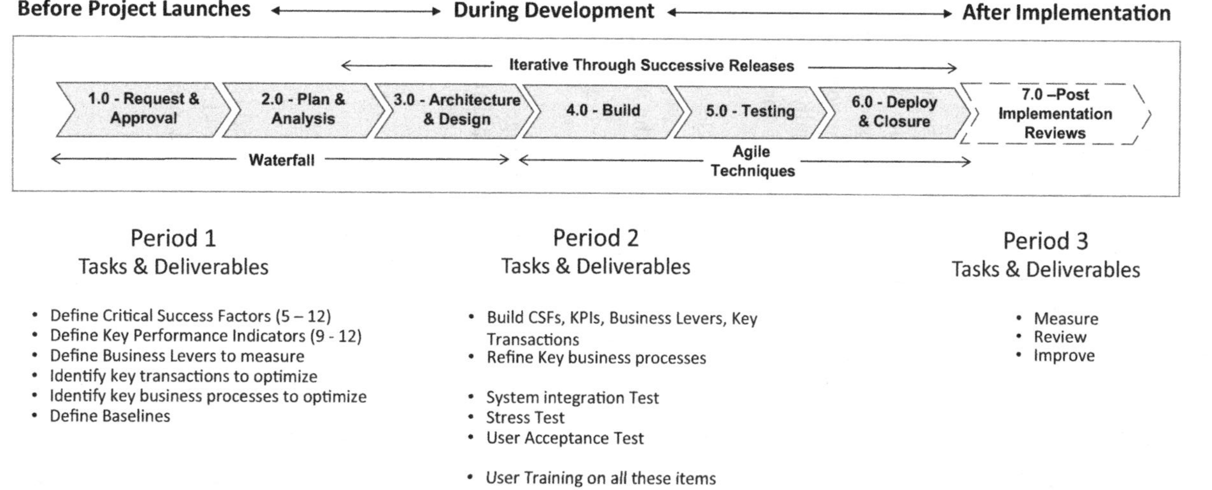

Figure 6.5 Before-during-after thread.

Define Key Performance Indicators (9–12 measures recommended)

KPIs can be used as specific targets to measure a new solution's ability to drive business value. These targets must be carefully assessed, beginning with a baseline of "As Is" and then setting realistic targets for after system implementation. Since these will be part of the Go/No Go discussions after user acceptance testing is successfully passed, they should be specific, critical, and measurable.

On one past health check for an ERP implementation, the process owner brought a list of over 100 KPIs to the 1-1 interview meeting with the health check manager. While many of the items were important, there were just too many of them to actually be critical. The items would certainly be business requirements and business rules. Test scenarios would be built to validate them. But problems with many of the supposed KPIs in the large list were not showstoppers or items which could drive business value significantly. The cost of not going live, the burn rate of the team, would exceed the benefits accrued individually by many of these items. Thus, some of them could be done as change requests for a follow-on release after Go-Live.

A recommendation coming out of the health check assessment was to reduce the number of KPIs down to 12. This was done and the project delivered against each of these and was implemented successfully according to the measures that the steering committee and board of directors approved.

Some examples of KPIs are as follows:

- Process 100+ customer orders a minute on average
- Process 90% of loan applications with no manual intervention
- Reduce the cost of each loan renewal by 10% compared to the pre-launch average
- Raise average google scores to 4.5 stars (confirm after system is live)

Define Business Levers to Measure

The preceding lists provided some examples of CSFs and KPIs that can be translated into business levers. The Business Owners and stakeholders need to identify all the levers that can be built to drive business value, by how much, and under what specific assumptions. Here are some examples:

- New Customer On-Boarding
- Loyalty Renewals
- Time to Collect Revenues
- Time to Close Month-End Consolidations
- Time to visualize, design, build, test, and deploy a new consumer product with the relevant regulatory approvals

Identify Key Transactions to Optimize

Most business processes generally have a small group of transactions that service the majority of their business (the classic 80-20 rule). It is these transactions that should be best architected, designed, built, and tested. For example, a user-entry transaction of an order drives the bulk of the business activity and some be optimized. An exchange transaction may be important to the business but only accounts for a small percentage of the overall traffic. If a tradeoff is needed, the former rather than the latter should win the prioritization contest.

Identify Key Business Processes to Optimize

A transaction is typically a component of an end-to-end business process, which may contain many transactions. The business leaders know which of these processes are the most important. The transactions within those need to be optimized. All the activities outside the system transactions will also need to be designed for efficiency. This list of key processes should be as automated as possible. Lesser used business processes would not be priorities.

Defining New Baselines

Baselines for each measure need to be established for end-to-end business processes, key transactions, and each of the business levers that were identified by the business for optimization. An "As Is" baseline is critical for each measure, otherwise there is nothing with which to compare the system's contribution against. How long does an order take to enter today? What would be the ideal time based on the expected volumes of growth?

Build CSFs, KPIs, Business Levers, and Key Transactions

Moving out of the definition phase, the team transitions into the very active build phases. The health check team needs to confirm that the definition of the KPIs, CSFs, Business Levers, and key business transactions are supported by the proposed business architecture. They should also be fleshed out in the business requirements deliverables with relevant business rules. The project plan should be reviewed to confirm that these are built or configured. Any gaps here should be included in the health check warnings section of the final report.

Refine Key Business Processes

With the metrics and levers defined, the business process team needs to reflect changes to the "As Is" business processes to support the "To Be" process versions that will support the enhanced business capabilities as the business value is achieved after system implementation.

System Integration Test

The business requirements documents pertaining to the business value levers should be translated to specific testing scenarios and test cases. These will then confirm, during the testing cycles, that the envisioned benefits are being addressed by the software solution. Of course, realization will be post-launch, but the testing validates that the development has included the code or configuration to support the planned business value.

Stress Test

As some of the business value levers will likely increase transaction volumes, there should be stress test scenarios to confirm the testing scenarios mirroring live expected data volumes after go-live with consideration for extra growth included. These can be automated and used alongside the regression testing solution.

User Acceptance Test

UAT is in the critical path for driving business value. The test scenarios corresponding to the highest value business requirements need to be prioritized and confirmed and verified. Defects found in the testing need to be reprioritized against the value each defect would bring back to the business. Ideally, 100% of the business levels, KPIs, CSFs would be tested and ready for production. The assessment team needs to review how this process is being handled or planned to be handled.

User Training on All These Items

The organization change management team needs to ensure that the training materials reflect the user training needed to support the KPIs, CSFs, and business value levers. The assessment team needs to confirm this thread is in place, including any process related training, otherwise they should issue a health check warning in the final report.

Sustainability

As mentioned earlier, it's in the sustainment period that business value begins to get realized. Some structures that need to be put into place to support this are as follows:

Center of Excellence

Some of the core team members are typically given new roles within a structure called the Center of Excellence. Staffing needs to be a mix of technical resources to

- Measure and improve business benefits
- Establish standards, governance and ensure compliance.
- Establish and utilize platform best practices.
- Manage releases, patches, upgrades for the platform.
- Maximize use of people, processes, knowledge, and technology.
- Ensure consistency across business units sharing platforms.
- Enable consistency with functions such as project management, training and operational support.
- Monitor tangible benefits after go-live
- Prioritize new functionality
- Manage relationships to vendors supporting the solution

Figure 6.6 Center of excellence.

maintain and enhance the system, business users to make business decisions, executives to align with the rest of the organization, and second- and third-level support from one or more vendors to provide specialized knowledge and skills. These all have to be pre-negotiated before go-live. Figure 6.6 shows the structure of one Center of Excellence solution with the following mandate:

- Measure and improve business benefits: Compare to the business levels from the business case.
- Establish standards, governance, and ensure compliance: These are established by the compliance group, risk group, and external regulatory bodies.
- Establish and utilize platform best practices: The contracted vendors should be asked to bring best practices from other clients to serve as a baseline.
- Manage releases, patches, upgrades for the platform: These can be on a frequent basis and could impact the development of new functionality or the resolution of important defects. The health check team should examine the process and prioritization for this as it's not uncommon and, in fact, unhealthy to let these pile up and not be processed for extended periods of time. This would be listed as a major warning flag in the final assessment report. Official audits will flag this situation as a major cyber risk.
- Maximize use of people, processes, knowledge, and technology: This should be assessed against industry targets.
- Ensure consistency across business units sharing platforms: This will involve the look and feel experience.
- Enable consistency with functions such as project management, training, and operational support. These can be measured through user surveys.
- Monitor tangible benefits after go-live: This will require management reports populated with accurate data captured at source.

- Prioritize new functionality: This should be done through a fact-based prioritization approach, otherwise, some executives will begin to feel like they are not getting any benefits from the new system.
- Manage relationships to vendors supporting the solution: The licensing costs are a major component of future system costs so these should be actively negotiated to be as low as possible without losing any other benefits. The best times for negotiations to occur from a client perspective have historically been at the vendor's financial year-end or quarter-end. The former is the most pressing for publicly traded vendors who are trying to maximize the revenue and profit for the street, and their own personal bonuses.

The Center of Excellence operates in conjunction with several other parts of the organization as shown in Figure 6.7, namely:

- Help Desk: There is often a help desk already in place in the organization. The new initiative can plug into this structure which involves some configuration work and training of the help desk resources. The health check team should review how the help desk resources have been trained to support the new solution and the deliverables (e.g. training summary sheet) they have been given to do this.
- The Steering Committee: The Steering Committee should have combined business and technology sponsors to prioritize functionality, remove obstacles, solicit funding, and to make decisions around the ongoing maintenance and enhancement of the solution. There should be a written mandate, organizational chart and a recurring cadence for meetings (e.g. Monthly to start).
- Software Vendor: The software vendor will continue to play an important role after a solution goes live. They will provide upgrades and patches that

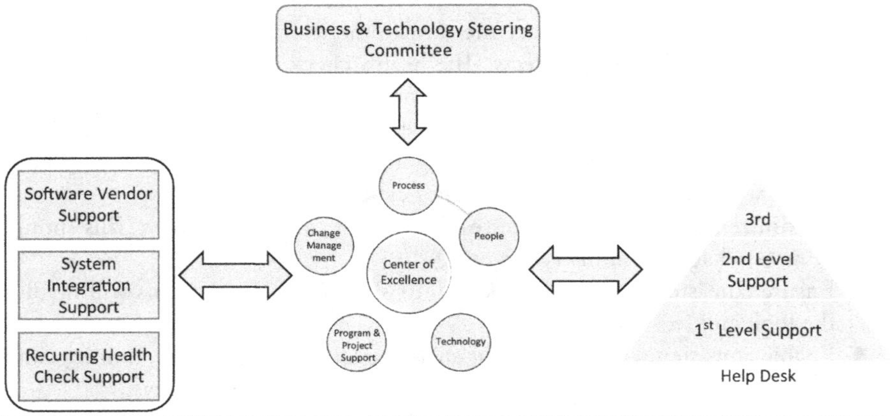

Figure 6.7 Sustainment organizational structure.

need to be planned for release around the other priorities on the project. They may have support and maintenance services they offer. They could also have resources that the help desk can call when specific information is required to respond to tickets.

- System Integrator (SI): The SI may be involved in maintenance activities that include defect fixes and change requests. They could be a third level of defense for the help desk to call if answers are needed to tickets. They would also be involved in delivering new functionality.
- Health Check Vendor: The Health Check Vendor can be retained to do regular or recurring checkups and ensure that recommendations are being implemented as intended.
- Other Vendors: These could include cloud vendors and other suppliers. The health check team may want to inspect the terms and conditions of any maintenance contracts that have been accepted to ensure equity. What are the costs of the services? How long is the contractual commitment? Is there a way to easily get out of the contract? How much was the price discounted? What other savings can be achieved?

Business Process

Business processes need to be documented, reviewed, signed off, and shared prior to implementation. These can be reviewed by the assessment team to examine the following:

- "As Is" and "To Be" processes
- Happy path
- Minimize manual interventions

Organizational Improvements

As stated previously, the people element has a tremendous impact on the business value extracted from an IT solution. The health check team should review the following:

- User training at launch
- Future training of new resources
- The training materials
- "To Be" Job descriptions
- "To Be" processes and alignment with job descriptions
- Surveys to the user base to see if they feel ready to support the system, how they felt about the user training, if they feel they are valued by the organization, and any other feelings they have.

ROI Improvements

Return on Investment improvements should be done as follows:

1. Identify and execute on the areas of cost savings
   a. During development—freeze tested code and reduce resource requirements
   b. After launch—implement a Center of Excellence (COE) to centralize and reduce costs
2. Bring resource capabilities more local and in-house where-ever possible
3. Justify future expenditures on a Benefits/Cost basis in writing.

Figures 6.8 and 6.9 show some very simplified examples of calculating ROI. As the figures show, the post-implementation sustainment period is the time period to greatly profit from the system implementation. Keeping the costs at a nominal level allows the profit to soar. In the example shown, the organization would be in the profit sometime in year two (2).

Component	Function (s)	Full Costs	Maintenance
ERP	Finance, Procurement, Warehouse	$61.1 Million	$8 Million
CRM	Marketing, Sales, Social Media	$18.7 Million	$3 Million
Total		$79.8 Million	$11 Million

The program vision to justify the expenditure included:
- ❑ Improved sales of existing product lines ($25 million/yr)
- ❑ New market capability ($9 million/hr
- ❑ Better warehouse management (savings of $5 million/yr)
- ❑ Improved auditing transparency
- ❑ Better public reputation

Hard Revenue Improvement: $34 million/yr
Cost Savings: $20 million/yr

Figure 6.8 ROI baseline.

Component	Running Cost + Maintenance Position	Revenue + Savings	Cost Position
Year 1	$90.8 Million	$54.0 Million	$36.8 Million
Year 2	$47.8 Million	$54.0 Million	($6.2 Million) Profit
Year 3	$11.0 Million	$54.0 Million	($43 Million) Profit

Notes:
- ❑ Amortization considerations not included
- ❑ Interest considerations not included
- ❑ Simplified accounting assumptions

Figure 6.9 Simplified example of calculating ROI.

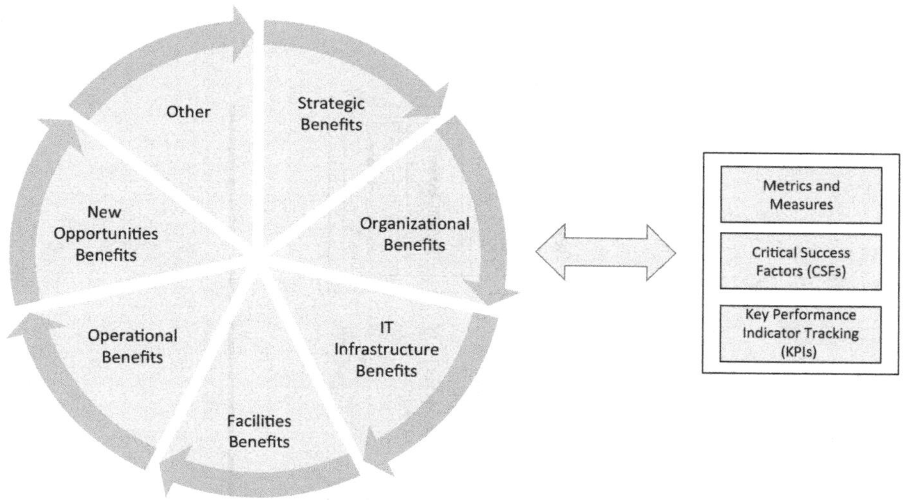

Figure 6.10 The business benefits pie.

The Business Benefits Pie

Business benefits value at the most basic, as shown in Figure 6.1 involving increased profit (revenue increase, cost decrease), corporate sustainability, and regulatory compliance. Additional benefits can be measured, but they are generally components of one of these items. The Executive Team will want a more detailed analysis of benefits than just final ROI as there are many pieces that drive this value. Figure 6.10 shows some of the pieces that make up the benefits pie.

Driving business value must be planned throughout the program lifecycle. Measurement criteria must be agreed to with business stakeholders and then tracked on a monthly basis to ensure that benefits are being achieved. It is important to realize that business process improvements must be continual and based on the results of the benefits tracking, as shown in Figure 6.11.

Business Drivers to Justify IT Projects

This book is focused on IT projects but those IT projects that ultimately serve a business interest. Even a Windows 365 upgrade has a business objective—support user productivity needs, secure access to their data, and collaboration with other users for example. This chapter examined the key drivers for business projects and how their value can be optimized in those and other areas. Figure 6.12 shows a list of business benefit drivers that can be used to justify approving projects or programs. For the purpose of driving business value, these can be used as a checklist

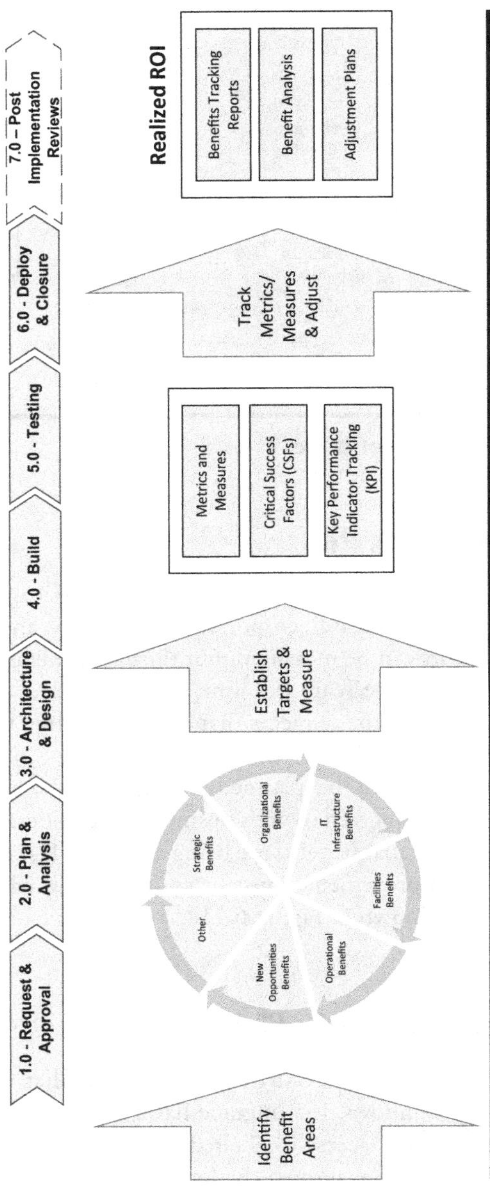

Figure 6.11 Benefits realization cycle.

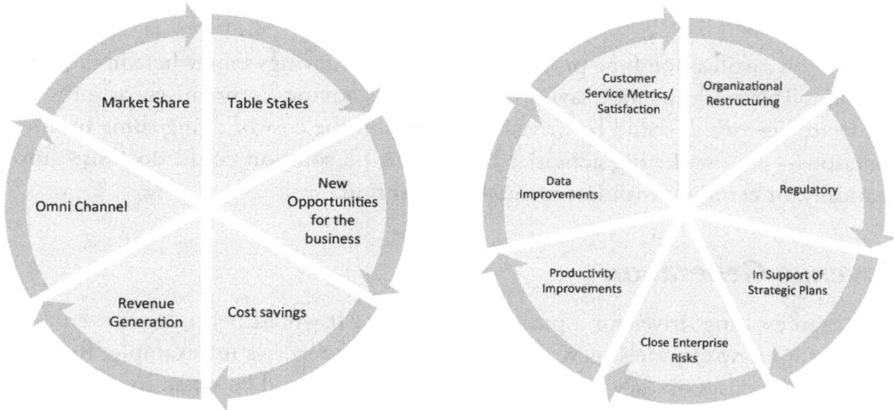

Figure 6.12 Business benefit levers.

and to baseline expectations for each relevant lever and to optimize these on specific projects. The Health Check Team should question if these are not included in the business case of the initiative being assessed.

Table Stakes

What used to be an advancement at one time actually becomes sustainability in the future. For example, the internet was an advancement not long ago, today it's table stakes. Most businesses cannot survive without the Internet. Similarly, some projects may be approved simply because the business has no choice but to do them. What might be negotiable is the cost of matching the table stakes established in the industry.

New Opportunities for the Business

Imagine a retail company that is used to storing inventory in multiple warehouses and building an automated supply chain which provides the following capabilities:

- Real-time knowledge of inventory counts in the distribution center and the warehouse
- Reduced need for actual inventory by 90%
- Automated purchase order for inventory items that drop below certain amounts
- Detailed reporting on items that are selling, their velocity, and returns
- Other related items that are also selling out

This subset of objectives for a new system could offer new opportunities for many businesses.

Cost Savings

A common justification for a project is to obtain cost savings somewhere in the organization. This could include savings in operations, savings in premises, or software/hardware licenses. It could be driven by savings in the cost of doing some business functions—e.g. marketing activities because an IT solution could do those automatically, or certainly with less manual intervention.

Revenue Generation

This is an exciting driver for a project or program. It would be to drive revenue by opening up new channels, new markets, and new categories for example. Revenue generation focuses on driving the top line, but care should be taken to ensure that operational expenses do not negate the value without executive support (e.g. a management decision to grow market share without driving profits in the near term).

Omni Channel

This is the desire to maximize customer service by allowing interaction through a variety of channels: at a store, on the Internet, mobile devices, and websites. The desire is to have the same look and feel and user experience through any channel.

Market Share

This is a desire to increase market share in specific categories for the organization. This could involve opening up new markets or new product lines. There would need to be process changes in the business to reach the new channels, as well as changes to the IT systems. Some systems become too difficult to change to support new products, driving the need for an entirely new system. In such a case, the additional business value projected is compared to the fully-loaded solution cost in the business case.

Organizational Restructuring

This can be in response to a merger/acquisition, new growth opportunities, more efficient ways of doing things, entering a new market somewhere in the world, and many other reasons. Organizational restructuring has many components to be reviewed in the health check assessment including Communication Plan, System Configuration, Security Permission Setups, User Training Plan, and other HR Processes for payroll, onboarding, and transfers.

Regulatory

Depending on the industry, regulations can play significant roles in business processes. For example, in the gaming industry there are specific regulations around customer privacy and sharing of information, and prevention of problem gambling. If these requirements are not met, an entire program will be delayed until they are.

In Support of Strategic Plans

An organization can decide on implementing a new strategic plan for long-term sustainability and growth. The assessment team should ensure there are technology plans to support the strategic plan.

Close Enterprise Risks

Some initiatives are specifically designed to deal with enterprise risks. For example, a reputation risk, a cyber risk, or pandemic risk.

Productivity Improvements

General productivity improvements across the organization or in specific parts of the organization.

Data Improvements

With data increasingly becoming currency, some projects are needed to benchmark data and validate its accuracy. Sustainable tools and processes are required to maintain data accuracy on an ongoing basis.

Customer Service Metrics/Satisfaction

Ensuring top, consistent satisfaction from customers is a consistent driver for new systems. Surveys have shown that it's up to ten (10) times cheaper to sell to an existing customer than to find a new one. Getting a multiple return on investment can be obtained by improving customer satisfaction so that loyal customers remain loyal and who introduce their friends to the organization. Customers can be influencers who can drive buying or boycott decisions through their social media platforms. Figures 6.13 and 6.14 show a simple survey that can be sent out from time to time to solicit meaningful information to improve service levels. Customer satisfaction surveys should have a small number of well-reasoned questions. Anything too long likely will not get a response. Essentially the survey should ask: (1) Are you satisfied with our work? (2) What could we do better? (3) Will you recommend us? (4) Will you use us again? (5) Is there something else we can provide?

The health check team should ensure that each of these are included or considered as business value drivers in the business requirements.

Resource Being Reviewed: ____________________
We would like to thank you in advance for your time in completing this feedback survey.

Your feedback is very important to us. We strive to meet all your expectations in every interaction and to overachieve as much as possible. Your feedback will allow us to improve our service to you and other customers in the future.

If we you like us to contact you directly, please provide the following contact information:

First Name: ____________________
Last Name: ____________________
Your Title: ____________________
Department: ____________________
Company Name: ____________________

Email: ____________________
Phone number: ____________________
Best time to talk to you: ____________________

1. On a scale of 1- 10 with 10 being very likely, how likely is it that you would recommend our organization to a colleague or friend? ____

2. Why did you provide the score you did? Specific examples are very appreciated.

____
____

3. What is an example of a service we provided with excellence?

____
____

4. If you had to pick one thing we can improve on what would that be?

____
____

5. Are there other areas of improvement you can recommend?

____
____

Figure 6.13 Customer satisfaction questionnaire (Page 1).

6. On a scale of 1- 10 with 10 being very high, how strong is our relationship to you? ____

7. Do you view us as a trusted advisor? ____ (Yes/No)

8. We consistently add value to your organization? ____ (Yes/No)

9. What you use us again? ____ (Yes/No)

Please explain?

____
____

Thank you for your time.
Please send this survey to .....@.....com

Figure 6.14 Customer satisfaction questionnaire (Page 2).

Closing Perspective

Business value realization starts at the business case level and cycles through the entire project development cycle in the post-implementation sustainment phases. Figure 6.15 shows the many different benefit pies that can drive business value. The health check assessment team can use these as a starting checklist to see if the business case has been well thought out.

Figure 6.16 shows some basic considerations in driving business value at strategic points in the project development lifecycle. These can be coupled with the slices

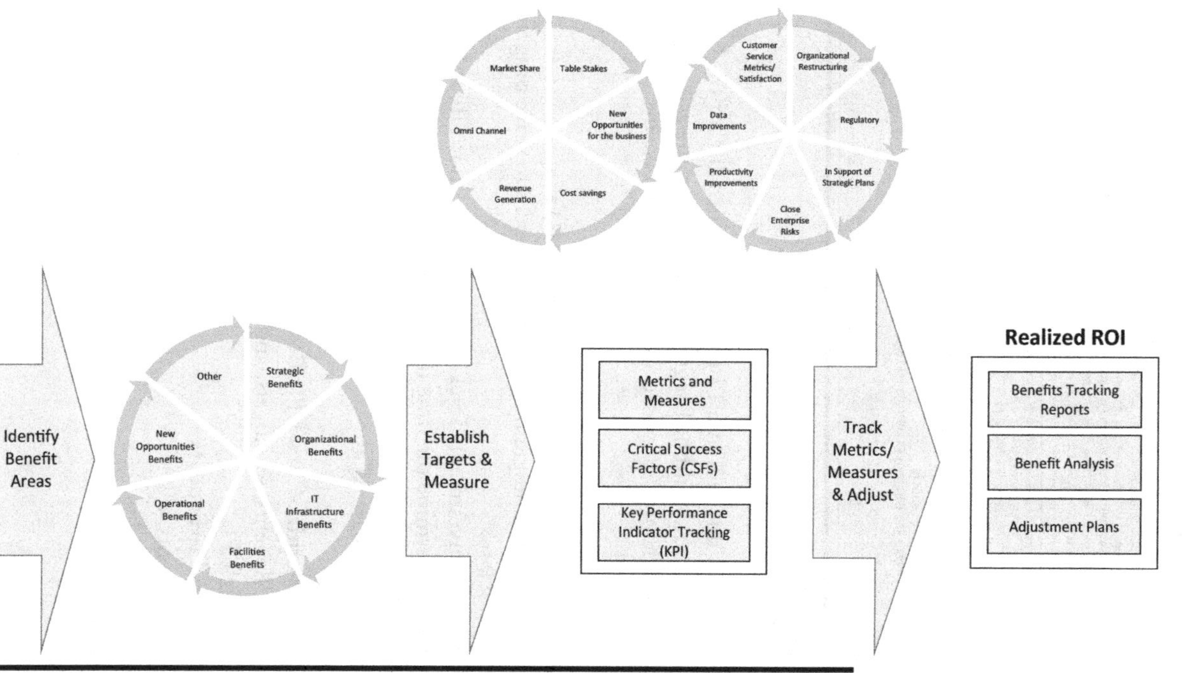

Figure 6.15 Benefits realization cycle and the business benefit pies.

Successful Implementation	1. On Time 2. On Budget 3. Key Features a. Measurable b. Identified on the Executive Dashboard
Business Process Improvements	1. Key customer and business user facing processes 2. Agree on the key business processes and supporting business transactions that provide the greatest benefits 3. Measure efficiency as a ratio on key transactions 4. Support substantial corporate growth year over year
Sustainability	1. Identify and execute on the areas of cost savings a. During development – freeze tested code and reduce resource requirements b. After launch 2. Bring capabilities local and in-house where possible 3. Justify future expenditures on a ROI basis.
Future Corporate Growth	1. System Scalability 2. Increasing efficiency to coincide with Revenue growth

Figure 6.16 Program benefits.

shown in the business value pies in 6.15 to serve as a checklist for the health check. Gaps in the business case should be flagged as a warning in the assessment report.

In summary, this chapter discussed driving business benefits in the following time periods;

- Before Go-Live: Envision and build for business value
- After go live: set up a program and then populate it to drive program benefits on an ongoing basis
- Maximizing the Investment: Track the value of functionality that is not being activated and determine the time it should be.

The process can be summarized as:

- Identify and prioritize CSFs/KPIs/Benefit Criteria
- Baseline KPIs/Benefits, set targets, and then set stretch goals
- Build for CSFs/KPIs
- Update CSFs/KPIs/Benefits
- Track KPIs/Benefits
- Measure KPIs/Benefits
- Enhance Benefit Realization
- Repeat

CONDUCTING THE HEALTH CHECK ASSESSMENTS

B

Chapter 7

Laying the Foundation for a Meaningful Health Check

As was discussed in earlier chapters, a methodology for conducting an IT Health Check is shown in Figure 7.1. The dashed box includes the activities within Period A and a small part of Period B to lay a foundation for a meaningful Health Check to be executed. This involves setting executive-level expectations, firming up a solid scope, signing a project charter-like agreement that contains a list of deliverables, and completing a thorough gathering of project information from a variety of disparate sources. This would include scouring documentation repositories, reviewing documents, building questionnaires, and doing rigorous one-on-one interviews with a cross-section of the project or program team. The subphases of these activities are discussed in more detail later in this chapter.

Commissioning Health Checks

IT Health Checks, as discussed earlier, are generally commissioned by a Business or Technology sponsor or some other senior executive on a project or program. This could be a CEO, CFO, COO, CIO, CDO, CRO, VP HR, other VP level resources, or other Director level resources. Recall that this could be for any number of reasons as shown in Figure 7.2. There may be more than one driver or trigger that calls for a health check as well, which needs to be established upfront between the sponsor and the assessment team, and included in the approach for the initiative.

DOI: 10.1201/9781003269786-9

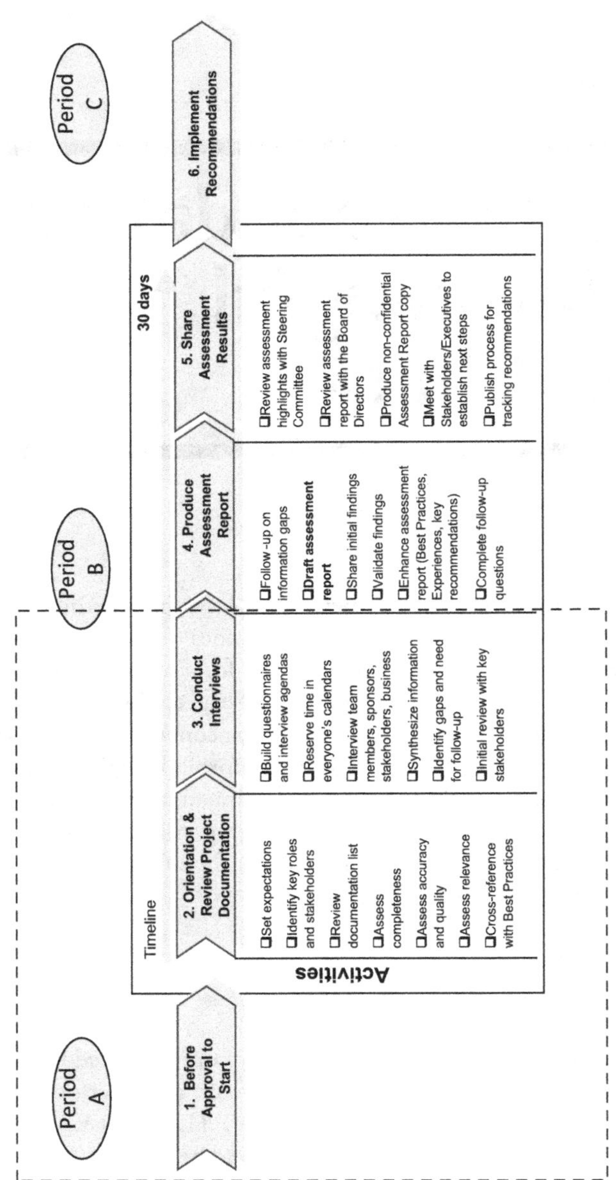

Figure 7.1 Health check foundational activities.

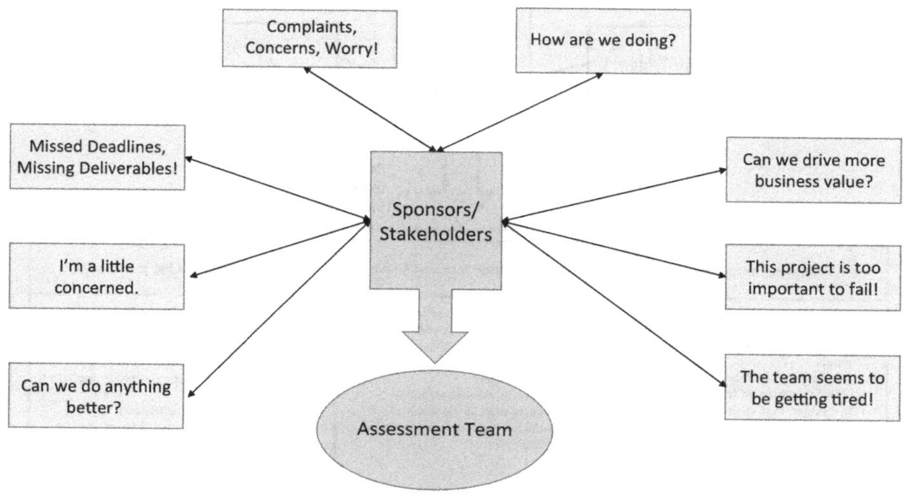

Figure 7.2 Proactive and reactive reasons for contacting the assessment team.

These drivers and triggers can be disparate. Some sponsors may be proactive and want to drive multiples of business value, while other sponsors may be reacting to one or more triggers suggesting some sort of warning signs are flashing on the project or program. If the motivation is trigger related, executives generally wait until more than one trigger is flashing in front of them, so the situation might be more problematic than the project team realizes. Some of the more common triggers that eventually get Executive level attention are as follows:

- Missing multiple project deadlines or deliverables
- Sprint test results are showing major defects, sprint after sprint
- Very poor morale where team members feel they are on a project hurtling towards failure
- The initiative has the attention of the board due to its importance or criticality to the organization as a whole
- There is some concern about the capabilities of key members of the project team
- An unusual number of resources resigning or requesting to get off the project
- People starting to question the business value of the initiative
- The initiative (s) are too important to fail and need reassurance about direction
- The Executive is looking for reassurance that everything reasonable is being done
- Need another opinion on what's happening on the project
- There are conflicting details coming out about the project
- There are a lot of political maneouvers occuring
- Make adjustments to get the project back on track because some incremental misses are being reported
- Need a Project Rescue to avert a pending project disaster

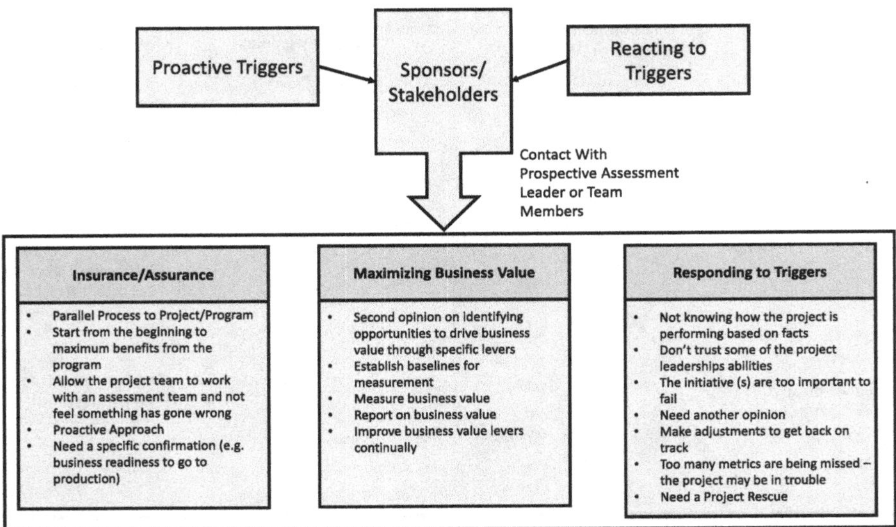

Figure 7.3 Triggers driving contact with the assessment team.

Figure 7.3 reminds us of the three major categories of these health check triggers, namely: Insurance/Assurance, maximizing business value, and responding to the triggers mentioned previously.

As a result of these drivers, the executive project sponsor (s) will reach out to one of the parties shown in Figure 7.4 for assistance. The type of output from the health check will vary greatly between these organizations. Each, of course, has their pros and cons to offer. These are discussed in more detail below:

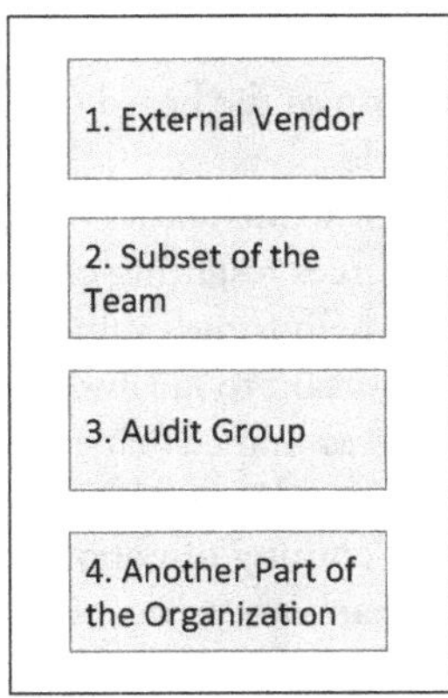

Figure 7.4 Sourcing the health check team.

External Vendor

These can be small consulting organizations that offer Health Checks as a service, a large consulting organization, or independent consultants that have extensive expertise and a strong track record in helping organizations drive business value through these initiatives.

Pros

- Independent expertise
- Bring external experience
- Offer choice in selecting an external vendor
- Will bring their own methodology and approach

Cons

- Incremental cost (but will generally more than pay for themselves with just one actionable recommendation)
- The project team will need to spend time and effort to select a vendor to do the health check
- Will need to learn the corporate culture of the organization

Key Considerations in Working with External Vendors

- Check their track record and get references
- Be clear in explaining the corporate culture to them
- Spend the time to properly onboard them

Subset of the Team

This option would select a cross-section of resources on the existing project or program and have them spend time doing a health check on the initiative and report the results back in a format similar to the reports shown in Chapter 4. There are clearly some very strong Pros and Cons to this approach.

Pros

- The individuals selected for the review already understand the project and organization
- Bring strong subject matter experience
- Costs may not have to be approved separately so the review can be done right away
- This could be built in as an ongoing process

Cons

- No independence
- The team may not know what they don't know
- Recommendations may be status quo
- Outside experience will be lacking

Key Considerations in Working with a Subset of the Team

- Stress that the team must be as independent as possible and that there would be no management retribution if they find problems
- Get external best practices
- Have them follow a proven health check assessment methodology
- Consider an external mentor to help the team from time to time

Audit Group

This option would leverage resources in the corporate Audit group to do a review of the project or program. While the resources may be readily available as they are internal to the organization, there are several challenges with this approach. Chief of all is that the output may not be what is needed from an independent, collaborative health check point of view.

Pros

- The Audit team will be using a proven methodology
- They already understand the corporate culture
- They have experience reviewing projects and interviewing project team members

Cons

- Audit functions will typically want to stay hands-off from the project and will not usually make recommendations.
- Their findings are generally focused on a lack of controls and failings. They do not typically provide specific advice on correcting the gaps as this would taint their future audits—they would essentially end up auditing the implementation of their own advice in the future.
- Members of the Audit Group may not have the technical and domain expertise to deliver a fully meaningful IT Health Check in terms of depth, breadth, and specificity.
- The Audit Team may not have availability until some later date as they are going through their standard audit cycle of different functions within the organization.

Key Considerations in Working with the Audit Group

- It will be difficult to rely on the Audit function for a collaborate IT Health Check that delivers actionable recommendations to drive business value or to adjust a project's trajectory.
- Consider one of the other sources to do a Health Check and leverage the Audit function to ensure that the recommendations are compliant with the corporate Audit standards.

Another Part of the Organization

Some companies, usually large, global organizations have a team that is dedicated to doing reviews of projects undertaken within the organization and which have certain attributes. These would include projects or programs above a certain budget, size, or impact, among other factors. The groups generally have dedicated resources using a well-defined methodology with specific deliverables. However, these usually are not the output needed from a collaborate and independent health check. This group's objective must be aligned with that of the request for the health check. Usually, the objectives of the group are to collect project status from different initiatives, do a risk assessment, and report the results to management – sometimes at an aggregate level. The part about actionable recommendations may not align with the needs of the sponsors requesting the health check from this group.

Pros

- There may be strong expertise inside the company to do Health Checks
- Members of this group will understand the corporate culture
- They will be in a good position to know impacts of the project outcome to other parts of the organization (e.g. another group needs the system to be implemented before they can implement their own system)

Cons

- Not entirely independent because the functions all roll up to the same CEO and Board of Directors
- They may not have any external best practices or learnings from similar projects from other organizations
- The resources may not have the technical skillsets for an implementation using a new ERP, CRM, HRIS, Cloud solution, EPM or other software solutions.
- The methodology used by the group may not produce the type of actionable recommendations required from the review this group completes.

- The group may be tied up with reviews of other projects and may not be available for some period of time
- The project may not meet the criteria to invoke this group to do a review

Key Considerations in Working with Another Part of the Organization

- Validate that the proposed team members have experience doing collaborative health checks previously
- Validate that the team will have the technical depth to do the Health Check
- Stress the need for them to use best practices for similar types of projects in the industry—have them look outside the organization
- Have them get external best practices
- Validate that the proposed team members have experience doing collaborative health checks previously

Initiating the Health Check

As stated previously, a senior member of a project or program will reach out to a member of a health check team to inquire about doing a formal health check. Figure 7.5 shows the type of resources on the project or program team that will be involved in the health check. Typically, any of the senior roles shown on this slide could proactively or reactively make the request for a health check. Many of them could be asking questions similar to the ones shown in Figure 7.5.

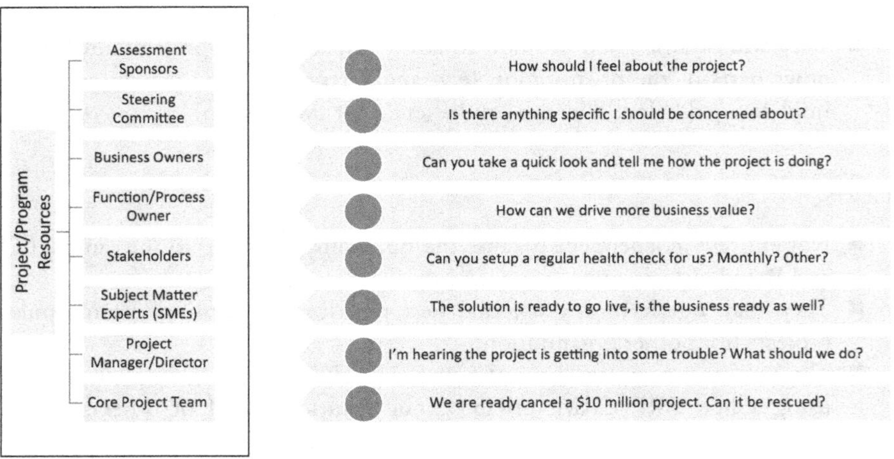

Figure 7.5 Questions from project/program resources.

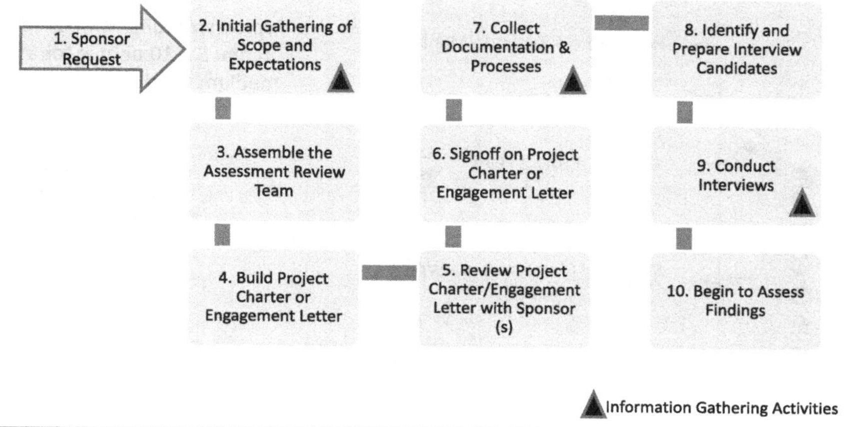

Figure 7.6 Initiating the health check.

Figure 7.6 shows the process that the Health Check assessment team will follow once a project or program team member has reached out for help with an IT Health Check. These processes apply for the following sources doing the Health Check:

- External Vendor
- Subset of the Team
- Another Part of the Organization

Sponsor Request (1)

Once a sponsor has decided that a health check needs to be commissioned, they will be dealing with a simplified organization like that shown in Figure 7.7. The roles shown here should exist in any of the three health check sources referenced earlier (e.g. not including the Audit function). The leadership in the assessment team will then follow the phases in Figure 7.6. The assessment manager (or equivalent) will use members of their team to build out the deliverables in those phases. The roles of these members are:

- Health Check Director/Manager: Overall leader of the assessment team.
- Project Lead: Lead streams on the project health check.
- SME Pool: Designated resources with specific and domain expertise that can be useful on the project health check from time to time.
- Business Analyst: Provides business experience to the team.
- Architect: Provides different types of architectural experience to the team (e.g. solution, data, technical, reference, business).

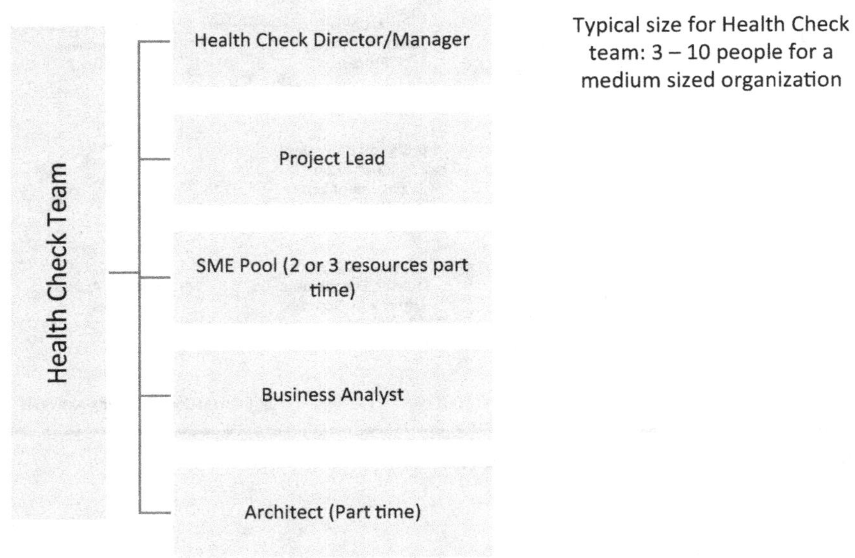

Figure 7.7 Health check team roles.

Initial Gathering of Scope and Expectations (2)

The health check team gets involved in this phase, with the manager generally taking the lead. The conversation will begin between the requesting sponsors and this resource. The objective of the initial discussions is to understand the scope of the project at a detailed level and the current project team's perception of the current state of the project or program potentially needing a health check. They also must ascertain the phase of the project development cycle the initiative has reached. It's always a good idea to pre-plan a list of questions to get at this information. The questions can be open-ended and even free flowing at this stage. Some examples are shown in Figure 7.8.

There may be a need to sign a mutual non-disclosure agreement to start the conversation. Any project documentation, especially the project charter, the corporate organization chart, and the project organization chart should be requested at this time if they exist. Figure 7.9 shows the type of information the assessment team should be gathering from the sponsors. This information will be used in Phase 4—Build Project Charter or Engagement Letter set out below.

Assemble the Assessment Review Team (3)

Assessment teams are not large by any standard as shown in Figure 7.7. They can be as small as one person, 3 to 4 members are common, or larger if the initiatives being assessed are unusually large or complex. There is also a pool of part-time resources

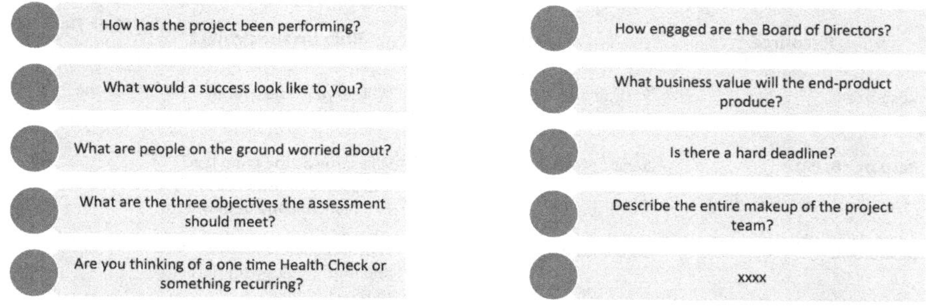

Figure 7.8 Sample questions to ask the sponsors.

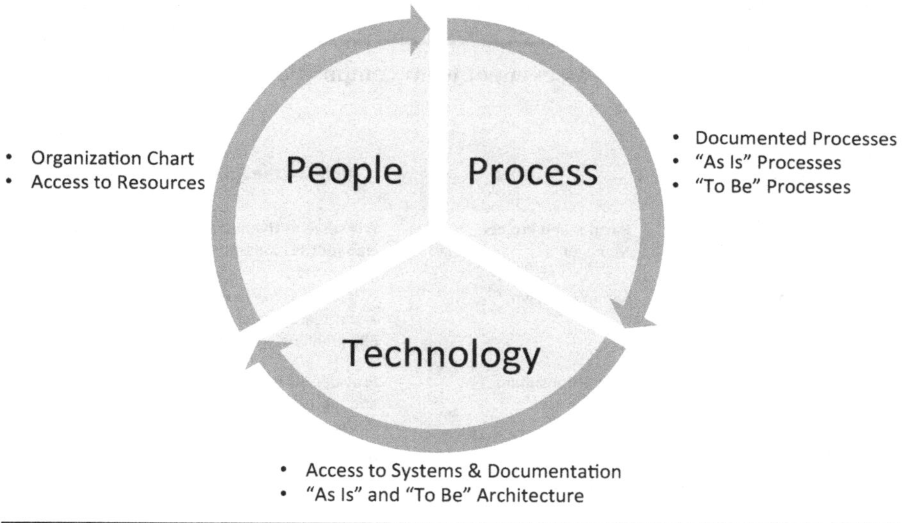

Figure 7.9 Assessment team needs of people-process-technology.

to provide specific domain or technical experience as needed. For example, someone with knowledge of the tax system in each US State or a Cloud Azure expert could be in this group.

Figure 7.10 shows a team that would be identified for a one-off Health Check assessment (e.g. to find out how to drive more business value for their investment). The team members can be identified at this time, but they do not all have to start until the health check assessment is formally approved to begin. In Figure 7.10, resources A and B are dedicated to the assessment full-time or near full-time. Resource A is the manager or leader of the initiative and will do most of the executive-level interaction. Resource B will provide substantial SME-type capabilities, review the documentation in detail, and do a lot of scribing in core team interviews. The other

Resource	Title	Role on the Project	% of Time Involved
Resource A	Partner and Project Manager	Will serve as the overall lead for the assessment.	90
Resource B, PMP	Senior Manager	Will serve as the team lead and subject matter expert for ERP planning and deployment.	100
Resource C	Senior Consultant	Provides subject matter and methodology support to the initiative.	50
Pools of SMEs	Varies	Act as subject matter experts.	50

Assessment team for a one off health check for a period of say three weeks.

Figure 7.10 Example of an assessment team composition (one off request).

Resource	Title	Role on the Project	% of Time Involved
Resource A	Partner and Project Manager	Will serve as the overall lead for the assessment.	20
Resource B, PMP	Senior Manager	Will serve as the team lead and subject matter expert for ERP planning and deployment.	25
Resource C	Senior Consultant	Provides subject matter and methodology support to the initiative.	15
Pools of SMEs	Varies	Act as subject matter experts.	25

Assessment team for a monthly health check.

Figure 7.11 Example of an assessment team composition (recurring request).

members of this assessment team are reserved for as-needed work. Their involvement will peak and ebb during this focused health check assessment.

Figure 7.11 shows an example of a team that could be assembled for a recurring health check. This team has peak involvement on the initiative usually before presentations, but their effort is more spread out across the entire assessment period. This would allow these resources to have time to be involved in multiple initiatives, as they would not be dedicated fulltime to this health check.

Figure 7.12 shows how the assessment team resources would be organized across the different types of health checks that were introduced in Chapters 1 and 2 of this

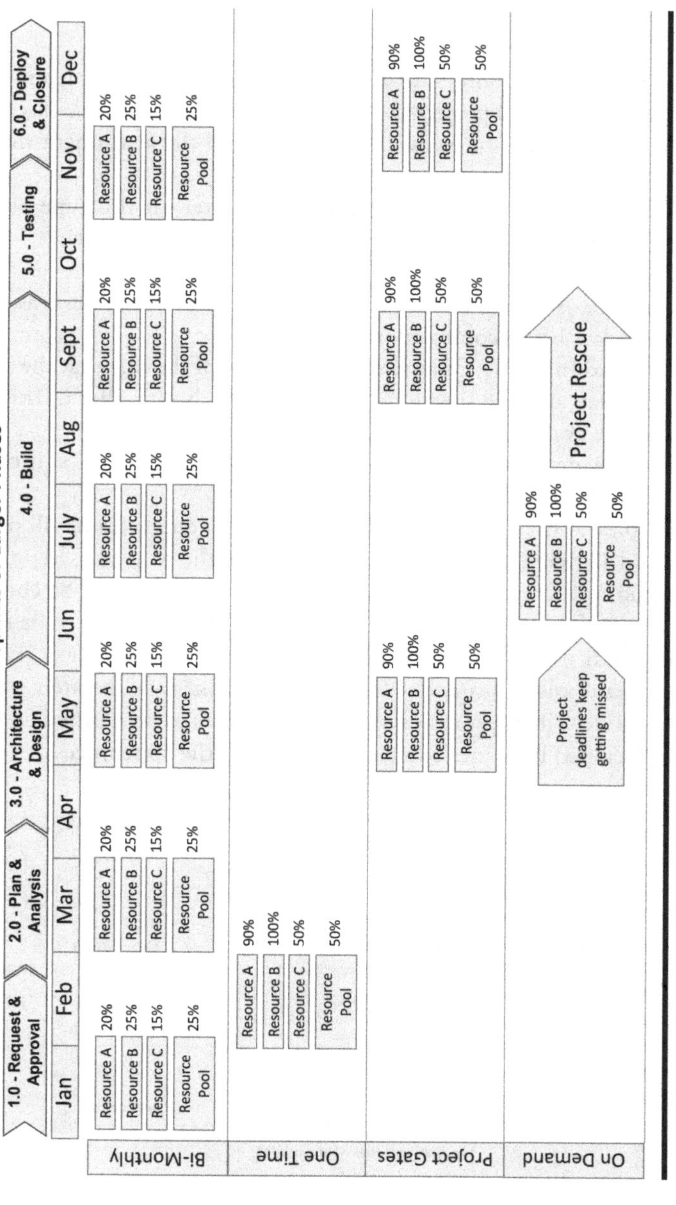

Within Sprints or Larger Phases

1.0 - Request & Approval
2.0 - Plan & Analysis
3.0 - Architecture & Design
4.0 - Build
5.0 - Testing
6.0 - Deploy & Closure

Jan Feb Mar Apr May Jun July Aug Sept Oct Nov Dec

Bi-Monthly
Resource A 20%
Resource B 25%
Resource C 15%
Resource Pool 25%

One Time
Resource A 90%
Resource B 100%
Resource C 50%
Resource Pool 50%

Project Gates
Resource A 90%
Resource B 100%
Resource C 50%
Resource Pool 50%

On Demand
Project deadlines keep getting missed
Resource A 90%
Resource B 100%
Resource C 50%
Resource Pool 50%
Project Rescue

Figure 7.12 Resource distribution by health check.

book. The On-Demand example shows that a Project Rescue intervention is started following the completion of the health check.

Build Project Charter or Engagement Letter (4)

Regardless of where the resources for the health check are coming from, it's highly recommended that a formal project charter and/or engagement letter is constructed and formally signed off by the assessment sponsor and the assessment manager (or a designate).

Figure 7.13 provides a template for a project charter for this type of initiative. There are several sections in the template which are described below:

- Introduction: A background on the project and high-level reasons why a health check is being commissioned.
- Our Role and Initiative Objectives: Description of the role that the assessment team will play and the specific objectives of the health check. This could be based on the evaluation dimensions shown in Figure 7.14.
- Approach: A detailed description of the approach that will be used to complete the health check.
- Deliverables: A list of deliverables that the health check team will produce.
- Scope and Timeline: A detailed confirmation of the scope, based on a customized version of Figure 7.14, and a timeline for the review to be completed in the context of the overall project plan for the initiative about to be the subject of the health check review should be included in this section. Figure 7.15 shows an example of a timeline for doing this. This is deliberately shown to fit into one slide to make it easier for all stakeholders to be on the same page at a glance. Detailed timelines could be included in the appendices.

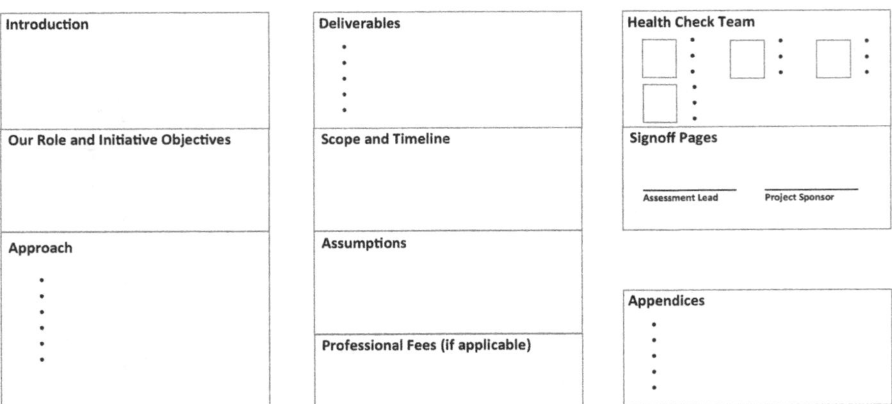

Figure 7.13 Project charter or engagement letter template.

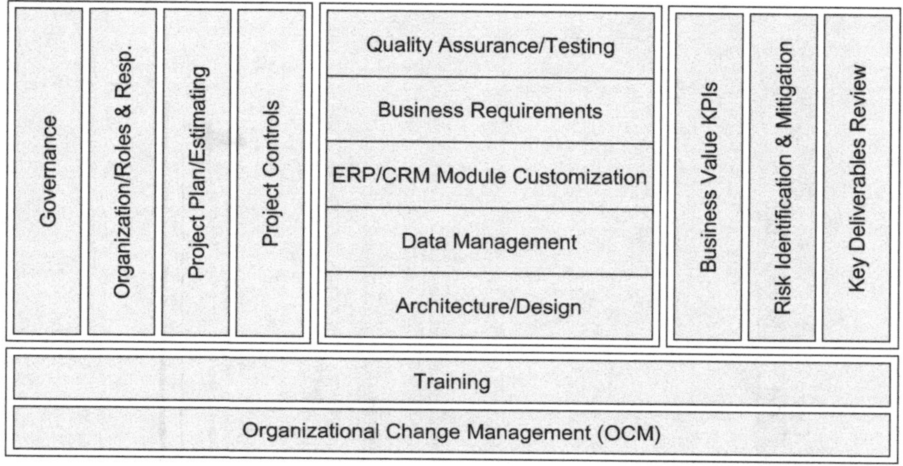

Figure 7.14 Sample customized health check framework dimensions.

- Assumptions: A list of assumptions for the assessment that the executive sponsors need to support. E.g. a meeting room will be reserved for the assessment team for the four-week health check. The information and access that the assessment team will need for the health check activities should be included here. This should include a list of the deliverables, documents, and process maps that will be needed for the review. A request for access to the systems supporting the project or program should also be explicitly included here.
- Professional Fees (if applicable): This would normally be applicable when external vendors are being commissioned to do the health check, unless there is an internal accounting process in the organization.
- Health Check Team: A list of the individual members of the health check team. Their photos can be included with a few lines of description around their background. Detailed resumes can be included in the appendices.
- Signoff Pages: Formal signoff from the assessment sponsors from the project side and the lead resource on the health check team.

Review Project Charter/Engagement Letter with Sponsor(s) (5)

In this phase, the health check team leads will meet with the assessment sponsors from the project to review the details of the health check initiative. They need to confirm the scope and objectives. The evaluation dimensions should be confirmed and will form the basis of the scope of the assessment. Recall that Figure 7.14 shows the evaluation dimensions and areas of scope that the review will examine.

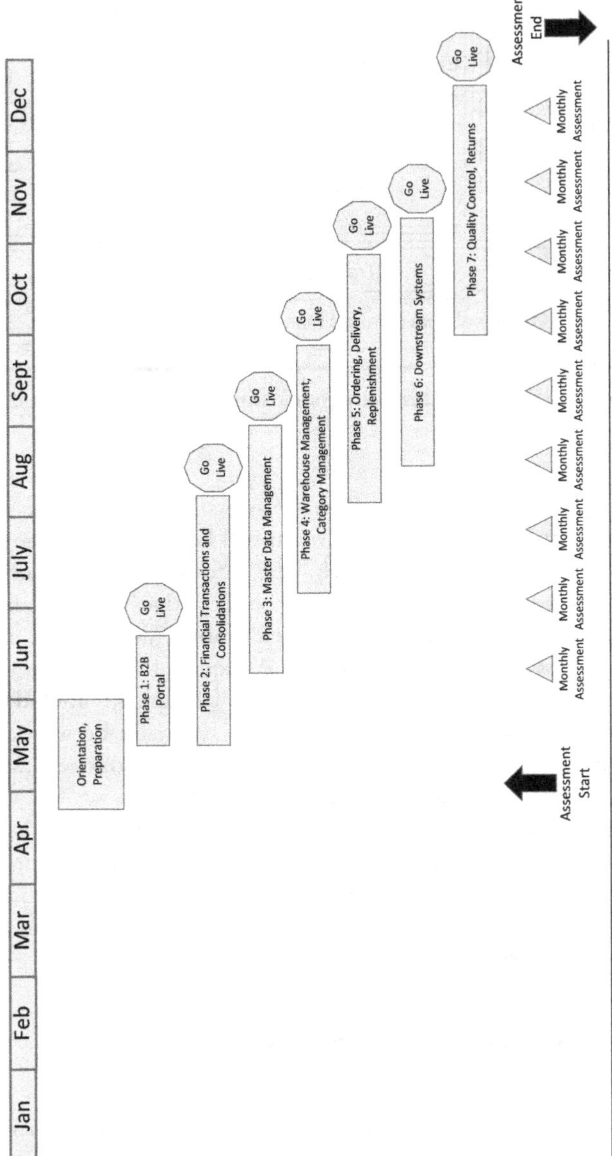

Figure 7.15 Sample timeline for a recurring health check.

These can be customized further when finalizing the project charter with the assessment sponsors shown back in Figure 7.5.

Signoff on Project Charter or Engagement Letter (6)

Despite receiving a verbal agreement to proceed, the assessment team should insist on getting a formal signoff from the assessment sponsors so that there is a written confirmation of their commitment to support this important initiative. The signoff should trigger sharing the information and the start of the other requests that were defined in the assumptions section of the health care project charter.

This signature will also trigger onboarding activities that the assessment sponsors will need to undertake, including the following:

- Setup email and system access for the individual members of the assessment team
- Provide access and directions to the requested deliverables
- Send out an introductory email introducing the health check team to the larger project team or even the organization if the initiative has that level of visibility. The sponsors need to unreservedly support the health check team and ask all members of the project team to make participation a top, mandatory priority. Any desired outcomes from the health check can also be shared in this executive level communication.
- The sponsors should make themselves available to answer any questions from members of the project team who have concerns or reservations of the process.

Collect Documentation and Processes (7)

Once formal agreement to start has been reached, the assessment team will go through collection and review of the documentation, deliverables, and process maps that are shared by the core project team. This will be the focus of "Chapter 9: Reviewing the Documentation & Other Deliverables".

Identify and Prepare Interview Candidates (8)

The organization charts and recommendations from the assessment sponsors are used to build an interview list. Questionnaires must be built in advance of the meeting based on the information collection activities. The sponsor will need to send an email to the identified candidates and inform them of the upcoming requirements of their time. The calendars will need to be reserved well in advance of the interviews. This will be discussed in more detail in Chapter 10.

Conduct Interviews (9)

Each user interview should be between 30 and 60 minutes on average. This process is also discussed in more detail in Chapter 10.

Begin to Assess Findings (10)

The last phase in getting started is to begin to assess the results of the discovery activities. As shown in Figure 7.16, this is just to the left of the midpoint of Period B. The assessment approaches are discussed in later sections of this book.

Project Charter Example

A template for the project charter was presented earlier in this chapter. This section provides a sanitized example for the sections.

Introduction

Here is an example of an introduction section:

> Dear (sponsor list names):
>
> On behalf of our team, we would like to thank you for considering us to conduct a health check. In this letter, we are providing an outline of project scope, deliverables, and timelines for this project to provide for the proposed health check.
>
> We understand that the NextGraph project has multiple stakeholders and tight timelines. This adds complexity to meeting your business objectives, timelines, and project costs. Studies and best practices have shown that running a recurring, independent Health Check will find many multiples of business value and reduce the risk and costs of project initiatives.
>
> Based on the documents we have reviewed and the meetings we have conducted, we understand that a key component of your project involves the implementation of an integrated ERP and Warehouse management system that will serve over 2500 users. A business case and selection process has already been followed to select this solution, as well as a discussion of high-level project costs and timeline. The scope of this implementation and for our health check will be: will be: MDM, Vendor APIs, Warehouse Management, HR, Finance, Procurement, Store Operations, Executive Reporting, and Category Management. The planned timeline for this initiative is currently October 25, 20xx to Oct 15 20xx+1. Key milestones are scheduled throughout this period.

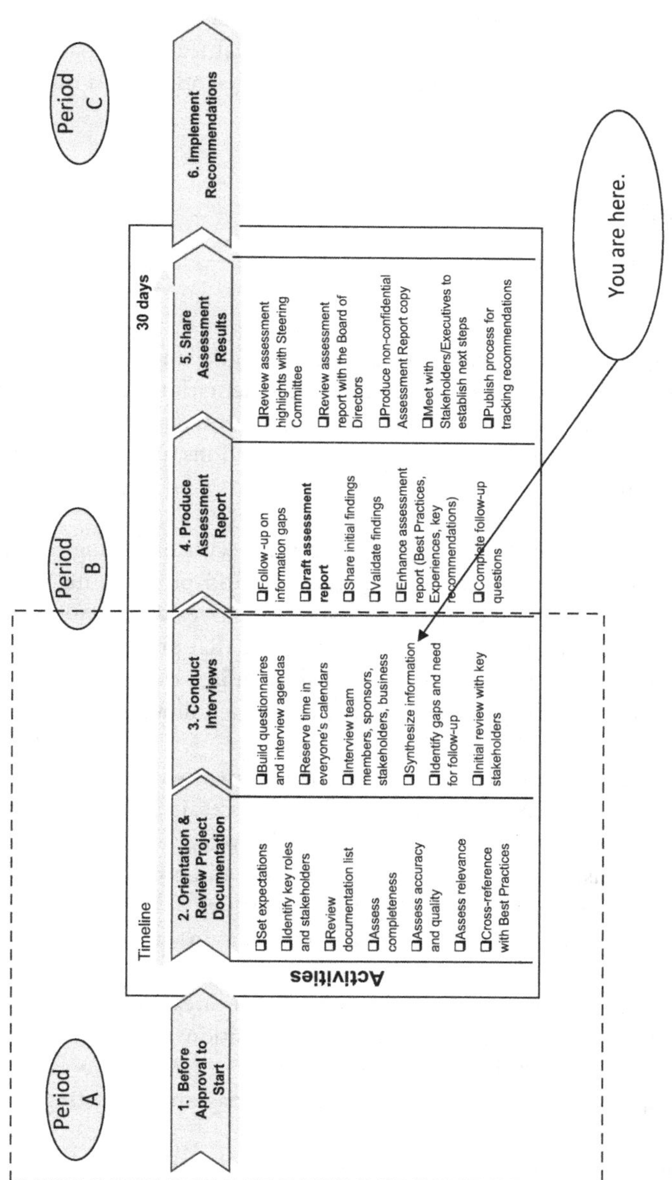

Figure 7.16 Completing the initial discovery activities.

Given our qualifications and experience with ERP implementation quality and risk assessment initiatives, we clearly understand and have experienced your key concerns and challenges that are inherent in executing a mandate of this magnitude. We have assembled a qualified local team that has delivered recurring program-level health checks in the past to work on this initiative.

Our Role and Initiative Objectives

Here is an example for this section of the letter:

Our role on this engagement is to provide an independent assessment of Project NextGraph in parallel with the implementation team. Our independent Health Check processes will create awareness and consensus related to issues and risks to ensure that decisions and actions are taken to prevent threats from materializing and threatening the successful implementation of the project deliverables.

Our primary objective is to assist your team with obtaining an understanding of and evaluating the various business and program management risks and quality issues that could impact your initiative. We also want to help you maximize business value. Our goal is to ensure that program/project risks and quality challenges are identified and dealt with in a timely manner.

The objectives of the Health Check are to do the following:

- Provide the project's leadership and management with a recurring independent assessment of the project risks, successes, issues, and opportunities at each stage of the implementation lifecycle
- Evaluate business and IT risks for the project and provide recommendations for appropriate risk management strategies
- Review key deliverables and documentation in order to provide an assessment and recommendations based on best practices
- Provide guidance and thought leadership in areas of systems design, implementation, testing, deployment, transition to sustainment, and overall project and risk management
- Participate in key project, executive, and management meetings

Conduct a monthly health check assessment and present our documented findings to your Steering Committee on a monthly basis

Approach

Here is an example for this section of the letter:

Our approach includes establishing baseline measures to help ensure that the project meets business requirements in the proposed timeframe, budget, and quality requirements. To be effective, we will take a long and wide view of the project and deliverables, but as issues and risks are identified we will provide recommendations to deal with the concerns. We will generally be on site a few days a month on average, participate in key meetings (e.g. The Steering Committee Meeting, Operating Committee, Project Status Meeting), and provide executive dashboards summarizing quality, risks, and other issues for the executive team.

We will review and evaluate the following on an ongoing basis:

- The overall project plan and detailed schedule
- Project Status Reports and dashboards (weekly, monthly, and executive versions)
- The methodologies being used by the different System Integrators and vendors
- The project management approach being taken by the lead System Integrator
- Documentation and deliverables.
- Issue logs and Risk/Mitigation strategies
- Change Management requests
- Program guidelines, processes (e.g. change management), and policies
- Our results will be included in our Monthly Executive Dashboard.

Deliverables

Here is an example for this section of the letter:

We will produce the following deliverables within the scope of this engagement:

A monthly health check dashboard that summarizes and characterizes the status of key project variables using a Red, yellow, and Green rating scale. Red and Yellow indicators will be accompanied by recommendations on how to bring them back to Green.

- Our review of your key risk and issue log on a monthly basis.
- Input into the ongoing project management activities including advice on establishment of governance, PMO, and management reporting structures.

- Provide an independent viewpoint to the risk, quality, schedule, scope, and cost.
- Review of Key Project Deliverables as they are produced.

We anticipate the need to have access to your technical and business users for about 12% of the elapsed duration each month.

Scope and Timeline

Here is an example for this section of the letter:

The scope for our health check review involves applying the dimensions in our evaluation framework to the following functions:

- MDM
- Vendor Portal
- Warehouse Management
- Human Resources (HR)
- Finance
- Procurement
- Store Operations
- Executive Reporting
- Category Management.

Our time involvement includes the following:

- The initiative runs between Oct 25, 20xx to Oct 15, 20xx+1.
- We expect that our resources will spend about 2-4 days per month on this initiative on average, with greater involvement at key points of the project lifecycle.
- We would request that we attend the steering committee meetings (monthly) either in person or by conference call, the weekly PMO meeting, and the regularly scheduled Operating Committee meeting.

Assumptions

Here is an example for this section of the letter:

Our letter is based on the following assumptions:

- The project team will provide access to resources and materials in a timely fashion.
- The documents corresponding to the deliverables list requested in our email of xx/xx/xxxx will be provided prior to the start of the health check
- Members of our resource team will be given access to your documentation systems and network
- The project team will provide representatives who are responsible for final approval and ownership of all documents and deliverables produced in this initiative.
- All interim deliverable reviews will be done in a timely fashion by designated client resources.
- The project team will identify key stakeholders and a project manager to work with the health check team.

Professional Fees (if applicable)

Here is an example for this section of the letter:

Our professional fees are based on the actual time required to complete the agreed-upon work at hourly rates identified for the professionals assigned to the engagement. Any taxes or expenses would be on top of these. We are providing two estimates to provide a range for our services, as follows:

- Low Estimate: This represents the situation where our team will provide focused effort at the beginning and end of each phase, but will ease up as issues that are discovered are minimal.
- High Estimate: This represents the situation where our team will expend the same level of work effort throughout the project lifecycle with little or no periods of reduced involvement. This situation will be driven by the number and size of issues we uncover.

Health Check Team

The health check team is generally very lean. An example that matches the scope and timelines above is shown in Figure 7.17. This health check is recurring, so the resources will be spending their time on the project every month.

Resource	Title	Role on the Project
A A	Project Manager	Will serve as Engagement Manager for this health check, as well at being the project manager.
B B	Senior Manager	Will serve as a team lead and subject matter expert for retail ERP planning and deployment
C C	Senior Consultant	Will provide subject matter and methodology support to the initiative.
D D	Architect	Expertise on the solution and technical architecture.

Figure 7.17 Health check team.

Please indicate your acceptance of the **health check assessment** arrangements for **project NextGraph** by signing and returning one copy of this letter to the undersigned. We are pleased to discuss this letter and our initiative with you at any time. We look forward to continue working with you on this exciting and challenging engagement.

Yours very truly,

Signature	*Signature*
A A	G G
Authorized Signatory	Project Signatory

Figure 7.18 Signature wordage.

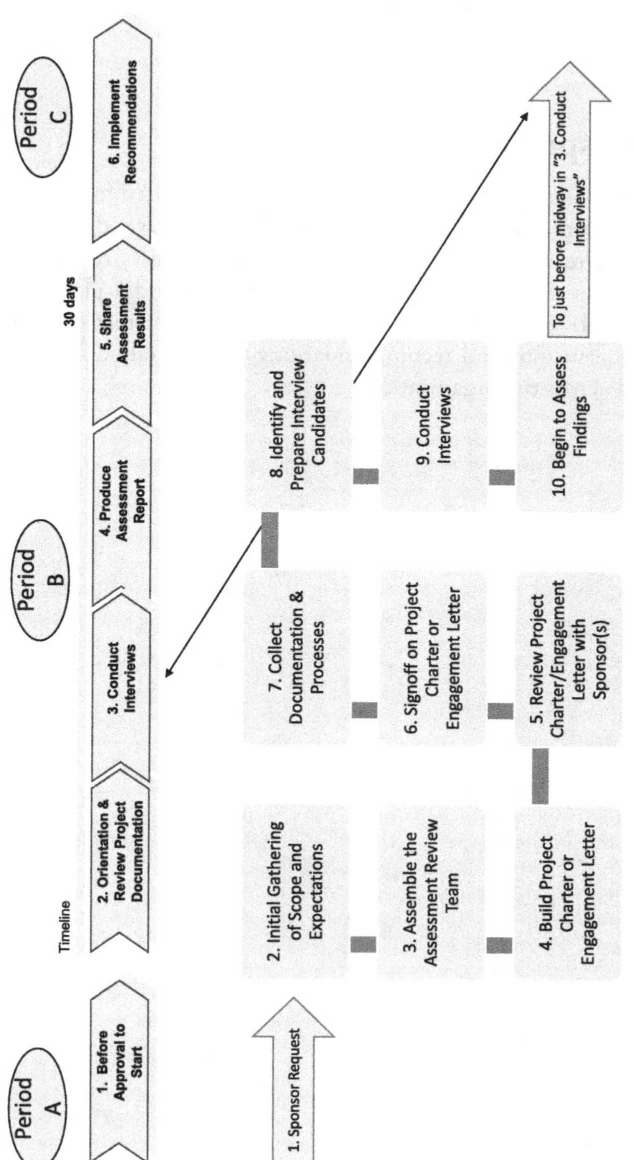

Figure 7.19 Setting up the health check.

Signoff Pages

Figure 7.18 provides a simplified example of the signature block. It is highly recommended for the reasons discussed previously that this portion of the letter be executed.

Closing Perspective

This chapter examined the activities and deliverables required for setting up a health check initiative from the point in time that project executives decide one is needed, to the point where relevant information is gathered and is ready for assessment. Figure 7.19 shows that these activities cover Period A and a portion of Period B. The remaining activities dive into making sense of the information gathered so that meaningful observations and recommendations can be drafted and then meaningfully socialized across the organization.

Chapter 8

Spotting Early Warning Red Flags in the Initial Stages of the Health Check

This chapter provides some best practices around identifying early warning red flags on projects or programs. The health check should look for these in each of the major project dimensions of: People–Technology–Process. Figure 8.1 shows some of the high-level points that a health check assessment team can start to look for when reviewing deliverables, documentation, and during stakeholder interviews. There are recurring patterns that can be spotted during these reviews which are flags to investigate further in those areas.

We are not trying to predict the future by identifying red or other warning flags. What we are doing is looking at past history and the likelihood that events will repeat. Using a red warning flag checklist is an accelerator to understanding the status of an initiative and what is likely to happen. The health check should not be limited to the red warning flags identified here, but should use them as a starting point.

For example, data conversion, as shown by past experience, is often underestimated in terms of effort, duration, and resources (all three elements of the project management triangle). A red warning flag that stands out is if the project plan shows the data conversion activities to be back-ended, meaning there is not enough time to deal with problems that may occur, and arguably do occur on most initiatives. Figure 8.2 shows a simplified view of this process. The figure shows that the data conversion process will continue until data validation shows that the data accuracy

DOI: 10.1201/9781003269786-10

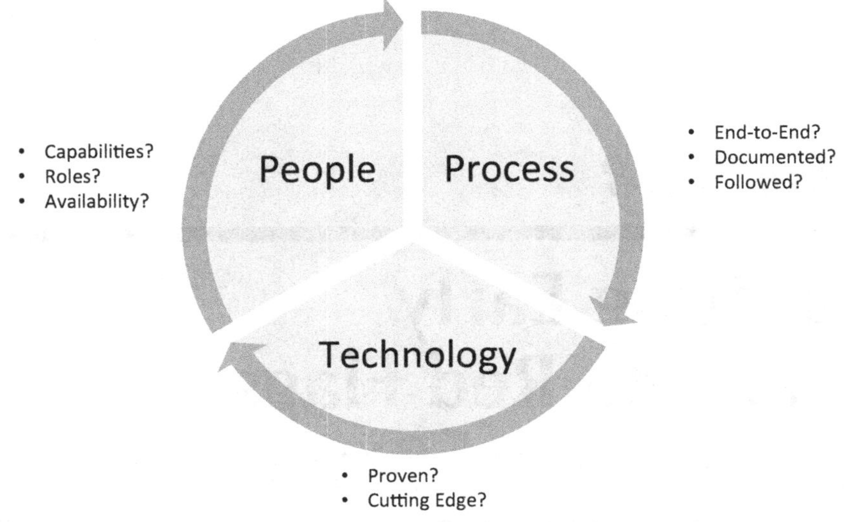

Figure 8.1 Red flag groupings.

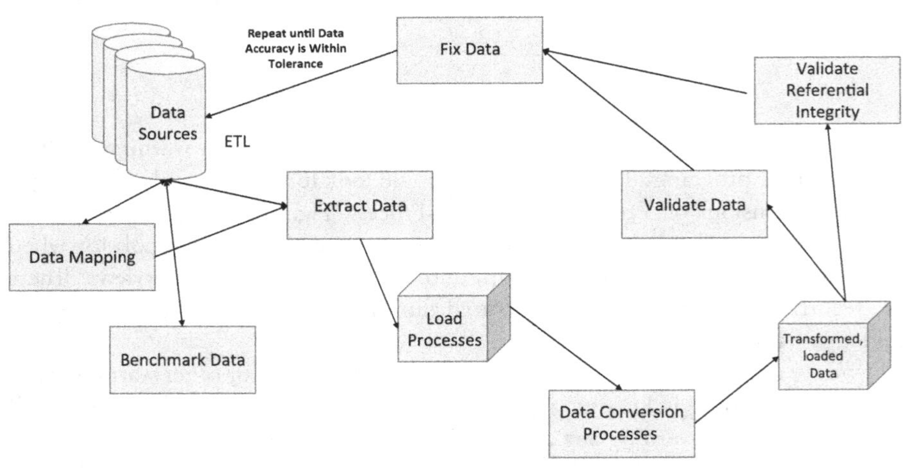

Figure 8.2 Simplified data conversion, ETL processes.

is within a specified tolerance (say 5%). This will be dependent on the data benchmarking findings, and the results of the data validation routines. Depending on these results, the data conversion process can be extremely time-consuming. There are a few more interesting points that we will discuss later in this chapter in the data conversion section.

The assessment team, in some ways is playing detective, reviewer, and referee. There should be no agenda to embarrass anyone or to be too picky and pedantic. The goal is to align with executive management's definition of project success and to assess whether that is happening and collaboratively arrive at solutions to drive more business value.

Consider this case study. An IT project for an entertainment company had missed multiple deadlines. The IT organization was also complaining about code quality and their ability to support the system after implementation. An independent executive was hired to conduct a health check over three months. The project sponsor (s) were at the "VP" and "C" level from the business and technology. The project was clearly very high profile and watched outside the company. Spotting several red warning flags, the reviewer quickly identified three reasons why the project could not hit the implementation deadline about 6 months away when the review started, as follows:

1. The data conversion activities had not started and there was no sense of the state of the data quality in the current system. The estimate for the amount of data in the system to be converted was generically four months. Experience tells us that there will be surprises during the data conversion process so two months of contingency—less if you assume a system freeze period of ten days—would not be enough.
2. The business requirements had not been signed off and were still changing. A lot of details around business rules were missing. Only a few business requirement documents had officially been signed off by the executives and business owners.
3. Testing activity experience coming out of the monthly sprints showed a great number of defects were being identified. Fixing these, while building new functionality, was splitting the core team and would likely slow the project down further with the completion of each monthly sprint.

Based on these observations, and from past project experience, the likelihood of successfully achieving the six-month implementation date with a quality product that would be sustainable after implementation seemed to be remote to impossible. The interim report, written and presented one month after the start of the assessment, provided these observations with a recommendation to plan for a new implementation date based on estimates made against a new bottom-up project plan that incorporated the recommendations from the review. These recommendations were accepted by the executive team.

The recommendations coming out of the health check review stopped the death march the project was on and stopped it from outright cancellation. By identifying the issues, an adoption of the recommendations contained the additional work effort required to complete the project to an additional 4 months. Existing overages already exceeded one year without delivering the project into production.

The Health Check saved the project from continuing on a costly path that was consuming resources and probably going to be outright cancelled in the future. The system went into production and met the business objectives and provided the customer loyalty metrics in the original business case. A two-month project health check assessment saved a 24-month project investment and delivered over 10x business value when all the final numbers were tabulated.

Sources of Project/Program Problems

The IT industry is unique in the sense that it combines elements of both science and art. We can argue about the exact split, and it varies from industry to industry, but both elements are present in IT initiatives. This is because of all the moving pieces within the three levers shown in Figure 8.1.

- Technology: For a long-time technology was considered to be the biggest risk. While the actual technology solution is obviously crucial, it's probably a smaller slice than the others in terms of risk. It's important to rely on proven technology solutions to meet non-functional requirements and have detailed plans and solutions when going outside that box. This will be discussed in more detail later in this chapter.
- Process: There must be a logical progression from an "As-Is" process view to a "To-Be" process viewpoint. Very often, the future processes do not go far enough to exploit the full business benefits that are possible. There is a tendency to mirror status quo, but on a new system. User training at the appropriate times (e.g. a few weeks before a project implementation) with the appropriate materials is needed to support process changes.
- People: This is arguably the largest slice on the red flag warning pie. There are so many potential red flags, that the people side of the project must start before the initiative is approved and extend well past the solution implementation. The HR organization must be deeply involved during these times.

Optimism–Realism–Pessimism

An organization implemented an ERP-CRM system for a mid-sized financial institution. The project required an extensive rescue intervention, which allowed it to be ultimately implemented on time and under budget for the revised metrics following the rescue. Optimism was used to build the original project plan. All tasks were given work efforts on the extremely optimistic side. Tasks were arranged with minimal dependencies, assuming many could be done in parallel, which turned out to have no basis in fact. Resources were assumed to be available and not involved in their day jobs. Week-to-week status reports were showing green—well, because everyone was optimistic and hopeful that the system integrator, internal staff, and many other vendors would somehow bring everything together. A project rescue was executed after a project health check and the project ended up going into implementation within the revised budget and timelines.

After the eventual implementation, for a time, when new projects were in the "Planning Phase" at the organization, executives started multiplying all the time and resource estimates by a factor of 5! They went from an unjustified optimistic viewpoint to an unjustified pessimistic one in terms of work effort and cost on new project initiatives.

Neither the optimistic or pessimistic viewpoints are the best way of thinking. The optimistic view is seldom met so the business value justification will always be invalid by being an overestimation. Similarly, the pessimistic view is also seldom justified and so projects and programs may not be approved for all the wrong reasons.

Project planning must be based on traceable and transparent estimates. It is true that things can go very well and so the project could beat expectations, just as it is true that a lot of risks could materialize and we could end up with the pessimistic scenario. But when assessing a project, it's important to look for realistic estimates that are based on logical facts. One approach is to try to come up with three scenarios shown in Figure 8.3, and use these to plan for the project. The difference between the optimistic case and the pessimistic one could be covered by contingency.

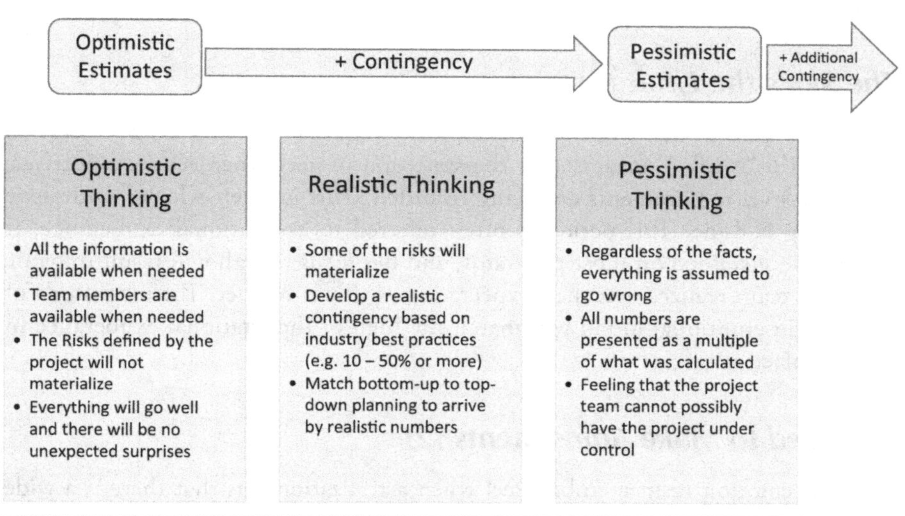

Figure 8.3 Optimistic-realistic-pessimistic thinking.

Understanding the Psychology Behind Emotional Roller Coasters on Project Initiatives

There are a common set of emotions many team members feel when a program is started. These emotions cycle through and repeat until a later phase when they become normalized. As part of the assessment team, as you begin the review expect to be in some part of this cycle and adjust your analysis and expectations accordingly. As shown in Figure 8.4, there are just over a half-dozen common emotional states you can encounter.

Depending on the type of methodology being used, the cycle can repeat again and again across sprints and releases, albeit the height and width will change over time. Ideally, with more experiences the intensity should be getting smaller as shown in Figure 8.5, but in some cases it could be the exact opposite as the team begins to lose complete control. The cycle may even repeat through a waterfall series of phases. The emotions may be balanced through the testing activities, but then panic sets in as soon as the team reaches deployment. Will the users actually be ready? Will the help desk be overwhelmed? Did we forget something?

Being able to recognize the actual emotional state that the project team members are in will allow the assessment team to form reasonable questions to get to real answers, and then to form recommendations that will be actionable by the project team so that the initiative can get to a balanced state as quickly as possible.

The "roller coaster of emotions" that team members experience are described in the sections that follow below. The assessment team needs to understand the state of the project team and provide recommendations to get them as rapidly as possible to the mode in Point 6 in Figure 8.4.

The Sky's the Limit (1)

Team members in this emotion will typically feel that nothing is impossible to achieve. This is often witnessed at the start of a project when scope, objectives, and high-level requirements are being recorded. This is when a lot of optimistic estimating is done. This period is often referred to as irrational exuberance. It will not be sustained on most programs, and like a sugar high will result in panic when the team realizes that their expectations will not be met. The magnitude of the drop in emotional mood will match the high of the irrational exuberance in the first place.

Prepared to Make Adjustments (2)

The next emotion team members feel when a realization hits that there is a wide delta between expectations and reality is to start making minor adjustments. Perhaps every report is not needed they will reason. Maybe some interfaces can be done

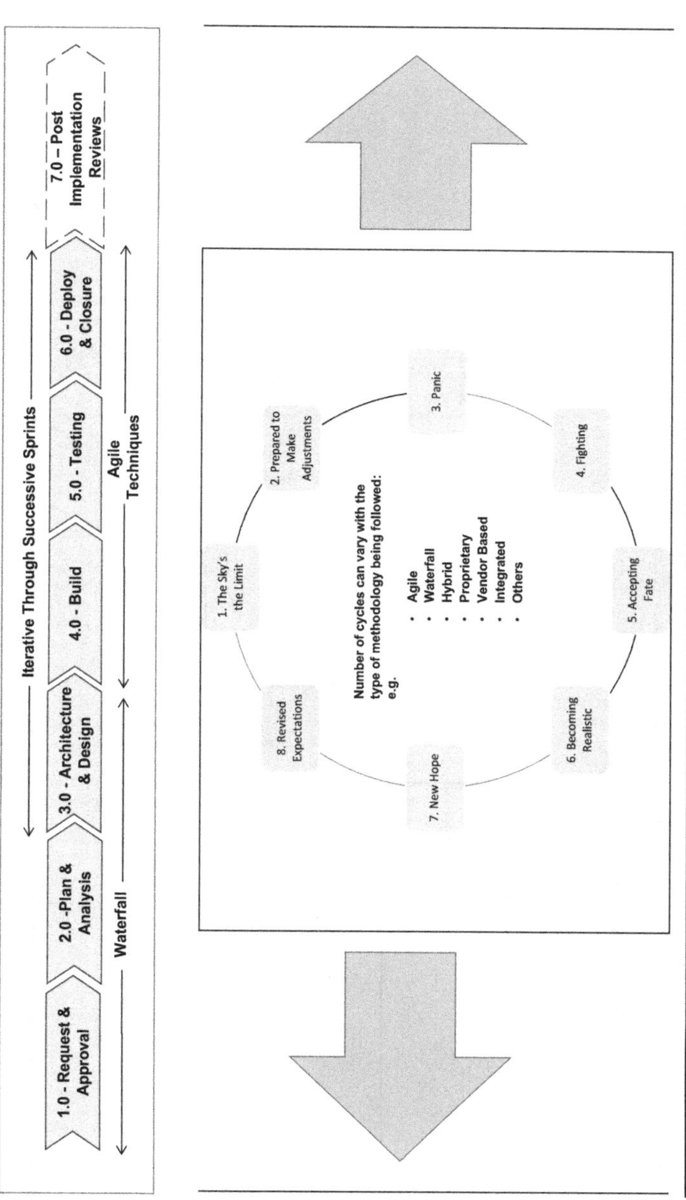

Figure 8.4 Emotional rollercoaster.

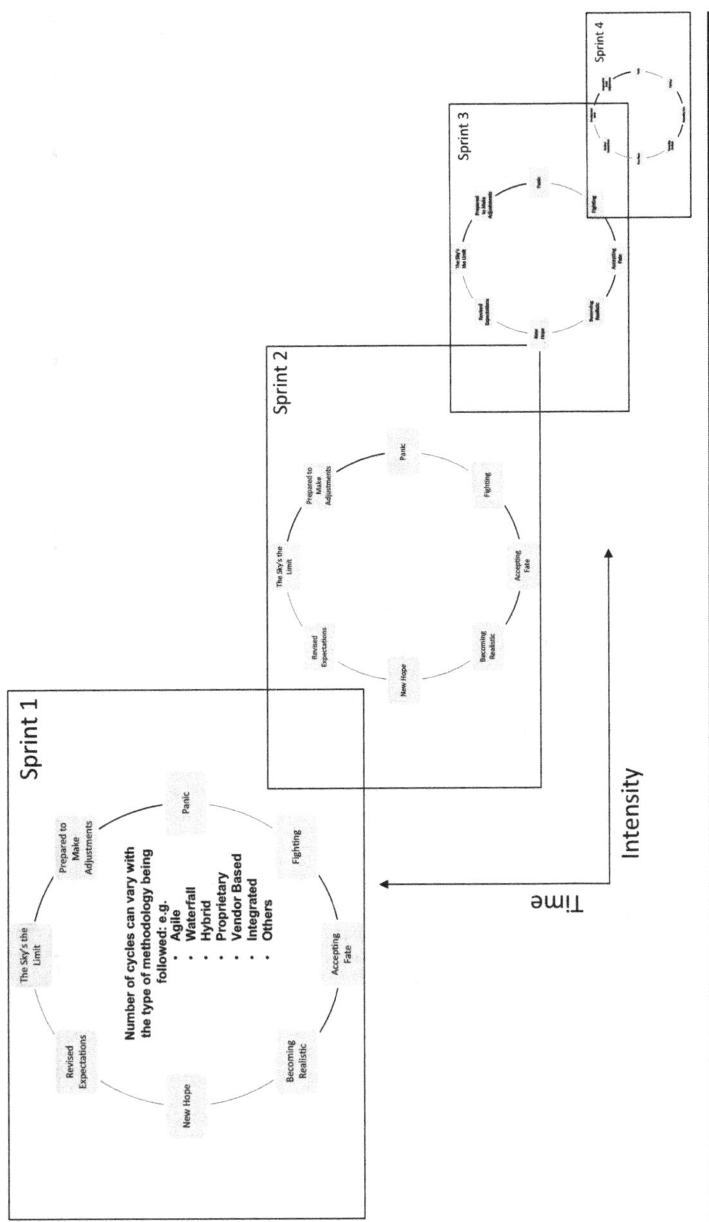

Figure 8.5 Emotional rollercoasters by sprint.

manually because the number of transactions is pretty small, and perhaps every process does not have to be automated. Maybe some functions can be postponed until sometime after the system goes live? This is when tradeoffs start to be acceptable, a situation that would be intolerable at point 1.

Panic (3)

In more complex programs, the team may begin to feel collective panic when the deadline and budget pressures become a reality when small tradeoffs are not seemingly saving the project. How much budget was spent to get to this point? Panic can be averted with "informed knowledge". The sooner the team gets informed knowledge the better aligned to realistic delivery they will be and the higher the business value that will be received by the organization. Figure 8.6 shows that the acknowledgement of best practices, health check observations and recommendations, or some other mechanism to quickly bridge the gap between irrational exuberance and realism will reduce the overall amount of wasted effort and resources. The "X" shows that the emotional rollercoaster will not continue throughout the project life-cycle and serves as a hard stop.

Fighting (4)

At some point the team will go back to a rough fighting form following the panic mode. Too many times, they will not be prepared to make the right decisions to remain consistent with the original business benefits and scope. This will result in more wasted effort, budget, and time until the next emotional mode sets in.

Accepting Fate (5)

After feeling panic and fighting, project teams then tend to go into an accepting, almost stoic mode, becoming prepared to accept a less than optimal solution. This mode can result in underestimating what's needed and becoming too pessimistic in terms of what is achievable. These wide extremes become an enormous energy drain on the team and contribute greatly to wasted resources.

Becoming Realistic (6)

With more knowledge and experience, the team will then start to become realistic. Many team members will figure out that there is a critical path acceptable and profitable for the business. This creates a sense of realism which results in revisions to the budget, timeline, and most importantly the functionality.

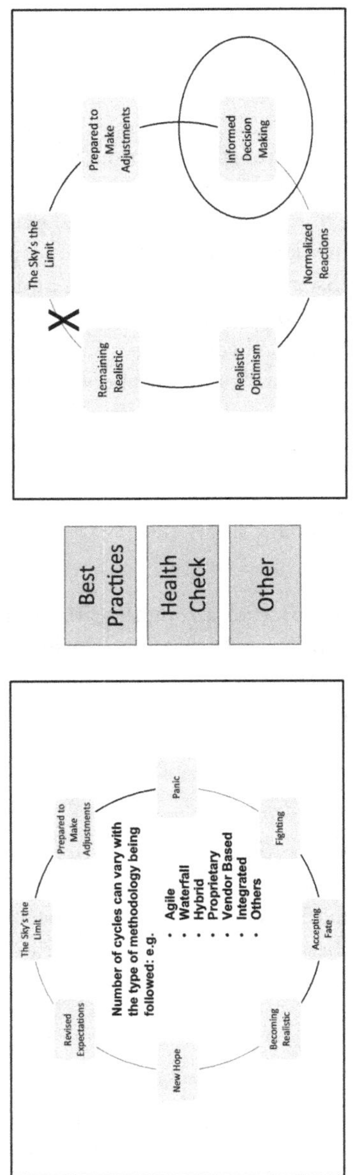

Figure 8.6 Informed decision making.

New Hope (7)

As new metrics begin to be met, the project team will begin to feel a new sense of hope. There may be some pressures toward optimistic exuberance again, but this is where the Steering Committee or a Health Check team needs to stay on course and focused.

Consider this case study. An HRIS system was being implemented for a services company. They had experienced the emotional rollercoaster modes and started to feel that the project was going to fail. A quick health check identified the need to add another skilled Project Manager to the team, one with skills in implementing global HRIS systems with financial backends. Within a few months, the project was back on track and the perception was that the sky was the limit again. Various stakeholders wanted to add functionality that would be good for business value. However, scope control was a discipline brought in by the new PM. Despite lots of pressure to expand, to be exuberant, the PM insisted on staying the course laid out and agreed to by the executive sponsors in the Project Charter. The project was implemented within the realistic contingency (well under the pessimistic number). The HRIS vendor provided feedback that it was one of the best implementations they had seen. It was due to the scope control and not going back to Mode 1 in Figure 8.4.

Revised Expectations (8)

The final emotional state we are examining is that of revised expectations. This will follow the "New Hope" feeling, and should ideally be realistic with fact-based reasoning. If the team has learned lessons throughout the entire cycle, the cycle will not go back to mode 1. The assessment team recommendations work best when the project team is in modes 6 or 8.

Psychological Drivers of Project/Program Problems

While being alert for red warning flags upon starting an assessment, the assessment team should also understand some of the psychological drivers that explain why there are project or program problems. Figure 8.7 shows some of the common reasons for why project problems are not detected or solved right away. The Emotional Rollercoaster can be driven by the psychological drivers discussed in this section.

Some of these can be resolved by instilling a culture of transparency and openness. However, the challenge is that until it becomes part of the DNA of an organization, team members will not internalize the approach and can default to the original way of thinking.

As show in Figure 8.7, here are some of the common psychological or human reasons behind issues that emerge on projects. The assessment team should look for

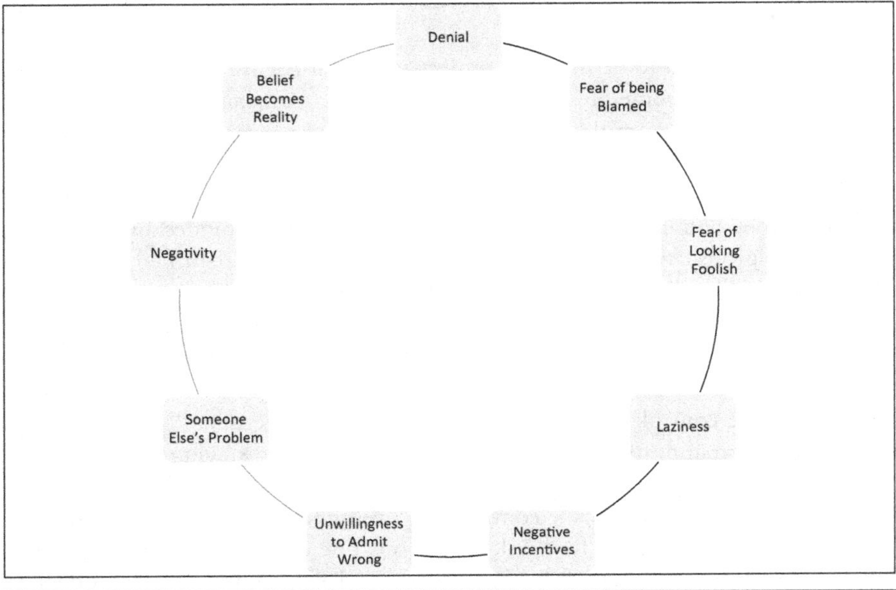

Figure 8.7 Psychological drivers of project/program problems.

evidence of these occurring in the project team and view these as red warning flags. Recommendations should include specific suggestions for dealing with the following cultural behaviors:

- Denial: Team members are denying reality, e.g. they argue that there is still more than enough budget left even though the project is far behind in delivery.
- Fear of being blamed: Team members may not speak up about problems for fear of being blamed by management for the problem in the first place.
- Fear of looking foolish: Have you ever known an answer to a question on a gameshow but said nothing because you did not want to risk the embarrassment of being wrong? The same thing happens on projects but on a higher level. Team members who may suspect something, e.g. the project timeline is not realistic, but may not speak up because they think they will be laughed at or ostracized.
- Laziness: Some team members are not willing to do the work to dig deep into the project or program issues.
- Negative incentives: Some members of the project team or expanded team may not want the project to succeed. For example, perhaps they will end up in a new role they do not want or be moved out of the organization altogether.
- Unwillingness to admit wrong: At some point in a project lifecycle, it becomes difficult for leadership and others to admit that they have made mistakes,

ignored warnings, and believed in the impossible. This is where a collaborative independent health check can remove the emotion out of bringing the project back on track and only focus on the results and not the blame.

- Someone else's problem: Some members may believe that if they wait long enough, it will be another group's problem. For example, the APIs do not work, but the project will never get past the data conversion in the first place so why say anything. They reason that the blame will be placed on the data conversion team.
- Negativity: Some members will be negative to all suggestions to improve the project's success possibilities. This can have a cascading effect that can bring morale down, and cause all sorts of problems. Sometimes, they have valid points, but never offer suggestions to deal with issues. For example, an architect on an ERP implementation was negative about every architecture, every deadline, and every decision. It was terrible for getting decisions made and getting team members on the same page. IT would reinforce the negative morale already on the team. Worse, the architect did nothing to deal with the issues he was raising! The new PM took this individual aside and said there would be virtual fines for every negative public statement without a corresponding solution. The situation quickly improved. No money needed to change hands.
- Belief becomes reality: On some projects, negativity becomes a self-fulfilling prophecy because no actions are taken to stop the project from failing.

Incubating Conditions That Drive Downstream Red Flags

While some of the incubating conditions can also be viewed as red flags themselves, their manifestation on a project will almost certainly spawn other problems, issues, and red flags in the future. Before even examining the details of the deliverables and documentation, the assessment team can do a high-level review of whether these exist, as shown in Figure 8.8. If them do exist, consider building a checklist in the areas shown below to drive deeper for other likely red flags during the interviews

- Everything is Perceived to be going Smoothly: This is an interesting observation after reviewing many projects. Just as seeing a project team panicked is a clear sign of problems, so too is a team that perceives the project is running too smoothly. There are usually challenges on IT programs due to their complexity with People–Process–Technology. Teams that do not experience that feeling of trepidation and start identifying concerns probably are not looking deep enough and have not yet fully understood the problem.
- Lack of Specific Documentation: If the documentation is too general and has not focused in on specific details, there is a chance that the project is

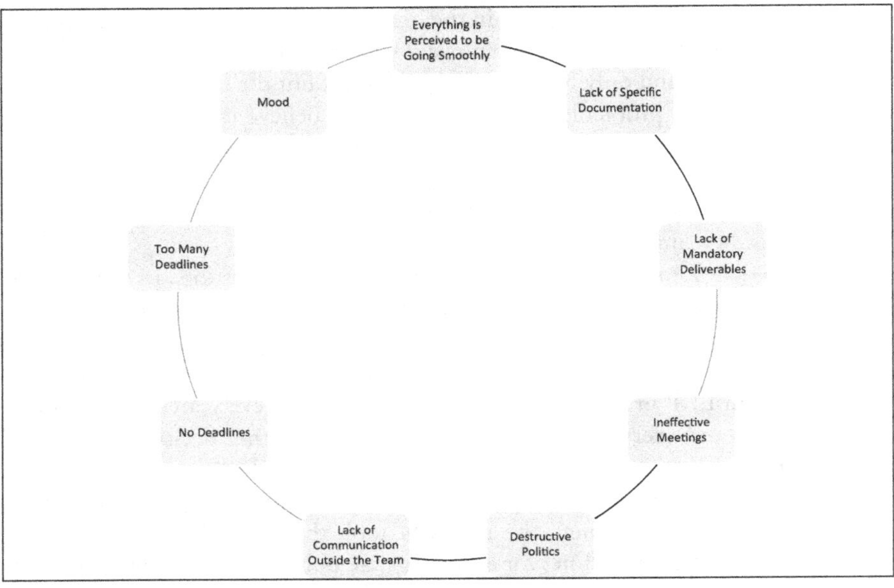

Figure 8.8 Incubating conditions for future red flags.

falling behind schedule. This is because the fact the documentation exists will be reported as "green". Only if someone looks at the detail will an issue be raised.

- Lack of Mandatory Deliverables: If some of the mandatory deliverables are missing past the point in time that they were required, downstream issues with dependencies, quality, resources, and timeline are going to start emerging in other areas of the project.
- Ineffective Meetings: By itself it may only be an isolated event. However, if the project is regularly having such meetings, important work and decisions are not being done. This will create many problems in other areas of the initiative.

Consider this case. A Project Director decided to attend a business requirements meeting. There were about 20 team members present, including Business Analysts, process owners, designers, and business users in the meeting. The Director came into the meeting in the middle of a discussion on whether a button on a user screen should have the world "Next" or "Continue". The conversation had been going on for two hours involving 20 users to make that single decision. This was accurately perceived to be a huge red flag on whether the business requirements would be done on time and have the level of detail needed to complete the design. The proper approach would have been to allocate the decision to the two User Interface (UI) specialists in the room, document an issue, and formally set a date for the decision. At an average cost of $100/hr for 20 people. The suggested action would have saved up to $4,000 on a simple wording decision.

- Politics: Politics are unavoidable. But there are politics, bad politics, awful politics, and destructive politics. The last three are the worst. It's hard to argue there are good politics, except maybe from the perspective that worse things would happen if politics did not exist. As an assessment team, it's important to understand the role that politics are playing on the key levers of the project, and include recommendations that will deal with the worst impacts. Are team members being open? Are they setting someone else to blame? Are they trying to prove that a project cannot succeed? Do they not want it to succeed? Are there other priorities that are cannibalizing the current project team?
- Lack of Communication Outside the Team: Projects that are not communicating key messages outside a core team will lead to other major downstream issues. For example, without support outside the team, how will users find time to be trained on the new system? There must be a sense of awareness and positive excitement throughout an organization for larger programs to succeed. This is a big assessment item and warning if groups outside the core team have no knowledge of the milestones in the project.
- No Deadlines: No deadlines means that there is no method available to track the success of the program. Unless the budget and timeline are effectively infinite, this is a situation where the assessment team needs to dig much deeper to understand the definition of success the organization has adopted.
- Too Many Deadlines: The flipside of having "no deadlines" is having too many of them. This creates a lot of unnecessary work as well. The team spends time trying to meet them all and deadlines that are not critical may cause suboptimal decisions to be made.
- Mood: The overall mood of the team is an indicator of respect for management, respect for each other, buy-in to the process, and general wellbeing of the project as a whole. Negative moods are an indication of many downstream red flags that are waiting to be discovered, or waiting to derail the project.

More Red Flags

Here are some more red flags for the health check team to spot in the initial period of the assessment. When the assessment team spots them, they will need to dig deeper to see if they are impacting the project's timeline, budget, or requirements, as follows:

- Final decisions are not being made: There is a list of decisions that are pending with dates that have passed and no decision recorded.

- Lack of priorities: There are no priorities on a list of issues, requirements, or change requests.
- Quality issues: Components being delivered are experiencing more than expected quality issues in testing or through walkthroughs.
- Expectations Management: No one is managing user expectations on the project.
- Personal bias: Objectives and priorities are driven by personal interest and bias. For example, someone hates the ERP selected and just does not want to devote team resources to getting the solution to work.
- Assumptions are incorrect: Key assumptions in the project charter are proving to be incorrect.
- Lack of clarity: Requirements and other parts of the program do not have crisp clarity and definitions.
- Optimism: There is a belief, with no proof, that the timelines and resources are sufficient to meet the project objectives.
- Lack of signoffs: Development and configuration work has started while there is no evidence that the designated executives have officially signed off on the required deliverables.
- No issue log: Issues are being raised but there is no evidence that they are being recorded or tracked anywhere. They are not being tracked in one place.
- No risk log: There is no risk log or mitigation strategies. Risks are not being recorded and tracked in one place. The risk management lifecycle is discussed in its own chapter in this book.
- Mixing methodologies: There is more than one methodology on the project or program. There may be a way to support them, but the assessment team needs to look deeper to see how they are effectively working in conjunction with each other.
- Changing requirements: Requirements are changing after signoff without going through a change management process.
- %complete is not going up in the project plan: Activities are not hitting complete week after week, even though status reports are showing that the timeline is in a green status.
- Technology: The technology has never been tested. Proof of concepts have not been completed to validate the key business transactions. Proof of concepts that have been done have not addressed key potential showstoppers. This is an area of improvement that must be included in the final report.
- Governance: These processes are not documented and there is no executive support for governance. There is no evidence that Steering Committee members are actively engaged in the program. Key processes like change management or escalation procedures are not documented or being followed.
- Planning: The project plan is not showing resources, dependencies and there is no justification for the durations. There are activities on the plan that in

themselves are discovery activities which will create more unknown work. There is no contingency in the plan.

- Data Conversion: Data conversion is planned too late in the project to allow time to clean up the data if it's worse than expected. There is no level of prioritization in terms of which data items are mandatory which require a high level of accuracy and how the accuracy will be measured. There is no tolerance number for the level of accuracy required in the converted data.

Closing Perspective

This chapter examined some early warning red flags that the health check team can use to drive a detailed investigative plan for the assessment. It also examined the different emotional modes team members will cycle through as projects proceed through the lifecycle. The chapter also examined optimistic–realistic–pessimistic thinking as red flags for further problems in the initiative. For example, a project where the team is tripling all their estimates because of pessimistic thinking will be making decisions that will create other problems on the project.

Here is a list of top key warning flags to look for when starting a health check assessment:

1. Members of the team you are meeting are only giving you good news.
2. The implementation is only a month or two away and there are no User Acceptance Testing results available for you to review.
3. There have been no hands-on demonstrations of the end-to-end working system.
4. Most of the team members you are meeting are complaining about the skill-sets of other team members, or some other parts of their behavior.
5. People are defending their own past decisions.
6. Team members are resigning before the assessment starts.
7. The initiative has already missed several deadlines.
8. The budget is being spent and cannot be tied to actual deliverables that have been provided.
9. It seems like you are talking to individuals who are not part of a project team.
10. The user community has not even heard about the project.

Chapter 9

Reviewing the Documentation and Other Deliverables

Reviewing the project documentation and deliverables is one of the key activities undertaken by the health check team to understand project background, history, current state, future state, requirements, and to begin getting a sense of how well the project or program is functioning. Is the project team cutting corners? Are there clearly defined business objectives? What are the key milestone dates? What are the key milestone deliverables? What does the organization look like? Are all the roles filled? Are team members splitting their time on too many initiatives? Are there regular meetings? How effective are they? Reviewing the deliverables will give the health check team an understanding of facts on the ground and give them a grocery shopping list of areas to dive into during other phases of the health check assessment.

Most of the deliverables to be reviewed in the health check assessment will be in the form of electronic or printed documentation, but some deliverables might be system prototypes or other interfaces. The project management and delivery methodology should be reviewed in the context of the deliverables review to know which outputs should be available and when. Deliverables should be reviewed in the context of the methodology timelines and dependencies, but also a sanity check on whether the business objectives will be met using the methodology that was selected by the organization.

The assessment team should be getting access to the deliverables and documentation even before the engagement is started, but certainly no later than the project kickoff. The documentation should be reviewed prior to any project team

DOI: 10.1201/9781003269786-11

interviews. The team needs to be prepared, and they need to ensure they are not giving the perception that anyone's time is being wasted.

The documentation review must be done by keeping the current phase of the project or program in consideration. This means that if the health assessment is being done in the Planning phase of the program, the deployment deliverables will not be available for review. As show in Figure 9.1, this reality must be part of the expectations that are set with the project sponsors and the assessment team.

In this example, clearly the test results that will be produced in the "Test" phase will not be available if the project is currently in the Architecture phase.

Starting the Deliverable Reviews

The assessment team can follow the process in Figure 9.2 to begin review of the documented deliverables. The members of the assessment team should use a checklist of deliverables to ensure nothing is being missed. For each item on the checklist, the following questions need to be asked:

- Should the document or deliverable exist at this time?
- When will it be available?
- Is it complete?
- What is missing?
- Is there justification to skip this deliverable?

As shown in Figure 9.2, the documentation set that should be examined first by the assessment team include the following:

- Project Charter: This deliverable should contain the business case, scope, objectives, high-level project plan, risk assessment, cost of not doing the initiative, budget, and justification for the project or program. Also check to see if a formal signoff was done by the executive team. This is a major assessment finding if this is lacking and the project team has initiated the project.
- Business Case: The business case could be a separate deliverable or incorporated into the Project Charter. It should contain a detailed justification, costs, benefits, and Return on Investment (ROI) expectations for the program.
- Project Plan: Look for an overall view of the major milestones, milestone deliverables, and dependencies and then jump into the detailed activities. Look for phases, activities, and tasks. Also look for resources attached to each activity. Are they over utilized? Does the plan seem achievable given the business objectives of the project?
- Organization Chart: This should correspond to the roles and responsibilities you would expect on the project given its scope. Which key roles are still not

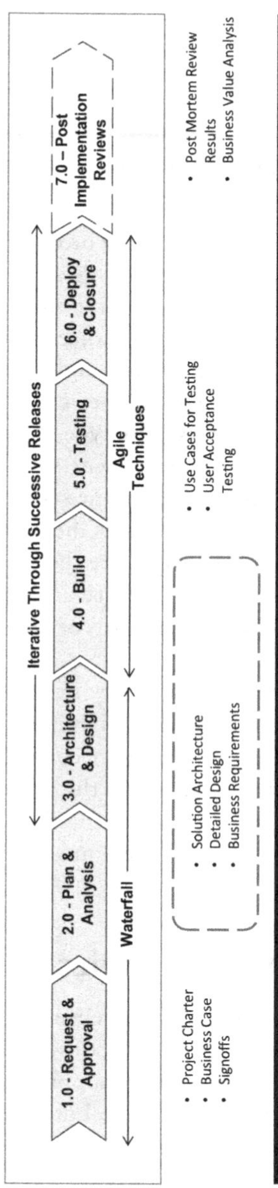

Figure 9.1 Sample deliverables by project delivery phase.

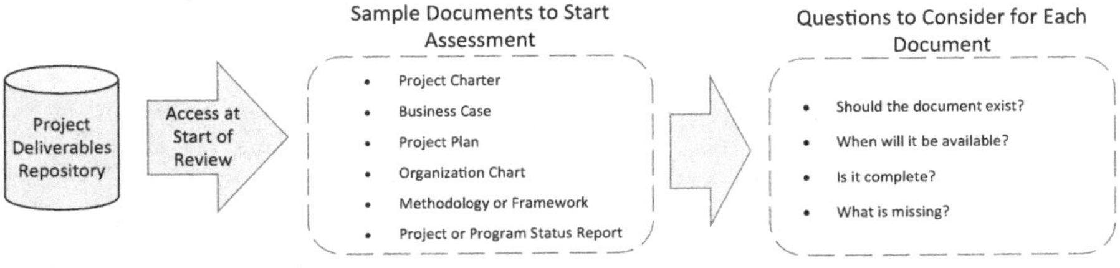

Figure 9.2 Process for inspecting documentation & deliverables.

filled? When are they needed to be on the project given the project plan? Will they be trained and fully onboarded by then? Will they have access to the systems and get their hardware by the time they are needed? Also, are there enough fully dedicated resources to the project or are most of them also doing other activities in the organization. These and other questions will need to be explored further during individual interviews.

- Project or Program Status Reports: Any type of status reports that have been produced for the initiative by management should be reviewed. These provide a lot of relevant information about the state of the program and history. Look for involvement of key executives. Is there an issue log? Are issues being addressed? Are decisions being made? Are they being recorded? What is the status of the project? If everything is "green" meaning smooth, look deeper. Is the team aware of the true project status or are they in a state of unrealistic optimism?
- Methodology or Framework: This is a very important baseline to understand, especially if there are multiple vendors delivering pieces of the system. If the methodologies are not aligned, the team communication will be jumbled. One team may have a widget ready while the other does not. One team's widget may be tested, the other is in an agile sprint. The methodologies do not necessarily have to be the same, but there must be points of alignment.

Applying Different Methodologies

In conducting a review of the documentation deliverables, the specific delivery and/or management methodology that is being used by the organization has to factor into the assessment that is being done. For example, a purely agile approach may not have detailed requirements documentation, but may have a prototype or sprint results to review. Similarly, if the team is implementing an ERP, CRM, ECM, HRIS, or other types of systems, the vendor they selected will have a project delivery, project management methodology that is customized for their product set. In this case, the deliverable hierarchies shown in this chapter should be customized using the deliverables defined in the methodology or methodologies being used on the project.

Organizations are also implementing hybrid solutions. For example, the objective of the project might be to implement an ERP, CRM, and a ticketing system in the cloud (e.g. SAP, Salesforce, and Service Now on Azure). In such instances, the assessment team should review the deliverables for each system as driven by the vendor methodology being used. However, the integration points of the solutions will also need to be reviewed with a hybrid methodology approach. This could mean abstraction from the process and timing, but a focus on specific gates where the integration from different vendors will be done. For example, the CRM team may be using an Agile approach to develop their solution, while the ERP is using a Hybrid Agile approach. The ERP and CRM teams will need to synchronize their deliverables at some point in order to allow integration between specific points in each solution. This would also apply to how system integration testing will occur.

Figure 9.3 uses entrance and exit gates to these integration points. The Gate perspective is not prescribing "how to" meet the entrance criteria (i.e. which methodology to use). But the process will not start until the entrance criteria are met. Similarly, the process will not conclude until the exit criteria are met. These would be health check assessment recommendations if the project teams are not doing this.

This was exactly the case on an initiative where an ERP team was using an approach that combined agile and waterfall principles, while the CRM team was using a purely agile approach. Each monthly sprint by the CRM team was performing well, but they could not share specific delivery dates with the ERP team on when their solutions would integrate. Given the CEO and the Board of Directors were not willing to provide unlimited funding, management needed to bring these two teams together and did so by specifying specific gates and criteria that were then incorporated into the monthly sprints. These items were prioritized based on milestone dates along with the gates. Documentation of the criteria made accountabilities very clear to the business users who were also providing requirements in the monthly sprints. Attempts were made to do this remotely, but in the end it was more effective, measured as faster, cheaper, and personally fulfilling, to fly thirty (30) people into the same city for six (6) weeks to get this planning work done. This may be a consideration in the future as remote work, around the world, is becoming more the norm than the exception.

Deliverable/Documentation Heat Maps

In addition to the short set of deliverables shown in Figure 9.2, other deliverables that could be available for review in the assessment are shown in Figure 9.4. This view categorizes deliverables across project phases and is presented in the form of a map. These could be produced using Agile, Waterfall, or hybrid methodologies.

The deliverable document lists contained in this section should be customized for the assessment project so that they correspond to the methodology or methodologies that are applicable to the project or program in scope. The list in Figure 9.4

Gate	Entrance Criteria	Exit Criteria
SIT 1	❑ Unit Test results available and reviewed ❑ The cloud test environment is ready for test. ❑ Testing User Id's have been setup. ❑ Data conversion for all functional areas completed. ❑ API Integrations are ready for test. ❑ All test scenarios have been added to the test environment.	❑ All test scenarios have been executed at least once (or are scheduled for SIT 2). ❑ 80% pass rate. ❑ No high defects remaining (e.g. all have been fixed, retested, & passed or there is a documented disposition).
SIT 2 (fix and test defects)	❑ Confirmation that test resources identified in the resource matrix are allocated to the effort .	❑ Remaining medium defects have a documented disposition (fixed, deferred until after go live, documented manual work around, cancelled).
SIT 2 (end-to-end testing)	❑ Test scenarios for each functional group are documented . ❑ Confirmation that test resources identified in the resource matrix are allocated to the effort.	❑ All test scenarios have been executed at least once. ❑ 80% pass rate. ❑ No high defects remaining (e.g. all have been fixed, retested, & passed). ❑ Remaining medium defects have a documented disposition (fixed, deferred until after go live, documented manual work around, cancelled
Payroll Parallel Tet	❑ Data Conversion has been executed within executable time period (e.g. 4 weeks) and validated.	❑ All cycles are fully executed and variances documented. ❑ No critical and higher defects remain without a documented and accepted work-around.
User Acceptance Testing	❑ Test scenarios for each functional group are documented ❑ Confirmation that test resources identified in the resource matrix are allocated to the effort ❑ Testers are trained and prepared to test	❑ All test scenarios have been executed at least once ❑ 80% pass rate ❑ No high defects remaining (e.g. all have been fixed, retested, & passed)

Figure 9.3 Project gates: Entrance and exit criteria.

A. Request & PMO Gate	B. Initiation	C. Planning	D. Architecture, Design, Analysis	E. Build	F. Test & Deploy	G. Sustainment
Project Charter	Scope Revision	Resource & Organization Plan	Reporting and BI Planning	Data Conversion Execution	Training Development & Delivery	Benefits Realization
Business Scope	Project Charter (approved)	Budget & Revenue Plan	Legacy Decommission Execution	Risk Management Execution	System Integration Testing	Centre of Excellence Implementation
Proposed Budget	Quality Plan	Project Plan	Requirements Management	Resource Management	Performance Testing	Integration / Interface Implementation
Risk Mitigation Strategy	Overall Test Planning	Communication Plan	Solution Architecture	Budget Management	Functional / Integration Testing	Reporting and BI Implementation
Program & Project Governance Plan	Vendor Support Planning	Organization Change Management (OCM) Plan	Technical Architecture	Scope Management	End-to-end Testing	Benefits Delivery & Tracking
Strategic Benefits Identification	Security Planning	Risk Management Plan	Data Architecture	Communication Management	User Acceptance Testing	Key Performance Indicator Tracking (KPI)
Business Benefits Analysis	Training and Communication Strategy	Benefit Realization Plan	API Design	Org. Change Management Execution	Security Testing	Help Desk Procedures
Vendor Management Approach	Integration / Interface Impacts	Data Conversion Plan	"As Is" and "To Be" Architecture Views	Unit Testing	Operations Transition Planning	IT Operations Transition
Security Approach	Schedule Management	Project Methodology Rollout	Security Architecture	Development Execution	KPI Testing	Vendor Support Agreements
KPI Definition	Risk and Mitigation Log	Sprint Planning	Detailed Design	Sprint Planning	CSF Testing	Disaster Recovery / Business Continuity Implementation
CSF Definition			User Interface Design	Centre of Excellence Planning	Deployment Signoffs	Governance Transition

Figure 9.4 Deliverable map.

is constructed from best practices and past project experiences that range from a half dozen resources to project teams of five hundred or more.

Not all the deliverables in the Deliverable Map are necessarily applicable to a specific project. Deliverables not required can be identified by a different color, as shown in Figure 9.5. Furthermore, the intent is to fit the deliverables onto a single page for presentation purposes. When presenting to larger teams, including Executives, showing priorities and key deliverables helps to guide conversations to meaningful conclusions. For the purpose of the deliverable and documentation reviews, and to serve as a checklist, another hierarchical format will be discussed later in this chapter.

The single-page view of the key deliverables allows heat maps to be produced for conversation and presentation to all levels of the core project team. At a glance, a lot of information can be conveyed, as shown in Figure 9.6. Each of the deliverable/documentation boxes can be color-coded, as follows:

- Grey: Deliverable is not yet available
- White: Deliverable is not in scope
- Green: Deliverable was reviewed by the assessment team who found it to have good quality
- Yellow: Deliverable exists, but quality is still a work in progress
- Amber: Deliverable exists, but the assessment team has serious concerns about its quality
- Red: Deliverable does not exist or the quality is completely unacceptable to the assessment team

In addition to color coding, the boxes can be further annotated with dates when the review was done, and dates when "Greyed" boxes will be available for review. You can also color the boxes and write the color next to the side of the box beside the optional date tag shown in the Legend in Figure 9.6.

Deliverable Hierarchy

For presentation purposes, the summarized view shown in Figure 9.6 is highly valuable and effective. It provides a heatmap, a sense of timing across the phases, and a visual depiction of project or program status. However, a more detailed view of the deliverables is helpful for tracking purposes. Figure 9.7 shows a hierarchical list of deliverables organized under a phase or a set of activities for categorization. This list of deliverables is based on best practices and experience over hundreds of projects. The list should be customized to reflect the methodology or methodologies on the initiative by the health check assessment team. If the deliverables are not available, a note should be kept for an explanation from the project team. It could be that the deliverable is late or not required. These findings will form a portion of the final recommendations.

A. Request & PMO Gate
Project Charter
Business Scope
Proposed Budget
Risk Mitigation Strategy
Program & Project Governance Plan
Strategic Benefits Identification
Business Benefits Analysis
Vendor Management Approach
Security Approach
KPI Definition
CSF Definition

B. Initiation
Scope Revision
Project Charter (approved)
Quality Plan
Overall Test Planning
Vendor Support Planning
Security Planning
Training and Communication Strategy
Integration / Interface Impacts
Schedule Management
Risk and Mitigation Log

C. Planning
Resource & Organization Plan
Budget & Revenue Plan
Project Plan
Communication Plan
Organization Change Management (OCM) Plan
Risk Management Plan
Benefit Realization Plan
Data Conversion Plan
Project Methodology Rollout
Sprint Planning

D. Architecture, Design, Analysis
Reporting and BI Planning
Legacy Decommission Execution
Requirements Management
Solution Architecture
Technical Architecture
Data Architecture
API Design
"As Is" and "To Be" Architecture Views
Security Architecture
Detailed Design
User Interface Design

E. Build
Data Conversion Execution
Risk Management Execution
Resource Management
Budget Management
Scope Management
Communication Management
Org. Change Management Execution
Unit Testing
Development Execution
Sprint Planning
Centre of Excellence Planning

F. Test & Deploy
Training Development & Delivery
System Integration Testing
Performance Testing
Functional / Integration Testing
End-to-end Testing
User Acceptance Testing
Security Testing
Operations Transition Planning
KPI Testing
CSF Testing
Deployment Signoffs

G. Sustainment
Benefits Realization
Centre of Excellence Implementation
Integration / Interface Implementation
Reporting and BI Implementation
Benefits Delivery & Tracking
Key Performance Indicator Tracking (KPI)
Help Desk Procedures
IT Operations Transition
Vendor Support Agreements
Disaster Recovery / Business Continuity Implementation
Governance Transition

Legend
In Scope
Out of Scope

Figure 9.5 Deliverable's not in scope.

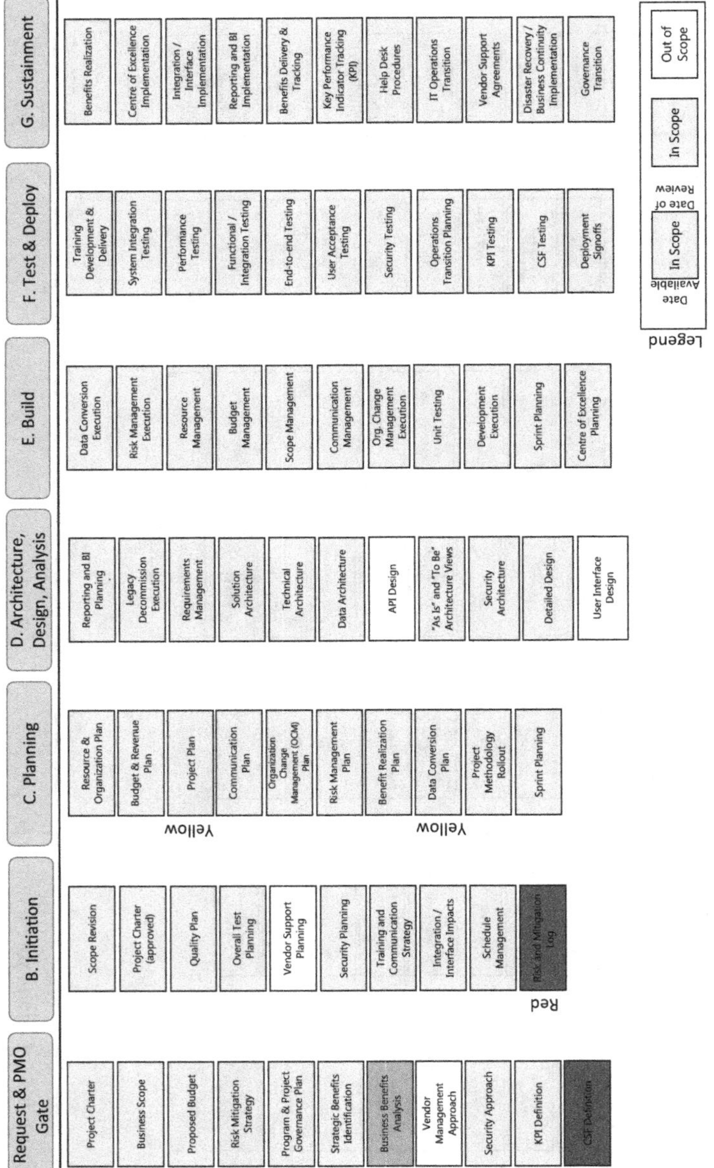

Figure 9.6 Deliverable heat map.

Pre-Analysis Case
❑Current Situation
❑Solution Outcome
❑Business Benefit
❑Initiative Risk
❑Resource Expectations
❑Reference Architecture
Business Case
❑Scope & Objectives
❑Costs, Benefits, Risks
❑Resourcing
❑Milestone Dates
❑Options
Executive Review
❑Decision & Executive Signoffs
Project Charter Outline
❑Conceptual Design
❑Project Plan (High)
❑Team Roles
❑Capital Effort
❑SG&A Effort
Executive Review
❑PMO Recommendation
❑Committee Signoff
❑Executive Signoff

Project Charter
❑ Scope and Approach
❑Business Case (signed)
❑Business Requirements
❑Technical Requirements
❑Project Plan
❑Quality Plan
❑Team Structure & Roles
❑Governance Model
❑Risk Assessment
Organizational Change Management Strategy
QA Strategy
Management Kit
Procurement Approach
Requirements
❑Business & Technical
Blueprinting Doc
Exec Approval
QA Test Plan
❑Test Scripts
❑Test Organization
OCM Plan
❑Training Plan
❑Communication Plan
❑Roles & Responsibilities

Architecture
Functional Specs
❑Detailed Design
❑Storyboards/Mockups
❑Information Architecture
❑Application Design
❑Application Rules
❑Security
Technical Specs
❑Programing Logic
❑Technical Architecture
❑Network/Hardware Topology
❑Database Model
Development
❑ Configuration
❑ Application Coding
❑ Data Conversion
Unit Testing
❑ Test Scripts
❑ Test Results
❑Functional Specifications (Updated)

Testing Cycles Prep
❑ Test Cases/ Scenarios/ scripts
❑ Test Data Preparations
Deployment Plan
❑ Cutover plan
Training
❑ Develop Course Materials
Communication
Test Cycles Execution
❑ Functional Tests
❑ Integration Tests
❑ Regression Test
❑ Stress Volume Test
❑ User Acceptance Test (UAT)
Sign Off
❑ Go/ No Go Review
❑ Business Sign off
User Training Execution

Deployed Applications
Initial Production Support
Project Closure
❑ Post Implementation Review
❑ Lessons Learned
❑ Project Closure Signoff
❑Business Value Realization

Figure 9.7 Deliverable hierarchy.

The following section identifies some key considerations in the assessment of each deliverable. Notes from the evaluation should be recorded in a suitable format, one of which is shown in Figure 9.8. This deck can then be used as input into the questionnaires for the team interviews and to form the final recommendations from the review. The assessment team should review each deliverable with the following in mind:

- Establish whether the deliverable is needed;
- Establish when the deliverable will be available for review;
- Review the deliverable for completeness;
- Review the deliverable for logistical consistency with other deliverables (e.g. test cases should have corresponding test scripts and be mapped to the business requirements)

The section below describes some other key considerations and questions the assessment team should consider when reviewing each deliverable.

Pre-Analysis Case

The deliverables in this category are required to determine whether the project should be given executive approval to proceed. This would mean funding is extended and a team can be formally assembled. These deliverables form the foundation for

Deliverable Documentation Review Reviewer: ____________ Review Date: ____________	Overall Observations: ____________ ____________

Business Case	Observations:	Recommendations/ Assessment Concerns	Deliverable Status:
❑Scope & Objectives			
❑Costs, Benefits, Risks			
❑Resourcing			
❑Milestone Dates			
❑Options			
Executive Review			
❑Decision & Executive Signoffs			
❑Executive Signoff			

Notes: Deliverable Status: Missing, Late, Expected Date, Not needed (with explanation)

Figure 9.8 Deliverable assessment.

driving business value from the project/program investment. The deliverables are discussed in more detail here:

- Current Situation: This deliverable will document the current business solution set, identifying key opportunities for improvement. This deliverable is needed so that a roadmap can be built for moving the organization to a "To Be" version of the situation. It is often missing or incomplete which causes more work for the project team later in the process.
- Solution Outcome: This deliverable should contain a clear description of objectives that will be achieved through the initiative. These should lend themselves to business benefit identification.
- Business Benefit: A clear listing of business areas that will benefit from the project with empirical data to support the business case. It should include baseline information if it is available so that future benefits can be compared and tracked to that baseline. For example, if 1,000 transactions are currently being processed at an operational cost of 18 cents each, that would become the baseline. Future benefits would be calculated using those numbers.
- Initiative Risk: A list of the risks the initiative may encounter with some consideration of mitigation approaches. These strategies will be fleshed out in future chapters.

- Resource Expectations: Roles and responsibilities needed in the initiative with some description of when and for how long. A list of roles that need to be full-time on the project. A high-level plan for filling those roles when they are needed should be included.
- Reference Architecture: Should include business and solution architecture both "As Is" and "To Be". Other architectures that can be included are technical architecture, infrastructure, solution architecture, network architecture, data architecture, and process architecture.

Business Case

The business case will leverage some of the deliverables from the previous section and could be a component of the project charter.

- Scope & Objectives: Look for clarity and precision in both of these areas. What are the specific domain scope items? The objectives should be quantifiable and measurable. Being the "best warehouse management solution in the market" is a vision statement, but not measurable. Adding specific criteria (e.g. cost per item to store in a warehouse) that would make it the best should be included instead. This will force the project team to research the industry standards.
- Costs, Benefits, Risks: These should be as detailed as possible with buy-in from the Finance Group.
- Resourcing: A continuation of the "Resource Expectations" deliverable with more detail including external vendor types if known. Can the business objectives be met with this resource list? Is there a detailed roles and responsibilities document as well?
- Milestone Dates: A logical list of milestone dates that the project or program will need to meet. How realistic do these seem with the resourcing to meet the scope and objectives?
- Options: Different options and details for meeting these to enable the scope and objectives of the initiative.

Executive Review

- Decision & Executive Signoffs: Are the Executives needed for signoff clearly identified? Is there a process documented to enable this?

Project Charter Outline

- Conceptual Design: Look for completeness in the business and solution design.

- Project Plan (High): Look for completeness in the major activities, appropriate contingency, logical dependencies, and appropriateness of the work effort that is being proposed. If possible, ask for how estimates were done. Also was there both a top-down and bottom-up analysis? This adds more credibility to the numbers.
- Team Roles: Look for completeness compared to other similar types of initiatives. These should also be documented as a separate roles and responsibilities document.
- Capital Effort: Breakdown of the budget that can be classified as capital and hence is capitalizable. This can have a big impact on how the project budget hits the bottom-line year over year.
- SG&A Effort: Breakdown of the budget that has be expensed and is thus not capitalizable. The Finance Group will have input on adopting and applying their policies for these. Compare the polices to what the Business Case is proposing. They should align otherwise make this an assessment warning. There have been many examples of projects where the alignment is not there and the situation results in big issues much later in the project cycle.

Executive Review

The Executive Review deliverables confirm that there is an appropriate level of executive governance on the project or program. The key deliverables are described below:

- PMO Recommendation: If there is a PMO and the PMO is involved in the initiative, confirm that the PMO has approved of the deliverables produced so far. If the PMO is not involved, consider including this question in the interviews to understand why they are not involved?
- Committee Signoff: Ensure that there is a formal signoff list that appears complete. This would be an assessment finding and recommendation if this is not the case.

Project Charter

The project charter has the following deliverables in its scope:

- Scope and Approach: This should align with the business case.
- Business Case (signed): The business case must have executive approval for the project to continue. This will be an audit item, so ensure that formal and traceable signoff of key deliverables like this one are being done.
- Business Requirements: Look for completeness and alignment with the scope and approach.

- Technical Requirements: Look for non-functional requirements such as performance of key transactions. Are there any Critical Success Factor's or Key Performance Indicators that must be met, e.g. system up time?
- Project Plan: Examine the detailed project plan for activities, work effort, and identification of resources. Examine how the estimation was done and if it is traceable.
- Quality Plan: A lack of this plan is a red warning flag. It should describe how quality will be maintained through the entire program, responsibilities, and timelines.
- Team Structure & Roles: Clear roles and responsibilities document listing accountabilities, responsibilities, and authority.
- Governance Model: Look for completeness in terms of a description of all the Steering Committees needed, change management process, decision-making process, escalation process, and signoff processes.
- Risk Assessment: Are the risks and mitigation strategies realistic, complete, and thorough. Are they being actively managed by the project team?

Organizational Change Management Strategy

The organization change management (OCM) strategy should include the following at a minimum:

- Communication Plan (e.g. schedule of townhalls, newsletters)
- Training Materials Identification
- Approach to Create Training Materials
- Process Maps (As-Is and To-Be)
- User Role Descriptions (As-Is and To-Be)
- Training Approach

QA Strategy

Approach for ensuring Quality Assurance in the entire program. This should include roles and responsibilities, tools, and milestone dates. This strategy should include all testing phases, code quality, deliverable quality, and any other quality issues that the project will need to address. This deliverable should be updated throughout the project. This deliverable drives the detailed QA Test Plan.

Management Kit

Complete description of the project management procedures, tools, and expectations. This includes when status meetings occur and who attends them. Also examine procedures for how change management requests will be handled.

Procurement Approach

Ensure that the procurement approach on the project or program is consistent with the practices published by the procurement department. Procurement of services, technology, or other items could be greatly delayed if these two processes are not aligned.

Requirements

Examine both the business and technical requirements and align to the objectives and scope of the program. This deliverable is the focal point of the project and it should be detailed, thorough, and clear. Look for evidence that business owners, executives, and others have reviewed the document and provided a formal signoff. This is a gap on too many projects and should be a critical assessment finding were it to be the case.

Blueprinting Documentation

This is applicable to some ERP implementations. Look for whether this deliverable can be turned into a global template and how well it aligns with the Requirements documentation. Also examine if the process for localization is included.

Executive Approval

Look for evidence of written signoff from appropriate levels for each of the documents. This is absent on too many projects. The process for signoff should be documented in the governance rules.

QA Test Plan

The QA test plan should be built early in the project development cycle. Here are some deliverables that should be included:

- Test Scripts: Look for alignment with the requirements. It is also helpful if there is some level of prioritization between the test cases for defect management purposes.
- Test Organization: Cross-check on availability to participate in the test cycles. Also examine how the testers will be trained to conduct the testing. What is the process for recording defects, prioritizing defects, and retesting them.

OCM Plan

A continuation of the OCM approach but with a detailed plan for each of the following:

- Training Plan

- Communication Plan
- Roles & Responsibilities

Architecture

Examine all the following "As-Is" and "To-Be" architectures:

- Data
- Technical
- Security
- Network
- Functional
- Solution
- Business
- Application

Functional Specs

The functional specification should be aligned with the following deliverables:

- Detailed Design
- Storyboards/Mockups
- Information Architecture
- Application Design
- Application Rules
- Security

Technical Specs

Contrast the technical and non-functional requirements with the following deliverables:

- Programing Logic
- Technical Architecture
- Network/Hardware Topology
- Database Model

Development

Examine the development process in terms of the methodology being used and ensure standards are being enforced, as follows:

- Configuration: Are standards being followed?

- Application Coding: Are standards being followed?
- Data Conversion: Is the data understood? How long will it take to complete the conversation processes? This is a time-consuming task so be convinced that the project plan accounts for all the activities needed to complete this.

Unit Testing

Ensure there is evidence that unit testing is being done and that test results are being captured and reviewed before other forms of testing are initiated, as follows:

- Test Scripts
- Test Results

Functional Specifications (Updated)

Map the business requirements to the functional specifications and align with the test scenarios.

Testing Cycles Prep

Align the testing deliverable to the requirements and ensure that there is direct mapping, as follows:

- Test Cases/Scenarios/scripts: Are they assigned to specific users? Was there user input in their design?
- Test Data Preparations: Is the data masked? Is the data complete? How is the data being prepared for each test?

Deployment Plan

How detailed is the deployment and cutoff plan in terms of user training and job preparation? Are there checklists and were they completed? Is there a Cutover Plan?

Training

Is the program getting ready for implementation? Review the course materials for completeness and contrast with the original plan. Here are some of the deliverables required to support the training stream:

- Develop Course Materials
- Develop the training schedule
- Finalize delivery methods

Communication

Ensure that communication is covered in the deployment plan for the cutover, post cutover, and help desk access. There should be detailed checklists to ensure that individual user needs are addressed, as well as those organized by departments across the organization

Test Cycles Execution

Ensure there is evidence of completion for each of the following tests. Align with scenarios, tests cases, test scripts, and resources to run the tests.

- Functional Tests
- Integration Tests
- Regression Test
- Stress Volume Test
- User Acceptance Test (UAT)

Sign Off

Ensure there is written signoff before a Go/No-Go decision is executed. The signoff pool must include the project/program sponsors, IT leadership, Business Owners, and other key stakeholders.

- Go/No Go Review
- Business Sign off

User Training Execution

Review the training plan which should align to all the users in the organization that will require training, how the training will be tracked, and how training can be retaken.

Deployed Applications

Evidence of how the applications will be deployed and managed in production.

Initial Production Support

Review of how users will be supported after go live. What will be the involvement of the Help Desk? How will the Help Desk be prepared?

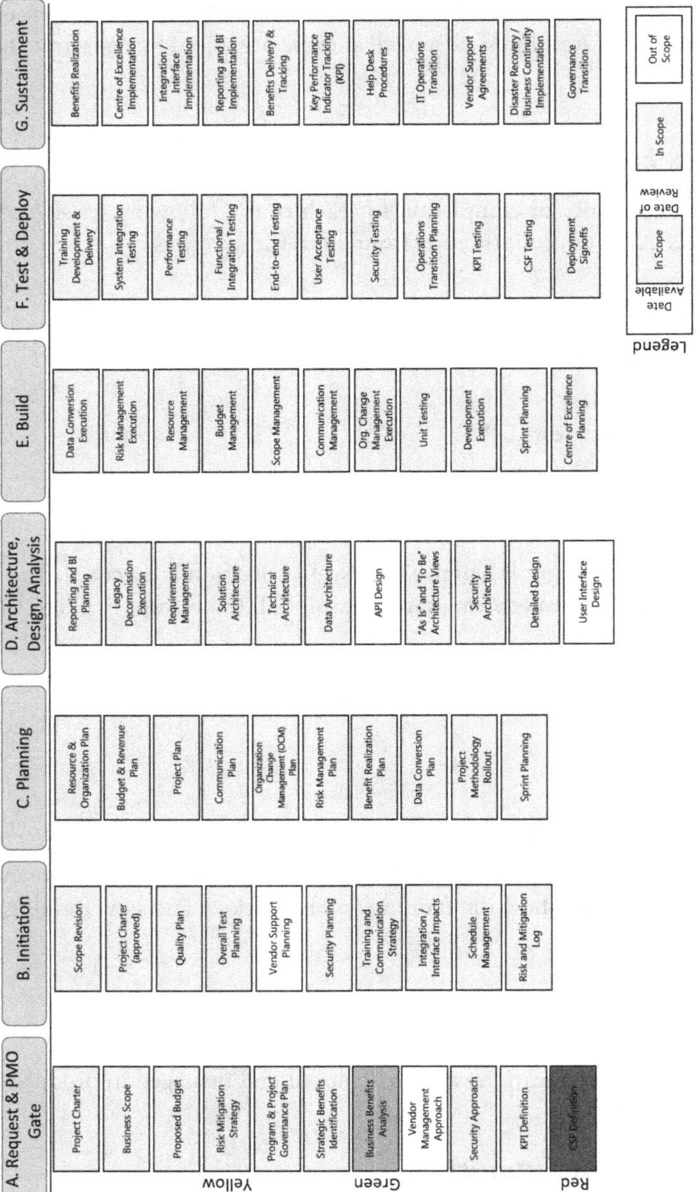

Figure 9.9 Deliverable heat map.

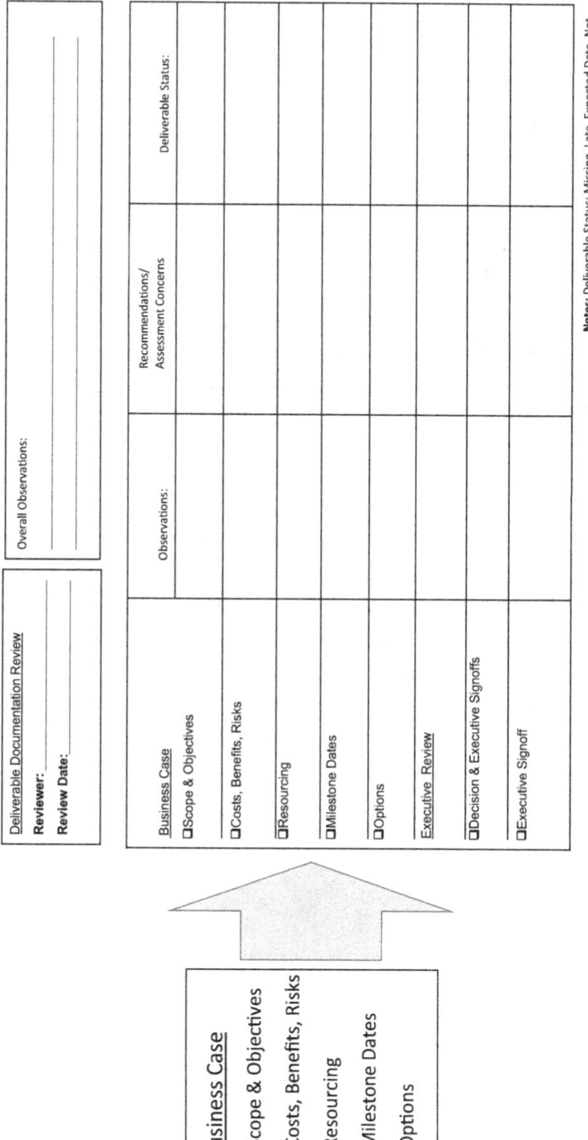

Figure 9.10 Deliverable assessment table.

Project Closure

Review how the business value will be measured after go-live and through the following deliverables:

- Post Implementation Review
- Lessons Learned
- Project Closure Signoff
- Business Value Realization

Closing Perspective

This chapter provided examples of heat maps that can be used to review the state of deliverables and documentation on project or program. These are useful to identify key deliverables and use the heat map to assess and measure progress across the project lifecycle. As shown in Figure 9.9, the heat map can be annotated with shading and other colors to show risks, potential failures, and good news. Specific date information can also be used to identify deliverables that will not be ready until that date is reached.

This chapter also examined a more detailed deliverable list built from best practices and project experience. The Health Check Team should augment this list using the specific methodology of the project being assessed. As shown in Figure 9.10, each category of the list can be used as a checklist and commentary can be included in a table similar to the one shown in the figure.

An assessment of the project deliverables generally finds areas of improvement that can provide substantial business value to the organization.

Chapter 10

Conducting Interviews of Key Project/Program Resources

The existing deliverables and documentation that the project or program provided for review are the first source of information that is available to the assessment team to start getting their arms around the initiative. These deliverables are instrumental in preparing for the upcoming individual team member interviews to continue the discovery activities. Figure 10.1 shows that the assessment team should be executing the activities included within the process surrounded by the dotted line square in the health check methodology. By this point, there should be a signed document, project charter, or engagement letter, that clearly defines the scope and deliverables for the commissioned health check. These define the scope of the interviews, and positions the health check assessment team to organize, analyze and structure the information that is being discovered in the investigation.

Interviews with key participants in the roles shown in Figure 10.2 offers the next key opportunity for the health check team to accomplish the following objectives:

- Establish a relationship with members of the project team
- Get a chance to hear directly from team members on the ground
- Hear a variety of perspectives on the project's background
- Hear a variety of perspectives on the project's true current state
- Get answers to questions about the deliverables and documentation
- Get a chance to cross-check different pieces of information they have received
- Offer anonymity to team members and get them to speak from their conscience
- Encourage transparent dialogue and openness to promote the good of the project

DOI: 10.1201/9781003269786-12

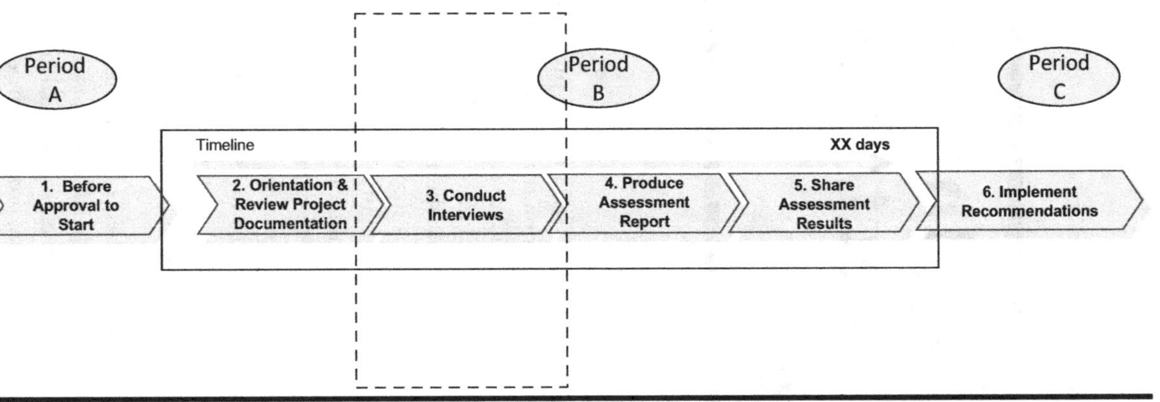

Figure 10.1 Conducting interviews phase.

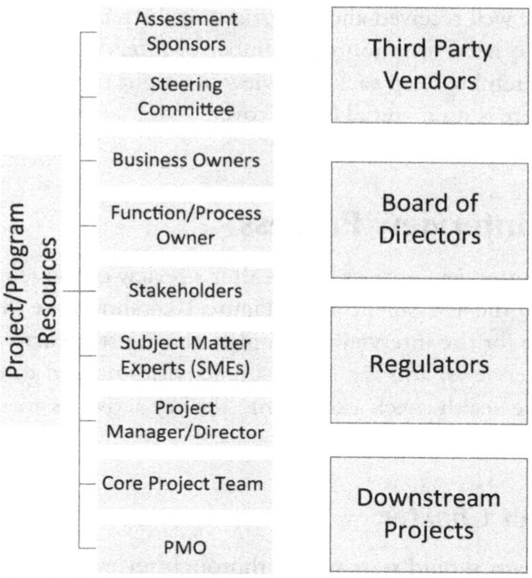

Figure 10.2 Sample roles to include in the interviews.

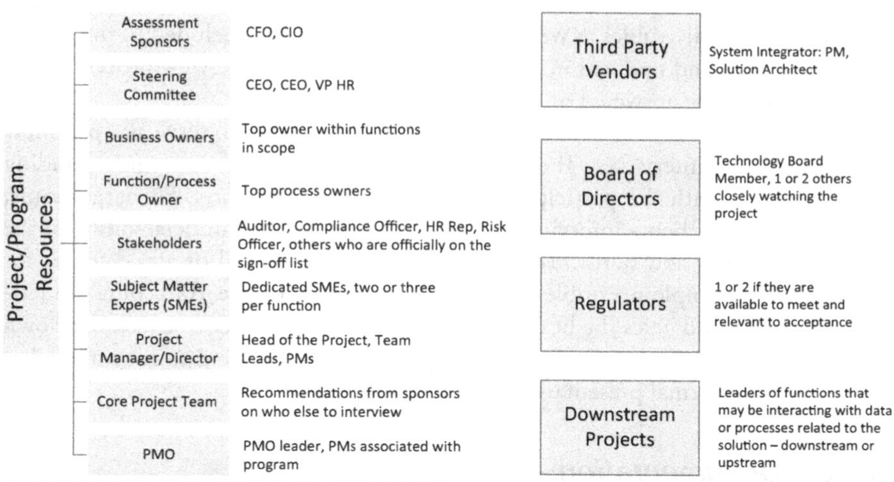

Figure 10.3 Sample titles to include in the interviews.

The health check team should work with the assessment sponsors, in conjunction with the project and corporate organization charts to identify specific individuals to interview. Figure 10.3 shows a sample cross-section of resources interviewed for a medium-sized financial company with a project size of 200 people. There were about thirty-two interviews in total for that health check. The author has found that interviews are well received and important to the reception of the health check results. There is no need to ration the number of interviews, but the health check team should be careful to keep each interview in a tight time boundary and politely wrap up when there is no material left to cover.

End-to-End Interview Process

The End-to-End Interview process begins after a review of the scope and documentation provided to the assessment team. Figure 10.4 shows the high-level activities needed to prepare for the interviews, complete the logistical activities, conduct the team member interviews, and the follow-up activities needed to complete the discovery phase of the health check assessment. The key activities are described in more detail in the subsections below.

Review Project Charter

The assessment team should start with a thorough review of the project charter or business case to understand the objectives of the initiative they are about to assess. Any questions should be recorded in a common log for the team, as shown in Figure 10.5. This format can be used to capture questions and answers about other documents and deliverables as well. The questions should be included in the appropriate interviews and updated in the log. By the end of the interview process all the questions should be answered or processed in some way.

It is also useful to start building a set of orientation slides to serve as a preamble to the individual interviews. These are used to baseline a common understanding of the initiative with the participants before the interview starts. For large teams, some of the people being interviewed may not have a detailed understanding of the project's objectives and status. They might be too embarrassed or afraid to ask for clarification. A sample preamble like the one shown in Figure 10.6, puts the participants at ease and gives the health check team an opportunity to check their own understanding of the project's objectives. It's better to be corrected at this time rather than during the formal presentations of the final report.

Review Documentation

The Project Charter establishes the baseline and should exist in some form regardless of when a Health Check is commissioned in terms of the project lifecycle. The health check team would have requested access to all the documentation that was built as part of the initiative, or related to it. Documentation related to past attempts at the project and related projects should also be provided to the health check team. Documentation and deliverables will be available in alignment with the phase of

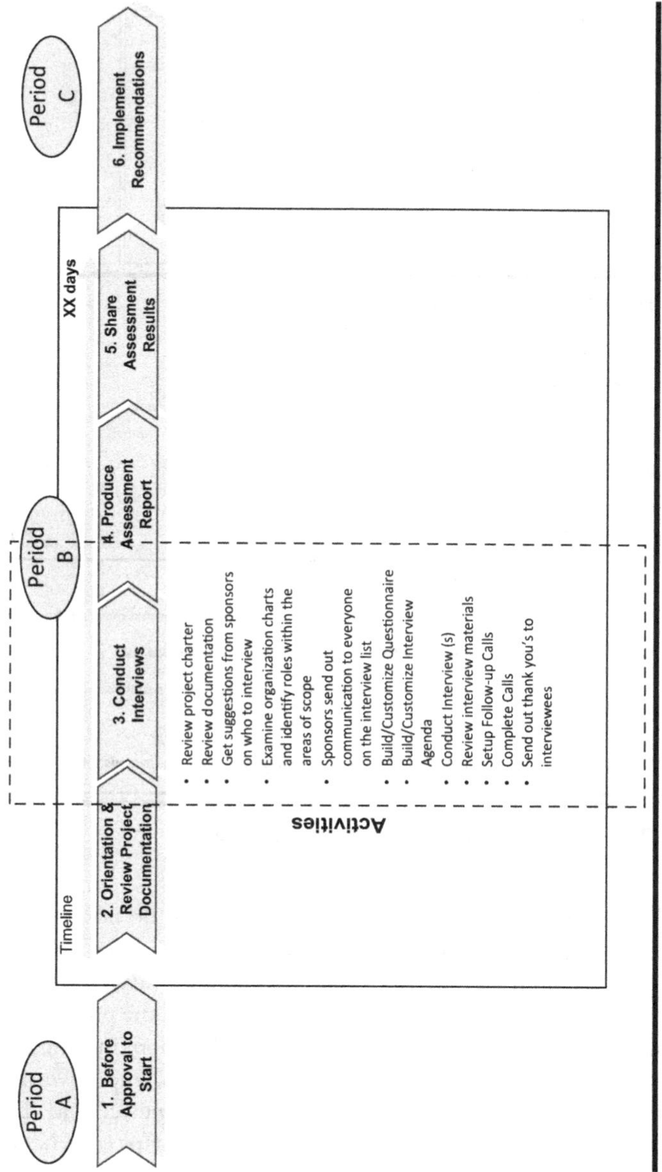

Figure 10.4 Conducting interviews—key activities.

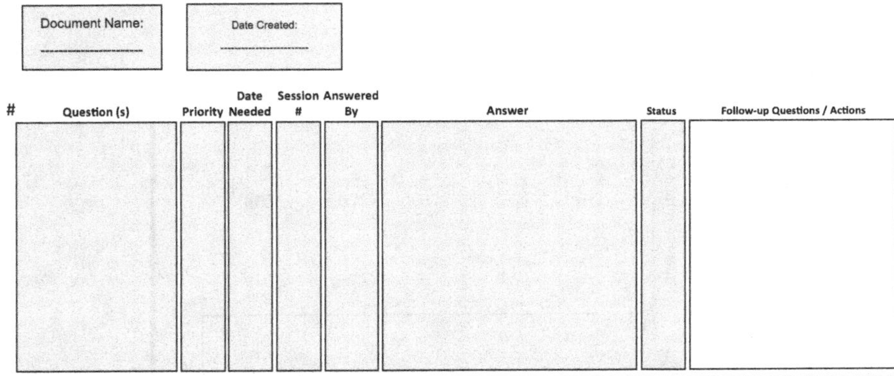

Figure 10.5 Health check assessment log.

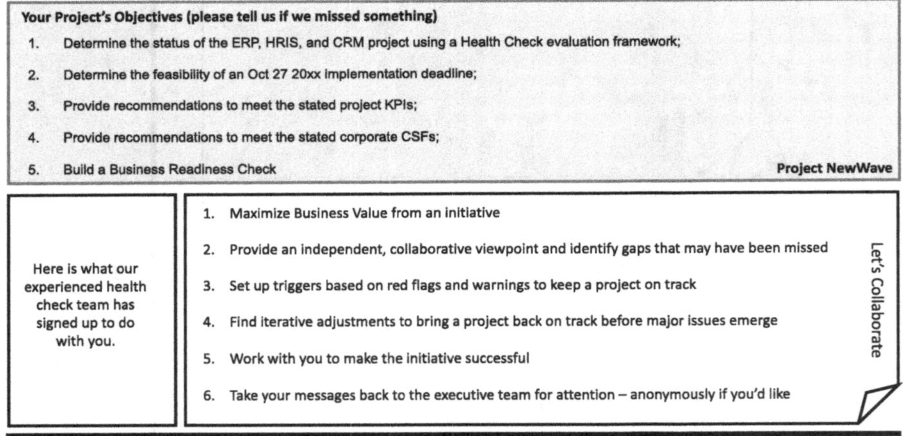

Figure 10.6 Preamble components to the health check.

the methodology the project has reached. Deliverables that do not have to be built at the given point in time, should be included in the plan with a date in the future. Figure 10.7 shows a sample of the deliverables that could be available for review.

The intention of the review at this stage is to understand the project background and current state. The health assessment team should be looking for key deliverables to be built, signed off by the correct representatives, and have the relevant information at the proper depth for the initiative being reviewed and the phase of the deliverable. For example, if there are only logical data maps (this happens!) and data conversion is starting in three weeks, this is a major red flag that needs to be escalated as a major finding and warning on the assessment review.

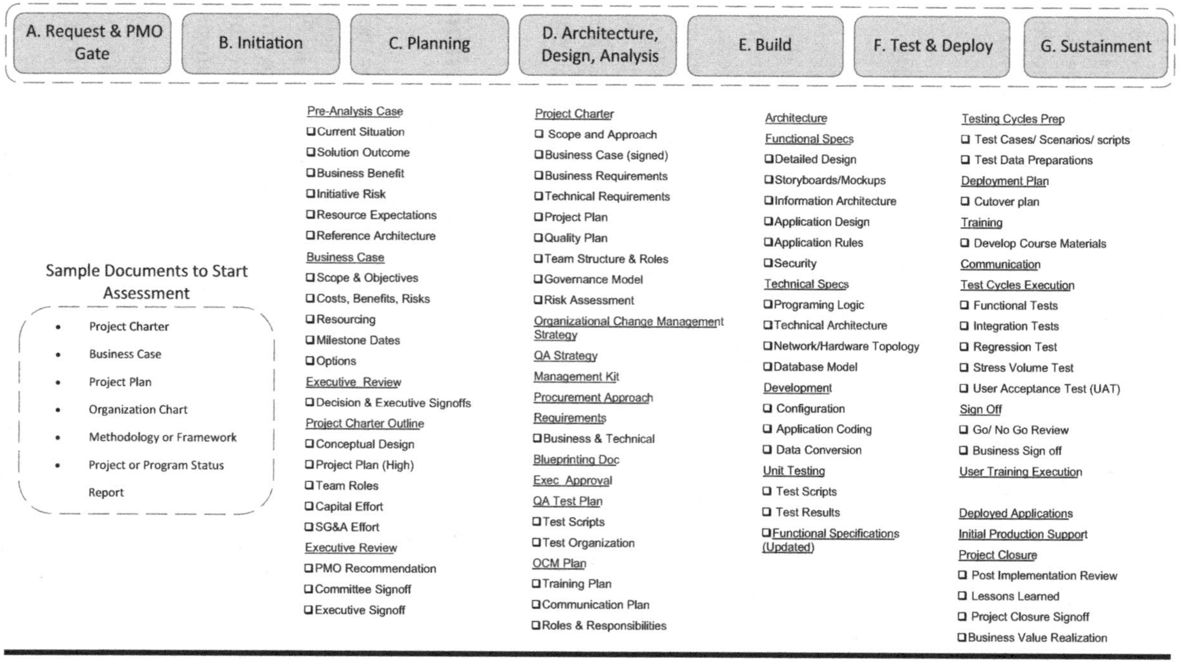

A. Request & PMO Gate | B. Initiation | C. Planning | D. Architecture, Design, Analysis | E. Build | F. Test & Deploy | G. Sustainment

Sample Documents to Start Assessment

- Project Charter
- Business Case
- Project Plan
- Organization Chart
- Methodology or Framework
- Project or Program Status Report

Pre-Analysis Case
❑ Current Situation
❑ Solution Outcome
❑ Business Benefit
❑ Initiative Risk
❑ Resource Expectations
❑ Reference Architecture
Business Case
❑ Scope & Objectives
❑ Costs, Benefits, Risks
❑ Resourcing
❑ Milestone Dates
❑ Options
Executive Review
❑ Decision & Executive Signoffs
Project Charter Outline
❑ Conceptual Design
❑ Project Plan (High)
❑ Team Roles
❑ Capital Effort
❑ SG&A Effort
Executive Review
❑ PMO Recommendation
❑ Committee Signoff
❑ Executive Signoff

Project Charter
❑ Scope and Approach
❑ Business Case (signed)
❑ Business Requirements
❑ Technical Requirements
❑ Project Plan
❑ Quality Plan
❑ Team Structure & Roles
❑ Governance Model
❑ Risk Assessment
Organizational Change Management Strategy
QA Strategy
Management Kit
Procurement Approach
Requirements
❑ Business & Technical
Blueprinting Doc
Exec Approval
QA Test Plan
❑ Test Scripts
❑ Test Organization
OCM Plan
❑ Training Plan
❑ Communication Plan
❑ Roles & Responsibilities

Architecture
Functional Specs
❑ Detailed Design
❑ Storyboards/Mockups
❑ Information Architecture
❑ Application Design
❑ Application Rules
❑ Security
Technical Specs
❑ Programing Logic
❑ Technical Architecture
❑ Network/Hardware Topology
❑ Database Model
Development
❑ Configuration
❑ Application Coding
❑ Data Conversion
Unit Testing
❑ Test Scripts
❑ Test Results
❑ Functional Specifications (Updated)

Testing Cycles Prep
❑ Test Cases/ Scenarios/ scripts
❑ Test Data Preparations
Deployment Plan
❑ Cutover plan
Training
❑ Develop Course Materials
Communication
Test Cycles Execution
❑ Functional Tests
❑ Integration Tests
❑ Regression Test
❑ Stress Volume Test
❑ User Acceptance Test (UAT)
Sign Off
❑ Go/ No Go Review
❑ Business Sign off
User Training Execution

Deployed Applications
Initial Production Support
Project Closure
❑ Post Implementation Review
❑ Lessons Learned
❑ Project Closure Signoff
❑ Business Value Realization

Figure 10.7 Deliverable review.

The next documents to review are the project plan, organization charts, methodology, and all the status reports. The project plan should tell a story about the initiative and show logical progression. There should be an executive version and a detailed version that rolls up to it. The detailed version is used to track at the task level, with dependencies and resource allocations considered. The executive level shows the high-level flow with high-level dependencies and resource allocations. The latter should be used at all Steering Committee meetings to keep the executive team aligned on the larger picture and needs of the project. Questions should be logged in formats like that shown in Figure 10.5 for each deliverable and included in the upcoming interviews.

Get Suggestions from Sponsors on Who to Interview

Using the project organization chart and the corporate organization chart, the health check team should begin to identify the resources that will be included in the interviews. One of the rules of engagement that must be settled with the assessment sponsors is for the health check team to have freedom in finalizing members of the attendee list. This is one level of their independence in the health check. The health check team may not get a 360-degree picture of the initiative if they only stick to an attendee list that someone affiliated with the project provides them. If there are resources off limits, the sponsors need to be clear upfront, and maybe even explain the reasons for this. Another way to approach this is for the health check team to build the list or interviewees they feel are needed and have the list vetted by the Steering Committee before the interview requests go out.

Examine Organization Charts and Identify Roles within the Areas of Scope

The health check team should identify a combination of resources for the interviews based on past experience, best practices, and suggestions from other team members of the initiative about to be assessed, similar to the sample are shown in Figure 10.3. They should be careful to include everyone they feel might be useful to provide information for the health check. A general principle to impress on the Executive Group is that the assessment team should have the authority to reach out to anyone they feel the need to speak with—unless there is a good reason not to do so.

Interviews, whenever possible, should be with individual members of the team so that they can speak candidly. Doubling up interviewees should not be the default. The health check team doing the interview, on the other hand, can have more than one person in the interview.

The interview team makeup can also change from interview to interview. The interview can be some combination of resources making up the health check team shown in Figure 10.8. In that example, there are three core health check team

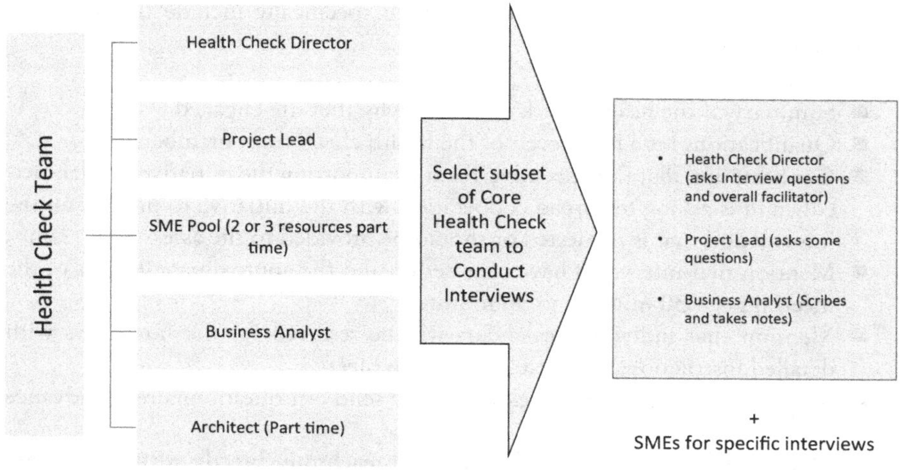

Figure 10.8 Deliverable review.

members in each interview. The overall facilitation is done by the Health Check Director, who will also ask some of the high-level questions. The team lead will ask questions in specific domains. The Business Analyst (BA) will take notes and minutes of the session. Additional SMEs can be included in some meetings or be brought in for just a portion of them. For example, for an architectural discussion, a Solution Architect SME from the Health Check team can be brought into the meeting to ask questions.

Sponsors Send Out Communication to Everyone on the Interview List

The sponsors should craft a communication email or letter that describes the objectives of the health check team and reinforces the message that specific members of the project team and perhaps other resources in and outside the organization have been selected to play an important role in the health check underway. While some team members may be stressed by this public acknowledgement, the communication is critical for getting support for the Health Check. Also, if the situation on the project or program is bad it is highly likely that a lot people in the organization already know, are already speaking about it, and will be relieved to hear that something is being done to try and fix the situation. In other cases, the health check can be called to improve business value and may not be because something is going wrong with the project. It is important to be realistic and transparent in the communication to set the appropriate tone for the assessment initiative.

The communication email or letter should specifically include the following information:

- Summary of the health check team and why they are engaged
- Qualifications (at a high level) of the health check team members
- Confirmation that the Executive Team is supporting the initiative wholeheartedly and is asking for broad cooperation with the initiative to provide all the information that is requested or should be provided to the assessment team
- Mention that interviews have been set up and the approximate lengths of the meetings e.g. 30 minutes to 90 minutes
- Mention that individual calendars will be reserved for the interviews with detailed instructions of where and how to meet
- Mention that the health check team may send out questionnaires in advance and to follow the instructions
- Mention that the health check team will reach out directly with any further information or questions
- Close the message by reiterating the importance of working with the health check team
- Reiterate that anyone with questions should ask the assessment sponsors or the executive team

The executive team should also ensure that interview rooms and/or video conference lines are reserved for each interview, and included in the calendar invite. Face-to-face interviews are preferred, if possible, followed in preference by video conference calls, and then phone calls.

Prior to sending out the email, the Steering Committee members may want to personally contact the managers of those included on the interview list and ensure they are aware of the time requirement, support it, and that there are no other obstacles.

The communication should be sent out to all those on the interview list with potential copies to the direct managers. An abundance of meaningful communication is generally positive.

Build/Customize Questionnaire

For each interview, the health check team should construct a questionnaire with some yes/no questions, but a lot of open-ended ones as well. If the questionnaires are more than 20 questions, they can be sent to the interviewees in advance so that they can have time to think of their answers and perhaps even bring materials to the interview.

Sources for the questionnaire should be the project documentation, input from the team members and executives interviewed to establish the scoping document, and the evaluation matrix that should have been approved and included in the

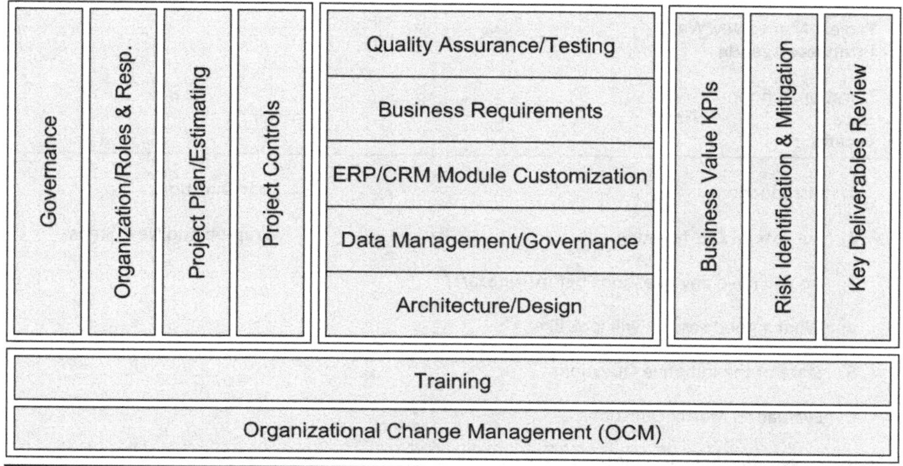

Figure 10.9 Build questions in each evaluation category.

Project Name: NewWave Inc. **Interview Questionnaire**

Interview Date: ______________

Interviewee: ______________

Interviewers: ______________

General

1. How well is this project going?
2. What could be going better?
3. Is the general feeling that the project is going to be on time and schedule?
4. Is the organization aware of and behind the project?

Business Requirements

1.
2.
3.

Architecture

1.
2.
3.

Governance

1.
2.
3.

Figure 10.10 Questionnaire subset sample.

Health Check Project Charter. Figure 10.9 shows the evaluation matrix exhibiting the specific dimensions that should also be included in the questionnaire. Some sample questions are included later in this chapter. A health check team should customize the questions that are relevant to the initiative being assessed.

These questions can be laid out in a format similar to that shown in Figure 10.10. This figure captures the date, who is being interviewed and the team members doing the interviewing. There is space for answers with each question. Additional questions can be added on the fly during the interview as new information is uncovered and new avenues for exploration begin to materialize.

Project Name: NewWave
Interview Agenda

Duration: 1 hour
Date: Time:
Location:

1. Introductions
2. Purpose of Our Meeting
3. Do you have any questions before we start?
4. What a good session will look like.
5. State of the Initiative Questions
6. Evaluation Matrix Questions
7. Deliverable Specific Questions
8. Your Questions
9. Wrap-up and Next Steps

Figure 10.11 Interview agenda.

Build/Customize Interview Agenda

An agenda should also be built for each interview. There is a lot of leeway in the format, but essentially the assessment team wants to ensure that there is some free time to follow new information that is discovered, while providing for a lot of structure during the interview. Figure 10.11 shows a simplified agenda for a one-hour meeting based on the evaluation matrix and documentation review.

Conduct Interview (s)

The interviews should be prioritized based on a review of the material and where some of the issues appear to be visible on the project. For example, start with the sponsors, members of the executive team, the business owners, the technology executives, and then members of the team based on the business value of the different areas to the organization.

Review Interview Materials

After the interviews are conducted, review the materials to see if any questions still remain unanswered, or if there were follow-up items. Highlight these so that they can be addressed in additional interviews or through more research into existing deliverables. Questions that cannot be answered can be included in the final health check report as items that require additional attention in the future and further follow-up.

Setup Follow-Up Calls

It is not unusual to need additional contacts with some of the interviewees to get additional information or clarify something that was said during the interview. Subsequent contacts can even be informal. Setup follow-up calls directly, if possible, to complete the discovery activities and to answer any remaining questions.

Complete Calls

Complete the calls for any remaining agenda items or remaining questions. This may be an iterative process and may require more than one conversation.

Send Out Thank You Notes to the Interviewees

The assessment sponsors or Steering Committee members should send out a thank you note to all the team members that were interviewed. They should especially express gratitude for the time the project or program team members spent in supporting the health check interview process and other activities that are pertinent.

Sample Questions to Include in the Questionnaire

This section contains some sample questions for common evaluation criteria that is typically included in health checks. These should serve as a starting point and be customized for a specific health check initiative. There will be different questionnaires for different interviews - customized for the specific attendees in that interview. For example, asking a business owner questions about network topologies might not yield much useful information. The questionnaire(s) can also be modified as a consequence of information gained in interviews. They can be living, breathing documents. Not all of these questions need to be included in the questionnaire. Select the ones that are the most appropriate and augment or change them based on the specific considerations of the initiative being reviewed. As shown in Figure 10.12, there are a variety of sources to provide input into the questionnaire, as follows:

- Questions from the assessment sponsors: These could have been provided during the scoping phase, and can be solicited again prior to the first interview.
- Questions from Steering Committee members: These could have been provided during the scoping phase, and can be solicited again prior to the first interview.
- Questions raised by any other stakeholders: These could have been provided during the scoping phase, and can be solicited again prior to the first interview.

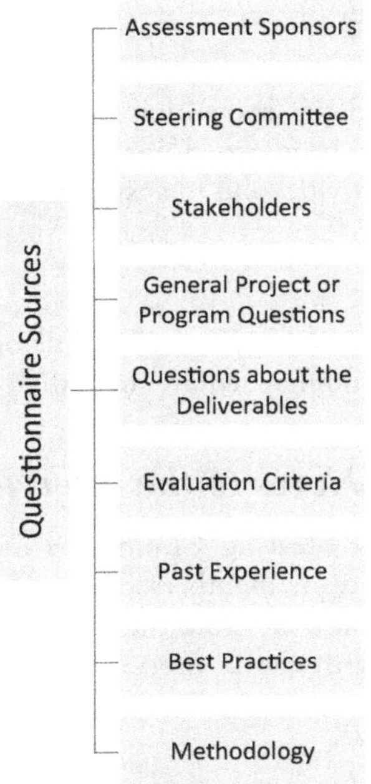

Figure 10.12 Questionnaire sources.

- General project or program questions: These are general questions about projects or programs. E.g. What business value will the project provide to the business? What major risks do you see? What would be appropriate mitigation strategies?
- Questions for deliverables in the documentation list: Each deliverable in scope should be reviewed and any questions or concerns should be included in the questionnaire. If a deliverable shown in the methodology has been labeled not in scope, the justification for this can be investigated in the interviews.
- Questions driven by the Evaluation Criteria: Each of the items in scope should be reviewed and included in the questionnaire if there are outstanding questions remaining.
- Past Experience: Past health check experiences provide a lot of information about where to look and which questions to ask. E.g. How do you know your data is clean? How much contingency is in the project plan? How do you know the business value business case is sound? Have the key risks been mitigated?
- Best Practices: Industry best practices should also be included in the questionnaire if they have not been raised by any of the other sources. E.g. What is your cloud strategy? How is AI going to be leveraged? How are you confirming the cybersecurity capabilities? Are permissions and roles clear?

- Methodology: Questions about the methodology or framework should also be included. E.g. Is the methodology appropriate for the project? How are the different vendors interacting when their methodologies are different? Is business value being created rapidly? Are people following the methodology?

Project or Program Scope

Recall how we were insistent to carefully and fully define the scope of the health check assessment in the health check project charter or statement of work. The scope of the project or program is critical. A constantly changing scope is one of the major reasons for project failure, so this has to be baselined and be solid. Here are a sample of questions to ask around project scope:

- Has the detailed scope been defined by the business?
- Has the detailed scope been approved in writing by the key stakeholders?
- Have detailed out-of-scope process areas been identified. Has this list been published and clearly communicated?
- Have detailed requirements been tied back to the scope?
- Has the scope changed since the project started?
- Is the scope adequate in your opinion?
- Is the scope driving maximum business value to the organization?

Executive Sponsor Support

Here are some sample questions to ask to determine the strength of the Executive Sponsor Support. A lack of Executive Sponsor involvement and support is another top 10 reason for project failure.

- Have key messages been developed for the Executive Leadership Team?
- Has the leadership team cascaded down their commitment, to ensure a good degree of buy-in at different management levels and in the organization as a whole?
- Does the leadership team have the capacity to fulfill their governance responsibilities?
- Has the leadership team shown commitment to the initiative?
- Has the leadership team removed obstacles to the project?
- Has the leadership team provided the resources needed for this initiative?
- Has the leadership team attended all Steering Committee meetings?
- Is this initiative a priority for the leadership team?

Business Case and Budgeting Strategy

The business case contains the drivers for the initiative. Too many projects start with a business case and then kind of leave it on the back burner. This impacts the level of business value that is derived out of the IT spend. Here are some sample questions to ask around the business case and budgeting strategy:

- Are benefits included measurable and have they been quantified in terms of the following:
- Revenue increases
  - Cost reduction
  - Improved customer service (increased service levels)
  - Expanded markets
  - Higher ROI
- What other areas have been included in the business case?
- Have the business units included the business benefits in their strategic plans after go live. Have they accepted accountability to meet those benefits?
- Has the business defined processes and roles to capture the business benefits?
- Is the organization ready to go after the defined business benefits?
- How will the business benefits be measured?
- Has a baseline been established to measure the business benefits against?

Risk Mitigation Strategy

Here are some questions to ask around the risk mitigation strategy:

- Is there a risk log?
- Are there mitigation strategies for each risk?
- What risks are you aware of?
- Has the risk management process been documented?
- Is there a risk escalation process?
- Have all the risks been included in a single repository or are they in multiple places such as emails, status reports, and other files?
- Is the risk log being maintained?
- Is the risk log reviewed during regular status meetings?
- Are there guidelines, detailing how to categorize each risk (high, medium, low for time, cost, quality, impact and benefit areas) and likelihood of risks e.g. High/Medium/Low probability?
- Is there a risk escalation and resolution process?
- What are the top three risks to the program? Are they mitigated?

Program and Project Governance Strategy

Here are some questions to include about the project and program governance strategy:

- In your opinion, would you suggest any improvements for the governance processes?
- Are the different management meetings well attended? Are they effective?

- Are there minutes of management meetings? Where are they kept?
- Are there any key decisions still outstanding?
- Do you know how to get on the management agenda?
- Is there an issue escalation procedure that is documented and shared?
- Are there weekly status reports?
- What are the regular management/governance meetings?
- Are the key decision-makers on the Steering Committee?
- Is there top-down support for the initiative?

Project Plan

The health check assessment team needs to continue cycling back to the project plan to ensure that it is a complete and workable deliverable. Like the business case, many projects have a plan but do not keep it current or actually use it on a week-to-week basis. Here are questions to consider including in the questionnaire:

- Does the project plan include all the items needed to go live, including OCM, and other systems that need to be integrated with our solution?
- How were the estimates for work effort calculated?
- Is there any contingency in the project plan?
- Are there any dependencies that are missing in the plan?
- Is the project plan being used to manage the project?
- Is there a summary and detailed version of the project plan? Where is the working copy kept?
- Are all the resources included in the project plan? Is their work effort realistically portrayed?
- What activities are missing from the plan?
- Is the project plan realistic? Is it too optimistic? Too Pessimistic?
- Are past project learnings reflected in the project plan?
- If we do everything on the plan, will we be successful?
- Is there a plan for post implementation activities?
- Are there any key assumptions we should know about?
- Does the project plan reflect personal vacations, statutory holidays, peak demand time such as quarter-end, year-end, and ad hoc time off?

Scope Refinement

Here are some questions to ask around scope management and refinement:

- Have all key program dependencies that have been considered included in the initiative's scope?
- What is the process to refine the scope? Are people following it?
- Who owns the project scope? Have they resisted refinement?

Management Toolkit

Here are some questions to ask around Program/Project Governance and Planning:

- How effective are the status reports?
- Are the status reports actively reflecting the state of the project?
- How well are the management tools being used?
- Is there a collaboration tool? Is it being used?
- Are key decisions, issues, action items being centrally recorded?
- How well is management communicating with the team? How transparent is the information?
- What are the key management tools?
- Are management processes clearly documented? What is included in their scope?
- How well is management performing? Do they need additional training?

Resource Planning

Here are some questions to ask around resource planning:

- Are there dedicated resources on the project team? Are there enough dedicated people?
- Is there enough management on the project team?
- Is there enough executive involvement?
- Are there the right mix of skills to get the project completed successfully?
- Are there backfills in the organization for the dedicated resources?
- What training is offered to the team resources to ensure that they can fulfill their duties?
- What is the morale of the resources on the project team?
- Are the resources engaged? Do they feel they are being heard?
- Is the project team the right size to deliver on the scope?
- How well are the vendors, employees, and contractors working together?
- What is done to promote team building?

Budgeting

Here are some questions to include about Budgeting:

- Has the budget been approved?
- Is there any contingency in the budget? How much? How was it determined?
- Who owns the budget? Is there a documented process to request changes to the budget?
- How is the project budget being tracked?

- How is the budget faring against the functionality that needs to be delivered?
- Is the budget the right size for the project scope?
- Have all the licenses, premises, and other costs been included in the budget?
- Are variances to budget being tracked and reported?

Project Planning

Here are some questions to include about Project Planning:

- Was a detailed work breakdown structure (WBS) completed and approved before the project plan was done?
- Have resource demands been leveled against the WBS? Is it reasonable?
- Has the executive team signed off on the WBS?
- What is missing in the WBS in your opinion?
- Is the WBS at the right level of detail?
- Is the project plan up to date?
- Is there a single integrated project plan?
- How well is the project tracking against that plan?
- Who is maintaining the project plan?

Organizational Change Management (OCM)

Here are some questions to include around Organizational Change Management?

- Is there an overall communication strategy? Has it been published and shared?
- Is the communication strategy being followed?
- Have townhalls been organized? How often are they held? Who is invited?
- What are the deliverables in the communication strategy?
- Is there a user training plan?
- Are there user training materials? How are they being developed? Who is signing off on them?
- Is there a regular newsletter? Who is approving the contents?
- How aware are people outside of the core project team about the initiative?
- How do people feel about this initiative?
- Are the "As Is" and "To Be" process maps documented?
- Are the "To Be" process maps being used to drive the training materials?
- Has the communication strategy been formally approved by key stakeholders?
- Have the new roles been defined and documented?
- What is the plan to implement the new organization?
- Have system permissions been tied to the new roles?
- Were any impact assessments done for the organization as a whole?

- What tools are being used for the following:
  - Surveys
  - Communication
  - User Training
  - Collaboration
- What are the plans for user surveys before, during, and after the program completes?
- How are the key executive stakeholders being kept in the loop?

Change Management Process

Here are some questions to ask around the topic of Change Management as it pertains to changes to scope or work:

- Is there a documented change management process?
- How many changes have not been processed?
- Do change requests consider business value as part of their approval?
- Where are the change management templates? Are they being used?

Architecture

Here are some questions to ask around the topic of Architecture:

- Have the different forms of Architecture been documented in both the "As Is" and "To Be" versions?
- Do you have any issues with the following Architectures:
  - Solution Architecture?
  - Business Architecture?
  - Technical Architecture?
  - Data Architecture?
  - Network Architecture?
- What are the key transactions that the architecture needs to support?
- Has the architecture been confirmed through meaningful Proof of Concepts? Are the results available?
- How were the different architectures selected? How were they validated?

ERP/CRM Modules

Here are some questions to ask around the topic of the ERP/CRM modules or other COTS (Consumer Off the Shelf) solutions:

- Why was the ERP selected?
- What was the CRM selected?

- Why was your COTS solution selected?
- How do you know the decision was the right one?
- Is the focus on configuration or customization?
- What level of customization is acceptable to the organization?
- How are you measuring the level of customization?
- Is there a process to determine whether a particular feature should be customized or configured?
- How will the customized code be supported in the sustainment period?

Project Controls

Here are some questions to ask around the topic of Project Controls:

- Are there timesheets for the different resources? Who reviews and signs off on them?
- How are security controls applied?
- How quickly is someone's account disabled when they leave the team?
- What is the expense management process for project resources?
- Are there satisfactory controls in the project? What are the risks?

Data Governance

Here are some questions to ask around the topic of data governance?

- Who owns the data?
- How clean is the data?
- Are there any data maps? "As Is" and "To Be" versions?
- Is there a data governance council?
- What are the requirements for a data conversion?
- Are key fields identified in the data conversion, that must be correct (e.g. someone's salary)?
- What is the tolerance for accuracy of the key fields for the data conversion?
- How will the converted data be validated?
- Who will do the data validation?
- Is there a detailed plan around the data conversion activities?
- Is there enough time to complete the data conversion?

Quality Assurance/Testing

Here are some questions to ask around the topic of Quality Assurance and Testing?

- What are the testing cycles?
- Who is involved in testing from the business side?

- How are you writing the test scenarios?
- Are the test scenarios being signed off by the business users?
- How is data being set up to support testing?
- Is production data masked to protect confidentiality?
- Who is running the testing activities?
- What is the process for reporting defects?
- How are defects prioritized?
- How are defects retested?
- How are defects reported? Daily? Weekly? By function?
- How will users be selected for User Acceptance Testing? How will they be trained?

Closing Perspective

This chapter examined the "Conduct Interviews" phase in the health check methodology. As shown in Figure 10.13, this is the last critical phase related to the discovery activities that give the assessment team the information needed to begin forming their observations, warnings, and recommendations. This will be the subject of the next part of this book.

This chapter examined the activities needed to conduct effective team interviews. These are generally set up as one person being interviewed by one or more people from the Health Check team. The chapter described an extensive amount of preparation activities prior to the actual interview. This included selecting resources to interview, ensuring their availability, communications from the top, booking times and venues, and preparing the agenda and questionnaires for each interview. Each interview offers an opportunity to update the questionnaires for subsequent discovery activities.

Following the interviews, the chapter described several activities to close the loop on any outstanding questions. The information gathered in the interviews, coupled with the documentation review, past experiences, and best practices, leads to the next phase in the Health Check methodology—to start forming observations, warnings, and recommendations.

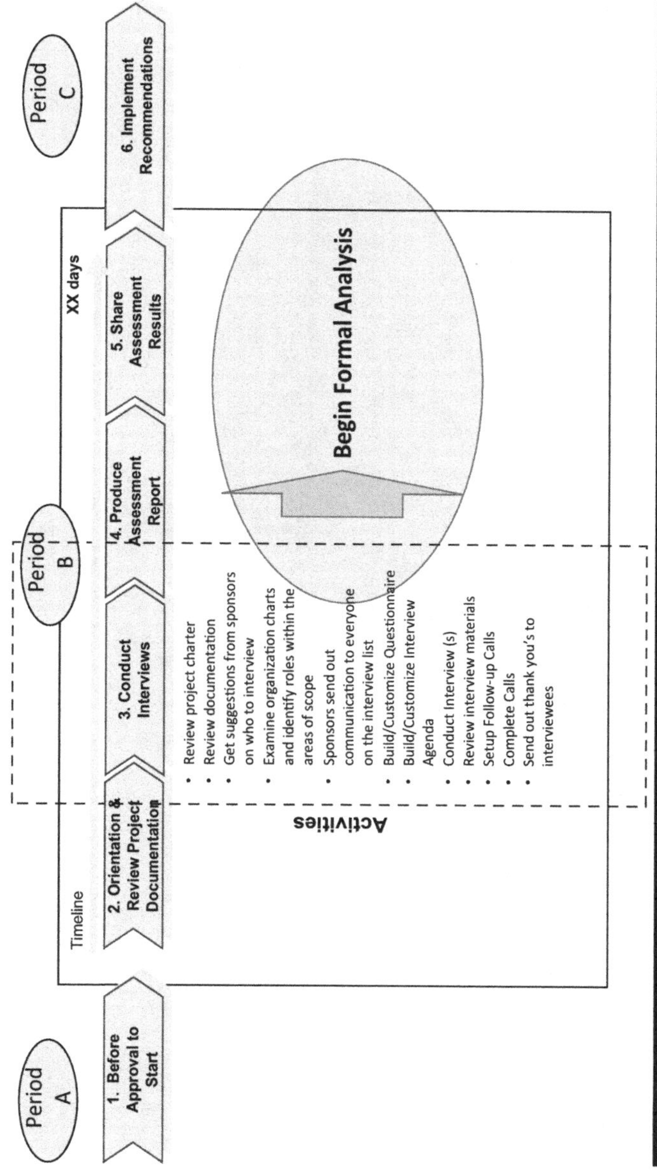

Figure 10.13 Finishing the discovery activities.

Chapter 11

Health Check Execution Considerations

The Health Check initiative is a project in itself. It should have a project charter that defines a scope, timeline, and resources. This forces us to question how we can make it successful and to drive multiples of business value. In a best-case scenario, a health check is commissioned by a steering committee with a duration of three to five weeks and a week or two to present and socialize findings in the organization. This can change dramatically from case to case. In the best-case example, the documentation is also available for review and the team members are available for interviews as needed. Everything is transparent and the result is a health-check report that identities what's going well and the areas that need improvement. The report highlights how to extract more business value from the initiative. This is the ideal case. In reality, there can be many more challenges facing the assessment initiative. Figure 11.1 shows some of the key dimensions that the assessment team must be mindful of to drive a successful outcome for the initiative, as well as providing useful best practices to apply in the health check itself.

Setting Expectations

Expectations have to be set across all the stakeholder groups. Start with the Sponsor(s) that are asking for the Health Check Assessment in the first place. That individual or individuals are likely very senior executives such as CEO, COO, CDO, CHRO, CFO, CIO, and others, and should be encouraged to open up as much as possible with the assessment team. The leader of the Assessment team needs to start speaking

DOI: 10.1201/9781003269786-13

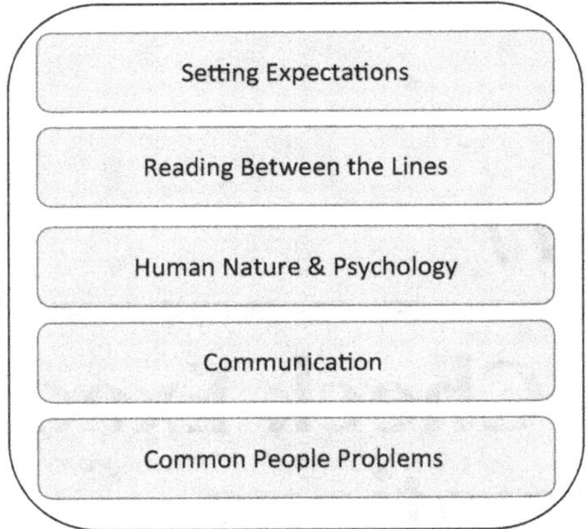

Figure 11.1 Health check execution considerations.

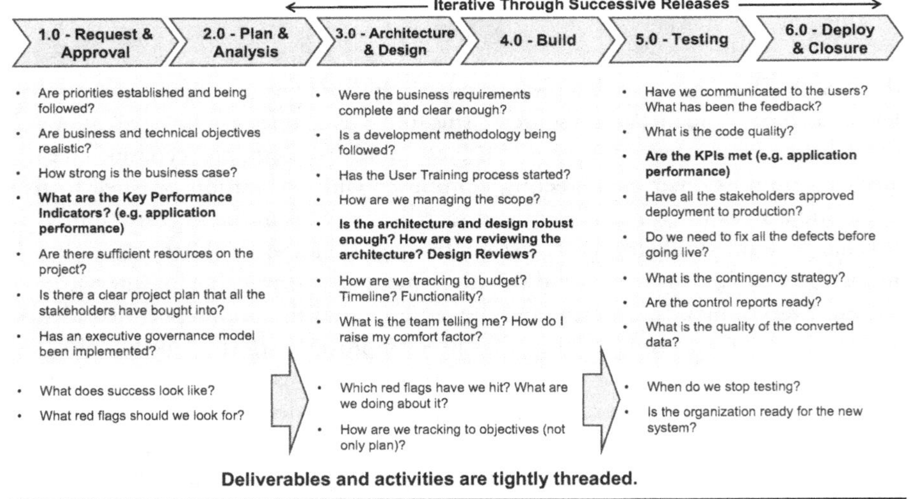

Figure 11.2 Explaining Dependencies.

with this senior resource (s) by confirming the reasons why the stakeholder should have confidence in the process, understand what can and cannot be delivered, and understand the complexity and the subtlety of the work about to be undertaken.

Figure 11.2 shows how dependencies in KPIs exist across a standard project delivery lifecycle. The figure shows that the KPIs must first be identified in the "Plan and Analysis" phase, then architected, built, and ultimately tested in the other phases. Some of the issues in the KPIs might not be discovered until the testing phase, and this could have ramifications with earlier assumptions and phases. This can be very eye-opening, especially to business leaders who do not have extensive previous involvement in systems projects. Use this time to set the expectation that this type of dependency will be reviewed across all aspects of the project, which may reveal new risks and issues that will have to be dealt with in the project plan. Since these are unplanned work activities, the core project team will need to find a way to resolve them within the parameters of the project—where possible. This sets expectations around the kinds of things the assessment may include in the recommendations coming out of the assessment and prepares the Executive Team in advance.

Taking time before the assessment formally starts and using it to provide examples of the work product to the assessment sponsors, as well as explaining why the answers from the review are not necessarily going to be a Boolean yes or no, will be important to build support for the recommendations coming later in the process. One of the critical success factors for an assessment to be successful is to set expectations and eliminate surprises.

Areas to Set Expectations

A detailed list of areas in which to set expectations with all the health check project participants is shown in Figure 11.3. Ensuring that these are understood, and ideally included in the health check engagement letter or project charter that was officially signed off ensures that both teams are on the same page. Differing expectations will derail the results or certainly ensure that the recommendations are not followed after the initiative ends. The health check assessment is a powerful tool, but it cannot be successful without buy-in from the Executive Team on the project or program.

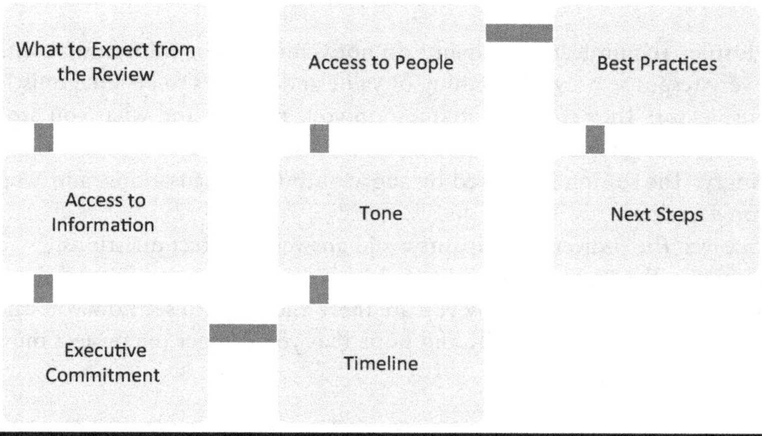

Figure 11.3 Areas to set expectations.

What to Expect from the Review?

From a contractual perspective, the engagement letter or project charter should have spelled this out clearly. However, that letter would not necessarily have been shared with the individual team members. It will be important to listen carefully and address any misinformation that exists. This could be anything like the following:

- The health check is trying to find someone to fire.
- The health check will get this project back on track within weeks.
- The health check is going to solve all of our problems.
- The health check is being used to spy on us.
- You're trying to find problems where there aren't any.
- You're just wasting our time.
- The project is going to fall further behind because of the time we're spending on this health check activity.
- You're trying to find a reason to cancel the project.
- What can you tell us that we don't already know?

The health check team should be prepared to answer questions like these as they start meeting members of the project team. For example, showing them briefly how your team solved similar problems on other similar projects in the past may set some of them at ease. It's also useful to stress that you both have the same end goal, namely the business success of the program which will require a unified collaborative effort. No questions should be viewed as too inquisitive or too threatening.

The tone and emotions coming from the project participants can fit into a very broad range, as follows. Some responses to deal with these is discussed later in this chapter.

- Hostile: The project participants do not want to share information with you. Every response provides nothing of value and appears to be antagonistic.
- Suspicious: They continue to question your motives and what you are trying to do to the project.
- Angry: The session is marked by angry outbursts, accusations, and tangential conversations.
- Evasive: The project participants avoid answering direct questions.
- Pleasant: They seem steady and to the point.
- Welcoming: They are happy you are there and want to see how you can help.
- Hopeful: They see as an ally and hope that you can get the project moving in the right direction.

In addition to clearing up misconceptions, the team should also reiterate that the review will not point fingers. Instead, the objective is to improve the project and raise business value for the organization. Recommendations will be constructive and actionable. The experience of the Health Check team over many other project or programs will be key to providing value on the current initiative.

Access to Information

All the assessment team members will need access to the working repositories of project documentation as well as historical ones. If there were previous failed attempts at the project, the deliverables from those efforts should also be made accessible. Look for any post mortem efforts to understand the reasons those projects failed. This will serve as an additional checklist in the current review and the health check team will be able to gain valuable insight into the culture and capabilities of the organization.

On one initiative, an HRIS implementation for a utility, two attempts at implementing the system were unsuccessful. The morale of the team was understandably very poor. What was unusual was the extent to which team members wanted to avoid being involved in any future projects with the Project Director. Many of the team members took demotions to move to other departments. The only constant remaining was the technology and the Project Director. A new System Integrator took over the initiative and understood that the biggest risk was that individual, and a mitigation strategy was adopted that provided executive coaching and pairing with another effective Project Director. This admittedly added costs to the initiative, but it did result in an implementation of the HRIS system on time and with the required functionality, with an increase in the budget that was acceptable to the organization's executive team. The critical path on this initiative indeed went through one individual in a 50,000 person organization. Without knowing the history of previous attempts at the project, both through the deliverables, but also through conversations with past team members, the incoming team would not have known where the true risks in the program lay had they only focused on the current deliverables.

Tone

The assessment team needs to establish the type of tone that should be conveyed in the assessment report. This decision should start in the initial meetings with the project sponsors and confirmed with them before the assessment report is written. As shown in Figure 11.4, the base approach for conducting health checks is to do a very collaborative health check that will provide information to populate the following sections on the final assessment report:

- Areas that are working and general observations: As shown in Figure 11.5, these should be listed as observations within specific dimensions. The general observations can be separated into their own section if desired. The decision here can be driven by the type of tone that the assessment team wants to portray. For example, if an aggressive tone is required, then separating the

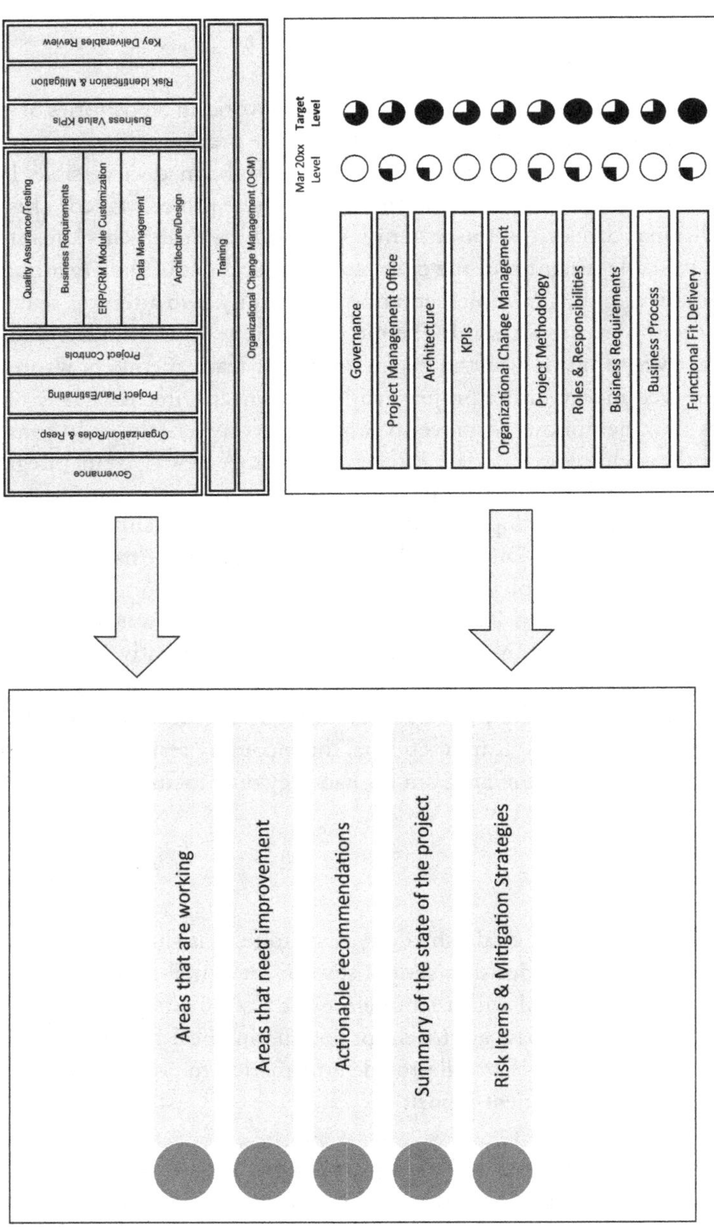

Figure 11.4 Standard health check deliverables.

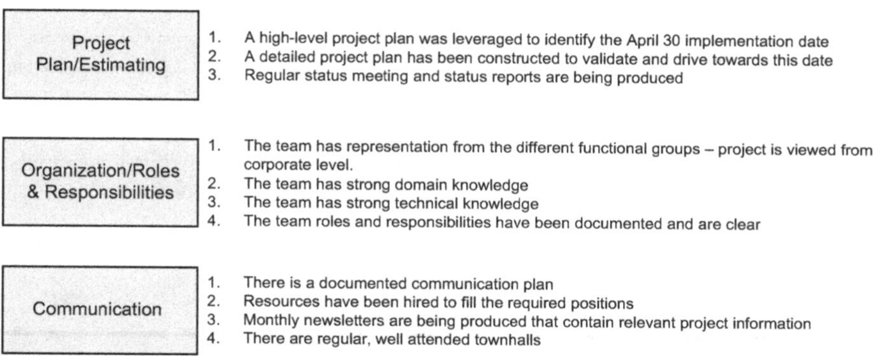

Figure 11.5 Areas that are working and general observations.

two sets of information into different groups sends a more terse message by reducing the number of items in the "Areas that are working" section. This can have a very big emotional impact on the reviewers. General observations are generally used to confirm facts and demonstrate that the assessment team has a good understanding of the initiative.

- Areas that need improvement: As shown in Figure 11.6, these should be listed as observations within the specific dimensions of the project. This is really the part of the report that creates the most apprehension in the project team because it is often viewed as a report card on them. The assessment team needs to make a decision on the tone being set here to maximize benefits to the program. If being moderate is going to let the team justify business as usual, then the choice of words should be carefully reconsidered.
- Actionable recommendations: As shown in Figure 11.7, these should be specific and measurable as much as possible. They can even be tied to a 30-60-90 day

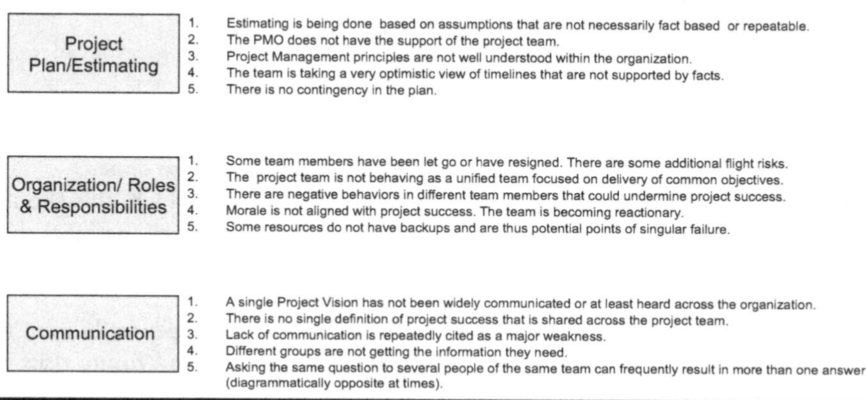

Figure 11.6 Areas that need improvement.

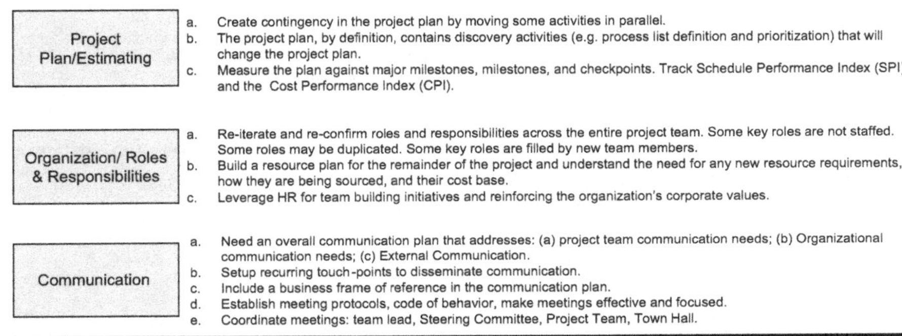

Project Plan/Estimating	a. Create contingency in the project plan by moving some activities in parallel. b. The project plan, by definition, contains discovery activities (e.g. process list definition and prioritization) that will change the project plan. c. Measure the plan against major milestones, milestones, and checkpoints. Track Schedule Performance Index (SPI) and the Cost Performance Index (CPI).
Organization/ Roles & Responsibilities	a. Re-iterate and re-confirm roles and responsibilities across the entire project team. Some key roles are not staffed. Some roles may be duplicated. Some key roles are filled by new team members. b. Build a resource plan for the remainder of the project and understand the need for any new resource requirements, how they are being sourced, and their cost base. c. Leverage HR for team building initiatives and reinforcing the organization's corporate values.
Communication	a. Need an overall communication plan that addresses: (a) project team communication needs; (b) Organizational communication needs; (c) External Communication. b. Setup recurring touch-points to disseminate communication. c. Include a business frame of reference in the communication plan. d. Establish meeting protocols, code of behavior, make meetings effective and focused. e. Coordinate meetings: team lead, Steering Committee, Project Team, Town Hall.

Figure 11.7 Actionable recommendations.

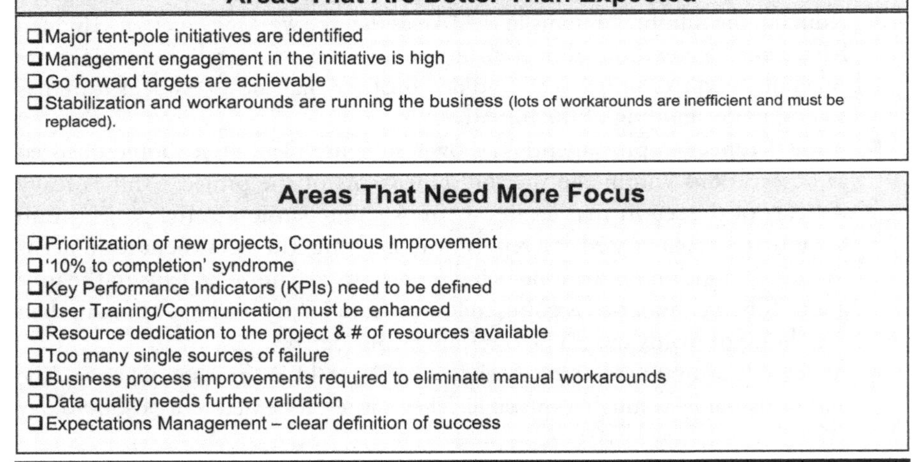

Areas That Are Better Than Expected

- ❑ Major tent-pole initiatives are identified
- ❑ Management engagement in the initiative is high
- ❑ Go forward targets are achievable
- ❑ Stabilization and workarounds are running the business (lots of workarounds are inefficient and must be replaced).

Areas That Need More Focus

- ❑ Prioritization of new projects, Continuous Improvement
- ❑ '10% to completion' syndrome
- ❑ Key Performance Indicators (KPIs) need to be defined
- ❑ User Training/Communication must be enhanced
- ❑ Resource dedication to the project & # of resources available
- ❑ Too many single sources of failure
- ❑ Business process improvements required to eliminate manual workarounds
- ❑ Data quality needs further validation
- ❑ Expectations Management – clear definition of success

Figure 11.8 Executive summary of the state of the project.

action plan. Getting the team to adopt these recommendations is the purpose of the assessment and so these have to be justifiable, precise, and clear. Including recommendations that do not help the project should never be done.

- Summary of the state of the project: As shown in Figure 11.8, this should include overall guidance for the executive team and other key messages that the executive team must receive. The messaging here tends to receive a lot of attention so this space should be used thoughtfully.
- Risk Items and Mitigation Strategies: The project sponsors generally want to understand the assessment team's perspective on existing and future risks to their initiative, as well as on how to respond to them. Figure 11.9 shows a

Risk Item	Project Risk	Mitigation Strategy
Sustainment team is multi-tasking between issue resolution and upcoming program events.	• Critical items are not resolved in a timely manner. • Certain pay components may not be correct on the paychecks.	• Prioritize most critical tickets • Communicate to the business on what's essential versus non-essential • Hire additional resources
Data quality and integrity fixes may need ongoing cleanup and synchronization with other systems.	• Could still have a high volume of tickets related to data inquires.	• Prioritize data elements that are the most critical and need to be addressed first.

Figure 11.9 Risk items and mitigation strategies.

high-level view of presenting just the top critical risks as part of the executive summary. Supporting information like timelines and responsibilities should be included in the main body of the report.

As mentioned previously, the tone of the wording and format of the report must also be discussed with the project sponsors during report writing. Even in a completely fact-based review, consider the following:

How will the report be received? Will it be acted on or simply put in a drawer (cloud) somewhere and the important recommendations ignored completely. While the Project Sponsors and team are responsible for implementation of the recommendations, as the assessment team, it's imperative to ensure that your message is being heard, incorporated, and executed. There are examples, the author has witnessed, where members of the steering committee counted the number of positive observations and compared that to the negative ones. They were comfortable with status quo as long as there were more positive observations than negative ones. In another case, a senior member of the team called to complain that there were not enough positive observations. Since the assessment is not an audit, it is necessary to consciously select a tone that will deliver the message that the experienced assessment team needs to deliver—impartial, fact based, objective but customized for the specific project or program at hand—raising benefits to the organization as a whole and bringing out the truth.

The tone of the members being interviewed will factor in the review as well. The assessment team must remain neutral and independent, and never get into an ego match regardless of the tone they are receiving. More on this later in this in the section "Human Nature & Psychology" later in this chapter.

Timeline

A lot of assumptions go into building a project plan. For example, Figure 11.10 shows a high-level rolled-up project plan. One of the key lessons learned from reviewing hundreds of project results shows the tendency for an inherent bias in estimating which can be from an optimistic viewpoint, pessimistic viewpoint, or a realistic/balanced viewpoint.

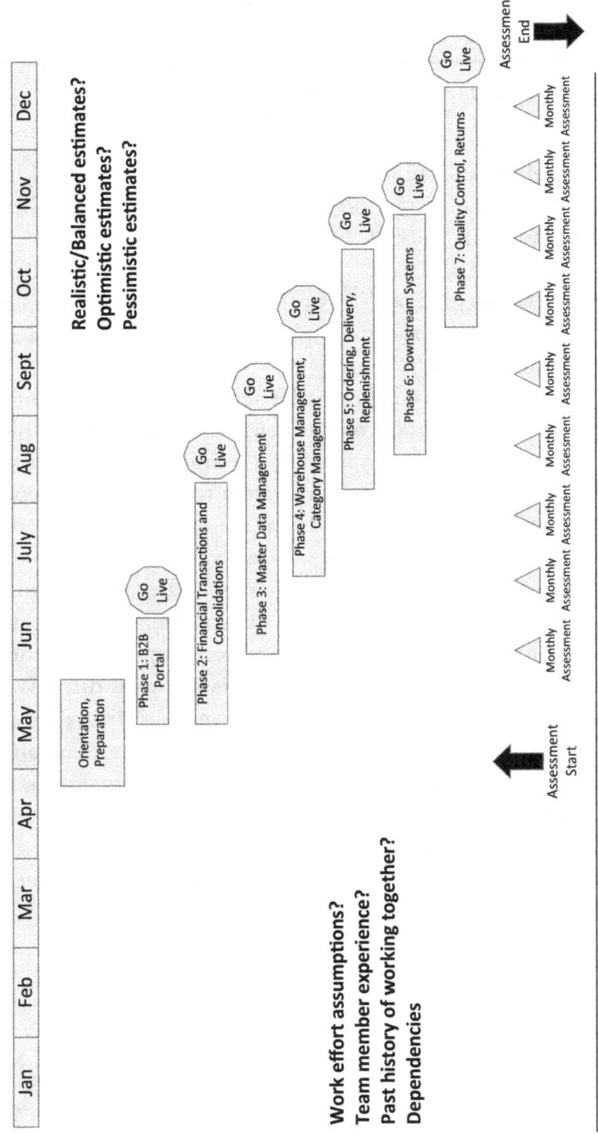

Figure 11.10 Timeline examples.

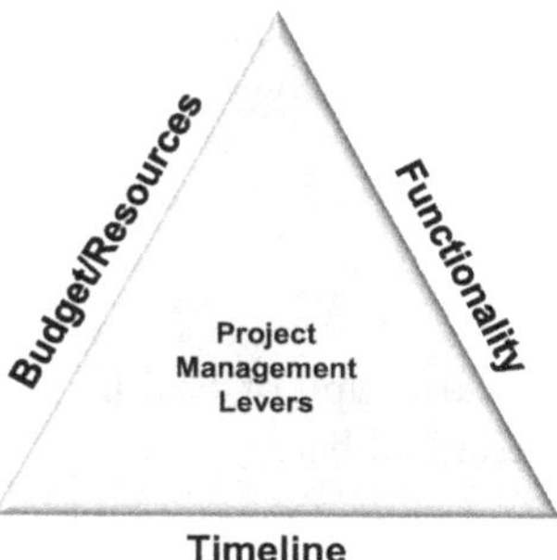

Figure 11.11 Project management levers pyramid.

When assessing the estimates, this inherent bias in estimating can be mitigated by incorporating other levels of rollup in the estimates. In addition to a bias in the optimism or pessimism, another source of potential issues is being given forced dates by the business executive. Was a date given and then subtasks were allocated work effort to meet the forced date? The familiar view in Figure 11.11, suggests that there would have to be tradeoffs to account for this. Look for evidence that this was the case. Is there contingency to account for this? If not, this will be a key finding of risk in the assessment findings. Were resources added to support the forced dates? Are they reasonable given the functionality and resources available?

Another approach to mitigate estimate bias is to do "bottom up" and "top down" estimates and to align them to get an average number for the tasks. Estimating was examined in the "Look Out for Red Flags" chapter. As the health check is executed, the precise nature of how timelines were established should be confirmed and included in the assessment report.

Best Practices

All the information gathered, assessed, and presented should not be done in a vacuum. Relevant comparable information needs to be incorporated in the messaging. If other projects have experienced similar issues, their lessons should be included in the observations and recommendations sections. Best practices can be sourced from the organization, industry, or both.

There are many examples where this would be relevant. Suppose the project is trying to support two vendors, one of which is using a pure agile delivery approach, while the other is using a waterfall approach. At some point in the lifecycle, their deliverables will need to connect. This could be a very difficult task as the agile group may not be able to define the state of their deliverables six months out, at least to the level of detail the waterfall group needs to setup their integration tests. Some best practices can be brought from other projects in the industry to build a solution for how these differences can be accommodated. The answer to this problem, by the way, was to customize a hybrid methodology to align deliverables in the project plan at specific integration points.

Next Steps

The next steps will depend on the type of health check, shown in Figure 11.12, being conducted. These are described below:

- Monthly/Bimonthly/Quarterly: Past recommendations should be tracked on whether they were accepted and their status of incorporation into the initiative. Recommendations that were not accepted should have a documented reason from Management. New recommendations should be added to the list, prioritized, resourced, and given deadlines.
- One Time: The assessment report should be published and socialized. An executive on the core team should be given the responsibility to execute on the recommendations section. Depending on the recommendations, additional resources may need to be hired on an urgent basis.
- Project Gates: The recommendations to complete the gate should be implemented on a priority basis. Other recommendations that were given will then need to be prioritized.
- On Demand: An executive will be given the accountability to own implementation of the recommendations.
- When a Project is Failing: The recommendations may call for adjustments or a full intervention. Additional key resources also may need to be hired. An executive on the team must take immediate ownership of next steps and execute the Project Rescue.

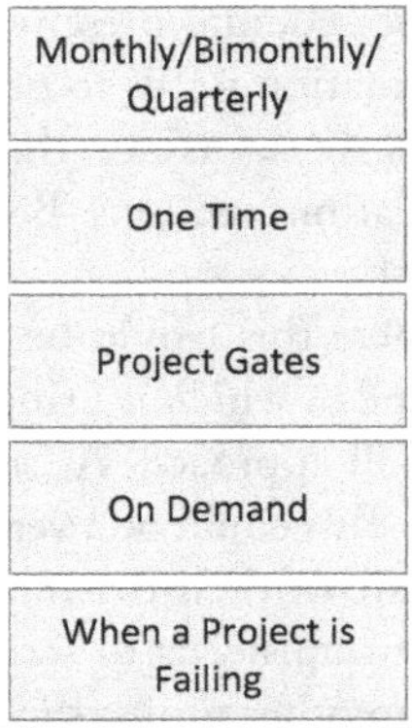

Figure 11.12 Types of health checks.

Changing Expectations

To be proactive, a change management process should have been included in the project charter for the health check assessment. However, changing expectations is more difficult than setting expectations at the start of the program. The sponsors may have heard exactly what they wanted to hear and might be unwilling to change their minds. This could make the assessment itself less than successful. When changing expectations, always lead with the original assumptions—that should have been shared in the first place—and show how they changed and why they changed, and finish by the best approach for dealing with the situation. For example, if the expectation was that a "Go-Live" needed to be confirmed with a simple "Yes" or "No". During the analysis, it's discovered that some activities will uncover facts that could impact the timeline, the explanation must include these details. This includes what is working towards the deadline AND what needs to work to meet that deadline. This positions the information in an active position and makes it more acceptable to the stakeholders. They have a choice to execute on the right side of the AND condition.

Reading Between the Lines

This is an important capability to develop for doing health check assessments successfully. This is not to say that the information being shared is not accurate and valid. The assessment team should be aware of things that are not said, or to read the meaning behind some of the opinions that are being shared. Some projects want the health check because the Board has asked for it. The sponsor may not be engaged as much as necessary. By reading this situation, the project team can better set expectations on outcomes and provide more meaningful recommendations.

This was exactly the case on a past project. The Board of Directors wanted an external team to conduct a health check for a project that had not moved forward. A business sponsor commissioned the external review, but did not complete all the onboarding activities. Some key stakeholders did not understand what the health check team was even trying to accomplish. The documentation was delivered for review but planned interviews were missed. Despite several conversations with the sponsor, it was clear that the team was not going to actively engage in the process. Writing of the health check report was accelerated and these findings formed the core of the recommendations.

Human Nature and Psychology

It's possible to argue that a lot of the management processes in IT projects and programs is based on human nature and psychology. In fact, as shown in Figure 11.13, while we speak of technology-process-people as a pie with equal-sized slices, the

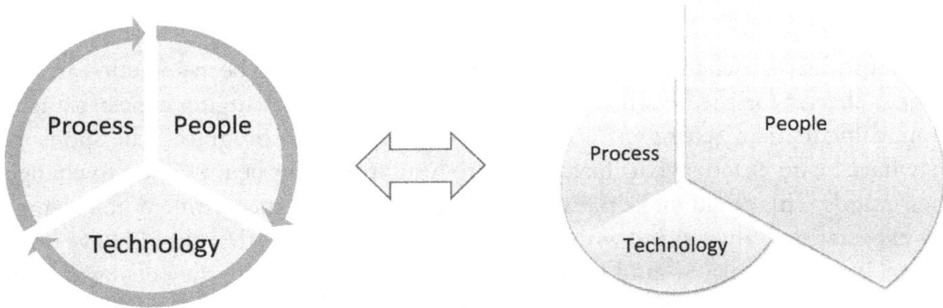

Figure 11.13 Adjusted people-process-technology view.

reality is that the people slice might actually be much larger than the others. This is not to say that technology and process are not vital to driving business value and project success. They tend to have issues but have corresponding solutions that can be implemented once identified. The people slice has many dimensions and drivers. There are solutions, but they need more work to discover and drive. Contrasted to Technology solutions, the people slice has decency expectations, rules, regulations, laws that all need to be factored into a solution. Different personalities respond differently to the same stimuli. Some resources are motivated by being the smartest person in the room, some will rise to the challenge, others will move away when met by the self-appointed smartest person in the room, and some will disengage too quickly when met with resistance.

All project teams have certain views for their initiative. Depending on their viewpoint, we will see certain behaviors and anticipate likely outcomes. The key ones are described in Figure 11.14. The assessment team needs to establish the type of view the initiative's team is taking and then adjust the approach accordingly. The "Cautious" or "Baseline" views represent team members who have gained the experience to recognize the complexities of the project and are engaged to meet these so that there will be a more likely successful outcome.

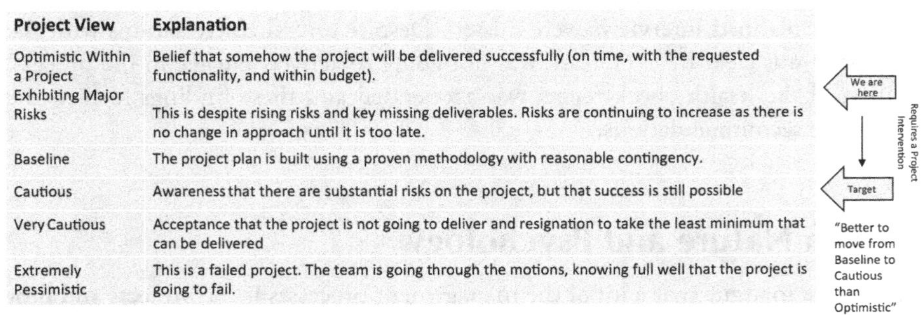

Project View	Explanation
Optimistic Within a Project Exhibiting Major Risks	Belief that somehow the project will be delivered successfully (on time, with the requested functionality, and within budget). This is despite rising risks and key missing deliverables. Risks are continuing to increase as there is no change in approach until it is too late.
Baseline	The project plan is built using a proven methodology with reasonable contingency.
Cautious	Awareness that there are substantial risks on the project, but that success is still possible
Very Cautious	Acceptance that the project is not going to deliver and resignation to take the least minimum that can be delivered
Extremely Pessimistic	This is a failed project. The team is going through the motions, knowing full well that the project is going to fail.

Figure 11.14 Team's perspective based on the project view.

Project View	Behavior
Optimistic Within a Project Exhibiting Major Risks	• No streamlining of activities is sought. • Focus on details that may be important, but are not significant towards successful delivery. • The assumption is that by fixing a few things, getting some resources to work differently will somehow fix the project. • Major moving pieces are considered at a high level, integration issues are not being resolved • People become afraid to speak up and continue to follow the herd.
Baseline	• The methodology is being followed. The project uses contingency to deal with unexpected issues. Communication is open, transparent, and frequent.
Cautious	• Looking for opportunities to streamline • Identify and stick to a critical path • Iterative &incremental approach to delivery • ONE team and business not as usual
Very Cautious	• Dysfunctional team • Business value is not sought • Even the simplest changes will not be accommodated.
Extremely Pessimistic	• Destructive politics • Shortcuts on quality • An Optimistic Within a project exhibiting major risks can move to this view without a proper project intervention.

Figure 11.15 Behavior's based on the project view.

Project View	Likely Outcome
Optimistic Within a Project Exhibiting Major Risks	At some point it becomes evident that the project is not going to be successful and then the project view becomes Very cautious or extremely pessimistic. The project is likely to fail on one measure – or more. This approach rarely works.
Baseline	The project is delivered on time and within the contingencies set aside.
Cautious	While the project will not deliver all the functionality the business wanted, the critical path provides highest value.
Very Cautious	Either the system will be delivered with substandard functionality or there will be major misses on budget/time.
Extremely Pessimistic	This is a project that is a significant failure.

Figure 11.16 Likely outcome based on project view.

The team members will exhibit certain behaviors based on which project view they are using, as shown in Figure 11.15. The objective of the recommendations will be to get to the behaviors exhibited in the baseline or the cautious views.

Figure 11.16 shows the expected project outcomes based on the prevalence of the project view that is being used by the project team members. As is clear, all the views besides baseline and cautious will lead to red warning flags that will need to be managed to bring the project to a successful conclusion.

Personal Expectations of the Assessment

Each member of the project team will have personal desires and expectations for the health check assessment. These should be understood by the assessment team so that they can interpret the information they are receiving. Also, the health check

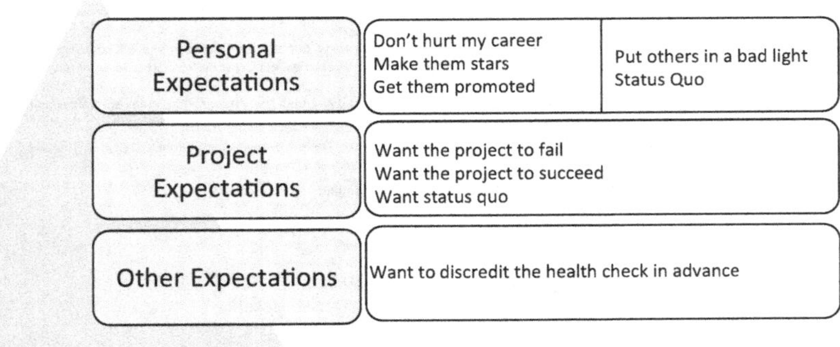

Figure 11.17 Expectations of the assessment.

team may not necessarily want or need to address these head on but rather build a preamble to start the interviews that would speak to those concerns.

Some common personal motivations are shown in Figure 11.17 and explained further below:

- Don't hurt my career: They do not want to be blamed for any issues on the project. They may be taking a very defensive posture and not making any difficult decisions that can be singled out later if things go wrong on the project.
- Make them stars: They want this process to bring them recognition and want to be singled out for the eventual success of the project.
- Get them promoted: They want an immediate promotion because they feel they are vital to the eventual success of the program and they feel they deserve the recognition and associated perks.
- Put others in a bad light: They want the health check to shed blame on those they feel are responsible for the current state of the project. They also might want to use this opportunity to get back at past grievances or remove competitors.
- Status quo: They do not want the health check to change anything on the project.

Some common Project Expectations from the core project team, as shown in Figure 11.17, are described below:

- Want the Project to Fail: Unfortunately, this happens from time to time. The assessment team can try to understand the motivation for this and make some recommendations in the final report. The phrasing that the author has used for such situations is:

> The project team is not behaving as a unified team focused on delivery of common objectives. There are negative behaviors in different team members that could undermine project success. Morale is not aligned with project success. The team is becoming reactionary.

- Want the Project to Succeed: Fortunately, this is the most common viewpoint among the majority of project team members. The assessment team needs to use their experience to draw out the information required to formulate recommendations that will drive business value and project success.
- Status Quo: This can happen when members of the project team feel help is not needed. They are confident in their ability to deliver the project or program and just want the assessment team to go away.

Politics

Project politics are truly inevitable. They are part of human nature and cannot be removed from the project. As mentioned previously in the book, there are politics, bad politics, destructive politics, and catastrophic politics. The assessment team needs to call out what they are seeing in the recommendations section—generally without pointing a finger at specific individuals.

There will be time when the Business or Technology Sponsors of the program want an in-camera or off-camera discussion with the assessment team. This is the exception where they might want to hear remarks about specific individuals on the program and how to manage them.

There are times when the business sponsors may have in fact asked for the health check specifically to get an independent viewpoint on key members of their project team. This might best be done behind closed doors directly to the Sponsors only.

Another approach for dealing with destructive politics is to use an options-based approach. Generally speaking, giving project teams a choice between a few options, as shown in Figure 11.18, will focus the conversation on just those choices. This can be a vehicle for breaking log jams.

Communication

As discussed previously, communication plays a crucial role throughout the health check assessment process. Key considerations include the following:

- Be transparent
- Be open
- Give credit where appropriate
- Use constructive terms

Impacts Elements	Option 1: Extend go-live date to first week of Oct	Option 2: Keep go-live dates unchanged
Description	❑ Extend some members of existing team for an additional month. Roll off others as they complete their activities and if they are not required for the remaining activities.	❑ Add no additional resources to the project team ❑ Require existing resources to engage to spend more hours and get paid overtime. ❑ HR to pre-approve overtime payments
Risks	❑ The project team is lean ❑ Multiple single points of failure as some skills only reside in one person ❑ UAT resources not identified	❑ The team is already showing signs of fatigue and disengagement ❑ Some members may leave the organization
Project Cost	❑ Additional one month of burn rate (approximately $1 million)	❑ The costs will be more than $1million ❑ There will be other tradeoffs
Resources	❑ Add resources strategically and look for opportunities to reduce resources over time.	❑ No additional resources required ❑ Morale on the project team is expected to plummet
Operations	❑ This approach will provide a strong position for sustainability following a strong implementation	❑ Will be costly if additional resources leave the organization and will have to be backfilled.
Tax Implications	❑ Amortize costs over 10 years	❑ Amortize costs over 10 years
Overall	**Recommendation is to proceed with Option 1.**	

Figure 11.18 Getting to green options discussion.

1. Determine the status of the ERP and CRM project using a Health Check evaluation framework;
2. Determine the feasibility of an April 30, 20xx implementation deadline;
3. Provide recommendations to meet the stated project KPIs;
4. Provide recommendations to meet the stated corporate CSFs;

Figure 11.19 Getting to green options discussion.

Also, by focusing on the objectives of the health check, as shown in Figure 11.19, also keeps the communication focused on what's important to the project. All conversation streams should lead back to how to optimize this list of business and project objectives.

Common People Problems

As discussed earlier in the chapter, the tone and emotions coming from the project participants can fit into a very broad range, as follows. Here are some approaches for dealing with these emotions to try and get value towards the assessment results:

- Hostile: Bring out the assessment objectives and go through them point by point, asking for any advice on achieving that objective. Ask for two or three specific actions that would help the project drive more business value.
- Suspicious: Discuss your prior experience with other similar clients and the results achieved. Reiterate that you are only successful if the project being assessed is successful.
- Angry: Follow the activities for the "hostile" emotion. Bring out the assessment objectives and go through them point by point, asking for any advice on achieving that objective. Ask for two or three specific actions that would help the project drive more business value.
- Evasive: Stick to the questions in the prepared questionnaire and don't be distracted by random comments being made by project team members
- Pleasant: Allow the conversation to take tangents. Use the questionnaire but put an emphasis on open-ended questions. Ask for specific actions that can improve the project and who else to interview.
- Welcoming: Allow the conversation to take tangents. Use the questionnaire but put an emphasis on open-ended questions. Ask for specific actions that can improve the project and who else to interview. Keep an open channel for follow-on questions after the formal interviews.

- Hopeful: Allow the conversation to take tangents. Use the questionnaire but put an emphasis on open-ended questions. Ask for advice on positioning the recommendations so that they have the best chance of being adopted.

Closing Perspective

This chapter focused on specific considerations for executing health checks. While it's true that there are considerations in the technology-process-people triangle, during execution, a lot of focus needs to be placed on getting the most accurate and detailed information from the stakeholders and core team of the project or program initiative.

Given the many different perspectives, motivations, and emotional makeup of different team members, the assessment team needs to prepare for the push-back, obfuscation, obstruction, and red herrings that might be put in their way. Conversely, the health check team might be overwhelmed with the information and ideas provided by willing and hopeful team members that welcome them with open arms to deal with a situation they might have given up on long ago.

Figure 11.20 reiterates some of the key considerations in preparing for the health check assessment and what to expect. Going through the categories, such as setting expectations, and preparing for the interactions with the culture of the organization in mind, allows the assessment team to gather accurate and meaningful raw information that leads into the subsequent phase of analyzing and assessing what they have learned.

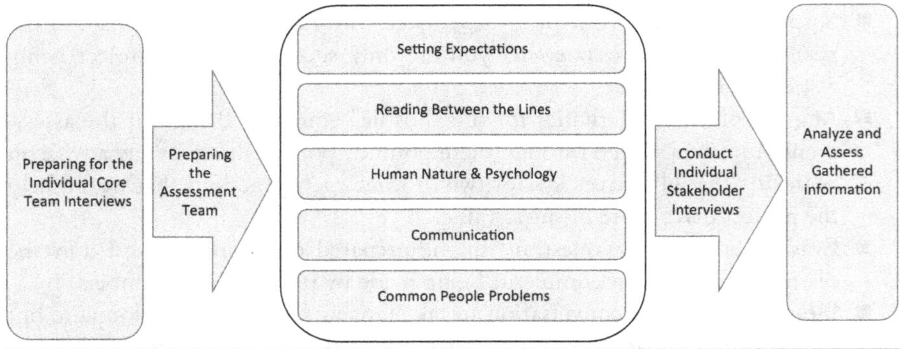

Figure 11.20 Emotional preparation for the interviews.

1. Eliminate surprises
2. Be firm in your resolve to improve the status quo
3. Be collaborative where possible
4. Listen intently
5. Look for win-win solutions
6. Put the Wellbeing of the project or program first
7. Understand the corporate culture to maximize the changes of the recommendations to be adopted
8. Prioritize the recommendations
9. Be transparent
10. Be thorough and detailed

Figure 11.21 Ten rules for executing health checks.

Figure 11.21 provides the top ten rules for executing health checks based on the discussions thus far in this book. These should be used an guidelines for building out a detailed health check execution strategy and plan.

Chapter 12

Risk Assessment and Mitigation Approaches

Managing risk is vital on projects and programs, but is often under evaluated or done sporadically by a core project team. Assessing risk is a vital part of the IT Health Check. Organizations that have not captured risk and how it is being mitigated have clearly not implemented an appropriate management and governance structure and are at risk of encountering many unexpected and negative events during the life of their initiative.

Figure 12.1 shows the focus of the Health Check assessment, namely the process itself, the existence of the deliverables, and the completeness and quality of the deliverable contents. It's not enough to perform a cursory examination of the deliverables in a Project Health Check. It's vital to get into the details and validate the logical elements that are being used. While a third-party project audit may only look for high-level information to put a checkmark on an action item list certifying that a deliverable exists, we must examine and comment on the information and processes more closely. There are three key questions to consider at the start of the review:

1. Are the initiative risks adequately captured?
2. Are the risks understood?
3. Are the risks adequately prioritized and mitigated?

The answer to these questions is never trivial and requires a methodical review of processes and information together.

A lack of a good risk assessment process or a sparse collection of risks is a strong indicator that the project team does not understand their project well enough. This is a huge red flag toward the success of the project and would form a key finding on an assessment report.

DOI: 10.1201/9781003269786-14

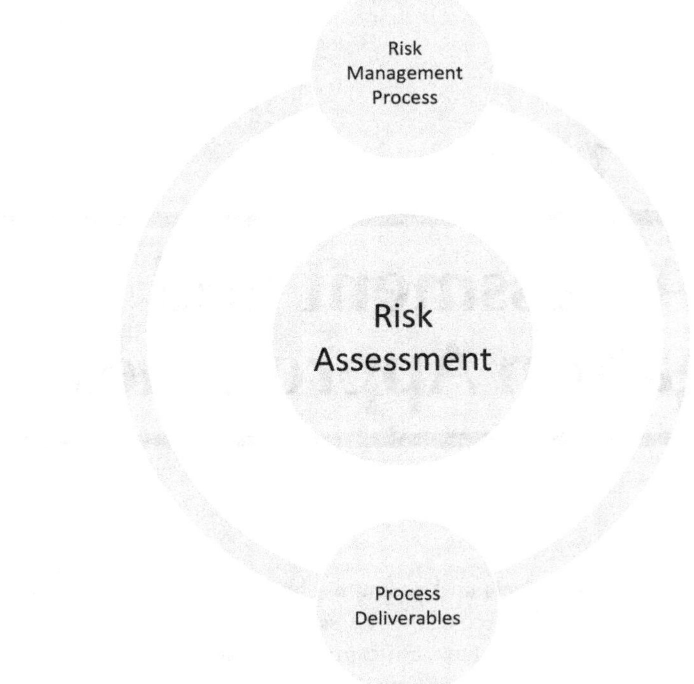

Figure 12.1 Risk assessment components.

There are four aspects of risk that must be assessed by the Health Check team. Weaknesses in even one of these can have a cascading impact on the entire project, so it is important to the health check team to identify and share these early in the health check assessment lifecycle. The four aspects of a risk assessment exercise are shown in Figure 12.2 and include the following major activities:

1. Risk Management Process: This must be published and shared with a project team. There must be evidence that it is being used on a regular basis.
2. Risk Register: A shareable list of risks that are identified and how they impact the project or program, along with key information. This is not a one-time collection activity. The risk register or log must be continually updated and shared. There must be evidence that risk mitigation activities are being completed.
3. Actionable Risk Mitigation Strategies: Each risk must have an actionable set of activities to mitigate the risk. For example, if a risk is identified as 'key staff may leave organization", a mitigation strategy would be to establish retention bonuses for each identified staff member. A second strategy would be to

Figure 12.2 Risk assessment details.

identify and train backup resources if it's felt that the first mitigation strategy is not enough insurance to fully mitigate the risk.

4. Ongoing Follow-Through: Many risk registers are completed once and then left unchanged for the duration of the initiative. This is not reflective of non-trivial projects, and is a huge and key red warning flag. There must be regular reviews of the register and evidence that risks are being mitigated. New risks should be added to the log on an ongoing basis. Risks that are no longer applicable should be marked as such. Prioritization of the risks should always be clear, as all risks do not have the same importance.

Risk Management Process Steps

There are different approaches to identify and mitigate risks, with different team members involved at different points of the project lifecycle. Some projects have a dedicated external team, while others rely on the Project Manager (PM) or designates to manage risk. To ensure there is no ambiguity, the process for managing risk should be documented and signed off at the executive level, and then widely shared. Typical risk activities that are usually included in a risk management process are shown in Figure 12.3.

As part of the health check process, a review of these activities should be undertaken. Some questions the health check team should ask are as follows:

- Is the risk management process documented and widely accessible to all the members of the project team?
- Is the risk management process signed off by the Steering Committee?

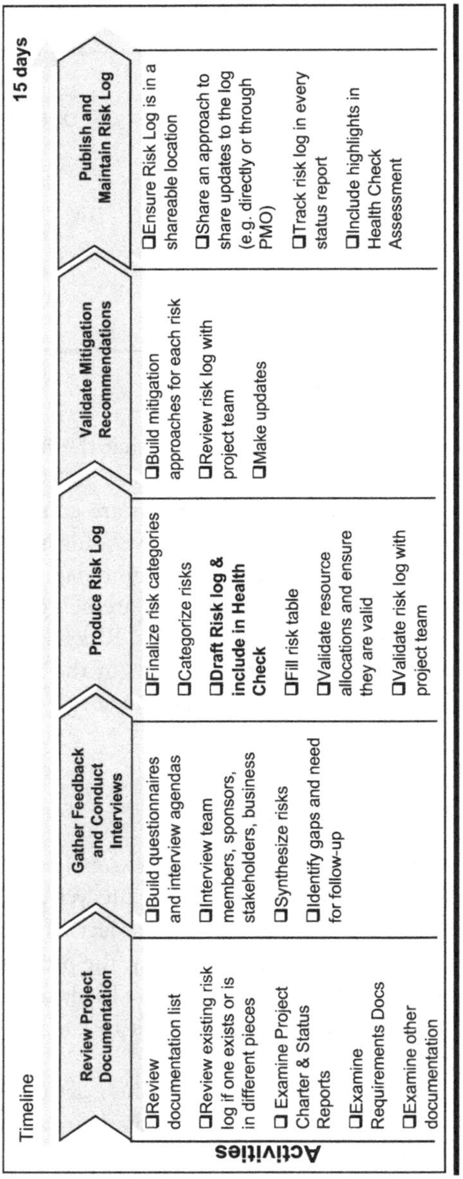

Timeline — 15 days

Activities	Review Project Documentation	Gather Feedback and Conduct Interviews	Produce Risk Log	Validate Mitigation Recommendations	Publish and Maintain Risk Log
	❑Review documentation list ❑Review existing risk log if one exists or is in different pieces ❑ Examine Project Charter & Status Reports ❑Examine Requirements Docs ❑Examine other documentation	❑Build questionnaires and interview agendas ❑Interview team members, sponsors, stakeholders, business ❑Synthesize risks ❑Identify gaps and need for follow-up	❑Finalize risk categories ❑Categorize risks **❑Draft Risk log & include in Health Check** ❑Fill risk table ❑Validate resource allocations and ensure they are valid ❑Validate risk log with project team	❑Build mitigation approaches for each risk ❑Review risk log with project team ❑Make updates	❑Ensure Risk Log is in a shareable location ❑Share an approach to share updates to the log (e.g. directly or through PMO) ❑Track risk log in every status report ❑Include highlights in Health Check Assessment

Figure 12.3 Risk management process steps.

- Was the risk management process shared with the Board of Directors?
- Who owns the risk management process? Is the owner capable and do they have the authority to manage risks by getting stakeholder buy-in across the organization?
- Is there evidence that the risk management process is being followed on projects?
- What are the highest impact risks to the organization?
- Are risks that are show-stoppers identified in the log? Are they mitigated?
- Which Risks Have Been Mitigated? Where is the Evidence?

Review Documentation

A corporate risk process should be built around a critical review of documented artifacts, and not verbal conversations. Auditors generally hold the view that something does not exist if it is not written down. This is a good starting point. The risk process should include a review of the following documentation at a minimum. The project health team should review these to confirm that the appropriate risks have been extracted by the project team, and included in the risk register. Some of the documents to look for in this process include the following:

- Project Charter
- Business Requirements
- Detailed Project Plan
- Solution Architecture
- Risk Register
- Sprint schedules
- Status reports (weekly, executive, monthly, Board level)

If these documents or deliverables are not available, the assessment team should examine the project plan to determine if these are scheduled to be delivered subsequent to the completion of the review. If they are not identified for future delivery, the assessment team should understand if they were not needed in the project at all, which is not unusual. If they are required, not built and not scheduled to be built, then this becomes a clear a health check finding, warning, and recommendation.

Gather Feedback and Conduct Interviews

While the deliverable documentation serves as the official record, individual interviews of stakeholders are the key to uncovering risks that are in people's minds but not being followed up. It's a safe assumption that most projects and programs suffer from this situation. The interview list should be broad and diverse and include representation from all the functional areas impacted by the project. Starting with members of the core team provides good background and so allows the interviewees to understand more about the project and the project team. From here, the interviews then should include key business and technology subject matter experts (SMEs) and then stakeholders. From a functional perspective, this could include the following sequencing, but the list should be prioritized for each initiative based on the focus of the program, and for groups within scope of the initiative:

- Operations Group
- Information Technology
- Human Resources
- Finance
- Sales
- Marketing
- Digital
- Legal
- Procurement

It can be time-consuming to conduct interviews, and there is a tendency to try and reduce the total number of interviews. However, as these can offer a wealth of information to the health check team, they should not be minimized. It is not uncommon for experienced health check teams to interview the members of the entire core project team and the first line of stakeholders and SMEs. However, the size of the interview list will depend on the size of the project and some tradeoffs may be required for the larger project teams.

Table 12.1 suggests the number of resources to interview based on the size of the initiative. Of course, this should be adjusted to suit the uniqueness of the initiative in question. The general rule is that the higher number of interviews the better, even if the information begins to repeat. The interview is an opportunity to build relationships with team members so are valuable even if no new information is uncovered. Each interview should last between 30 to 60 minutes as a guideline. Be careful to respect the time of the interview participants and do not drag the interviews out if there is nothing left to discuss.

Table 12.1 Interview Team Sizing

Initiative Team Size		*% of Team to Interview*
Small	1–100	25–100
Medium	101–500	15–50
Large	Over 500	5–25

Using Questionnaires and/or Interviews

An alternate approach to standalone interviews is to send a questionnaire to core team members and stakeholders. This can serve as an advance information collection exercise that becomes an agenda for individual interviews, or can be used as an information source in itself. In building the questionnaire, divide the questions into risk categories with a combination of Yes/No answers and some open-ended questions. Your objective is to give team members a chance to express what they have not been able to share before, either because they were reluctant to do so, or were never given an opportunity to do so. The reluctance can emerge from several places. Sometimes, individual team members do not want to feel like they are rocking the boat, causing problems, feeling like they are wrong, or just afraid to express an opinion. The questionnaire should offer a chance for anonymous feedback so that respondents feel protected and unafraid to share their concerns.

Figure 12.4 shows a set of questions under groupings designed to understand the state of the project scope, stakeholder involvement, and team capability. Each question is given a weight out of 100. The resource completing the questionnaire provides a Y/N response and points for each Y response (say out of 5) on how well the risk is being mitigated. The overall score (expressed as a percentage of the total points available) provides an idea of how well risks are being managed on the program.

Produce Risk Register or Log

This is one of the key deliverables produced and maintained in the Risk Management Process. This will be discussed further in the sections below with a review of the key information that should be captured and maintained in this important artifact. Figure 12.5 shows a snapshot of a register showing key risks as they ae being identified. Other important details, such as mitigation strategies and ownership will be added to this table as further investigation uncovers more information.

As part of the Health Check assessment, a review of the risk log needs to look for the identification of risks uncovered in the interview processes. It is not uncommon for team members to understand the risks, but these are not recorded or processed in anyway or shared with the management team. A mismatch should be identified on the final health check report.

Validate Mitigation Recommendations

Once risks are identified and understood, mitigation strategies should be developed for each, based on priority, and communicated to the project team. Senior leadership approvals for the strategies should be recorded for audit purposes. It's vital that the mitigation strategies be followed to offset the occurrence of the identified set

Success Criteria	Answer y or n	Score
1. User Involvement		
Do we have the right users?	y	3.8
Did we involve the users early and often?	y	3.8
Do we have a quality user relationship?	y	3.8
Do we make involvement easy?	y	3.8
Did we find out what the users need?	y	3.8
2. Executive Management Support		
Do we have the key executives?	y	3.2
Do the key executives have a stake in the outcome?	y	3.2
Is failure acceptable?	y	3.2
Do we have a well defined plan?	n	0
Does the project team have a stake?	y	3.2
3. Clear Statement of Requirements		
Do we have a concise vision?	y	3
Do we have a functional analysis?	y	3
Do we have a risk assessment?	y	3
Do we have a business case?	y	3
Can we measure the project?	y	3
4. Proper Planning		
Do we have a problem statement?	y	2.2
Do we have a solution statement?	y	2.2
Do we have the right people?	y	2.2
Do we have a firm specification?	y	2.2
Do we have attainable milestones?	y	2.2
5. Realistic Expectations		
Do we have clear specifications?	n	0
Do we have prioritization of needs?	y	2
Do we have small milestones?	y	2
Can we manage change?	y	2
Can we prototype?	y	2
6. Smaller Project Milestones		
Are we using the 80/20 rule?	n	0
Are we using top-down design?	y	1.8
Are we setting time limits?	y	1.8
Are we using a prototyping tool?	y	1.8
Can we measure progress?	y	1.8
7. Competent Staff		
Do we know the skills required?	y	1.6
Do we have the right people?	n	0
Do we have a training program?	n	0
Do we have incentives?	n	0
Will the staff see it through?	y	1.6
8. Ownership		
Do we have defined roles?	y	1.2
Do we have a defined organization?	y	1.2
Does everyone know their role?	y	1.2
Are incentives attached to success?	n	0
Is everyone committed?	y	1.2
9. Clear Vision & Objectives		
Is the vision shared?	y	0.6
Is the vision aligned with company goals?	y	0.6
Are the objectives achievable?	y	0.6
Are the objectives measurable?	y	0.6
Do we have honest sanity checks?	y	0.6
10. Hard-Working, Focused Staff		
Are there incentives?	n	0
Are we concentrating on quantifiable deliverables?	y	0.6
Does each member have part ownership?	n	0
Does everyone work together?	y	0.6
Are we building confidence?	y	0.6
TOTAL (100 max)		**85.8**

Figure 12.4 Sample questionnaire topics and weighting criteria.

Significant Risks as identified in Q1 20xx

The following are the major current risks for the project. Major risks are those where the probability of occurrence is High and the severity of impact to project is High if the risk materializes.

Risk #	Risk Event	Risk Response Strategy & Timing
1	**Growing customer involvement**	With several customers signaling a strong interest in being involved in the functional specification process (and other parts of the lifecycle), there will be an impact to the project schedule if these requests are accommodated. Need to agree on the level of involvement (low, medium, and high) and when to reflect it in our project plan. **This** risk is becoming more prominent. Customer requests have required support from different members of the team. Additional requests are also being made and will continue to be accommodated to maintain high customer and prospective customer satisfaction.
2	Claims entry productivity	Claims entry from paper receipts demands a high-speed, keyboard-only interface. Design priorities (e.g. security) will compete with system response time. Need to agree on the acceptable response times. Need to price out solutions that offer increasing response time. Also, will search the market for companies that have demonstrated this capability as a r eference point.
3	Scope Control	Functional Specifications are not complete, so some of the development estimates may be affected by details identified in the Business Workshops. Will need strong change management and scope control, but some flexibility in scope may be required if functions turn out to be more complex than initially thought. Want to freeze scope by May 1.
4	Converting customers	Effort to convert a customer can vary and needs more details. The cost and complexity will need to be managed and is being reviewed. Sample customers must be identified and brought into the process (no later than Dec). Overly complex processes will need to be segmented.
5	**Resource availability**	There are two aspects to this risk. The first is the availability of resources (Users and IS) when they are needed, dedicated to THB, and not competing with other projects in the organization. Mitigation of this is a management responsibility to make and keep these commitments. The second risk is the retention of resources in the same role for an extended period of time. This will be mitigated by ongoing personal reviews and checkpoints. Key resources will also share knowledge with other team resources. **We have experienced several instances –working on backfilling positions.**

Figure 12.5 Building the risk register.

of risks. As part of the assessment, evidence that this is happening is reviewed and assessed for consistency. The health check should look for consistency and completeness in this information. They should also look for evidence that mitigation strategies, as documented, were applied in the project or that there is a plan to do so in the future.

Publish and Maintain Risk Register

Too many initiatives take the time to produce a risk register, perhaps as part of a Project Charter to get funding, however, there is insufficient effort to maintain and use the information that was captured. The Risk Register should be published on a shareable media (e.g. JIRA, Confluence, Sharepoint). It should be maintained with regular reviews and updated with new information. It is a good idea to list and review risks as part of a project or program status report and meeting. The Project Manager needs to ensure that mitigation strategies are being followed. All relevant risks cannot be identified upfront. They evolve over time and are driven by circumstances that can arise during the length of the project cycle.

Getting Detailed with Risk Registers or Logs

As stated previously, an absence of a risk log is a huge red flag in itself and would be reported as a key finding by the assessment team. However, when the log exists, additional degrees of assessment must be done. Some questions to consider are as follows:

1. Does the Risk Register have sufficient information to be meaningful to the initiative?
2. Are all the known risks captured?
3. Are all the risks captured in one place?
4. Is there sufficient detail for each risk to be actionable?
5. Who's maintaining the information in the register and updating it as needed?

There may be a distributed risk log in terms of risk items tucked away in emails, status reports, requirements documents, and other repositories. If you're checking the health of a project, you will need to get access to all of these. An assessment finding here would be to have all the risk items collected into one spot—to serve as the single source of truth.

The end goal of a risk assessment process is to build and maintain a living risk log that identifies key actionable attributes of interest to the organization. The columns should be customized project to project. Figure 12.7 provides a fairly standard starting point for areas to examine for risks. Each risk is recorded as a row of information

Risk #	Risk Name	Risk Description	Priority	Occurrence Likelihood	Impact	Responsibility	Date	Mitigation Approach

Legend:

Priority:	Occurrence Likelihood	Impact
Critical (C)	Imminent (I)	Catastrophic (C)
High (H)	High (H)	High (H)
Medium (M)	Medium (M)	Medium (M)
Low (L)	Low (L)	Low (L)

Figure 12.6 Example of a risk register and mitigation strategy.

and columns can be adjusted according to the communication and audit needs of the project. In the example given, the columns are used as follows (Figure 12.6):

- Risk#: A unique identifier for each risk. The value can simply be a numeric counter, or an alphanumeric code that further classifies each risk (e.g. InfraXXX would be risk associated with Infrastructure).
- Risk Name: A short name for the risk (e.g. Organizational Risk)
- Risk Description: A detailed description of the risk that is identified.
- Priority: One-word description of the importance of a risk (e.g. regulatory approval not received).
- Occurrence Likelihood: One-word description of how likely the risk is to occur.
- Impact: In conjunction with the Occurrence Likelihood, the impact field is used to prioritize how the risks are mitigated. A 'high' likelihood with 'Catastrophic' impact must have mitigation immediately. These are the types of risks that would cause the project to fail massively. An example could be 'running out of funding' which would cause everything to come to a halt.
- Responsibility: The name or ID of the individual that is responsible for mitigating this risk. It is usually better to identify the main person responsible. Others can be listed, but perhaps not bolded or displayed in the same way.
- Date: The date by which a mitigation strategy is required and executed. The date field can be used for other purposes as well (e.g. the date that the risk was recorded).
- Mitigation Approach: A detailed description of how the risk is being mitigated. This should include dates and measurement criteria. The field can also be updated with execution details and any obstacles that are being encountered.

The legend can be modified to the organization's culture. In essence, the fields of "Priority, Occurrence Likelihood, and Impact" can be described using three (3) or four (4) items each to represent difficult levels of intensity. Any further breakdown usually begins to lose meaning. For example, what would be done differently between assigning a 7 or 8 (e.g. Important or really important) to a risk? The headings can also be renamed. For example, some practitioners prefer to use "Severity" instead of "Impact".

Most non-trivial business/IT projects will be audited after going live. A complete Risk Register in one place is one of the mandatory business artifacts the auditors will review to ensure that risks were understood and mitigated on the project.

Categorizing Risk Dimensions

Fortunately, the IT industry has enough experience to identify most categories of risk with extensive knowledge of the risks in each category. The project assessment should look for completeness in each risk category and each risk description. A list of risk categories is shown in Figure 12.7 and discussed further in this section.

Executive Leadership Risk

The assessment team must determine if the Executive Team is appropriately involved in the initiative. They must be engaged in Steering Committee Meetings, available to make decisions, remove obstacles, and provide adequate resources on an as needed basis. The Executive Team must demonstrate that they are supportive of the initiative. If they are not available for an interview in the project assessment activities, then it's difficult not to conclude that this is a grave concern to the health of the project. Some key questions to consider are:

- Who is the Project or Program Business Sponsor?
- Who is the IT Sponsor?

Figure 12.7 Common risk areas.

- Who are the executive Stakeholders?
- Are there scheduled regular Steering Committee meetings?
- Are there scheduled regular Operating Committee meetings?
- What is the involvement of the Chief Risk Officer?
- Are the escalation procedures documented?
- Are the stakeholders responsible for the identified business outcomes?
- Is success of the program demonstrably important to the stakeholders and sponsors?

Business Value Risk

The purpose of every project is to drive business value. Unfortunately, this is not commonly done that well on many projects or it is not given the priority it deserves. As part of the assessment, the team should review the Project Charter and other documents and ensure there is evidence that business value is identified and tracked. Some key questions to consider are the following:

- How is the project driving business value?
- How is the business value going to be identified?
- How is the business value going to be measured?
- How is the business value going to be optimized?

Governance Risk

Project and Program Governance is critical to the heath of a project. The assessment should review the deliverables being produced for the management stream including the weekly status reports, executive status reports, and any reports going to the Board of Directors. The review should also examine how decisions are being made on the program, escalation procedures to the Executive Team, and how decisions are communicated.

Business Requirements and Functional Risk

An examination of the business requirements should be done to assess the level of completeness and alignment with the scope of the initiative. The functional documents should be reviewed and assessed in terms of alignment with both the scope and the documented business requirements. Also assess the signoff process in terms of consistency of signoff and the involvement of appropriate stakeholders. Project auditors will look at the signoff trail so ensure this is part of the assessment. Some questions to ask in assessing this risk are as follows:

- How well understood are the business requirements by the stakeholders?
- Are the business requirements complete?

- What could be missing?
- Have the business requirements been signed off by the business owners?
- Does the delivery team understand the business requirements?
- What is the procedure to capture requirements that were missed?
- Are there any outstanding items that need to be resolved?

Technical Risk

This is a large area of risk to most initiatives. The assessment should examine the technology architecture in terms of proven capabilities, standardization, and scalability. There must be a plan to validate the technology perhaps through a proof of concept. The key performance success factors must be validated in the Technical Risk plan. An example that comes to mind was a program that underwent a health check about a quarter of the way through it's original timeline. One of the findings was that although a technical proof of concept (POC) was completed and signed off, a key performance measure for a pivotal transaction was not included. The requirement for the solution was to process consumer transactions in under one second from the time the data appeared at the firewall. Anything more than this would be rejected by the intermediate provider and would be a showstopper for the solution. This was a key risk and there was no evidence it was going to be resolved in time for launch. The assessment highlighted this and allowed the team to focus on a solution earlier than they originally intended.

Data Risk

System solutions are all about data and processes. They are everywhere. The assessment should examine the data management lifecycle from inception to eventual archiving or deletion. Some questions to ask include the following:

- Has the data been benchmarked? Do we know what's in it?
- How is the data being used for testing? Is it masked to protect confidentiality?
- How accurate is the data?
- Is there a data governance model?
- Are data owners identified?
- Is there a data management center of excellence?
- Is there a data conversion plan?
- Does the data conversion plan fit the project timeline?
- Is the data trusted? How do we create more trust in the data?

Resource Risk

There are many components to the resource risk. Are the roles and responsibilities well defined and documented? This must include clear definitions and expectations for each role. A RACI (responsible, accountable, consulted, and informed) matrix would be a good way to ensure the completeness of the descriptions. The project resourcing (bodies in roles) should align with the project plan. There should also be an examination of how skill sets are assessed and enhanced to align with the initiative's needs. Other risks to consider include resource retention and flight risks.

Funding Risk

A lack of funding would stop the project so in many cases this is one of the most impactful risks. The funding should be sufficient to cover the entire project and to address risks. A reasonable contingency bucket should be included in the budget. This can be anywhere from 10% to 100% of the budget with a personal sweet spot being between 20% and 30%. The exact amount is based on the specifics of the project and should be justifiable with facts.

The pattern of the budget spend tells a story. There should also be an analysis of how much budget was spent versus the functionality that was delivered for it. This shows whether the initiative is ahead or behind versus budget. Some key questions to consider include the following?

- Is there a process to solicit additional funding?
- Who approves the funding requests?
- Is the funding changed year over year?
- How do costs relate to business value?

Organizational Change Management (OCM) Risk

OCM does not always get the attention this important stream deserves. It is a key set of activities that drive business value, successful implementation, and adoption. In fact, a lack of adoption means a project delivery cannot be described as successful. A system is only as powerful as the features being used for driving business value.

Too often, this stream of work is starting too late, does not go wide enough, is not be complete enough, or remains understaffed. Here are some of the key questions to ask when assessing the health of this stream of work:

- Is there a Change Management plan?
- What is the communication plan?
- How are the business users and groups organized to receive communication?
- What is the user training plan?
- Who is producing the user training guides and what are the delivery mechanisms?
- Who is available to provide help to users? How will they be trained?
- Will there be Super Users? What are their responsibilities?
- How do new employees get up to speed?

- When will the training be provided versus the project implementation date?
- Is there a support desk for post-implementation help requests?
- How is the support desk going to be staffed and trained?
- What are the hours the support desk will be available?

Regulatory Risk

The regulatory risk varies by industry. For example, we reviewed a project in the gaming industry that had not actually gone to the regulator for approval. That approval step took eight (8) additional months to get, because the project had not been brought to them sooner. The assessment of this risk involves understanding regulations (e.g. residency requirements) and ensuring that the project will be compliant with all of them. This activity should not be left too late in the project cycle as noncompliance will result in additional costs in the best case, and project failure in more serious cases.

Process Risk

Process risk is applicable before, during, and after implementation. A review of all the processes in these time periods should be done in conjunction with the RACI diagrams that should be available as part of the Resource Risk assessment. Some critical processes to review for this assessment are as follows:

- Change Management Process
- Change Request Process
- Organizational Change Management Process
- Project Approval Process
- Organizational Process
- Business Readiness Process
- Escalation Process
- Decision-Making and Decision Sharing Process
- Signoff Process

Vendor or Supplier Risk

Vendor or Supplier risk can be outside the control of the project team once a project is started. For this reason, it is vital that a selection be done with the proper due diligence to select vendors and suppliers that have the stability and resources to be fully solvent players on the project. Once a selection is made, risks to the outside parties, which are an example of external risk, the team should capture risks associated with their ongoing needs. Before committing to longer terms for support after implementation, any lessons and issues encountered with the vendors or suppliers should be a key part of the selection criteria.

Challenges with Assessing Risk

There are inherent risks associated with the risk management process itself. By definition, these are often not detected by members of a project team. An independent project assessment, however, is a good opportunity to ensure that a thorough risk process is being followed. Some of the inherent risks are as follows:

- Project Culture does not reward identification of risks: Many people will not communicate risk for fear of reprisals. This often means that risks are not being communicated to management.
- Lack of formal signoffs: Too many times, there is reluctance to physically or digitally sign anything. A signoff process removes ambiguity and builds support and momentum.
- Design Decisions: Teams sometimes want to design the absolute best widget, when a solution 30% as rich would do. Ensure that the design assumptions along with the Project Charter and business requirements are documented and signed off. Identify a design that is being too over engineered and hence costly.
- Lack of Dedicated Resources: Even though an organization chart may look complete and well-staffed, a deeper look is required to ensure that the resources are actually dedicated and involved in the project. There should be evidence that most of the team is spending full-time hours on the initiative. It's a big red flag if the team is staffed with part-time dedicated resources who also have a lot of other responsibilities.
- Alignment with Standards: The processes, data, and technology should align with corporate standards or be driving a set of standards on their own. As part of the assessment, review the selection criteria used to make decisions and the reasons given. There should be a direct map to corporate standards.
- Insufficient Number of Key Performance Indicators (KPIs): This concept has been mentioned many times in the book. It is that important. Every initiative should have a handful (e.g. 6–12) of key performance indicators that must be met before the system can go live. Too few or too many KPIs are equally a problem. Only select those that must be met on a mandatory basis. It's the same for Critical Success Factors (CSFs).
- Critical Path: Look for a critical path on the project schedule. Everything being equal is a red flag and a risk that should be included on the assessment report.

Closing Perspective

In this chapter, we focused on understanding the risk management process that must exist on most initiatives, regardless of the implementation methodology that is used. An absence of one would be a key finding of the assessment and a huge red warning flag for management to understand. Where the process hopefully exists, the assessment examines the breadth, depth, and detail of the risks that are identified and how they are being mitigated. The assessment also examines evidence that the risk process is actually being followed and documentation is being updated as new information becomes available.

WORKING WITH THE ASSESSMENT RESULTS

Chapter 13

Interpreting the Discovery Results, Interview Answers, and the Warning Flags

The previous sections in this book described a detailed Health Check assessment methodology which included assessment deliverables, assessment artifacts, discovery activities, questionnaire-based user interviews, and documentation reviews. Undoubtedly, most health check teams will begin their analysis during the discovery activities, and even modify their discovery activities depending on what they are learning (e.g. a project's planned implementation date is threatened by a new regulatory requirement that was not known when the project requirements were signed off). Some observations might be so compelling that there may need to be immediate feedback to the Steering Committee (e.g. a key member of the team is about to leave the organization taking a lot of knowledge with them, or that the disaster recovery implementation is not working) and can be shared in the activity: "Initial review with Key Stakeholders" which is a summary of high-level thoughts, direction, and thoughts on urgency.

As shown in Figure 13.1, the assessment team starts to formally assess the information that has been gathered thus far in the initiative. Questions that remain unanswered can still be pursued or they can become an important part of the final

DOI: 10.1201/9781003269786-16

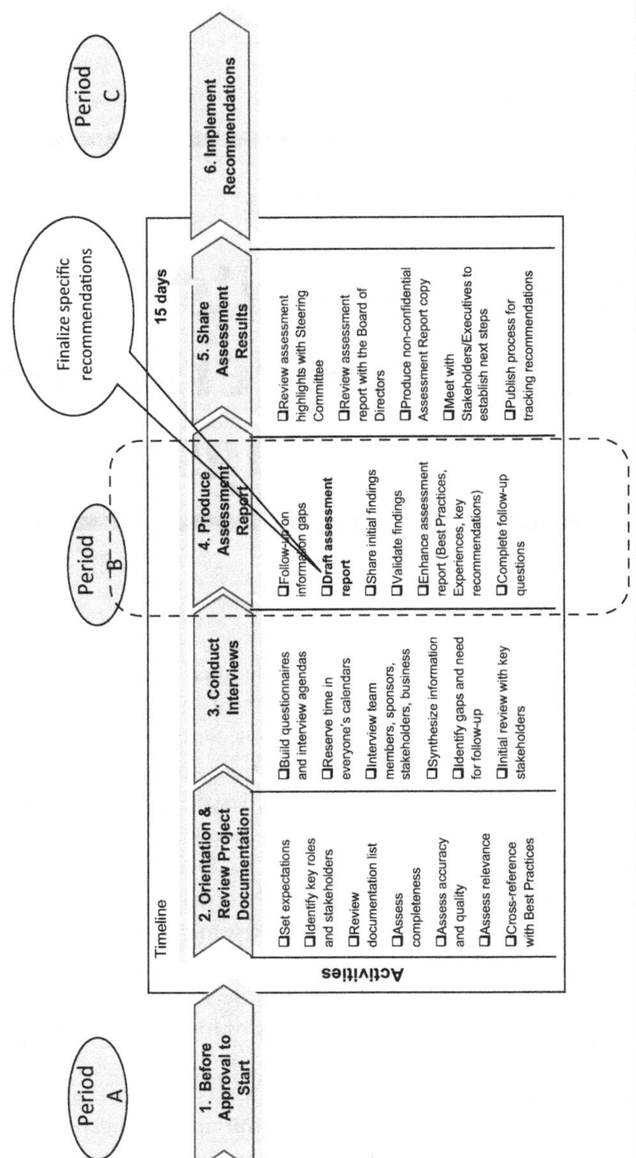

Figure 13.1 Analysis activities.

presentation with recommendations wrapped around them. The key activities in this phase are as follows:

- Follow-up on information gaps: Process the open question log through follow-on interviews, calls, and the review of additional documentation.
- Draft assessment report: Start to build sections of the Health Check Assessment Report using the observations and evolving conclusions.
- Share initial findings: Begin to review findings with stakeholders to get and incorporate their feedback without changing the tone of the health check findings.
- Validate findings: Confirm your findings and conclusions with key stakeholders, best practices, and past experiences.
- Enhance assessment report (Best Practices, Experiences, key recommendations): Add to the report using best practices and past experiences to flesh out justifications.
- Complete follow-up questions: Book final calls to resolve or confirm any outstanding questions on materials, tone, and intent.

By this point in the health check lifecycle, the assessment team will have revised multiple sources of information and produced several documents of collated notes, minutes, and summaries, as shown in Figure 13.2. These are now used to begin building out the draft report on an iterative basis. It is important for the health check team to confirm findings before making them final. This process is shown in Figure 13.3.

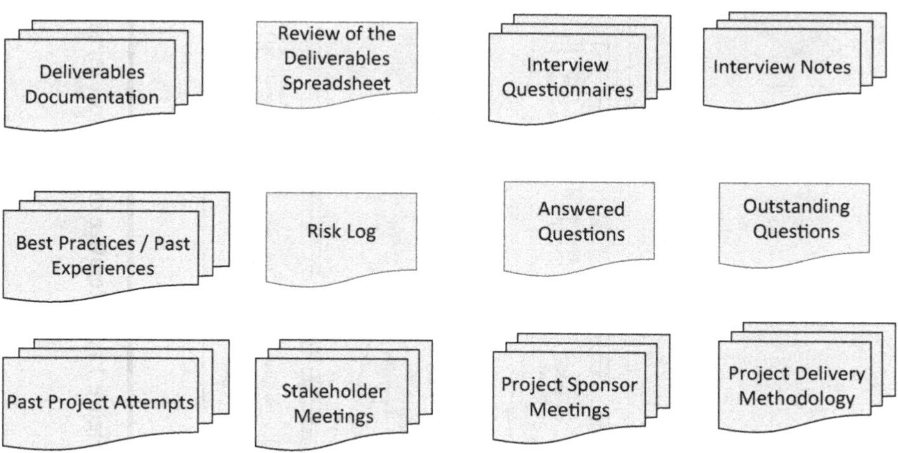

Figure 13.2 Collected information to analyze.

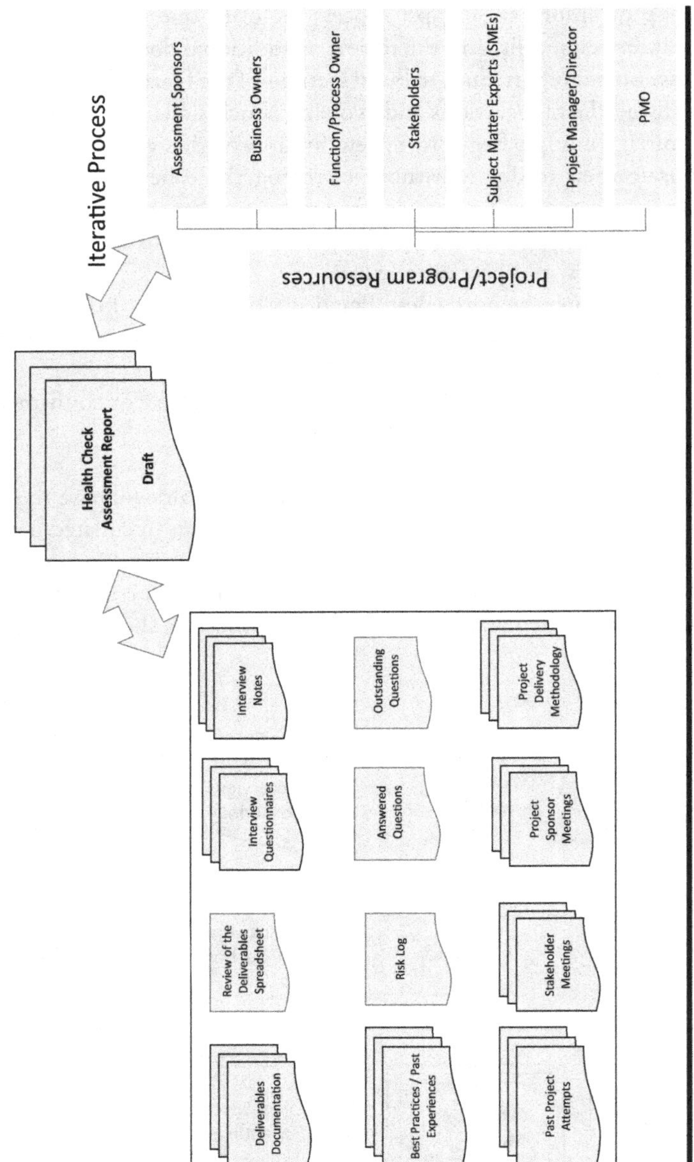

Figure 13.3 Iterative draft report revisions.

Positioning the work as 'draft' and bringing it to some key stakeholders for review and comment on an informal basis will accomplish several goals as follows:

- Confirm your understanding of the facts.
- Not set this up as a report card that is presented with no input at the end of the process.
- Begin to socialize your messages as you are not looking to surprise or jolt the organization with your findings, but rather to persuade and gain agreement to implement recommendations that will help the organization.
- Give stakeholders an opportunity to provide input that can or cannot be incorporated into the report at the discretion of the health check team. For example, some suggestions might enable a recommendation to be implemented from a political perspective if presented with certain prerequisites. Stakeholders could also recommend additional resources to meet with at this stage to also get their input on a report that is still in draft form and underway.

The States of the Health Check Assessment Report

Recall that the Health Check Assessment Report has several states as shown in Figure 13.4. The buildup and processes surrounding each of these states is important to the final acceptance of the health check assessment report. Following these states allows the process to be perceived to be inclusive, fair, and transparent and

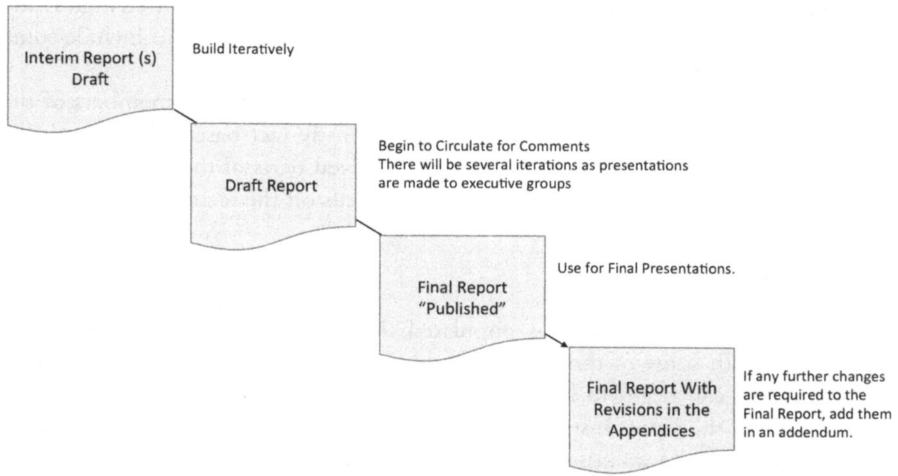

Figure 13.4 Health check assessment report.

increases the likelihood of gaining support for the recommendations. These report states are as follows:

Interim (Draft) Report

This is a work in progress, with some sections of the report filled in, others empty. The team should start with a skeleton report with a table of contents and fill in sections, perhaps divvying them up between core health team members to complete using a collaborative tool (e.g. Sharepoint). These sections can be walked through with project stakeholders to get their early feedback. The report is clearly labeled as Interim and Draft. These tags save the health check team from the unpleasant situation where pages of the report are circulated, without context, and project team members begin to think the report is final too soon.

On one specific health check, an interim report was reviewed with the two senior project managers on a large project initiative. Within a few minutes, the conversation turned into an argument over the tone of the report. No facts were being questioned, but the senior managers argued that many good things were happening on the project, while the report only identified weaknesses. Their caution was that Senior Management would shut the project down based on the tone of the report, and asked whether this was the conclusion health check team was recommending? The answer was 'no'. While there were certainly issues on the program, the health check was not recommending that the program be canceled. The health check reviewers wanted to assure the executive management team that specific recommendations would allow the program to succeed and be implemented successfully. This information from the project managers, while helping them personally, was also important for the rest of the program to succeed. Without changing any observations or recommendations, the health check team was able to include some more balance in the observations.

One of the earlier parts of the report that can be shared with members of the project team are the observations. As these are mostly fact based, they should be verified with the team so that when the other derived parts of the report are being delivered, those will not be challenged and take focus off the recommendations.

Draft Report

Once the health check team has populated the interim (draft) report and have socialized it with some of the key stakeholders, the interim label can be removed and the report can begin to be shared as a Draft Report. It is preferable to walk people through the report instead of just sending it to them. That can be done, with revisions on, after the walkthrough. There should be a number of walkthroughs to ensure that the messaging is consistent, facts are facts, and there would be no surprise when the Final Report is delivered.

Final Report

Once the report draft has been socialized to key stakeholders and resources, and their feedback incorporated where appropriate, it's time to be bold and remove the draft label from each page of the report. At this point, any recommendations or comments will now have to stand on their own. The health check team must be able to defend every recommendation or comment past this point.

A series of presentations is done in front of different groups in the organization. Figure 13.5 shows how the original project/program resources can be divided into different groups categorized by function, role, or authority. It is better to avoid doing a presentation to a very large group all at once, as this situation can lead into different tangents of conversation that would not be of no interest to many of the attendees. It's preferable to do a series of presentations to small groups first, and then to have a presentation to a larger group.

Feedback received during these sessions should be captured in minutes by the core health check team. No commitments to change anything in the report are usually made at this point.

Final Report with Revisions in the Appendices

The feedback received during the report presentations should be carefully reviewed by the health check team and either responded to directly and/or summarized and included as an appendix to the Final Report.

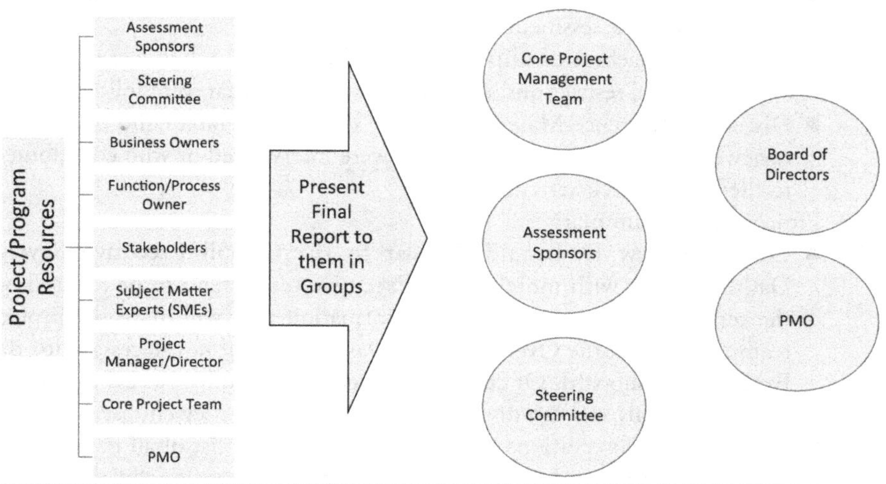

Figure 13.5 Final health check report group presentations.

Health Check Report Sections

Recall that the health check assessment report had a table of contents similar to that shown below. There are, of course, many variations to the format of this report, but the essential subsections that serve as a starting point are shown in Figure 13.6. The specific look and feel can vary dramatically with the documentation templates of each organization and can be more pictorial, more wordy, or a combination of both.

1. Executive Summary
   - Objectives: Summary of the key objectives of the project or program being assessed are included in this section.
   - Assessment Methodology: The process followed to execute on the health check assessment is described in this section.
   - Overall Executive Review Dashboard: Dashboard with the summary observations on the state of the evaluation criteria, key activities going well, key activities needing work, key warnings, key red flags, and key recommendations.
   - Action Plan for the First 30 Days: A list of activities that must be started in the 30 days after the recommendations are accepted. There can also be additional sections for 60 days, 90 days, and other frequencies appropriate to the organization.
2. Evaluation Guidelines
   - Critical Success Factors (CSFs) for Business & Shareholder Value: A list of the top CSFs that were identified during the review to make the project successful in the definition agreed to by executive management.
   - Evaluation Framework: A list of the evaluation criteria dimensions being reviewed in the assessment.
   - Review Approach: A description of how the health check was executed and any guidelines, restrictions, or special instructions that were followed.
   - Discovery Reference Material: A list of all the deliverables and documents reviewed as well as the resources that were interviewed or who contributed to the health check activities.
3. Project Review Summary
   - Overall Review Dashboard: Similar to the Overall Executive Review Dashboard but with more details. Executive teams tend to be focused on the results so there may be some information that will drive the project team included in the Overall Review Dashboard, but not necessary for the Executive Dashboard. Of course, the executive team has access to the full review materials and can dive into any of the details they choose.
   - Summary of Observations & Recommendations: A list of all the observations and recommendations categorized by the dimensions in the evaluation criteria.

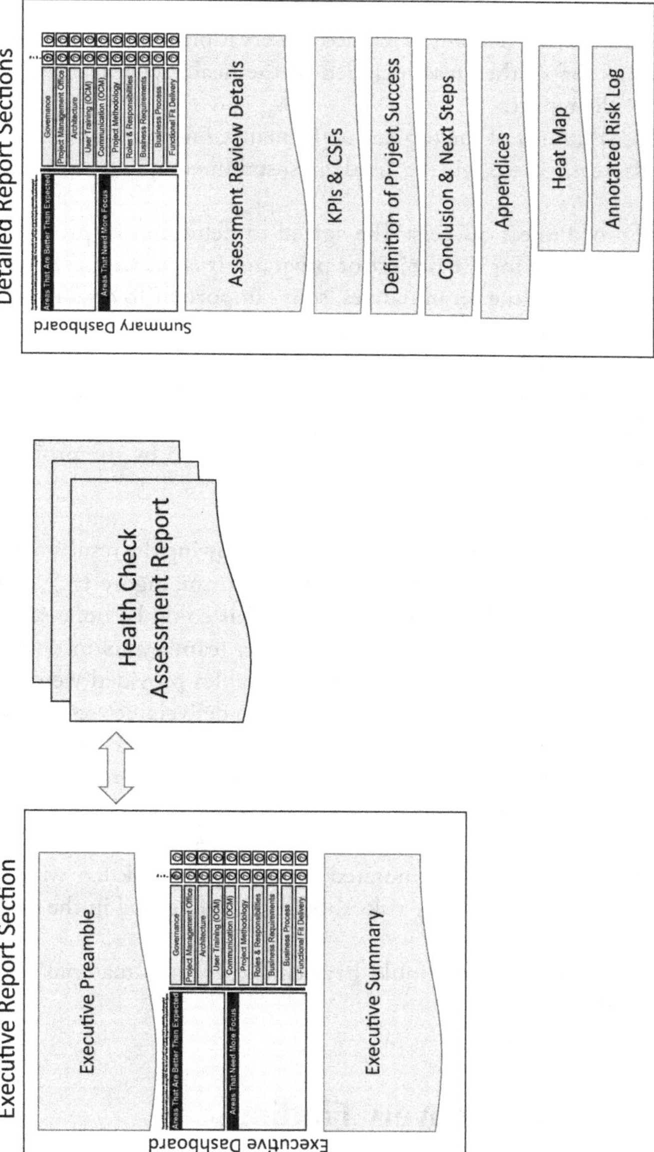
Executive Report Section
Executive Preamble
Areas That Are Better Than Expected
Areas That Need More Focus
Governance
Project Management Office
Architecture
User Training (OCM)
Communication (OCM)
Project Methodology
Roles & Responsibilities
Business Requirements
Business Process
Functional Fit Delivery
Executive Summary
Executive Dashboard
Health Check Assessment Report
Detailed Report Sections
Areas That Are Better Than Expected
Areas That Need More Focus
Governance
Project Management Office
Architecture
User Training (OCM)
Communication (OCM)
Project Methodology
Roles & Responsibilities
Business Requirements
Business Process
Functional Fit Delivery
Summary Dashboard
Assessment Review Details
KPIs & CSFs
Definition of Project Success
Conclusion & Next Steps
Appendices
Heat Map
Annotated Risk Log

Figure 13.6 Health check report table of content sections (high level).

- Summary of CSFs for Business & Shareholder Value: A more detailed summary of the CSFs that will drive business and shareholder value in the initiative. Baseline information and specific numbers should be included if known.

4. Assessment Review Details: Detailed observations, comments, and recommendations for all the areas included in the health check. This is a detailed section of the report.
5. KPIs & CSFs: A list of the top key performance indicators and the key critical success factors. These will be used in sustainment phase to track business benefits.
6. Definition of Project Success: The agreed to definition of project success by the executive team for the project or program. It is sometimes surprising how this changes over time on initiatives, so it's important to document and share it among all the stakeholders to remove any doubts and to ensure everyone is on the same baseline.
7. Conclusion & Next Steps: Action-oriented conclusion and key messages coming out of the health check assessment. A list of activities to execute next, some even while the rest of the report is being evaluated by the project executive team.
8. Appendices
   - Heat Map: a heat map for the deliverables showing the results of the detailed review of each document by the assessment team. Figure 13.7 shows that all the sustainment deliverables are at risk. This could be because details have not been included yet and the assessment team wants to ensure that the project team understands that the deliverables provided were insufficient. However, there may still be time to fix the deliverables so they are not yet red. Some projects introduce an "Orange" state that is just shy of red.
   - Additional Materials to Review: Suggestions to the project team on other documents they may want to review and which could benefit the initiative. This could include industry-wide best practices.
   - Detailed Risk Log: An annotated version of the risk log with mitigation strategies. Some of the key risks should be highlighted in the overall assessment recommendations.
   - References: References should be included for any material referenced in the report.

Interpreting the Discovery Findings

As the Health Check Assessment report is being built, the story of how the project is performing begins to unfold. Will it be implemented on time and budget? How stable is the list of functionality and business requirements? Are important functions

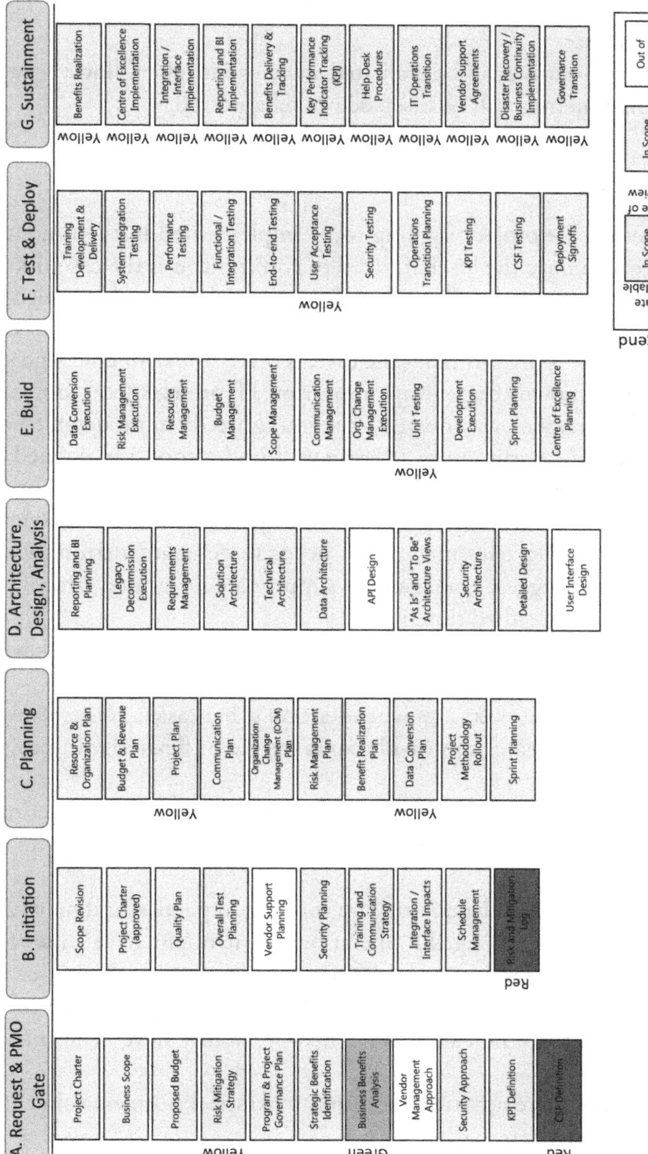

Figure 13.7 Deliverable heat map—sustainment warning.

being delayed or being positioned after the project is implemented? Is the change request log growing with no process on managing it in place? Are the KPIs as far reaching as they could be? Are there stretch goals that are still attainable? What else can be done to help the business grow value and improve ROI? What is the plan for the sustainment phase?

The state of the initiative can be evaluated starting with the following key project metrics. Additional metrics will be discussed in Chapter 16.

Timeline

Understand whether the project is going to be implemented in the timeline given. Does the project plan have the level of detail to confirm this is the case? Do the estimates make sense in terms of the team's abilities, availability and knowledge of the functional and nonfunctional business requirements? Is there a true drop-dead date when the project must be live? If that's the case, is there sufficient contingency in the plan to cover the unknowns that always appear on IT projects (e.g. someone needs time off, a key requirement was missed, something needs more detail, the performance is not sufficient)? A minimum 10% on well-understood and defined projects, 30% on projects with some uncertainty, and higher for projects with higher levels of uncertainty are places to start with timeline contingency. If there is no contingency and a drop-dead date, the assessment team needs to generate a strong warning in the final report and to suggest management support a streamlined critical path that ensures delivery in the specified timeline.

Other considerations for evaluating the project plan include the following:

- Dependencies: What tasks are dependent on other tasks? Is there any slack in their start and end dates to provide some degree of flexibility in project planning activities?
- Resources: Are the resources allocated to tasks? Are resources over allocated? Have they been freed up from other commitments so that they can focus on these tasks?
- Parallel Activities: Which activities are running in parallel and may cause contention with resources (e.g. IT operations) that might have to serve two or more groups on the project or in the organization at the same time?
- Past History: How have similar projects fared at the organization in the past? Is there any evidence that lessons learned previously have been incorporated into the plan?
- Critical Path: Is there a critical path that maximizes business value and minimizes project duration?
- Slack: Are there any activities that can be rearranged in the plan without impacting other activities?
- Estimating: What approach was used to estimate activity duration and is there evidence to support the accuracy of the approach? Was it too optimistic or too pessimistic?

Based on an evaluation of the project plan, the assessment can confirm that the project is on track, or how off track the details reveal it to be.

Budget

The budget should also be evaluated against the current project burn rate and what needs to be available to complete the project, including the contingency. The assessment team needs to examine how the budget was structured and whether it's delivering value proportionately to what is being delivered sprint to sprint or month to month. This topic will be discussed in more detail in Chapters 14 and 15.

Functionality

The assessment team should start with the original business objectives and tie these to the following deliverables to ensure that they are threaded right through the test scenarios and user training activities:

- Business Functional Requirements
- Non-Functional Requirements
- Architecture/Design
- Test Scenarios
- User Training

Quality

The assessment team needs to evaluate the quality coming out of the test plan, test scenarios, test cases, and the test results. This is the place where all the streams come together. The assessment team can base their analysis on best practices for similar projects and their defect rate as well, as well as how the defect list is being handled from test cycle to test cycle. Many projects or programs are reported as being in 'green' until the first test cycles begin to show otherwise.

Business Value

Just like the functionality, the assessment team needs to start with the KPIs and CSFs that were identified in the Business Case document and see if they are threaded through the following deliverables:

- Business Functional Requirements
- Non-Functional Requirements
- Architecture/Design
- Test Scenarios
- User Training
- Sustainment Metrics

Other Evaluation Criteria

Review of the other evaluation criteria will also be a key consideration in the final recommendation of the health check. For example, is the solution architecture scalable? For example, it may be sufficient to work for one year, but what happens after that? Will there be a project to enhance it before the year is up?

Each of the evaluation criteria dimensions should be evaluated with observations of fact (e.g. the project is using a hybrid cloud environment and implementing an ERP, CRM, and HRIS system with 24 APIs to back-end systems), ability to support the requirements (both functional and nonfunctional), ability to scale into the future to support projected growth estimates (+contingency), and cost-effectiveness. Any other impacts on ability to deliver or total cost of ownership should also be included in the assessment.

Chapter 15 examines additional evaluation criteria that should be included in the final health check assessment report.

Assembling the Health Check Report

As mentioned previously, the Interim Draft report is the place to start the assembly. A report template with the table of contents should be placed in a collaborative tool so the entire team can start to modify its contents. All the discovery materials and commentary, shown in Figure 13.2, should also be included and organized in the common drive. The dimensions contained in the Evaluation Criteria should be populated—first with observations, then with what is going well ("Going Well"), and then with areas of improvement ("Focus Needed"), as shown in Figure 13.8. After some reflection, the recommendations section can start to be populated. The circular balls can be used to highlight recommendations that would provide the most value or which are deemed to be mandatory.

Sources of Information

By this point in the Health Check assessment, there would have been many sources of information that would allow the assessment team to understand the state of the project and begin to form recommendations. The sources of information are described below:

What People Revealed

At every interaction with team resources, they would have revealed information that would lead to conclusions and ultimately recommendations. It's important to verify any information from one source with other sources, documentation, and experience, but this is an excellent source of collaboration and place to start. On one

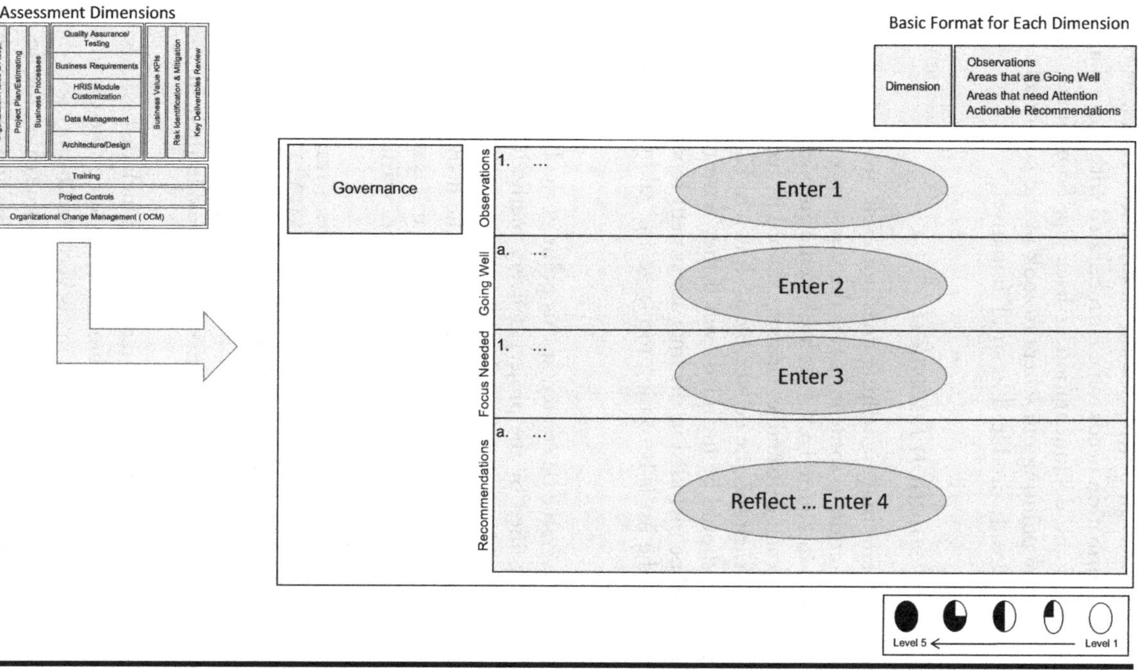

Figure 13.8 Detailed evaluation section template.

health check, one of the process specialists provided some warnings to the Health Check Manager. After a few hours, the same source back and totally reversed gears and said the opposite. In this case, the source took responsibility for the information and corrected bad advice. In other cases, the health check reviewers may not be so fortunate. All the information needs to be corroborated with more than one source, and hopefully with some documentation as back up. Sometimes, the interviews offer a great service by pointing out where to look in the potentially tens of thousands of documents already produced in an IT initiative.

What the Documentation Revealed

Auditors repeatedly state that something does not exist "unless it's written down". Deliverable documentation in some format is the surest way to understand the state of a project. As shown in Figure 13.9, here are specific questions the assessment team needs to consider for each deliverable. Answers should be recorded in a format that can be traced back to each specific deliverable as shown in Figure 13.10. Each of the deliverables in scope should be included even if they have no gaps. The collection of this review should be included in the final assessment report in the detail section or the appendices if the list is becoming too large and taking attention away from other salient points.

- Should the deliverable be created at this point in the lifecycle? This relates to the timeline specified by the project delivery methodology and the point in time the review is being conducted.
- When is it expected to be ready for review? If the deliverable is not supposed to be built at the time of the review, confirm that it is in the project plan with a delivery date. If not, issue a key consideration or warning in the health check assessment report.
- How complete and thorough is it? This requires a reading of the deliverable by a knowledgeable Subject Matter Expert (SME). Time should have been reserved when the health check team was assembled for part-time utilization of SMEs over the duration of the program. Have the relevant experienced SME(s) review the relevant documents and provide their impression of the contents.
- What are the gaps? Gaps should be recorded and included as assessment warnings or red flags. The assessment team needs to determine the impact of a gap (e.g. missing architecture components is very significant) and the impact on the project metrics or future business value. In some cases, the document may not have been updated, which generates a warning and caution that the deliverable needs to be reviewed again when it's ready.
- Should it be formally signed off? Project Management should be clear on which deliverables need to be formally signed off. If such a list does not

Inspecting Deliverables

- Should the deliverable be created at this point in the lifecycle?
- When is it expected to be ready for review?
- How complete and thorough is it?
- What are the gaps?
- Should it be formally signed off?
- Has it been signed off?
- What impacts does this have on other parts of the project?
- How can it be improved?
- What are final recommendations for the deliverable?

Update this deliverable list using the specific Project Delivery Methodology being used on the initiative.

Pre-Analysis Case
❑Current Situation
❑Solution Outcome
❑Business Benefit
❑Initiative Risk
❑Resource Expectations
❑Reference Architecture
Business Case
❑Scope & Objectives
❑Costs, Benefits, Risks
❑Resourcing
❑Milestone Dates
❑Options
Executive Review
❑Decision & Executive Signoffs
Project Charter Outline
❑Conceptual Design
❑Project Plan (High)
❑Team Roles
❑Capital Effort
❑SG&A Effort
Executive Review
❑PMO Recommendation
❑Committee Signoff
❑Executive Signoff

Project Charter
❑ Scope and Approach
❑ Business Case (signed)
❑ Business Requirements
❑ Technical Requirements
❑ Project Plan
❑ Quality Plan
❑ Team Structure & Roles
❑ Governance Model
❑ Risk Assessment
Organizational Change Management Strategy
QA Strategy
Management Kit
Procurement Approach
Requirements
❑ Business & Technical
Blueprinting Doc
Exec Approval
QA Test Plan
❑ Test Scripts
❑ Test Organization
OCM Plan
❑ Training Plan
❑ Communication Plan
❑ Roles & Responsibilities

Architecture
Functional Specs
❑Detailed Design
❑Storyboards/Mockups
❑Information Architecture
❑Application Design
❑Application Rules
❑Security
Technical Specs
❑Programing Logic
❑Technical Architecture
❑Network/Hardware Topology
❑Database Model
Development
❑Configuration
❑Application Coding
❑Data Conversion
Unit Testing
❑Test Scripts
❑Test Results
❑Functional Specifications (Updated)

Testing Cycles Prep
❑ Test Cases/ Scenarios/ scripts
❑ Test Data Preparations
Deployment Plan
❑ Cutover plan
Training
❑ Develop Course Materials
Communication
Test Cycles Execution
❑ Functional Tests
❑ Integration Tests
❑ Regression Test
❑ Stress Volume Test
❑ User Acceptance Test (UAT)
Sign Off
❑ Go/ No Go Review
❑ Business Sign off
User Training Execution
Deployed Applications
Initial Production Support
Project Closure
❑ Post Implementation Review
❑ Lessons Learned
❑ Project Closure Signoff
❑Business Value Realization

Figure 13.9 Inspecting deliverable documentation.

exist, an overall warning should be issued under the "Deliverables Evaluation Criteria" in the summary dashboard.

- Has it been signed off? Confirm that key deliverables are formally signed off by the designees on the signoff list. An absence of formal signoffs of key deliverables is a major issue and should be flagged as a major red flag. Even if the project is seemingly running successfully, a lack of signoff means that the results can be challenged at any time. This can create lots of extra work that will directly impact the project's success. Missing signoffs are flagged by any future audits and raise major issues for the project executive team and project management.
- What impacts does this have on other parts of the project? This becomes more difficult to assess, as it requires meaningful past experience and best practices to diagnose correctly. It may be useful to have an SME to review these types of interdependent issues. The assessment team needs to also flag downstream impacts of gaps they are seeing in the documentation. For example, missing a test strategy will impact the testing cycles. A lack of a data strategy will impact how test data is assembled. A lack of a documented architecture can impact licensing costs as these may be left too late into the process to negotiate from a position of strength. The impact of this is significant to the bottom line. If negotiating from strength, it's not unusual to at least argue for discounts north of 50% – at least for periods of time. Similarly, a missing decommissioning strategy will impact the costs of operations where two systems are being supported after the project goes live.
- How can it be improved? Suggestions to improve the deliverable should be included.
- What are the final recommendations for the deliverable? A final assessment flag or comment reflecting the nature and severity of the findings for each deliverable should be included, as shown in Figure 13.10.

Past Experience

A major source of interpretation of what's being observed, of course, comes from past experience. While there is no guarantee that what happened on a past project will repeat on the current one even if there are similarities, it is an impetus to dig deeper and potentially put some guard rails in place to ensure that negative experiences do not repeat.

For this reason, the health check team needs to have some highly experienced practitioners who can connect remote dots. On one project assessment, the data conversion plan was presented to the health check reviewer. The plan had dependencies, resources, and at first glance seemed fairly complete and satisfactory. However, the health check reviewer, based on past experience picked up that the start date of the data conversion phase was too close to the implementation date (six months out) to allow any chance of remediating data problems if they were encountered.

Deliverable Documentation Review **Reviewer:** ________ **Review Date:** ________	Overall Observations:

Deliverable Name	Observations:	Recommendations/ Assessment Concerns	Deliverable Status:	Red Flags:	Assessment flag:
❑Business Case					
❑Scope & Objectives					
❑Costs, Benefits, Risks					
❑Resourcing					
❑Milestone Dates					
❑Options					
❑Executive Review					
❑Decision & Executive Signoffs					

Notes: Deliverable Status: Missing, Late, Expected Date, Not needed (with explanation)

Assessment flag Legend: Level 5 ← Level 1

Figure 13.10 Deliverable assessment.

The reviewer felt that given the size of the organization, the legacy nature of the data being converted, and the critical nature of the data that the data conversion should be started five months earlier. The recommendation was accepted and, in fact, the data cleanup took about ten months to complete. That implies the project would have been implemented at least four months late, possibly longer as deadline panic leads to other issues that further compound project delays. As shown in Figure 13.11, with a monthly burn rate of $2 million, a four-month overage would

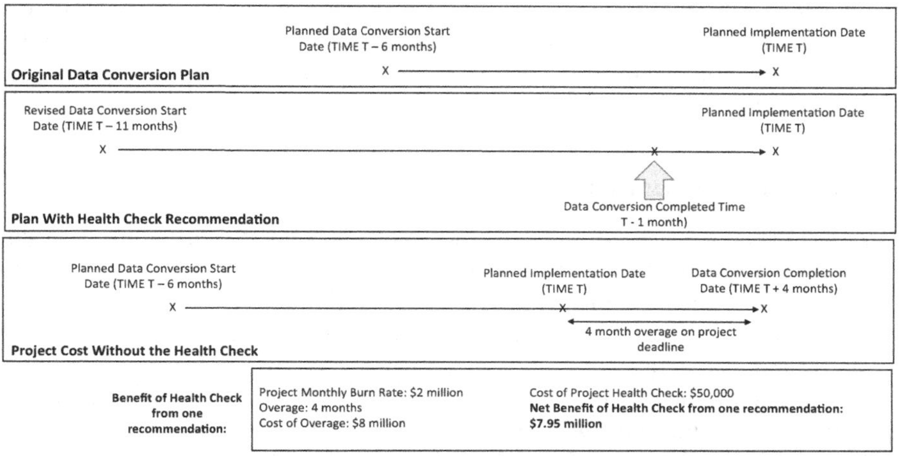

Figure 13.11 Impact of health check on project timeline and budget.

cost the organization $8 million. The cost of the health check was in the neighborhood of $50,000 for an assessment lasting a few weeks. That is a staggering benefit to the project of $7,950,000 from one recommendation alone.

Best Practices

The conclusion and recommendations should be compared to industry best practices as another sanity check. Examine how long other projects take to complete that have similar features. What were their budgets? What were their lessons learned? This information should be factored into the health check evaluation.

Detailed Entries

Entries in "Focus Needed" are often paired directly with an entry in "Recommendations", though one recommendation can sometimes cover more than one observation. These can also be tagged as the most important or mandatory, as shown in Figure 13.12. Looking at that figure, reviewers will often just zero in on the larger number of "Focus Needed" items which exceed the items in the "Going Well" section. This sends an immediate message that there are a lot of issues in the QA dimension, which in reality there were. Immediate changes needed to be made, otherwise there would be a significant impact on the project metrics.

This risk of not doing something can also be included in the analysis as shown in Figure 13.13. Including this information at this level can be overwhelming depending on the size of the report, so in some cases it's preferred to save only top risks for the summary dashboard and applying those to the key recommendations.

There are a lot of diverse formats that could be used for sharing this information and the format selected should be consistent with the message that the Assessment Sponsors set in terms of tone. For example, separating the areas that are going well from those that need improvement can show a lot of weakness at a glance. Will this get the best buy-in for the recommendations or result in the report being sidelined? This should be a conscious decision on part of the assessment team.

Summary Dashboard

There will be at least one set of observation tables for each dimension in the evaluation criteria matrix. The top most recommendations or observations can be summarized in a dashboard similar to that shown in Figure 13.14.

The summary of observations dashboard can be augmented with a rating scale to create a simplified dashboard in the interim report, as shown in Figure 13.15. With this information, the Interim report can begin to be socialized with members of the project team to validate the observations and other information.

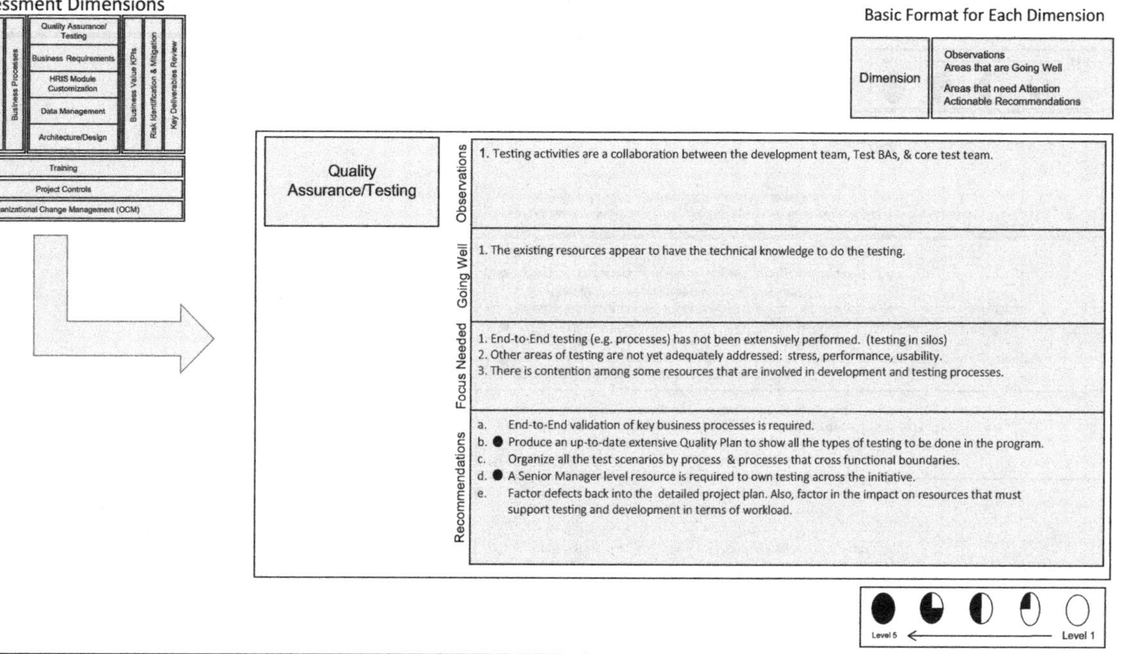

Figure 13.12 Annotated detailed section for one dimension (partial).

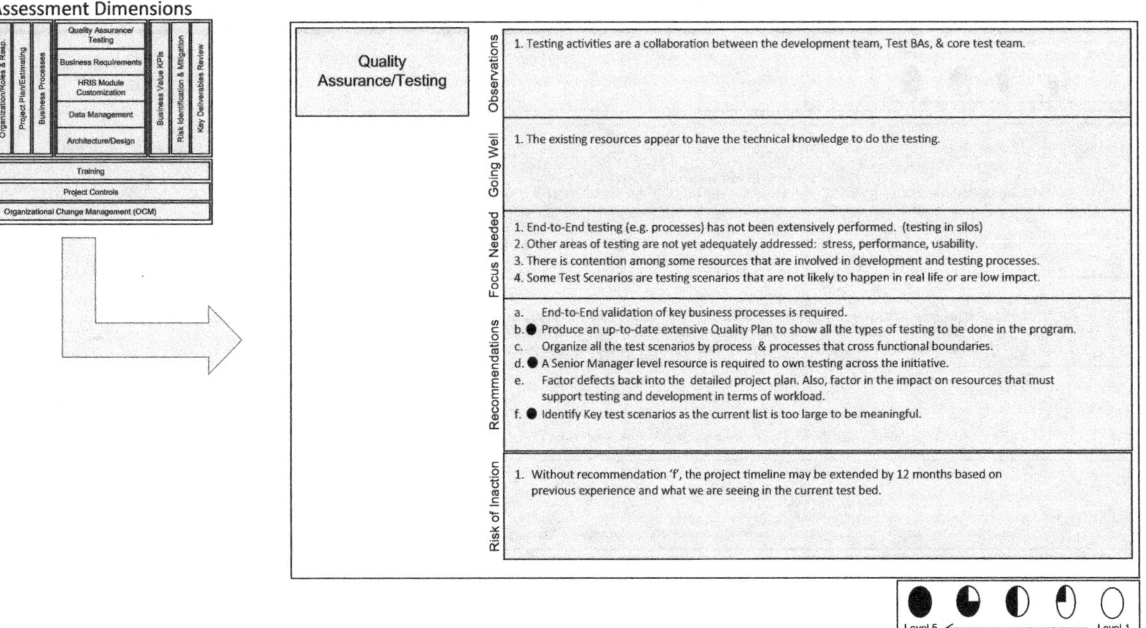

Figure 13.13 Including risk of inaction in the evaluation criteria.

The set of dimensions shown here are inter-related elements of a well run program that is sustainable, well accepted organizationally and which provides a strong probability on time, on budget, high quality delivery. The 'As Is' maturity level is shown for each dimension.

Dimension	Observation
Governance	Governance is shared between three different vendors, with no clear idea of who is leading. There is no single point of accountability, responsibility & authority.
Risk Identification & Mitigation	Significant risks remain on the project. Eg, delivery of the base system to meet the Pilots is a key risk as user stories were still being finalized in Jan/Feb and not signed off by all the member organizations. There are many such risks given the fixed delivery date of Sept 30 20xx.
Architecture/Design	The architecture is changing and relies on interfaces that are being developed. Order entry was built and tested in an earlier cloud environment.
User Training (OCM)	User training materials rely on functionality & configuration that is not yet built and 'To Be' business processes that are still being defined. Training has to be rolled out to 42 locations + their peripheral locations.
Organizational Change Management (OCM)	The Organization design has started in Dec/Jan by all accounts, but is not yet supported by agreed to 'To Be' processes. Once done, these will need to be accepted at the association level and then rolled out.
PMO & Methodology	The development team is using an agile methodology. The client is expecting a turnkey solution, with proven tasks and activities. Such a plan was not available in early Dec 20xx & requires months of effort to drive out. **There is no critical path defined.**
Project Plan/Estimating	There was no end-to-end project plan. The new version is relying on updates from an iterative process, which, by definition, contradicts the expectation of a waterfall implementation approach. There is no reasonable contingency in the estimates.
Business Requirements	Business requirements were still being signed off in January. In some cases, the user stories (590+) were being defined for the first time. These will need to be localized for the different associations.
Business Process	The 'To Be' business process has not been designed yet. The objective appears to be to drive it out as the sprints are done. This leaves little time for user training, refinement, or testing. The "As Is" version has not been signed off the business.

Figure 13.14 Summary of observations.

Possible Recommendations from the Review

Based on the evaluation criteria, the health check review can reach several conclusions. This will be impacted somewhat by the cadence of the health check. For example, if the health check is recurring, the recommendations will have a month-to-month orientation, while if the health check is a one-time request, the recommendations have to cover a longer period of time.

Here are some of the states the project or program can be in and how to respond appropriately. For each of the responses below, the organization needs to also focus on implementing the recommendations for the previous state.

The Project Is on Track

Based on the health check evaluation, no major risks were identified. The health check team should focus on the business benefits, inserting guard rails, and removing costs from the development where possible.

Some Metrics Are at Risk

Based on the health check evaluation, some metrics, e.g. functionality, are at risk. The health check team needs to focus on the adjustments needed to bring those items back to green or at least yellow. As shown in Figure 13.16, the assessment team can assemble a matrix that examines different options for getting the project back

● ◕ ◑ ◔ ○

Level 5 ← Level 1

The set of dimensions shown here are inter-related elements of a well run program that is sustainable, well accepted organizationally and which provides a strong probability on time, on budget, high quality delivery. The 'As Is' maturity level is shown for each dimension.

Dimension	Description	Maturity Level
Governance	Governance is shared between three different vendors, with no clear idea of who is leading. There is no single point of accountability, responsibility & authority.	◔
Risk Identification & Mitigation	Significant risks remain on the project. Eg, delivery of the base system to meet the Pilots is a key risk as user stories were still being finalized in Jan/Feb and not signed off by all the member organizations. There are many such risks given the fixed delivery date of Sept 30 20xx.	○
Architecture/Design	The architecture is changing and relies on interfaces that are being developed. Order entry was built and tested in an earlier cloud environment.	◔
User Training (OCM)	User training materials rely on functionality & configuration that is not yet built and 'To Be' business processes that are still being defined. Training has to be rolled out to 42 locations + their peripheral locations.	◔
Organizational Change Management (OCM)	The Organization design has started in Dec/Jan by all accounts, but is not yet supported by agreed to 'To Be' processes. Once done, these will need to be accepted at the association level and then rolled out.	○
PMO & Methodology	The development team is using an agile methodology. The client is expecting a turnkey solution, with proven tasks and activities. Such a plan was not available in early Dec 20xx & requires months of effort to drive out. **There is no critical path defined.**	◔
Project Plan/Estimating	There was no end-to-end project plan. The new version is relying on updates from an iterative process, which, by definition, contradicts the expectation of a waterfall implementation approach. There is no reasonable contingency in the estimates.	○
Business Requirements	Business requirements were still being signed off in January. In some cases, the user stories (590+) were being defined for the first time. These will need to be localized for the different associations.	◔
Business Process	The 'To Be' business process has not been designed yet. The objective appears to be to drive it out as the sprints are done. This leaves little time for user training, refinement, or testing. The "As Is" version has not been signed off the business.	○

Figure 13.15 Summary dashboard (draft).

Getting to Green: Options for Consideration

Decision Considerations	Option 1: Reduce Functionality	Option 2: Add Resources	Option 3: Move Go-Live Date by two months
Description			
Risks and Mitigation Strategies			
Project Cost			
Resource Impact			
Sustainability after Go-Live			
Other Considerations			
OverallRecommendations			

Figure 13.16 Getting to green.

to Green or yellow Status. A number can be assigned to each decision consideration and the top scoring option could be the appropriate recommendation to proceed.

The Project Is Going to Fail

If the health check is suggesting that a major intervention is required based on the number and type of red flags, there are several options to proceed, as shown in Figure 13.17. These include some stop-gap measures to a full-scale project rescue intervention. Chapter 14 focuses on the types of project rescue interventions that the assessment team can recommend, along with key considerations and recommendations that can be included in the summary report. Chapter 15 then brings all the recommendations together to produce the Final Health Assessment Report.

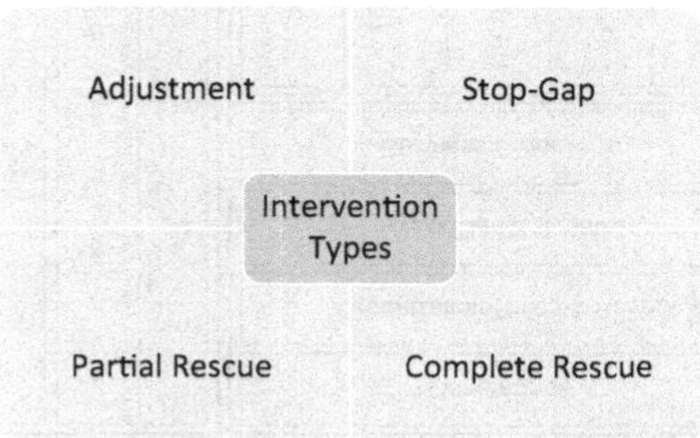

Figure 13.17 Types of project/program interventions.

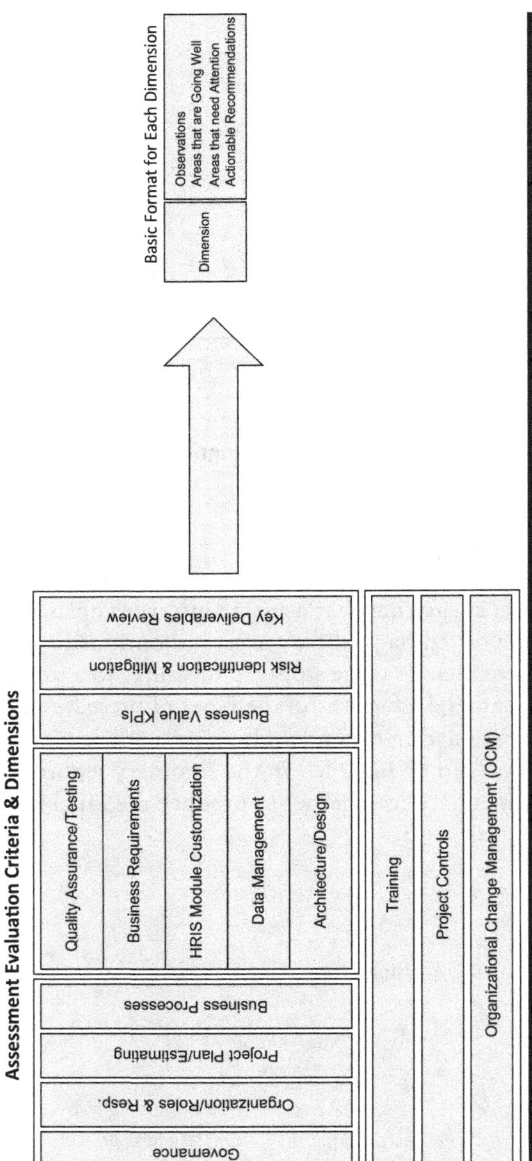

Figure 13.18 Leveraging the evaluation criteria for the detailed report.

Closing Perspective

This chapter focused on evaluating the information and feedback that was collected in the discovery activities. The chapter focused on several states that the health check assessment report can take during the course of development and socialization. This chapter described the process of building the interim (draft) report based on the evaluation criteria, as shown in Figure 13.18, and then summarizing the findings in a summary dashboard. This includes the following information:

- Observations: Fact based commentary on what the health check team saw in the trenches and which is confirmed by documentation or other sources in the program.
- Areas that are Going Well: Commentary around what is going well in the criteria being evaluated. There may be an opportunity to further optimize business value.
- Areas that Need Attention: Identification of specific areas that need attention, otherwise the project metrics will suffer or fail entirely.
- Actionable Recommendations: Often paired with items in the "Areas that Need Attention" section, actionable recommendations can be categorized with start dates (say within 30 days, 60 days) and the cost of not accepting them by the project team.

This chapter also examined what actions to start recommending at the entire project level. If the assessment demonstrated that the project was on track to deliver on the defined project metrics, the assessment team can focus on driving additional business value as will be discussed in Chapter 15. If the project needs some type of intervention to rescue it from failure, the assessment team needs to look deeper at root causes and find specific recommendations to streamline a critical path. Figure 13.19,

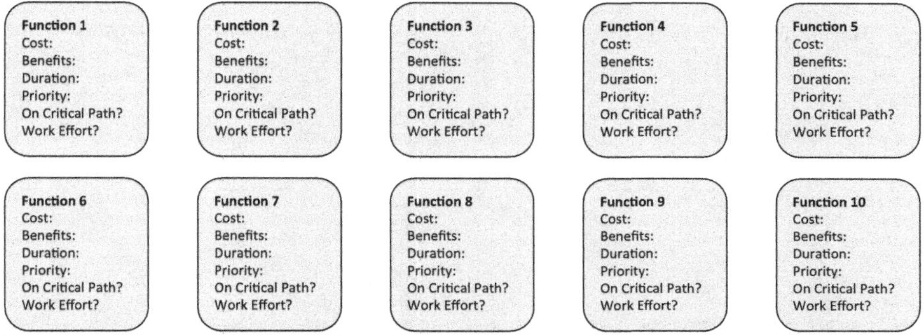

Figure 13.19 Prioritized functionality.

for example shows a deep dive into each element of functionality that was included in the scope of the project. The assessment team would work with the business owners and SMEs to define the benefit of each function to determine whether it is on the critical path or not. Chapter 14 focuses on project intervention techniques in more detail.

Chapter 14

Mounting a Project Rescue Intervention

As the previous chapters demonstrated, the information gathered in the discovery sessions can be used to construct some meaningful executive dashboards and provide detailed observations and recommendations to the project initiative being assessed. Figure 14.1 shows that the health check is getting to the end of Period B—finalizing the assessment report.

At this stage in the assessment lifecycle, the health check team should have prepared an interim draft report or be at the beginnings of building a draft report. Parts of this report should have been socialized and all the factual observations confirmed. That should be establishing that the team knows what they are talking about and they have understood the facts of the initiative.

If the summary dashboard in the interim report is showing that there are no major issues on the project, the assessment team can focus on recommendations to improve efficiency as well as drive business value. These recommendations also apply to projects that need a rescue intervention but those points will be supplanted by the immediate action items to get the project back from the disaster it's hurtling toward.

One of the key recommendations in most health checks is to change some set of parameters on the initiative to improve the budget, resourcing, or functionality, or to tighten up delivery in some way. As shown in Figure 14.2, the assessment team needs to get very specific with several types of questions as follows:

- Do we need a project intervention?
- What type of intervention is needed?
- What are the intervention activities we should execute?
- How do we know the revised approach will work?

DOI: 10.1201/9781003269786-17

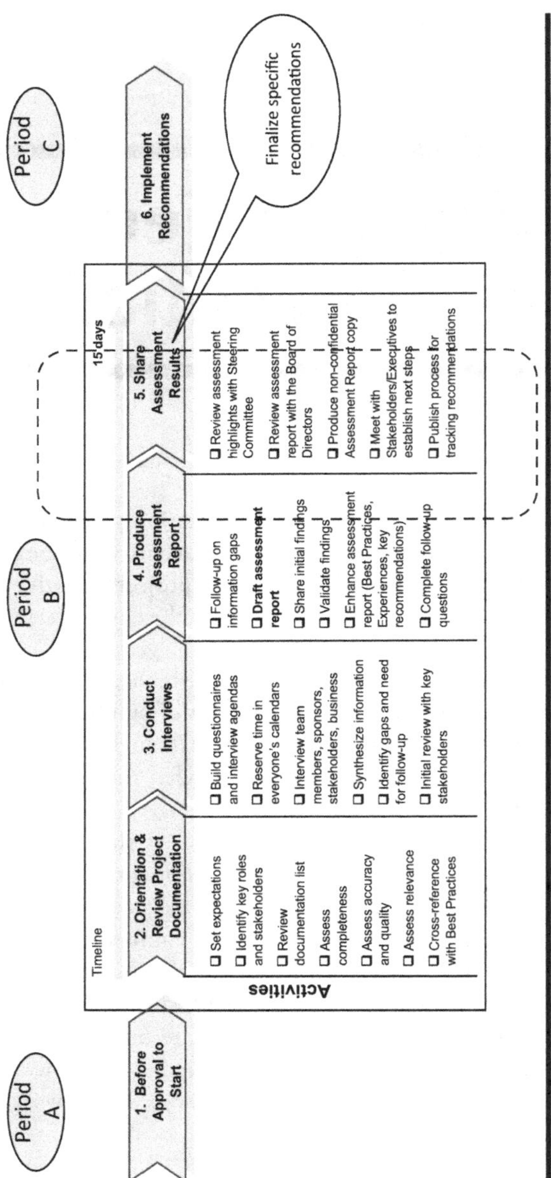

Figure 14.1 Completing the health check assessment report.

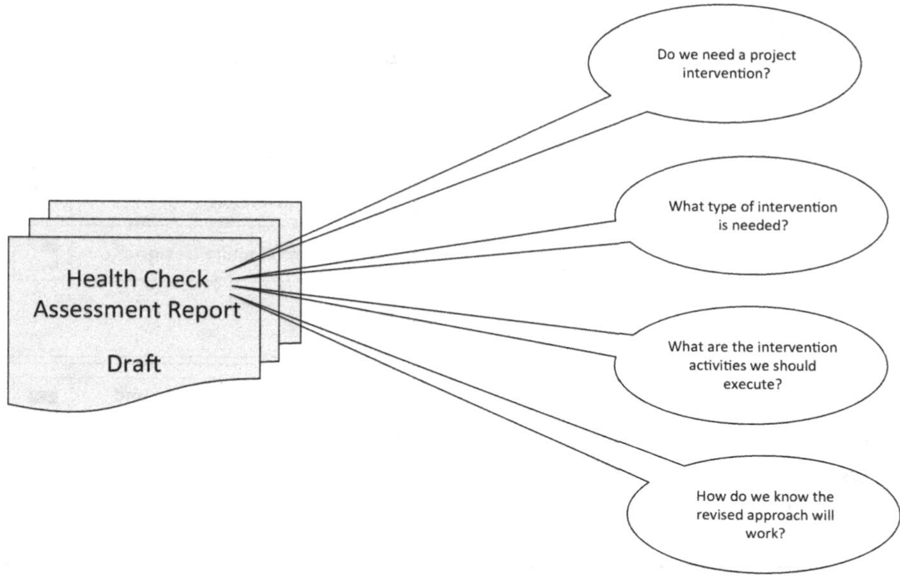

Figure 14.2 Considerations for completing the assessment report.

This chapter discusses activities associated with recovering or saving projects from failure as measured against the metrics established with the Executive Sponsors. The recommendations from the health assessment team need to be specific and based on the type of intervention required to correct the issues. This section discusses these approaches in more detail and the sections that follow describe project techniques to recover projects or programs that are in various stages of failure. These techniques should be turned into specific recommendations to be included into the Health Check Assessment Report before it is turned into a Final State.

Positioning Project/Program Interventions

Figure 14.3 shows a sample executive dashboard for a review that was done for an ERP project. Based on the results shown in the figure, there would be the need for a full intervention and project rescue. The project is about a year away from implementation, and as the figure shows, based on the legend, several evaluation dimensions are rated at 0—"wholly, wholly inadequate". Important dimensions like "Communication" and "Project Controls" do not even register with a reasonable score. Other important dimensions, such as Project Planning and Governance, among others are sitting at 25%. A good rating would be at least 75%, with maybe a few at 50%, and some at 100%. Without a significant intervention to reset this project it's going to fail pretty much on all the key project measurement metrics.

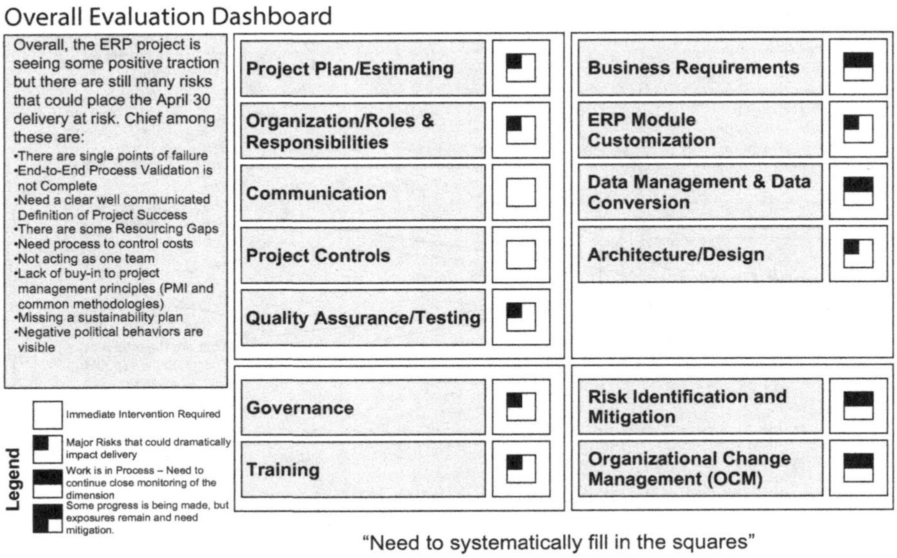

Overall Evaluation Dashboard

Overall, the ERP project is seeing some positive traction but there are still many risks that could place the April 30 delivery at risk. Chief among these are:

- There are single points of failure
- End-to-End Process Validation is not Complete
- Need a clear well communicated Definition of Project Success
- There are some Resourcing Gaps
- Need process to control costs
- Not acting as one team
- Lack of buy-in to project management principles (PMI and common methodologies)
- Missing a sustainability plan
- Negative political behaviors are visible

Project Plan/Estimating

Organization/Roles & Responsibilities

Communication

Project Controls

Quality Assurance/Testing

Business Requirements

ERP Module Customization

Data Management & Data Conversion

Architecture/Design

Governance

Training

Risk Identification and Mitigation

Organizational Change Management (OCM)

Legend

Immediate Intervention Required

Major Risks that could dramatically impact delivery

Work is in Process – Need to continue close monitoring of the dimension

Some progress is being made, but exposures remain and need mitigation.

"Need to systematically fill in the squares"

Figure 14.3 Sample health check dashboard.

But not before tens of millions of dollars will be spent, many resources fired, and a dramatic hit to the bottom line of the organization's value will occur.

Coupled with the warnings coming out of the assessment, and the upcoming implementation target date, this project needs an intervention. Having determined the need for an intervention on the project, the assessment team needs to determine the type of intervention the initiative needs, as this will drive the specific recommendations that the project team will need to follow to recover their program. Figure 14.4 shows four types of interventions that can be applied to a project or programs, as follows:

- Adjustment: This type of intervention can be performed without committing to an all-encompassing change to the basic management processes being followed on the initiative. Specific recommendations to surgically nudge the project to a better state are provided to the project management team to execute. These actions can also be designed to drive higher business value.
- Stop-Gap: This type of intervention looks for short-term actions that may not fix all the issues on the project, but serve as stop-gap measures to take the initiative to a point of success where the team can take stock of their current situation and then take actions for longer term success. It is an approach to buy some time before making all the decisions as there may not be enough information available to support those at the current time in the project.
- Partial Rescue: This diagnosis points to a more extensive change to the way a project is currently running—perhaps in project management processes,

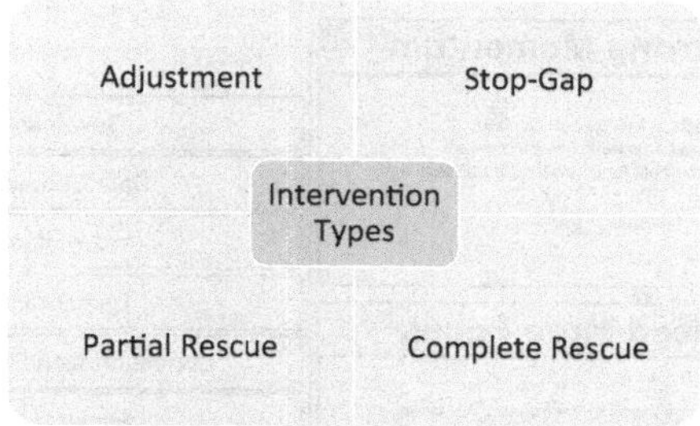

Figure 14.4 Types of project/program interventions.

training, priorities and in other ways that will approach but not quite reach a complete project reset. These are surgically focused activities that only need to reset specific streams in the project.

- Complete Rescue: This is a full and intensive reset of the project or program to rescue it from the failure that is currently in its future as discovered by the health check assessment. It's usually not a surprise to project team members that there are major issues with the program when this is announced at this point in the health check lifecycle. There are just usually too many problems with the project metrics that are openly being discussed. The discussion revolves around the nature of the reset and the specific recommendations that come out of the health check activities. The good news is that project rescue efforts have been shown to be very effective in saving projects – especially if they start early in the lifecycle.

Positioning an Initiative Adjustment Intervention

Many dashboards have been presented in this book and most have shown projects that needed medium to high levels of intervention to correct problems with the initiatives metrics. Figure 14.5 shows an example of a project where management had proactively commissioned a health check as insurance and to be another set of eyes to review and suggest anything the project could do better.

The evaluation criteria shows that the project is above 50% in each dimension that was reviewed. Many are at 100%. Yes, these types of projects do exist! Essentially, the assessment team found the situation that is described below.

Areas the Initiative Is Showing Strength

The initiative is showing strength in all the key project metrics, specifically:

- All the deliverables that were reviewed, including project charter, business requirements, status reports, solution architecture, project plan, risk log, and others were consistent, complete, and aligned to best practices.

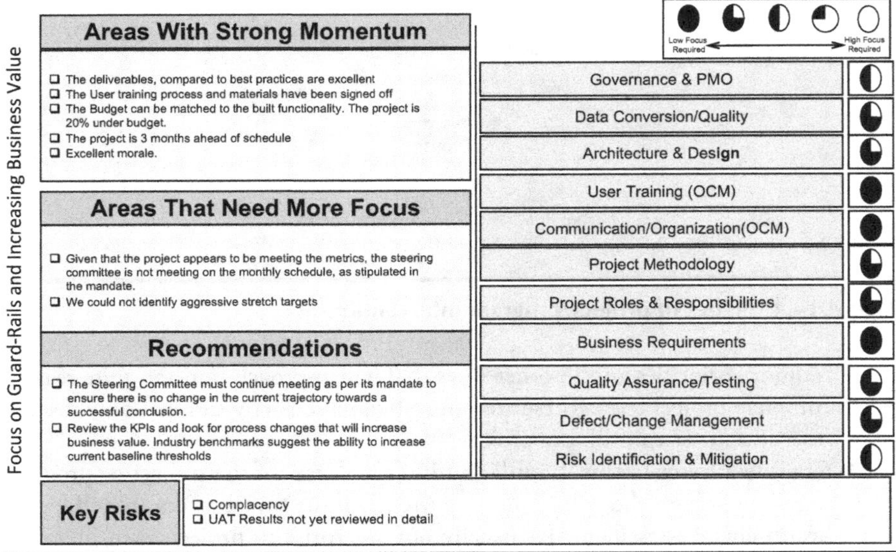

Figure 14.5 Example of a project executing well.

- The organization has completed all user training materials, scheduling, and identified user roles. The User training process and materials have been signed off by executive management across all impacted divisions.
- The budget could effectively be tracked against functionality and is well ahead of schedule. The project is 20% under budget, and there is still a 15% contingency remaining.
- The project is three months ahead of schedule and the assessment team could not identify any risks that would impact the current deadline.
- All the members of the team are showing commitment, buy-in, and excitement. Based on their personal plans, executive management has aligned the success of the initiative to individual goals. This has created excellent morale on the entire project team.

Areas for Improvement

The project health check team did not identify any significant areas of improvement. Two items to note from an assurance perspective were as follows:

- Although the project was tracking well and the assessment team did not see any significant risks, there were still eight months to the go-live date. The recommendation was for the team to remain vigilant and not become complacent. Given that the project appeared to be meeting the metrics, the steering committee was not meeting on a monthly schedule, as stipulated in its mandate.

- While the team was currently meeting KPIs, the assessment team made it clear that they did not see evidence that attempts were made to build more aggressive targets that would allow the team to massively over achieve. There is an element of playing it safe and losing an opportunity to drive more value into the business.

Recommendations

Here are some recommendations to protect the current positive trajectory of the program, as well as to drive higher business value.

- The Steering Committee must continue meeting as per its mandate to ensure there is no change in the current trajectory toward a successful conclusion.
- Review the KPIs and look for process changes that will increase business value. Industry benchmarks suggest the ability to increase current baseline thresholds.

Risks

The assessment team reviewed the risk log and found it to be complete with reasonable mitigation strategies for each risk. There was also evidence of continuous updates and reviews during weekly status meetings. The assessment team would caution on the following remaining project risks:

- We noticed a sense of complacency at the executive levels. They may be disengaging too soon in the project lifecycle.
- User Acceptance Testing (UAT) is not yet complete so the team needs to stay engaged and prepared to resolve defects as they arise.

Positioning a Stop-Gap Intervention

In this example, the Health Check Assessment team found that the project was in deep trouble as the budget spent did not correlate with the functionality that was delivered. 65% of the budget was spent and only 30% of the functionality was built (and not yet User Acceptance Tested). Project resources were also being pulled into their day jobs and could not focus on the project fulltime. It was not clear whether more budget was going to be available, or if any of the project management dimensions shown in the familiar management triangle shown in Figure 14.6 could be modified to save the entire project. The figure also shows some of the contributing factors for the current trajectory toward project failure, which are shaded

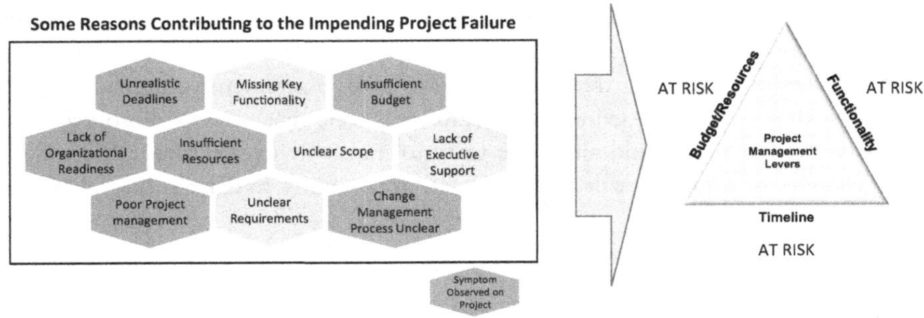

Figure 14.6 Causes impacting the project management triangle.

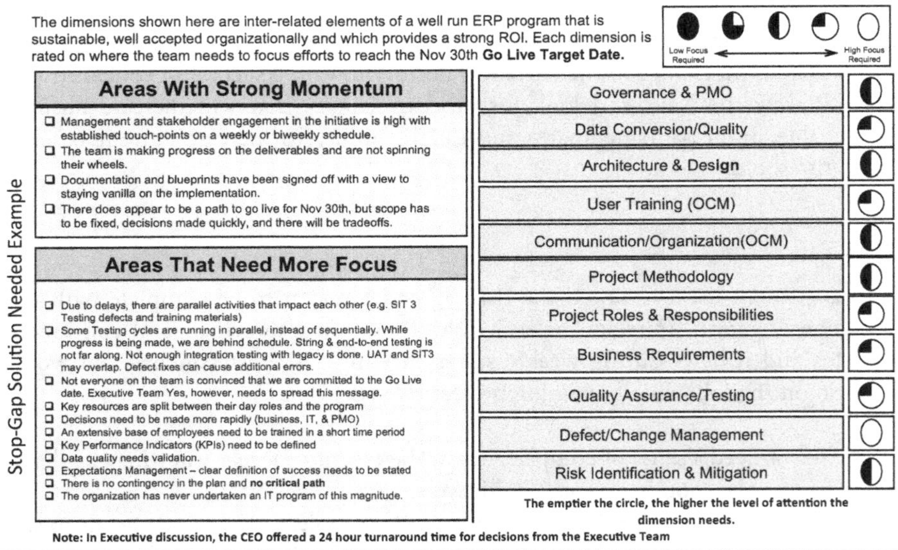

Figure 14.7 A stop-gap intervention example.

dark. The deadlines were not realistic, and root case analysis showed that the budget was never allocated the proper contingency to reflect complexities in the business requirements nor changes to the technical architecture.

Figure 14.7 shows the Summary Dashboard for the initiative. Executive Management needed to make tradeoffs in either timeline, functionality or budget, but were not in a position to do so at the time of the review. The morale was low, and most interviewees expressed their doubts about ever making the deadline. Cancelling the project outright was not a desired outcome because of the large money already spent. Continuing without a realistic rescue plan was not an option that anyone being realistic could support.

The assessment team realized that the program team needed to do the following:

- Get a quick win. After 18 months on the project and nothing tangible delivered, the team needed to drive some business value back into the business to raise morale.
- Gain some time to determine which management levers they could leverage to create a path for the project to be implemented.
- Look for cost savings to reduce the exorbitant monthly burn rate.

The evaluation criteria in Figure 14.7 shows that there were no dimensions rated higher than 50%. Many were between 0 and 25%. These weaknesses were reflected in the written summary sections. Some of the key items on the summary assessment are discussed below:

Areas the Initiative Is Showing Strength

While the project was executing poorly, the Health Check team did identify some strengths as follows:

- Management and stakeholder engagement in the initiative was high with established touch-points on a weekly or biweekly schedule.
- The team was making progress on the deliverables and not spinning their wheels.
- Documentation and blueprints have been signed off with a view to staying vanilla on the implementation.
- There does appear to be a path to go live for Nov 30th, but scope had to be fixed, decisions made quickly, and there would be tradeoffs in the functionality that could be delivered.

Areas for Improvement

The Health Check team uncovered many issues on the program, many volunteered during interviews, others gleaned from documentation that was incomplete and inconsistent. Some of the key areas for improvement were as follows:

- Due to delays, there were parallel activities that impact each other (e.g. SIT 3 Testing defects and training materials)
- Some Testing cycles were running in parallel, instead of sequentially. While progress was being made, the team was behind schedule. String & end-to-end testing was not far along. Not enough integration testing with legacy was being done. UAT and SIT3 activities may overlap. Defect fixes could cause additional errors.

- Not everyone on the team was convinced that management was committed to meeting the Go Live date. They had seen too many other dates come and go with no implementation.
- Key resources were split between their day roles and the program activities
- Decisions needed to be made more rapidly (business, IT, & PMO)
- An extensive base of employees (over 5,000) needed to be trained in a short time period
- Key Performance Indicators (KPIs) needed to be defined
- Data quality needed validation.
- Expectations Management—clear definition of success needed to be stated
- There was no contingency in the plan and no critical path identified
- The organization had never undertaken an IT program of this magnitude.

Recommendations

The recommendation formed with input from the steering committee was to implement a stop-gap solution that would put some functionality into production, affecting a subset of the user base. This would allow some business benefits to start accruing, provide a quick-win to show that the team could move forward, and allow some of the existing investment to be amortized on the books. This would also allow senior management to focus on a new direction for the project.

The recommendation was accepted and the team did realize the quick-win. Ultimately the project was recast and implemented. The team spent more than the original budget, even with an appropriate contingency. The situation would have been much better, based on other experiences, if the Health Check had been commissioned from the start of the initiative. The initiative was complicated enough to suggest a recurring health check just to provide ongoing guard rails for the project.

Positioning a Project Rescue (Partial or Complete)

A project rescue, whether partial or full, can have many common elements. In the example shown in Figures 14.8 and 14.9, the summary dashboard was built using a slightly different format to highlight the specific recommendations for each dimension in the evaluation criteria as there were issues throughout that matrix. The health check team felt that a stop gap solution was not workable and wasted money, and that a rescue intervention could be started with executive approval.

Recommendations

In this example, the tone was focused on the recommendations, mixed with areas of improvement, as follows:

- Governance: Governance was shared between three different vendors, with no clear idea of who was leading. There was no single point of accountability, responsibility & authority.

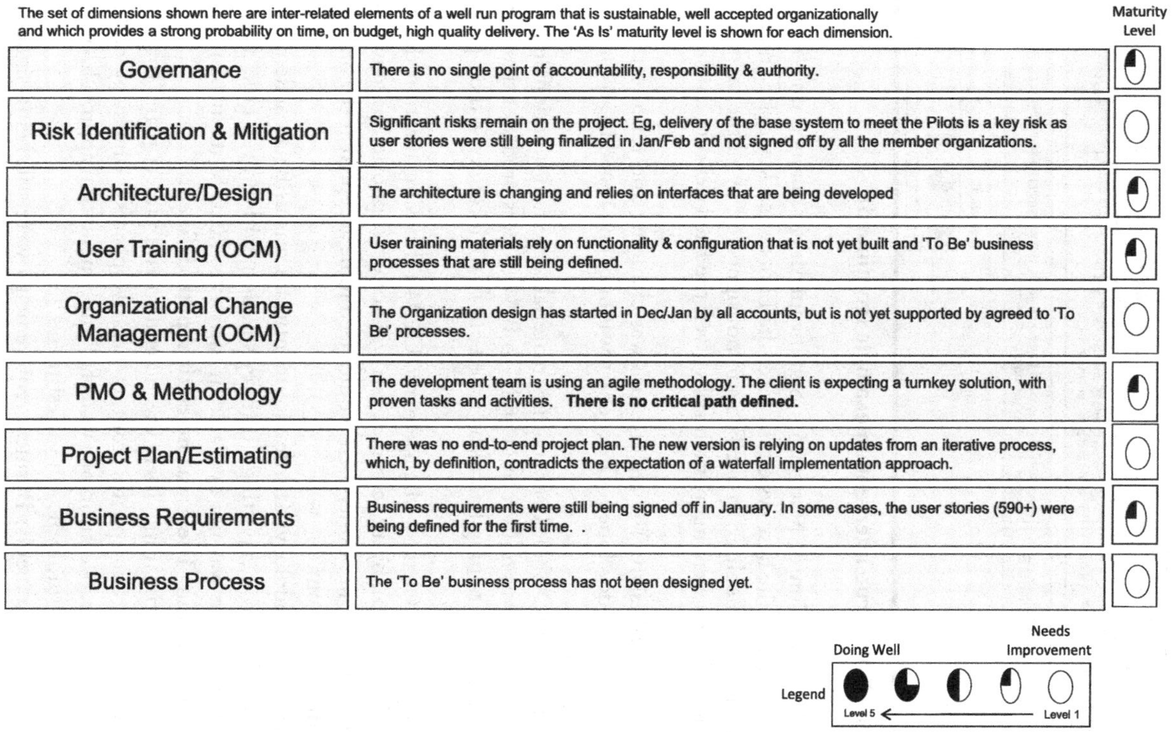

The set of dimensions shown here are inter-related elements of a well run program that is sustainable, well accepted organizationally and which provides a strong probability on time, on budget, high quality delivery. The 'As Is' maturity level is shown for each dimension.

Dimension	Description	Maturity Level
Governance	There is no single point of accountability, responsibility & authority.	
Risk Identification & Mitigation	Significant risks remain on the project. Eg, delivery of the base system to meet the Pilots is a key risk as user stories were still being finalized in Jan/Feb and not signed off by all the member organizations.	
Architecture/Design	The architecture is changing and relies on interfaces that are being developed	
User Training (OCM)	User training materials rely on functionality & configuration that is not yet built and 'To Be' business processes that are still being defined.	
Organizational Change Management (OCM)	The Organization design has started in Dec/Jan by all accounts, but is not yet supported by agreed to 'To Be' processes.	
PMO & Methodology	The development team is using an agile methodology. The client is expecting a turnkey solution, with proven tasks and activities. **There is no critical path defined.**	
Project Plan/Estimating	There was no end-to-end project plan. The new version is relying on updates from an iterative process, which, by definition, contradicts the expectation of a waterfall implementation approach.	
Business Requirements	Business requirements were still being signed off in January. In some cases, the user stories (590+) were being defined for the first time. .	
Business Process	The 'To Be' business process has not been designed yet.	

Legend: Doing Well — Needs Improvement; Level 5 ← Level 1

Figure 14.8 Full rescue intervention example.

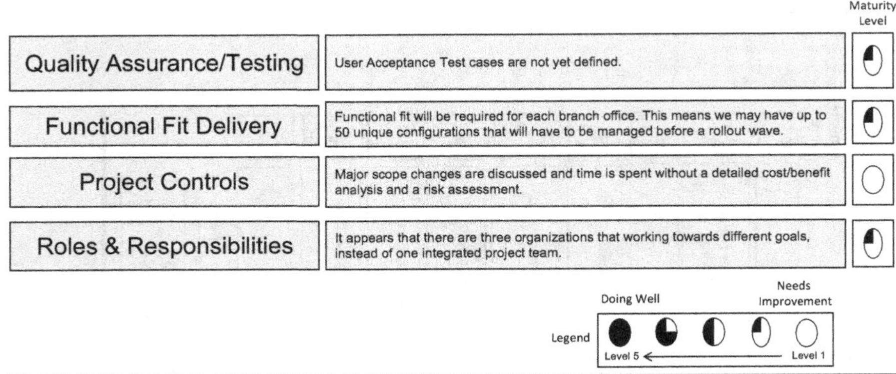

Figure 14.9 Full rescue intervention example (continued).

- Risk Identification & Mitigation: Significant risks remained on the project. E.g, delivery of the base system to meet the Pilots was a key risk as user stories were still being finalized in Jan/Feb and not signed off by all the member organizations. There were many such risks given the fixed delivery date of Sept 30 20xx.
- Architecture/Design: The architecture was changing and relied on interfaces that were being developed. Order entry was built and tested in an earlier cloud environment.
- User Training (OCM): User training materials relied on functionality & configuration that was not yet built and "To Be" business processes that were still being defined. Training had to be rolled out to 62 locations + their peripheral locations.
- Organizational Change Management (OCM): The Organization design had started in Dec/Jan by all accounts, but was not yet supported by agreed to "To Be" processes. Once done, these would need to be accepted at the branch level and then rolled out.
- PMO & Methodology: The development team was using an agile methodology. The client was expecting a turnkey solution, with proven tasks and activities. Such a plan was not available in early Dec 20xx & required months of effort to drive out. **There was no critical path defined.**
- Project Plan/Estimating: There was no end-to-end project plan. The new version was relying on updates from an iterative process, which, by definition, contradicts the expectation of a waterfall implementation approach. There was no reasonable contingency in the estimates.
- Business Requirements: Business requirements were still being signed off in January. In some cases, the user stories (590+) were being defined for the first time. These would need to be localized for the different associations.

- Business Process: The "To Be" business process had not been designed yet. The objective appeared to be to drive it out as the sprints were done. This left little time for user training, refinement, or testing. The "As Is" version had not been signed off by the business.
- Quality Assurance/Testing: User Acceptance Test cases were not yet defined. They would be built by a team that had never done a project of this magnitude. Every branch would have the ability to UAT their implementation. There was very little time available to deal with defects.
- Functional Fit Delivery: Functional fit would be required for each branch office. This meant that there could be up to 50 unique configurations that would have to be managed before a rollout wave.
- Project Controls: Major scope changes were discussed and time was spent without a detailed cost/benefit analysis and a risk assessment. This could have a devastating impact on project delivery. Segregation of user duties was not defined.
- Roles & Responsibilities: It was not clear who the single point of overall management was and who could clear obstacles encountered by the project team. It was not clear who the overall solution architect was either as the solution was cobbled together by three different solution providers. It appeared that there were three organizations that were working toward different goals, instead of one integrated project team.

Project Rescue Intervention Methodology

Key considerations and potential recommendations to include in the health check final assessment report are discussed in the sections that follow below. Figure 14.10 shows a project rescue intervention methodology that has successfully been used on a significant number of project rescue initiatives in the past with outstanding recovery results. There are seven phases in total. The project health check framework already followed by the assessment team to get to this point provides the raw data for phases 1 and 2. The health check assessment team can use this data to focus their recommendations to do a project rescue in phases 1 and 2 and then begin in phase 3 of the project rescue intervention methodology to finalize specific recommendations and possibly even a 30–60–90-day action plan to rescue the initiative.

The phases in this framework are discussed in the sections that follow.

Rescue Phase 1: Detection of Warning Flags

As part of the health check, the assessment team will try to detect specific warning flags that can be classified by Red, Orange, Yellow, Green, as shown in Figure 14.11.

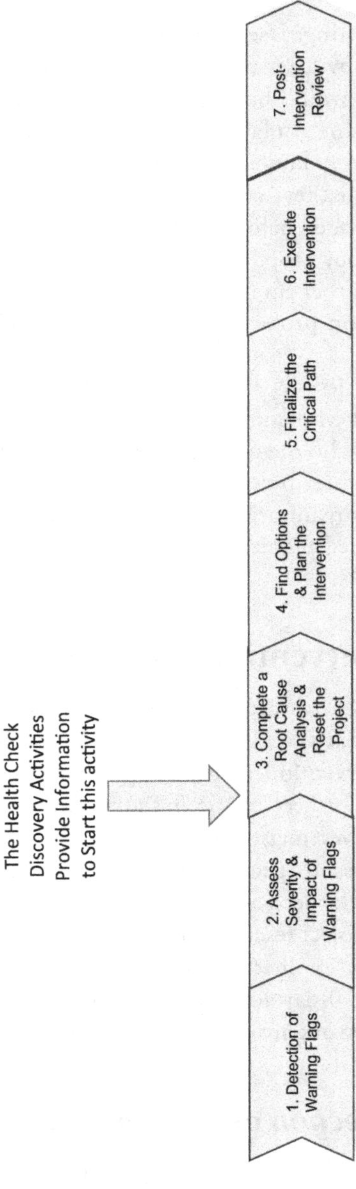

Figure 14.10 Project intervention and rescue framework.

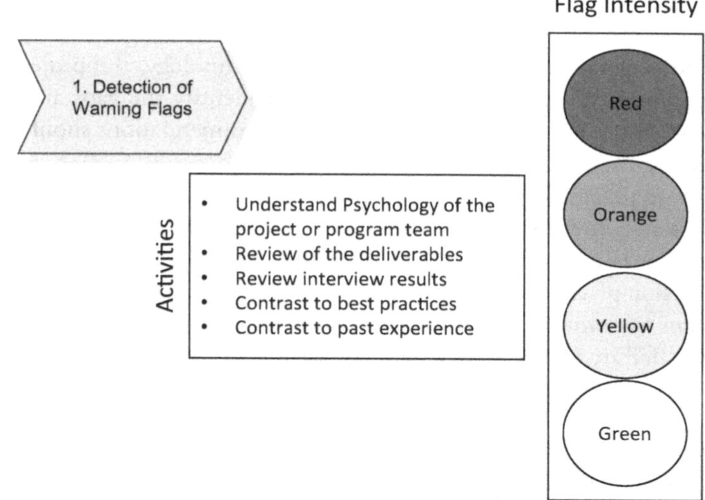

Figure 14.11 Detection of warning flags phase.

As discussed previously in this book, the sources of information the health check team will review to detect these warning flags are as follows:

- Understand Psychology of the project or program team: Various emotions on the project, such as irrational exuberance, panic, and unbridled/unjustified optimism are drivers for other problems in the project. When these types of emotions, discussed in earlier chapters, are visible, the health check team needs to look more closely at the project plan and dependencies to determine how realistic the timelines are for implementation. If they demand a project rescue, the health check recommendation should include "setting realistic expectations" to deal with the emotional perspective that is keeping the team from understanding the true picture—which is a prerequisite for any type of project rescue to be effective in the future.
- Review of the deliverables: A detailed review of the deliverables was done as part of the discovery activities. If by the start of the assessment activities in the Health Check methodology it is clear that a project rescue is going to be recommended, the health check team needs to prioritize the deliverables that must be corrected to support a critical path for project completion. For example, the business requirements will need to be complete, prioritized, and signed off (very important) as a prerequisite to any successful project rescue.
- Review interview results: The detailed interviews results will also be available. These would provide input into the morale and functioning of the project team, point to specific areas of concern, and validate some of the findings from the review of the documentation.

- Contrast to best practices: The findings of the documentation review and interviews should be contrasted to what is expected on a project at other organizations of a similar size, projects of similar technology, and projects of similar complexity. The assessment team should identify the gaps and then find fact-based reasons for their existence. The recommendations should be aimed at closing these.
- Contrast to past experiences: Past project experiences are the best tool to understand how to deal with the issues uncovered by the team interviews. An earlier example was given of the insufficiently planned start time of a data conversion phase. Similarly, the assessment team must rely on past experiences to form recommendations on how to deal with the reasons for the impending project failure (e.g. start the data conversion phase five months earlier than shown on the flawed project plan).

During project rescue planning, the warning flags identified in the discovery activities should be labeled with one of the colors: Red, Orange, Yellow, and Green. Once all the Red or Orange Flags are detected, the health check assessment team needs to focus on phase 2 of the project rescue methodology to assess the severity and impact of each flag.

Rescue Phase 2: Assess Severity and Impact of Warning Flags

Some of this work would have been done during the discovery activities of the health check assessment, but now that the team has decided that a project rescue is being recommended, the team needs to better understand the severity and impact of each Red or Orange flag sooner than they would have outside the need for a project rescue, and to begin to prioritize their recommendations. Figure 14.12 shows some of the key considerations for this phase. The final prioritization can only be done after the reset parameters are conceptualized in Phase 3 of the Rescue Intervention Methodology.

The prioritization needs to be aligned with those use cases that provide the key, mandatory, or highest business value. Figure 14.13 provides a template that can be used to elaborate on key meta information for each use case. These can be collated and sorted on key metadata keys as shown in Figure 14.14. Three were selected based on knowledge of the executive priorities in the organization. Three of the use cases are left in an "Other" category and so would be prioritized last in the activity sequence.

Rescue Phase 3: Complete the Root Cause Analysis and Reset the Project

Phase 3 is a completely new set of activities now that the Health Check team has determined that a project rescue intervention is needed. This means that the determination in the Interim Draft report points to a significant negative spiral for the

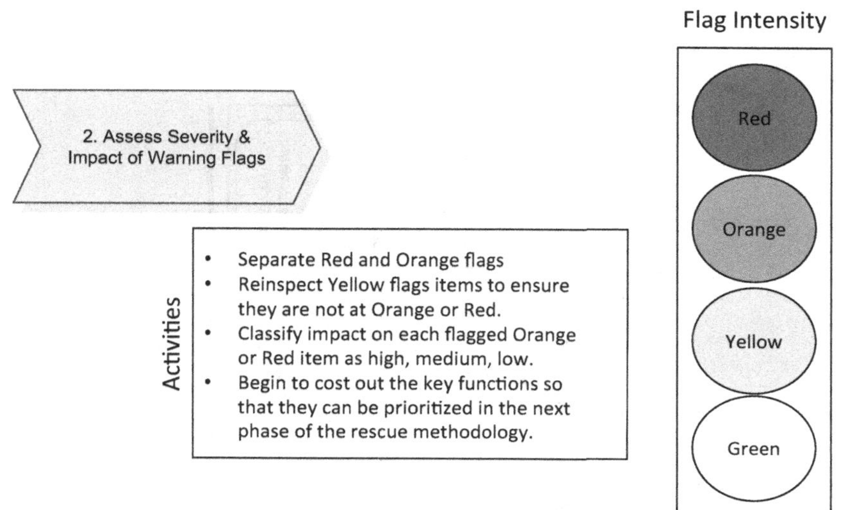

Figure 14.12 Assess severity and impact of warning flags.

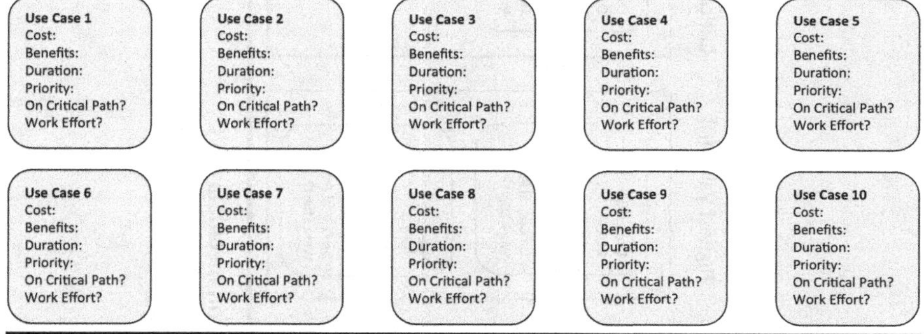

Figure 14.13 Use case metadata information.

project or program that is hurtling towards outright failure. In some cases, this could be catastrophic to the organization as a whole. Imagine a system that is costing north of $100 million or even $1 Billion that is needed to support major new business initiatives at a specific point in time in a very competitive market with the eyes of the stock exchanges focused on the initiative. This scenario will almost certainly get executives and decision-makers fired or demoted, and could cost the company in terms of reputation, security, revenue, market share, and other attributes.

A partial or full rescue becomes a call to action! A signal that business as usual was not working on the initiative and that a reset needs to be done. Figure 14.15 shows a set of activities that need to be completed in this phase. These are described in the subsections that follow.

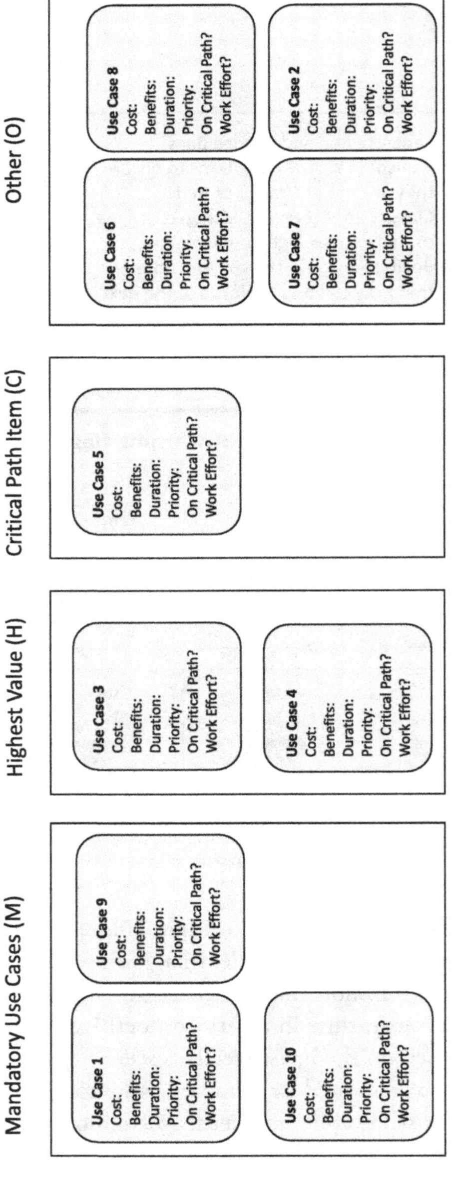

Figure 14.14 Sorted use cases on metadata keys.

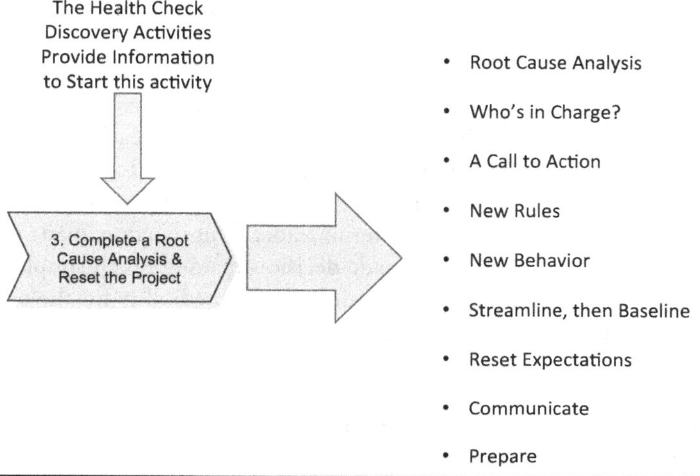

Figure 14.15 Complete a root cause analysis & reset the project.

Root Cause Analysis

Depending on the scope of the Health Check assessment, the recommendation could simply be to conduct a complete project rescue. However, this recommendation is only kicking the can down the road. For a fulsome health check, at this point the health check assessment team can either recommend a root cause analysis be performed or start the initial steps themselves beginning with the Red and Orange flags. They may have to reconvene with members of the project team to understand the causes of those flags and begin to look at options for addressing those and turn these into recommendations contained in the final health check report.

Who's in Charge?

At this point a recommendation will be to clarify who is making the decisions. If the current management team does not have the skill set to deal with the project issues, an interim leader may need to be brought in as part of the recommendation on the Final Health Check report. This leader must be paired with an executive sponsor who is prepared to lend complete support to the individual in charge to reset and execute on the initiative.

In a past instance of a health check, the assessment team made the recommendation to bring in a new leader that would essentially be the focal delivery executive for a North-America-wide ERP/Leasing implementation. All the current VPs would report into that individual. A member of the Executive Leadership team, COO, agreed to be the sponsor on the program—which was crucial to the survival of the organization. The project was a hot potato, heading toward a complete failure, and that event would be heard on the street and investors would likely flee for the foreseeable future. The COO and the interim leader crafted the reset path.

The first issue was to establish the power and credibility of the interim leader among a group of powerful and hard-headed executives. Each of them essentially ran organizations with several hundred people reporting into each of them. At every steering committee meeting, the COO would sit just next to the interim leader, and slightly behind. The VP-level members of the steering committee would look toward the COO and would see the interim leader. This dynamic made it clear that the two were linked at the hips and made decision-making much simpler. This was the first step, a small and subtle step, but it built the credibility for the other activities to be implemented. There were additional hurdles, but the project did implement by the due date and within 12% of the original budget.

The interim leader does not necessarily have to replace anyone already on the project team, but could instead become an additional member of the team for the duration of the project rescue. Conversely, the person could flip to a permanent leadership role and bring expertise inhouse for future projects in the organization.

A Call to Action

A call to action must be the recommendation after the reset. This requires the project team and the organization to accept new ways of thinking and new solutions. The call to action must be initiated by the executive sponsor with a clear communication plan of where the project is currently, the new interim leadership approach, why they were selected, and that many other changes that will be coming to support a complete rescue of the program. The call to action must make it clear that everything is on the table depending on the nature of the reset about to be done to save the project.

New Rules

The assessment team should look for red or orange flags and see if new rules could be crafted to combat the reasons for these problematic ratings. Some areas to examine for this are shown in Figure 14.16. Each of these can be plagued with bad and lazy habits that contribute to the project morass. These should be included in the 30–60–90-day action plan so that the new rules can be finalized, posted, and distributed.

- Running Meetings: Ensure they are running effectively and leanly. In projects that are heading to failure, a common issue is the execution of meetings and the time that is wasted without making decisions, a lack of people contributing, and having no agendas. People are talking over each other and sometimes arguing. The meeting culture is one of the first items to address and improve.
- Management Toolkit (also the project rescue toolkit): The common deliverables that are vital to a well-run project and a project rescue are: an end-to-end

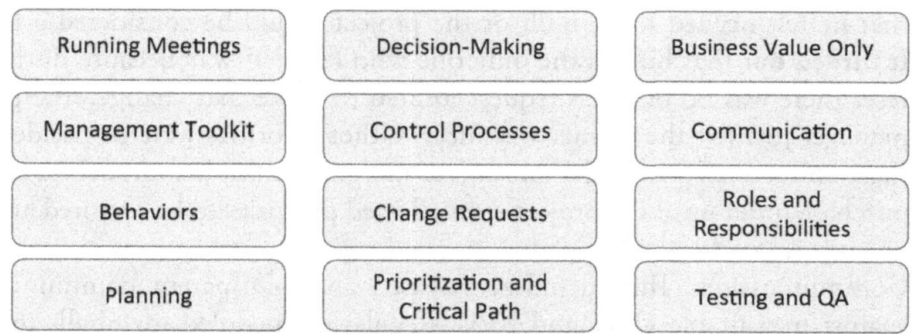

Figure 14.16 Areas to examine for new rules.

project plan, weekly status reports, project charter (signed off), organization chart, change management log, solution architecture, and an active risk log.

- Behaviors: A written set of behaviors that are acceptable going forward and those that are not. For example, no negativity for the sake of negativity. Speak openly, but offer options and solutions to problems, or raise a problem and ask people to think of solutions instead of stating that there are none.
- Planning: Detailed planning with realistic estimates and a reasonable contingency. Slack must exist in the plan to allow tasks to be shifted. Proper dependencies between tasks and resources need to be represented. For example, tasks that are dependent on each other should not be running in parallel. This happens on a lot of projects and it's amazing that there is surprise when the tasks have significant overage because team members are not available to work on the activities originally planned.
- Decision-Making: There has to be a commitment from executive management to make decisions in a timely manner (e.g 48 hours from the point a decision request is logged and shared).
- Control Processes (e.g. Signoff): There must be a commitment to control processes that add value, while those that do not must be removed as a bottleneck. For example, signoffs on key deliverables must be mandated, while others such as meetings that run for a full two hours even when there is nothing to resolve should be reduced to the length of time needed to cover the meeting agenda.
- Change Requests: Change requests must follow a documented process and justify business value to be considered. There must be active management of the log.
- Prioritization and Critical Path: All scope items must be prioritized so that a critical path can be defined through the project plan. Items not on the critical path should be descoped to a later phase.
- Business Value Only: Only items that add measurable and desirable business value will be scoped and included in the critical path. For example, on one initiative, a project manager made a big point of a merged purchase order

that he felt needed to be built or the project would be considered a failure. It turned out that he was the only one who felt that way because during the reset there was no business request located to make that change. The project manager just felt the format was nicer. Other priorities were put aside while the architects tried to find a solution to merging multiple sources into a single purchase order until the project reset allowed priorities to be revisited and this one was immediately dropped.

- Communication: This includes increased and transparent communication against measurable CSFs and KPIs. Regularly scheduled townhalls to share progress and expectations as well as regular newsletters, blogs, and other sources of information sharing.
- Roles and Responsibilities: Clear definition of accountabilities and tasks in the reset program must be reviewed and established. These must be documented and shared across the team to ensure that every team member understands their deliverables and the timeline they are going to be held to meet.
- Testing and QA: Realignment on the key transactions, use cases and scenarios that need to be tested to meet the CSFs and KPIs. This stream of activity must be streamlined as it's not unusual to have too many test cases that may be examining conditions of low impact or which may never arise in the real world. Also, look at the activities for defect review, prioritization, resolution and retesting. These should be daily activities. It's also important to examine how testers are selected, trained, and allocated to activities, especially in UAT.

New Behavior

As shown in Figure 14.17, the assessment team should identify the new behaviors needed from the team members in terms of the following:

- Mood and Morale: Examine activities and information that maintains a strong mood among the team members so that they are not destroying the collective will to complete the initiative successfully.
- Momentum: Look to identify and plan quick wins to build a culture of success and momentum toward the deadline. The assessment team should explicitly mention the ones they can identify in the health check final report.
- Politics: Explicitly discourage destructive politics by not rewarding such behavior. Demonstrate that executive management is not going to tolerate finger pointing, self-promotion activities, and any acts that hurt morale.
- Responsibility: Encourage team members to take responsibility to deliver solutions and to find answers to issues instead of raising them as showstoppers.
- Accountability: Encourage team members to take accountability for their actions and look for solutions instead of blaming other members of the team.
- Transparency: Encourage top-down transparency on deadlines, risks, and scope. This must be done at all levels of the program. Bottom-up transparency

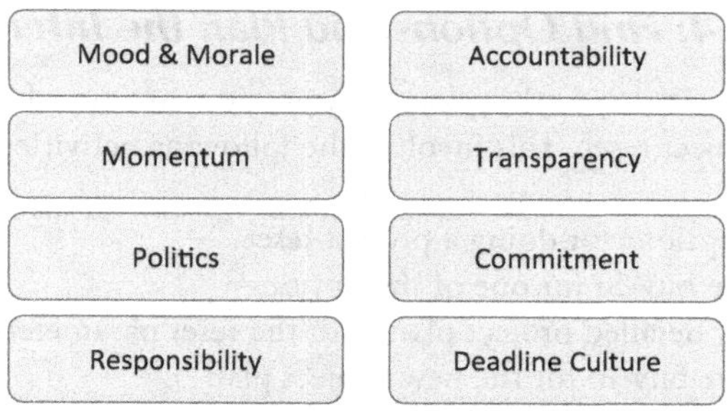

Figure 14.17 Focusing on behaviors.

in terms of what is actually happening in the trenches should also be encouraged.

- Commitment: Demonstrate commitment to meet the deadlines by looking for solutions.
- Deadline Culture: Executive management must demonstrate that they are going to get serious about the project deadlines. They can do this by placing incentives for meeting them and removing obstacles that are impeding progress.

Streamline, Then Baseline

The assessment team should look for opportunities to streamline the project plan and deliverables to the critical path and recommend making that a new baseline.

Reset Expectations

The scope should reflect the program reset. A process to get business and stakeholder signoff should be followed to make the new scope official.

Communicate

A regular channel for communication of the reset specifics should be recommended. This can be done through the OCM team. Team members, and even other parts of the organization, will want to understand if the Project Rescue is making a difference to the outcome of the project. Their buy-in and contributions will be dictated by the amount of information they are receiving about the project reset.

Prepare

The last activity in this phase is to prepare to finalize the integrated project plan with the critical path, key milestones, and contingency clearly identified.

Rescue Phase 4: Find Options and Plan the Intervention

As shown in Figure 14.18, in this phase, the assessment team should identify some options for the project reset. This involves the following activities:

- Document options for doing a project reset
- Get executive buy-in for one of the options
- Create a new detailed project plan with the reset parameters
- Get Executive buy-in for the new project plan

Rescue Phase 5: Finalize the Critical Path

As shown in Figure 14.19, in this phase the assessment team should complete the following activities to create a streamlined project plan to implement critical path activities:

- Align revised scope with the end-to-end project plan
- Identify and highlight activities that are on the critical path
- De-prioritize activities that are not on the critical path
- Using the business value criteria, identify activities that can be prioritized as the critical path items are completed to maximize delivery of business value

Rescue Phase 6: Execute Intervention

As shown in Figure 14.20, the assessment team should recommend approaches for executing a revised, high-level project plan reflecting the project reset. Figure 14.21 shows a project plan that was recast for a financial project with a firm deadline to produce the financial statements. This project, which was originally heading toward

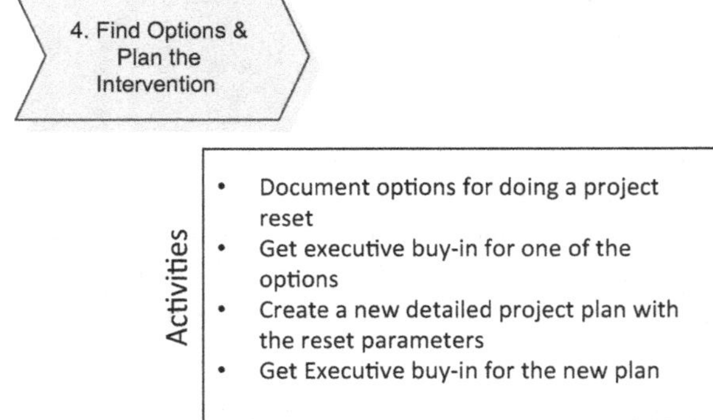

Figure 14.18 Find options and plan the intervention.

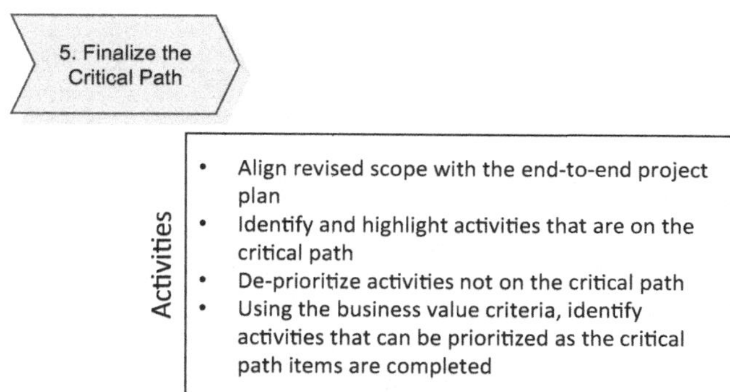

Figure 14.19 Finalize the critical path.

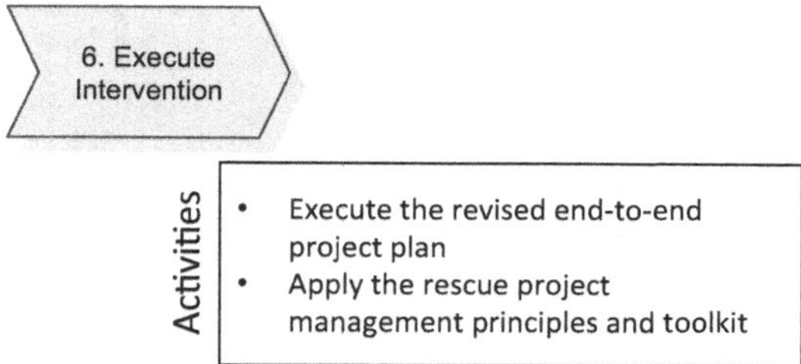

Figure 14.20 Execute intervention.

failure was successfully rescued by the clarity in the critical path shown in that project plan which allowed the team to understand and execute on their accountabilities without confusion. It was easy to explain and easy to track, even while the project was staffed with three different large System Integrators and permanent staff. Here are some of the key activities in this phase:

- Execute the revised end-to-end project plan
- Apply the rescue project management principles and toolkit

Rescue Phase 7: Post Intervention Review

As shown in Figure 14.22, the assessment team should finish this part of the project rescue planning by identifying recommendations on how the project team can expect to do the following:

- Get lessons learned
- Apply to remaining activities

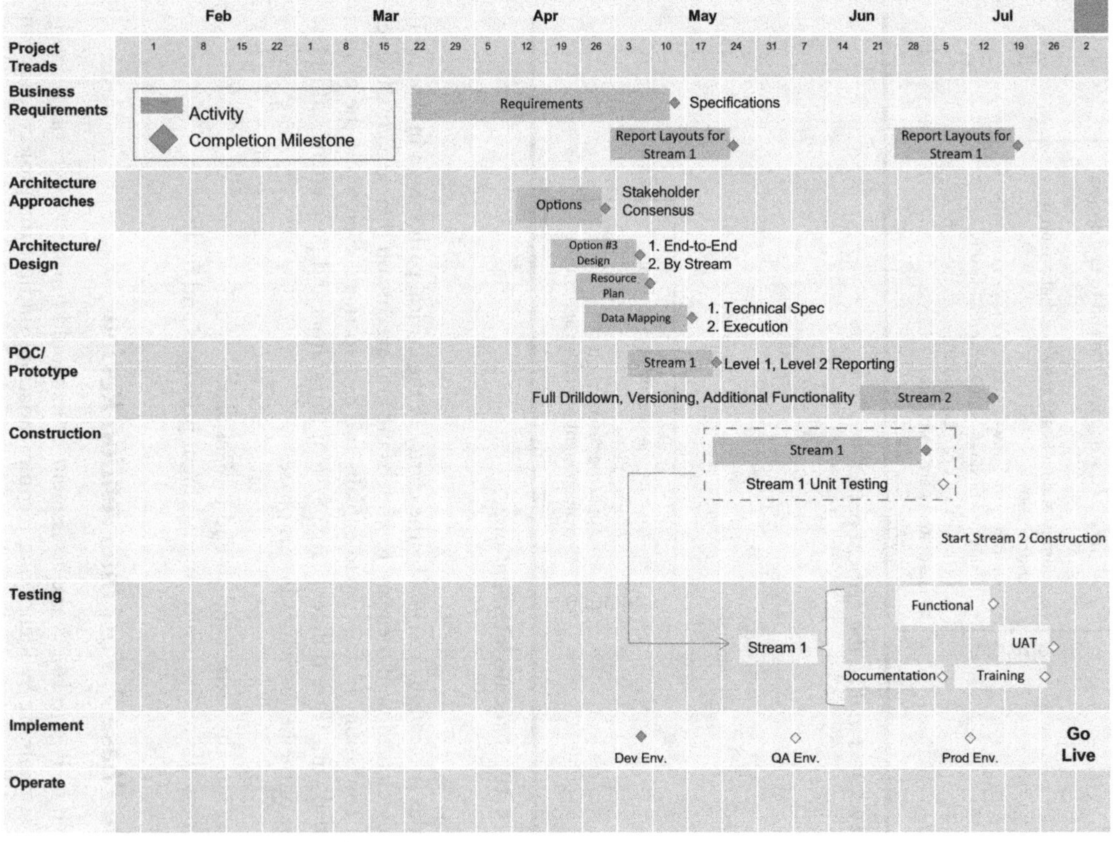

Figure 14.21 Revised financial reporting phase 1 timeline.

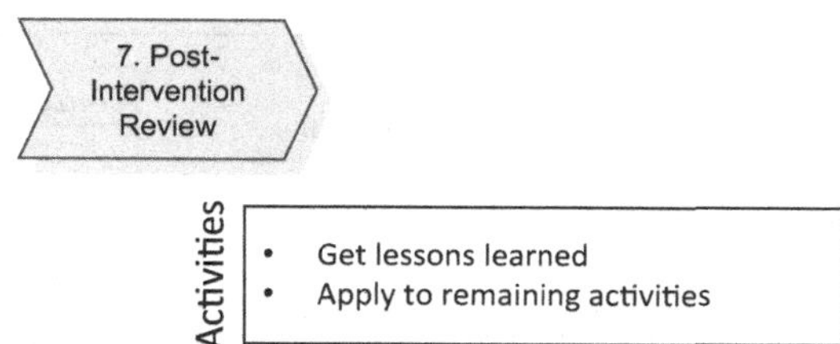

Figure 14.22 Post-intervention review.

The Importance of Understanding Psychology on Projects

It may seem strange to some readers that so much is made of human psychology and emotions on technical projects, even if they are delivering business-related value throughout this book. Afterall, technical solutions should be predictable, there are so many examples to draw on that the industry practitioners should have seen everything and know everything. On the contrary, there are so many subtleties and variations on projects that delivery may sometimes seem as an impossible mission to complete. The people element and emotions must be major considerations in the health check assessment process as well as any project rescue interventions. For example, if a majority of a team does not believe a deadline is possible to meet, they will not make the decisions or manage their time to meet the deadline. The cause and causation factors will make the project fail due to the human interpretation of the events, even if some well-timed actions could make the project successful. This is the importance of the health check—to identify the obstacles and make specific recommendations to overcome situations that could be impeding success due to faulty belief systems.

Going to Orange Then Yellow

A common aspect of many project rescue attempts is to build a "go to green" plan. While this is something that is desired and sometimes achievable, it may be better to start with a less aggressive approach, or a "go to orange" plan, instead. As shown in Figure 14.23, once the project gets to orange status, the focus should then be to get it to a Yellow status, and then if possible to get to a Green status. Sometimes, trying to get to Green from the start, discourages the team because they are unable to do this fast enough. Many projects sit in a yellow status until they are implemented successfully.

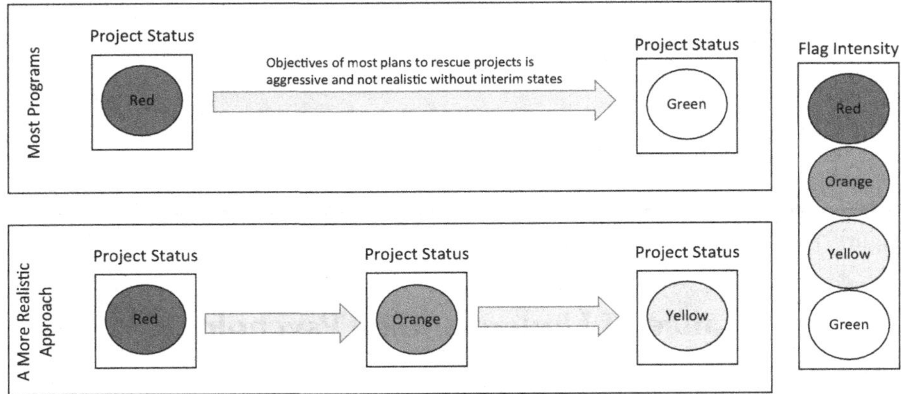

Figure 14.23 Going to yellow.

Top 10 Prerequisites for a Successful Project Rescue

Here is a list of top prerequisites that the assessment team must recommend to support a successful project rescue:

1. Demonstrated executive management support, including from the business owners
2. A critical path must be visible in the revised project plan
3. Sufficient levers to be flexible in planning and replanning from time to time
4. Minimum number of CSFs and KPIs that will maximize business value
5. A streamlined organizational readiness approach
6. Mitigated risks on the risk log
7. Positive morale and minimized destructive politics
8. Do not look for scapegoats to blame
9. Trust but verify all information on the critical path
10. Use Proof of Concepts to validate all technical challenges on the initiative

Closing Perspective

This chapter focused on how the health check assessment team could make recommendations to adjust the trajectory of a project or program that was hurtling toward failure. Four situations were discussed where interventions could occur, as follows:

- Adjustment
- Stop-Gap Solutions
- Partial Project Rescue
- Full Project Rescue

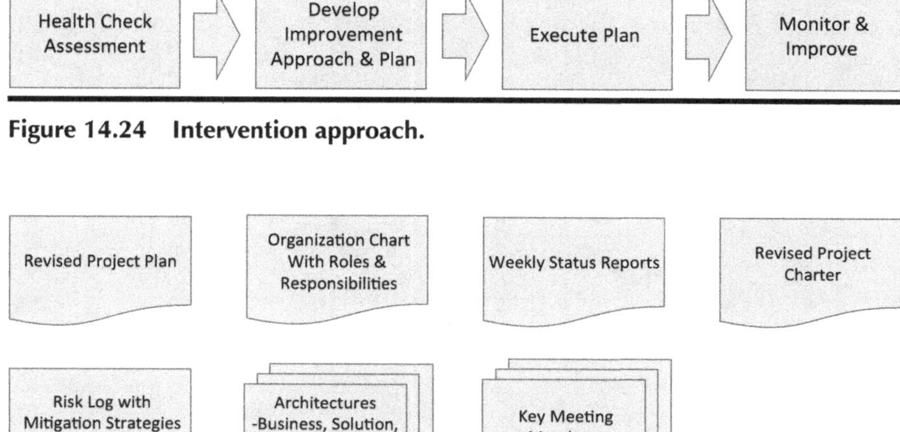

Figure 14.24 Intervention approach.

Figure 14.25 Project rescue management toolkit

Figure 14.24 shows a summary of the phases that can be used to plan different types of interventions. The health check discovery activities provide the information needed to build meaningful recommendations to the project team.

The primary project rescue management toolkit is shown in Figure 14.25. Each of these deliverables should be reset with a new scope to maximize business value on a critical path when a project rescue is required for a failing project.

Chapter 15

Bringing It All Together

How do you build trust with executive sponsors, stakeholders, users, or clients? This is a prerequisite for delivering the Project or Program Health Check assessment results. By this point in the health check assessment lifecycle, as shown in Figure 15.1, members of both teams have interacted with each other at various levels. There have been 1–1 interviews, debriefs, initial reviews, and extensive and possibly intense conversations. All of these will contribute to building trust in what is going to be presented in the final report. Also, the experience of the assessment team, their track history, and how well they have reviewed the deliverables will build trust in the results and show that the team appreciates the time offered by the core team members.

Figure 15.2 shows the assessment report states that were introduced in previous chapters. At this point in the health check lifecycle, the team is close to producing a final report. With the information presented in Chapter 14, the assessment team can update the Draft Report with recommendations reflecting the type of intervention that is needed for the initiative, be it driving more business value, minor adjustments, a stop-gap intervention, or a full project rescue. Are there risks that must be highlighted? These need to be added to the detailed sections of the report and the key items filtered to the Summary Dashboard and then further distilled into the Executive dashboard.

Finalizing the Assessment Report

With inclusion of the recommendations surrounding the type of project adjustment that might be needed, as well as including relevant feedback received during the socialization activities, the assessment team can begin to build the Final Report. Figure 15.3 shows the table of contents the assessment team started with in Chapter 4. Key considerations to include in each section are highlighted below.

DOI: 10.1201/9781003269786-18

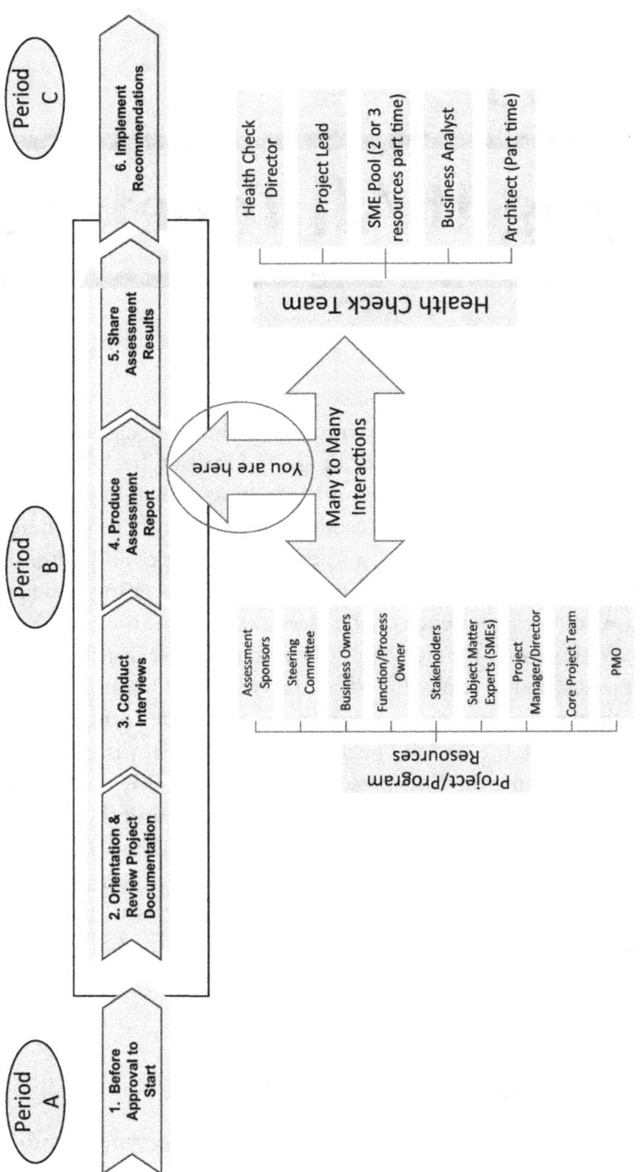

Figure 15.1 Preparing the final assessment report.

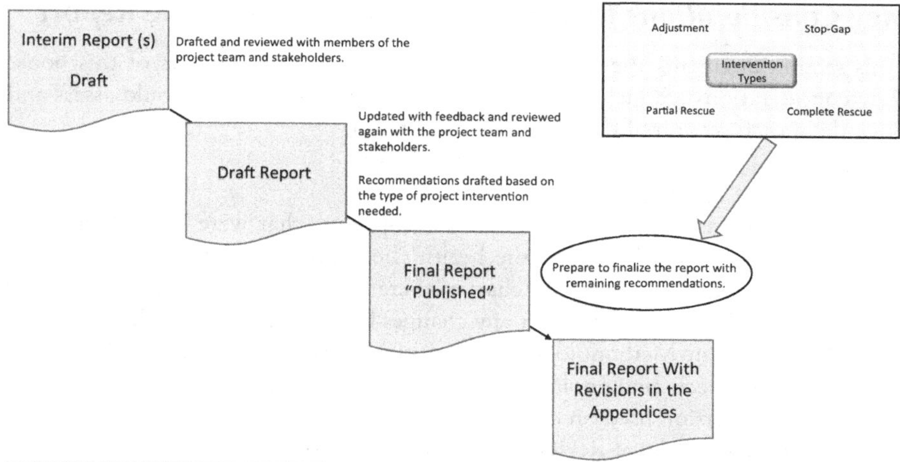

Interim Report (s)
Draft
Drafted and reviewed with members of the project team and stakeholders.
Draft Report
Updated with feedback and reviewed again with the project team and stakeholders.
Recommendations drafted based on the type of project intervention needed.
Final Report "Published"
Adjustment
Stop-Gap
Intervention Types
Partial Rescue
Complete Rescue
Prepare to finalize the report with remaining recommendations.
Final Report With Revisions in the Appendices

Figure 15.2 Finishing the final report.

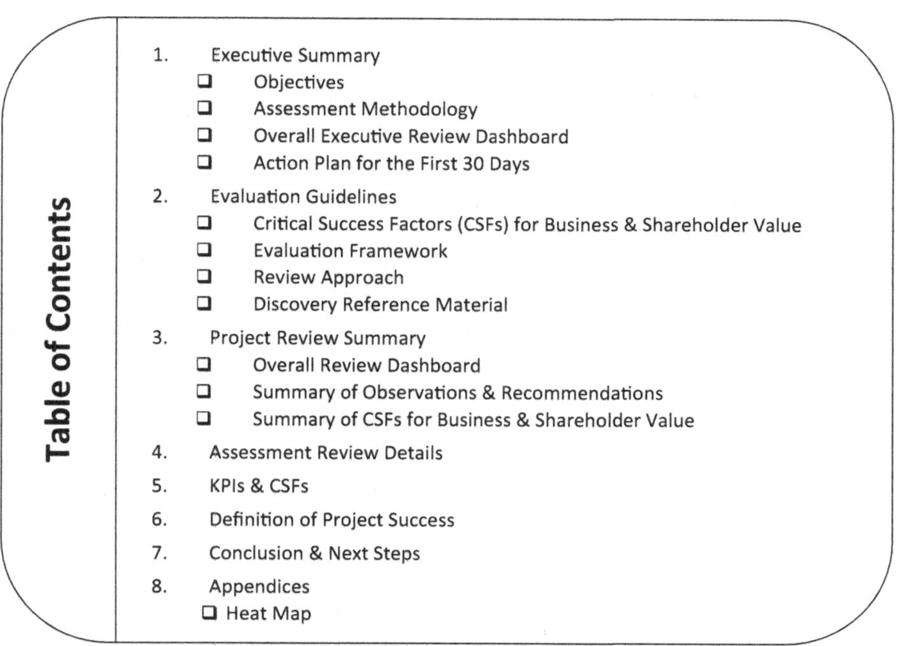

Table of Contents
1. Executive Summary
❑ Objectives
❑ Assessment Methodology
❑ Overall Executive Review Dashboard
❑ Action Plan for the First 30 Days
2. Evaluation Guidelines
❑ Critical Success Factors (CSFs) for Business & Shareholder Value
❑ Evaluation Framework
❑ Review Approach
❑ Discovery Reference Material
3. Project Review Summary
❑ Overall Review Dashboard
❑ Summary of Observations & Recommendations
❑ Summary of CSFs for Business & Shareholder Value
4. Assessment Review Details
5. KPIs & CSFs
6. Definition of Project Success
7. Conclusion & Next Steps
8. Appendices
❑ Heat Map

Figure 15.3 Finalizing the report.

Key Considerations to Include in Each Section of the Report

This section augments the information shared in previous chapters of this book. Key considerations are included below that the assessment team should assess and include in each section of the report at a minimum.

1. Executive Summary
   - Objectives: Be sure to include the objectives that were refined and possibility finalized through the health check process. If these have deviated from those in the project charter, there must be proper signoffs from the Executive Team to support any changes before they are official.
   - Assessment Methodology: A description of the customized version of the health check methodology is shown in Figure 15.1. This should be updated to the version used on the project.
   - Overall Executive Review Dashboard: After all the interviews and discussions, include the top two or three recommendations that must be implemented to drive business value. Also include the key risks that must be brought to the attention of executive management for mitigation.
   - Action Plan for the First 30 Days: This is an optional section. It can be expanded to additional periods or just include the recommended key activities as part of an action plan.
2. Evaluation Guidelines
   - Critical Success Factors (CSFs) for Business & Shareholder Value: include the top CSFs here as well as evidence that they were signed off by executive management.
   - Evaluation Framework: This is a customized version of the evaluation criteria. Some versions are shown in Figure 15.4. These should be revised with the assessment sponsors and customized for their needs. However, do be careful if they are underestimating the dimensions that should be reviewed. For example, some sponsors may argue that their problem is with reporting accuracy and not realize that this is a symptom in at least five other areas (e.g. business requirements, solution architecture, design, and others). As a general suggestion, additional dimensions can be added to those examples in Figure 15.4, but taking the ones shown away should be avoided. Those are important dimensions in any project and should have at least a high-level examination to look for red flags that might warrant a deeper dive.
   - Review Approach: Highlight the discipline that is built into the methodology to build trust with the project team. There is a reason for every document or interview request. Also, the methodology has been successfully used on other projects with good results.
   - Discovery Reference Material: Highlight the depth and breadth of material that was reviewed and the full number of specific resources interviewed.

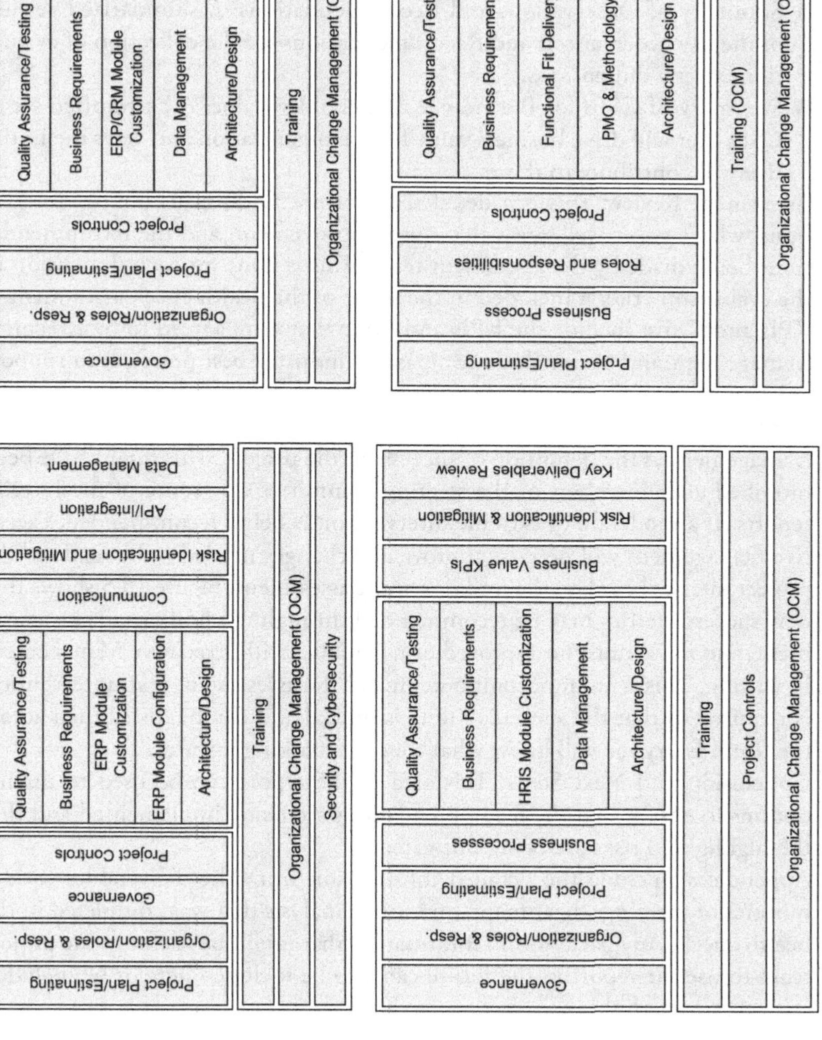

Figure 15.4 Customized versions of the evaluation criteria.

This is always appreciated and demonstrates concern for the team's time as well as professionalism. It also gives credit to members of the team for the time they have contributed to the health check process.

3. Project Review Summary
   - Overall Review Dashboard: This is a detailed overall summary dashboard that contains the key observations, scores for the evaluation criteria, key recommendations, key risks, and key action items. A subset of this dashboard is used as the Executive Dashboard.
   - Summary of Observations and Recommendations: A summarized version of the key observations and Recommendations for the collection of evaluation criteria dimensions.
   - Summary of CSFs for Business & Shareholder Value: A customized set of CSFs that will drive business value for the organization and ways the initiative will contribute to those.
4. Assessment Review This is a detailed list of the findings including observations, what's going well, areas that need improvement, and the recommendations being made by the assessment team. This is done for each dimension in the evaluation criteria included in the scope of the health check assessment.
5. KPIs and CSFs: Include the KPIs and CSFs that were agreed to by Executive Management and also include comparable industry best practices to support any stretch goals that could be justified.
6. Definition of Project Success: This is the final criteria accepted by Executive Management as the definition of success for the project. This might have been modified after members of the steering committee saw some of the interim reports. If a moderate to extreme intervention is being recommended, executive management will need to approve any changes needed to be made to the project metrics based on the findings of the assessment. Figure 15.5 shows that new success metrics may be recommended through the findings of the assessment, and those must be approved or negotiated with Executive Management in writing. This is an important outcome of the assessment, if an intervention is required so that the success criteria is official and can be distributed across the team. Everyone will know what they are working towards.
7. Conclusion and Next Steps: This area of the report can be used to discuss options to ensure that the recommendations are being implemented and that the highlighted risks are being mitigated.
8. Appendices: Include the detailed information from the deliverables review, minutes of meetings, heat maps, and other analysis that was completed in the health check. Any background information that might be useful to the project team to use the report in the future can also be included here or be included as a set of hyperlinks.

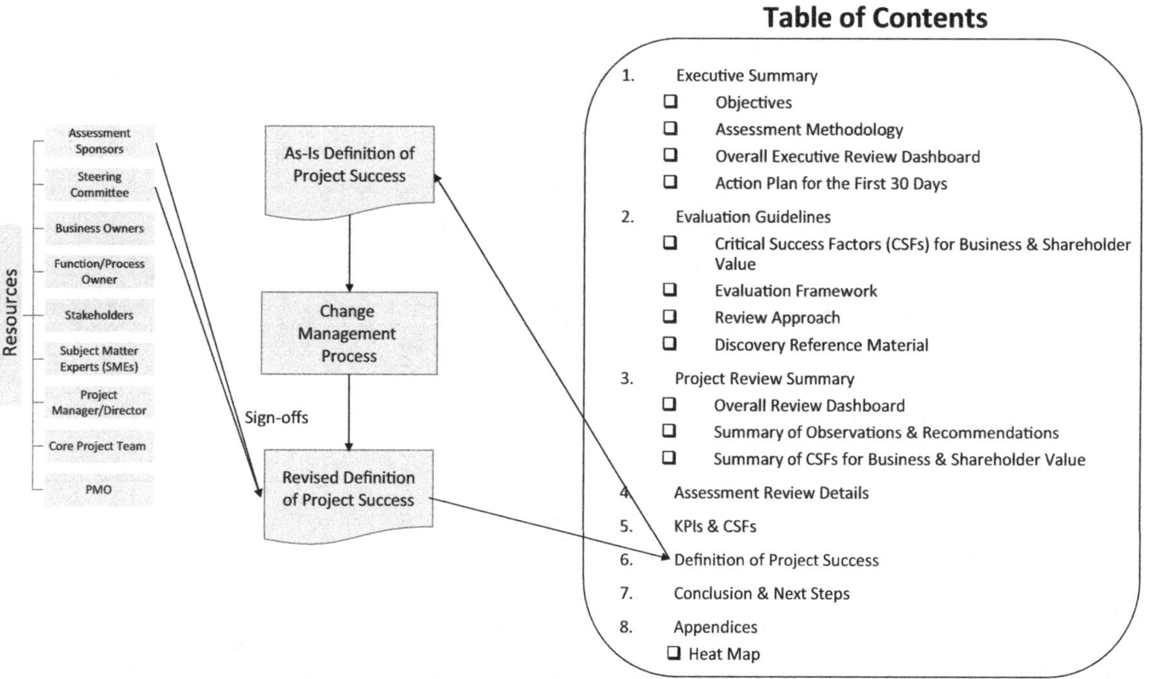

Figure 15.5 Setting the new success criteria.

Issuing the Final Report with Revisions

Once the assessment team has had an opportunity to update the draft report with all changes, it can be renamed to a final state. Reviews can be started with the project team members and the assessment sponsors. After that, the assessment moves to Phase 5 of the health check methodology.

Share Assessment Results (Phase 5)

By this point in the health check methodology, the final health check assessment report is assembled and has been revised with feedback from the business sponsors, the PMO, project management, and different members of the core project team. It is time to move to a process of making presentations to various members of executive management. Figure 15.6 shows the activities and processes that are relevant for each presentation to be done in Phase 5. The activities are being labeled as presentations/meetings because we want to make it clear that while a presentation of the final health check assessment results is the focus on the event, the intent is to have open discussions and to arrive at conclusions.

The subphases in Phase 5 are described below:

Review Assessment Highlights with Steering Committee

The Steering Committee must buy-in to the final action items, recommendations, and outcomes of the health assessment report. The presentation is also a meeting that facilitates an open discussion, under the auspices of the pre-set rules of engagement, so that the discussion can be effective.

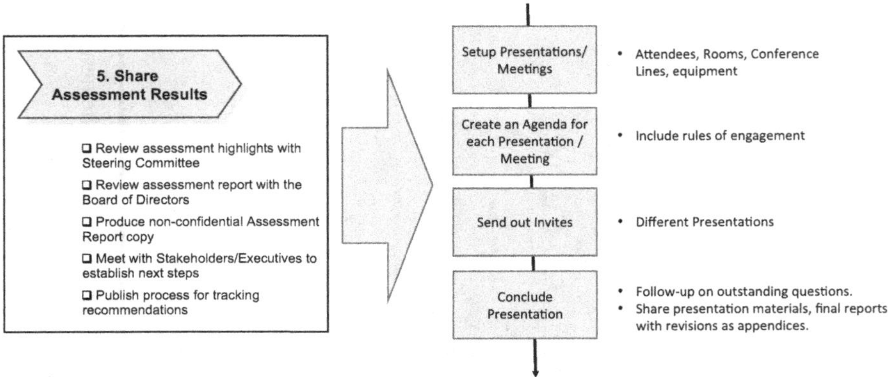

Figure 15.6 Preparing for Every Presentation/Meeting

Review Assessment Report with the Board of Directors

This is not always included in the mandate of a health check assessment. However, some initiatives have the attention of the Board of Directors (e.g. a core banking implementation or a global warehousing solution), and if it was perceived to be in trouble, they will likely want to hear the presentation as well. The agenda and material are essentially the same as those presented to the Steering Committee.

Produce non-Confidential Assessment Report Copy

As there may be confidential information that could not be included in the full public assessment report, aa confidential portion of the report should be developed and reviewed with the assessment sponsors. For example, there may be salary information as part of the analysis and this certainly should not be widely distributed. It needs to be included on pages that are marked "confidential" and saved for only a select audience that is identified by the Steering Committee, as shown in Figure 15.7. The non-confidential assessment report can be shared widely, while the confidential versions are closely held.

Depending on the nature of the confidential data, the splitting of the reports could have also been done at the draft stage or at the start of the program. For example, if the assessment sponsors wanted a review of the CIO, for example, while the criteria would likely be transparently shared, the actual review might be deemed confidential for some period of time.

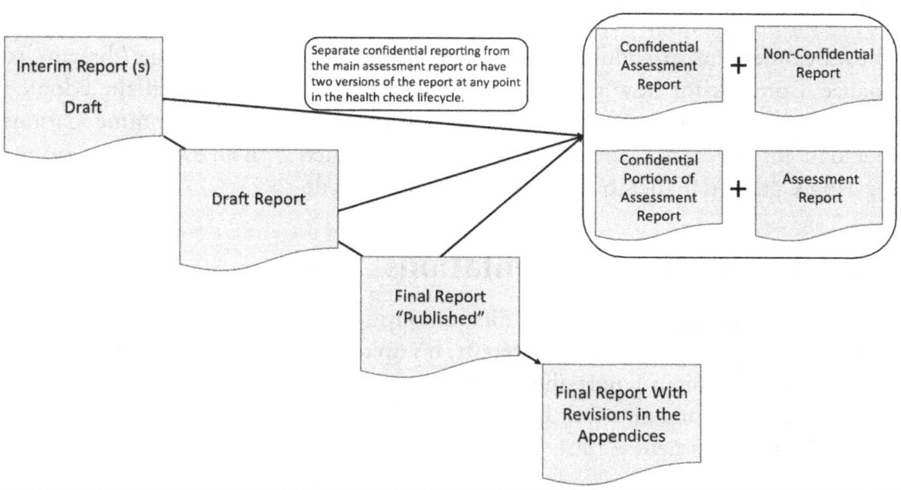

Figure 15.7 Confidential and non-confidential assessment report versions.

Meet with Stakeholders/Executives to Establish Next Steps

After the collection of presentations/meetings, the health check team should meet with the stakeholders to finalize next steps and the assessment team's continued involvement in the initiative—if there is any. The options to consider here are discussed at length in Chapter 16.

Publish Process for Tracking Recommendations

Regardless of the nature of the role that the assessment team will play after the health check report is finalized, the assessment team should extract all the recommendations into a common work area and allow progress to be tracked against each of those, as well as having a process for the project team to manage all the recommendations. This would include several items that have to be discussed and approved with project management, as follows:

- Sharing a link to the recommendations and where they are centrally stored.
- Defining a process for how the team will determine which recommendations are to be adopted and criteria for determining which ones are not.
- Identifying the final approvers at the Steering Committee level (it may be all the members of the steering committee, or the business owners that are impacted by the recommendation, or some other subset of the team).
- Determining how to assign recommendations to members of the team who will own them and the timeline for implementation.
- Documenting the acceptance criteria for each recommendation that will be accepted.
- Identifying impact on the project plan for each recommendation that is accepted.

The assessment team should work closely with the project manager/director to finalize a process for how the project team will report and close off the adopted recommendations. Part of the process should include updating recommendations metadata for the cases where they are not being adopted with an explanation from a Steering Committee member for the decision not to do so.

Running the Final Presentations

The actual final presentations to the different groups are a good opportunity to build momentum for the contents of the report. It's up to management whether they want to share the assessment report ahead of the meeting. The decision may be driven by the culture of the organization. Here are some pros and cons of each decision if it's left up to the assessment team:

- Pros: Meeting attendees will have an opportunity to review the materials in advance and come to the meeting prepared with knowledgeable questions. They will also have an opportunity to review, understand and synthesize the information in advance.

- Cons: It may be difficult to keep the group focused on an agenda as they may be impatient and preoccupied on the items that impact them and be very dismissive about the other parts of the report. They are already in a zone to find solutions or respond to negative observations. However, this can be mitigated by including in a preamble in both the message where they receive a link to a report in advance, and at the start of the session.

Presentation Logistics and Agenda

As with the interviews during discovery, there needs to be organization around meeting invites and the information that is sent out before and after the presentations. There will likely be several presentations as discussed previously so keeping the attendees at each individual meeting, as well as the times, locations, and conference chat lines, all clear is important. The invites should be sent out separately by one group.

Someone will also need to ensure that the rooms are set up for in-person presentations, as well as for providing links to video conference lines. Supplies that should be brought to the room include Flip charts, fresh markers, masking tape, projection equipment for laptops, and any food or beverages that the sponsors want to keep in the room. For virtual presentations and discussions, food can be delivered to the participants at their home offices.

Attendees

For each session, the attendees are selected by the Steering Committee and the health check leadership team. The health check team can be invited to most of the sessions, but with approval from the Steering Committee. For some sensitive presentations, only the leader of the assessment team might be invited to attend. One member of the Health Check Assessment team must be appointed as the facilitator.

Agenda

A standard agenda for a final assessment report presentation is shown in Figure 15.8. Start with soft introductions to all the participants. Follow this with key points around what success will look like at the end of the meeting. This list can be finalized with the Assessment Sponsors. This could include points such as the following:

1. Go through all the material
2. Get feedback from the attendees
3. Get commitment to pursue the recommendations
4. Get agreement on mitigation strategies for the key risks
5. Finalize next steps with dates and ownership

Health Check Presentation Agenda
1. Introductions
2. Discuss Rules of Engagement
3. What Success Will Like at the End of This Meeting
4. Evaluation Guidelines
❑ Evaluation Framework
❑ Review Approach
❑ Discovery Reference Material
5. Executive Summary
❑ Objectives
❑ Assessment Methodology
❑ Overall Executive Review Dashboard
❑ Action Plan for the First 30 Days
6. KPIs & CSFs
7. Definition of Project Success
8. Definition
9. Conclusion & Next Steps
Definition of Success For the Meeting
1. Go through all the material
2. Get feedback from the attendees
3. Get commitment to pursue the recommendations
4. Get agreement on mitigation strategies for the key risks
5. Finalize next steps with dates and ownership

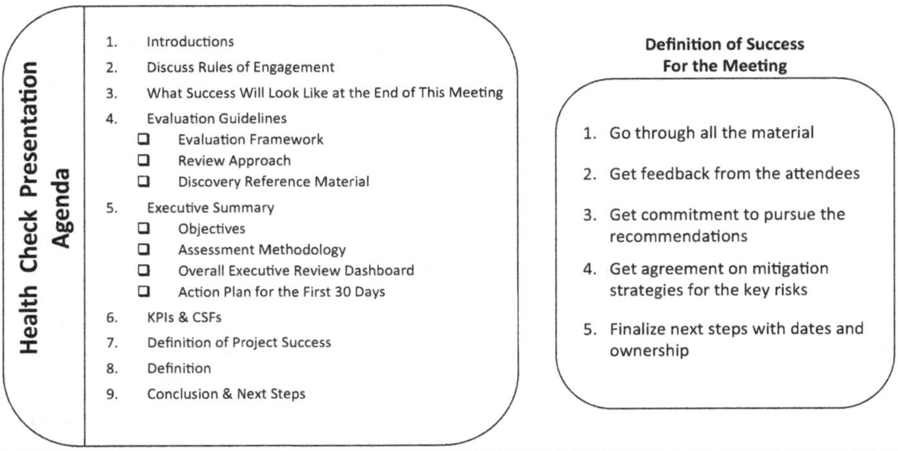

Figure 15.8 Final health check presentation agenda example.

Rules of Engagement for the Presentations/Meetings

There may be many participants in the room at some meetings, with different levels of intensity and management styles. It's useful to be very clear, up front, what the rules of engagement during the meeting are going to be in order to have a constructive and meaningful dialogue. Here are some examples to consider including in your own rules of engagement that will be shared at the meetings:

1. Show up on time
2. Everyone is encouraged to participate
3. No question is irrelevant
4. Assume best intentions in other participants
5. No personal attacks
6. The facilitator will stop discussion if it is starting to circle and will record the open issues for follow-up
7. Listen to all ideas
8. Do not interrupt—let people finish their statements
9. Contribute in a construction way
10. No shouting or raising your voice

Emotions and Attitudes to Expect

Similar to preparation for the interviews that were conducted during the discovery phase of the health check, the health check assessment team must be prepared for the avalanche of emotions they may encounter in the final presentations of the health check report. Figure 15.9 shows some of the more common emotions and attitudes that the health check team is expected to encounter. Techniques for interpreting and responding to these are described below.

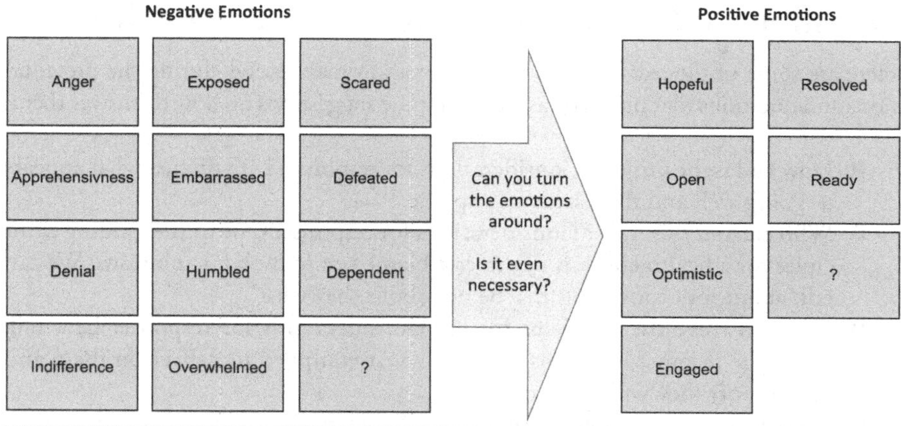

Figure 15.9 Emotional divide.

Figure 15.9 divides emotions into two categories for discussion: (1) Negative Emotions; (2) Positive Emotions. The reality is that it is not necessary or even commonly possible to turn negative emotions into positive ones in the span of meeting. In fact, some of the positive ones might be just as damaging as negative emotions. For example, executives that are hopeful and engaged might expect the health check to solve all of their project problems. Which is not possible. However, knowing and recognizing these emotions will allow the assessment team to stay on message. Some members of the audience might even swing through different emotional states multiple times in the same meeting as shown in Figure 15.10.

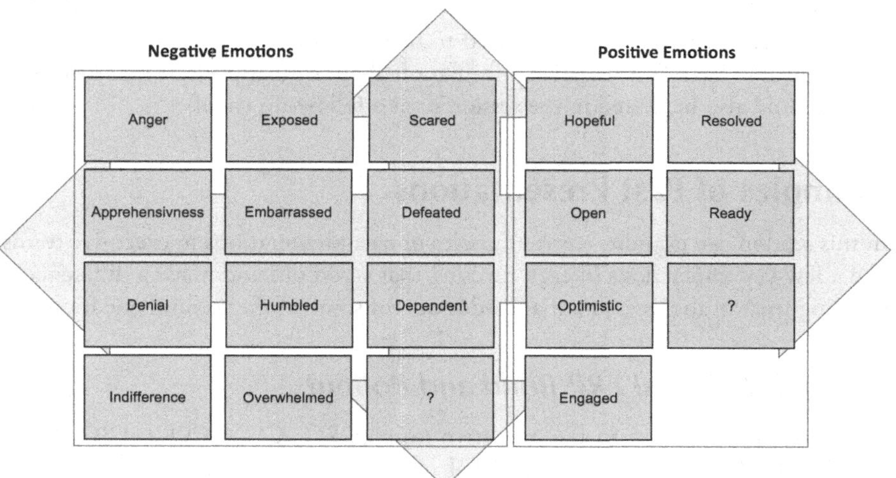

Figure 15.10 Emotional transitions.

Questions to Expect and Possible Answers to Give

Here are some of the reactions the assessment team may receive during the presentations and questions that might be asked, and some suggestions on how to answer them:

- How bad is the project? Considerations for response: Let's discuss what appears to going well and then areas to improve.
- Who created this mess? Considerations for response: One of the guiding principles for a health check is not to cast blame but to look for solutions. We can talk about root causes but maybe not about the "who".
- Can you solve the problems for us? Considerations for response: Let's talk about the recommendations and who's best equipped to deliver on them and the support they will need to succeed.
- We've been through this before, nothing happens? Considerations for response: A lot of people, even in this room, have spent a lot of time with us to craft out current recommendations to improve the direction of the project. We are not going to let their effort go to waste.
- Why should we believe you? Considerations for response: We're presenting findings that were assembled based on past experience, best practices, and input from the project team here. Provide comparative information about similar projects that were helped by Health Checks. Isn't this project doomed? Why are we throwing good money after bad? Considerations for response: This may be a very loaded question. On the surface, the requestor might be right, or might be in a pessimistic frame of mind. On a more nefarious level, there will be team members who do not want to be proven wrong. They view the health check as an opportunity to suggest that the project cannot be successful, for whatever reason, so they or other members of the organization should not be blamed. This might be to retain power or certainly not be lose it. A response to this question, without knowing more details would be to say that that decision would need to be made after all the facts are presented and absorbed. Comparative information about similar projects that succeeded should also be shared in the session or as a follow-up email.

Examples of Past Presentations

In this section, we examine some examples of past presentations to executive teams, and a few key interactions in each meeting that stood out and made a difference to building trust in the assessment and adoption of some of the recommendations:

Example 1 Global ERP Build and Rollout

This was a presentation to the executive team (CEO, CFO, COO, CIO, CRO, CMO, CHRO, and others) of a global organization that had just implemented many of the modules of an ERP solution in one country. Some of these executives are well known and frequently in the news. Solving IT project problems was not their first choice for spending their time, but they clearly recognized the importance this initiative had in their overall organization and profitability.

The ERP implementation was not textbook easy and many executives in the organization felt that the implementation was not successful or at least was more painful than it needed to be. A global System Integrator (SI) was in charge of the implementation and management had brought in an experienced health check expert to provide recommendations to roll the ERP out globally. Three major interactions at various times in the presentation are described below:

Interaction 1: One of the executives asked directly whether the SI had misled the executive team and if they were the reason for the problems in the implementation. The health check expert answered with past experience, stressing that these types of implementations were always challenging and that the SI had a fixed price budget to work with and operated within those limits. The reviewer offered that the SI could have been clearer about the tradeoffs that would need to be made in the confines of a fixed price but usually it is not entirely a one-sided blame in these situations.

Interaction 2: How can you fix the problem? This demonstrated a transition from anger to hopefulness. The danger here is setting unrealistic expectations that when not met would result in extreme distrust. The answer was to stress that the team has learned a lot through the health check that was just being completed and that the lessons learned would be used to fix current problems and be used to plan for the global rollout.

Interaction 3: The meeting concluded with a request for a firm date for the global rollout to be completed. The response to this was to again point back to all the lessons learned and to state that a date could not be finalized until the business requirements and global solution architecture was fleshed out. The only commitment that could currently be made was to build a detailed global rollout plan once the requirements were signed off.

The presentation ended on a high note and the health check team was asked to leave the room, but not go too far. About half an hour later they were thanked for the good report and presentation and told that their recommendations would be implemented. The team was retained for more work.

Example 2: An ERP at a Financial Services Institution

By the time the presentation was being made to the Steering Committee, the assessment report had already been socialized with the Operating Committee and other executives. The observations were 100% substantiated and the recommendations had support across the team, however, there were a surprising number of executives that were taking the situation personally. Some of them even wanted the health check report to state that the project should be canceled and that the organization was never ready for it. This would be an exoneration for them, even though the health check team was not trying to lay blame and were only looking for solutions. Furthermore, if one of the recommendations was to bring in more talent, the result would be a loss of control for some executives.

Interaction 1: You are telling us what we already know! This is a classic line to put reviewers on the spot and become defensive. Afterall, the reviewers have just spent the better part of one to two months in reviewing the project and formulating recommendations. Yet, after the first slide is presented, one of the top executives dismisses the effort with one line or shakes up the agenda so that the presenter cannot just follow the agenda. The response in this situation was to acknowledge the question, flip a few slides to show some of the coming meat, but then to return to the same point in the agenda to argue the case that the background had to be set for each recommendation to have meaningful appeal. The executive was squirming in his chair at this but did allow the meeting to proceed.

Interaction 2: What can be done immediately? This line of questioning, indeed, shows the urgency of the situation. It could be from a place to put pressure on the presenter or it could be due to the stress the project team was feeling. This is the reason there should always be 30-day recommendations included in the report. Turning to these puts a stick in the ground and demonstrates that real deadlines are going to be established that can be measured.

Interaction 3: Can you help us get the project over the finish line? After 60 minutes of intense conversation, the last notable interaction was to then acknowledge that the recommendations made sense and to open the door to get more help—in fact, to openly request the help. The answer was certainly a "yes" and a willingness to work with the assessment sponsors to determine what that would look like. It's important not to leave the health check sponsors out of the discussion as they were conceivably the first supporters who saw the need for a project health check.

Example 3: Retail Implementation

This was a replacement of a legacy system with an integrated ERP that would support stores, warehouses, the back office, eCommerce, and a customer-focused omni-channel. There were at least three large vendors involved, a separate organizational change management team, and a recurring health check team. Project management was using highly optimistic estimates and not focused on the business side of the implementation, only the technical perspective of getting the system into production. The health check team presented their findings to the Steering

Committee which consisted of the CEO, CFO, COO, CIO, VP HR, and various other executives.

Interaction 1: The project team is saying the project is in green, you are saying it's yellow teetering on red. How do you explain the difference? The question came from the well known CEO. The answer to this question involved addressing several points. The first was based on experience. There was no integrated project plan. Each of the vendors had their own plan. There was no attempt to build a single integrated one with dependencies and resources mapped out. This meant that when it was necessary to connect two systems, for example, a plan would have to be fleshed out and there is no guarantee that the two sides were going to align. Another issue was the growing backlog of key decisions that the team needed and no one was addressing. These would add to the workload and may even cause rework in the future. The health check team was arguing to escalate the project status to yellow until these were resolved, with an argument that the status would be red if the situation was not resolved within three (3)-weeks.

Interaction 2: What's wrong with the project timeline? The answer again was that optimistic estimating meant that the plan was a best-case scenario. Furthermore there was no contingency in the project plan to handle any surprises or work effort related to defects. The health check team demonstrated what they meant by showing how each implementation resulted in two streams of activities. One was a solution put into production that would have associated defects and change requests. The other stream was the next phase of development. Depending on the number of defects and change requests, team members and business users would be drawn in separate directions delaying the project. Then with the subsequent implementation the workload would magnify yet again. The recommendation given was to use realistic estimating to get defendable milestone dates and to add contingency on top of those. It is more expensive by many times to deal with a project that has slipped a deadline, than to increase a deadline in the first place based on solid evidence and add resources up front.

Interaction 3: Should we replace the SI? This was in response to the situation that there was no integrated project plan. The challenge in doing this was that the SI had knowledge and experience that would be lost if they left the project. The health check team recommended that a clarification to the contract was needed to include the end-to-end project plan mandate in their scope.

Closing Perspective

This chapter focused on the final activities required to complete the Health Check Assessment Report and to do a presentation roadshow to various levels of the organization as shown in Figure 15.11. As the figure shows, the presentations start with

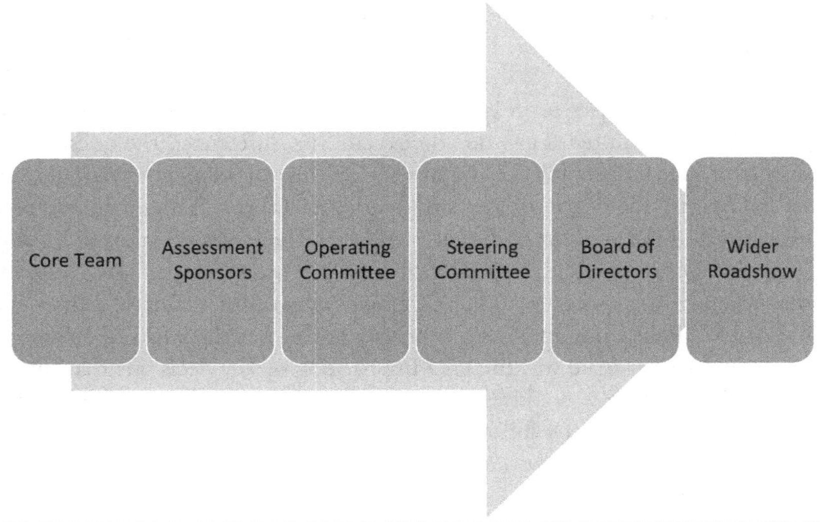

Figure 15.11 Presenting the final IT health check assessment report.

members of the core team and then head into management. The report can be revised until the Steering Committee level presentations are completed, after which it should be considered final. Changes to it at that point should be done through a "change request procedure" and be included as appendices instead of just continuing to revise the report. Confidential information should be separated from the report and follow a different line of dissemination under the direction of the Steering Committee.

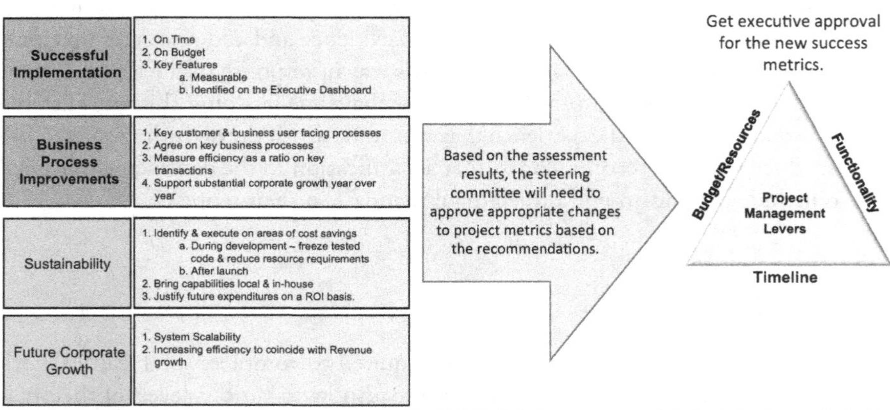

Figure 15.12 Setting the new success criteria.

There may have been changes to metrics originally defined in the project charter. These cannot just be accepted into the record. They must go through a formal change management process and then be formally approved by the project sponsors and/or steering committee as shown in Figure 15.12. The same type of process would be followed for other parts of the project charter or business case that required changes due to findings in the health check review.

AFTER THE ASSESSMENT AND NEXT STEPS

Chapter 16

Monitoring Progress Through the Health Check

Reaching this stage of the project or program health check means that the final assessment report has been delivered to one or more groups in the organization, their feedback has been received and included in an appendix where appropriate. Figure 16.1 shows the three periods in the health check methodology. A new phase to "Monitor" can be inserted into Period C. There are several directions this can take which are influenced by the type of health check that was commissioned (e.g. recurring, one time) by the assessment sponsors, as well as the organization which performed the assessment.

Options to Monitor Progress

The assessment team's involvement in monitoring progress will depend on the nature of the assessment that was commissioned and also what the assessment sponsors want to do next. It will also depend on the point of time in which they were commissioned in the general project development lifecycle. As shown in Figure 16.2, the assessment could have been commissioned at the start of the initiative, anywhere during the development lifecycle, closer to implementation (perhaps as a business readiness check), or even on a recurring basis. This timing of the health check will also play a role in determining the activities that follow the health check report delivery.

Before diving into the details of 16.2, there are some questions that need to be answered between the assessment sponsors and the assessment team leadership.

DOI: 10.1201/9781003269786-20

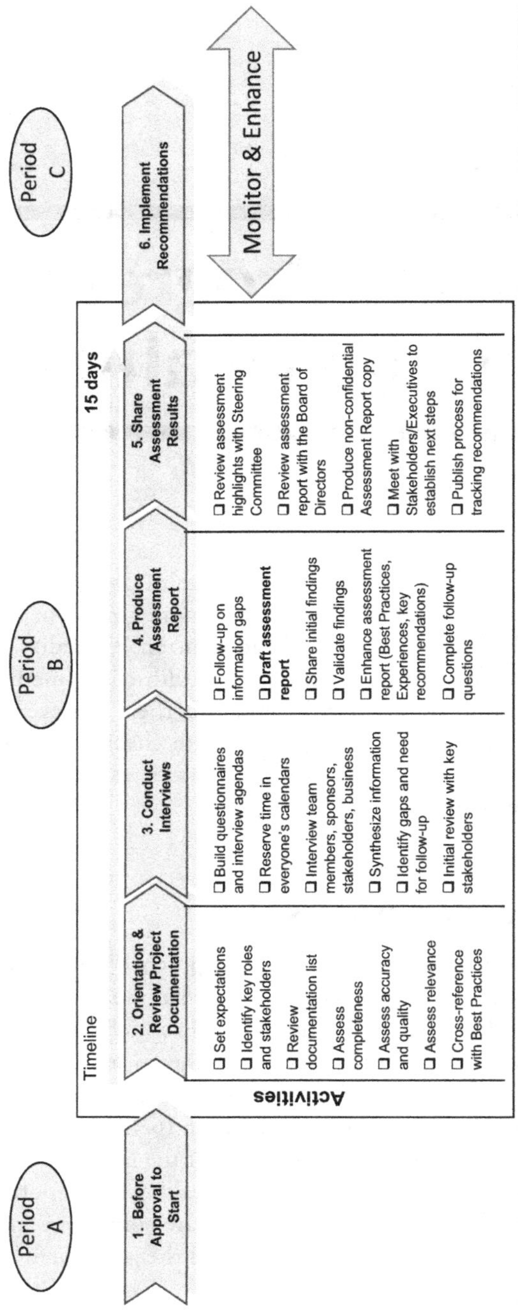

Figure 16.1 Monitor and enhance phase.

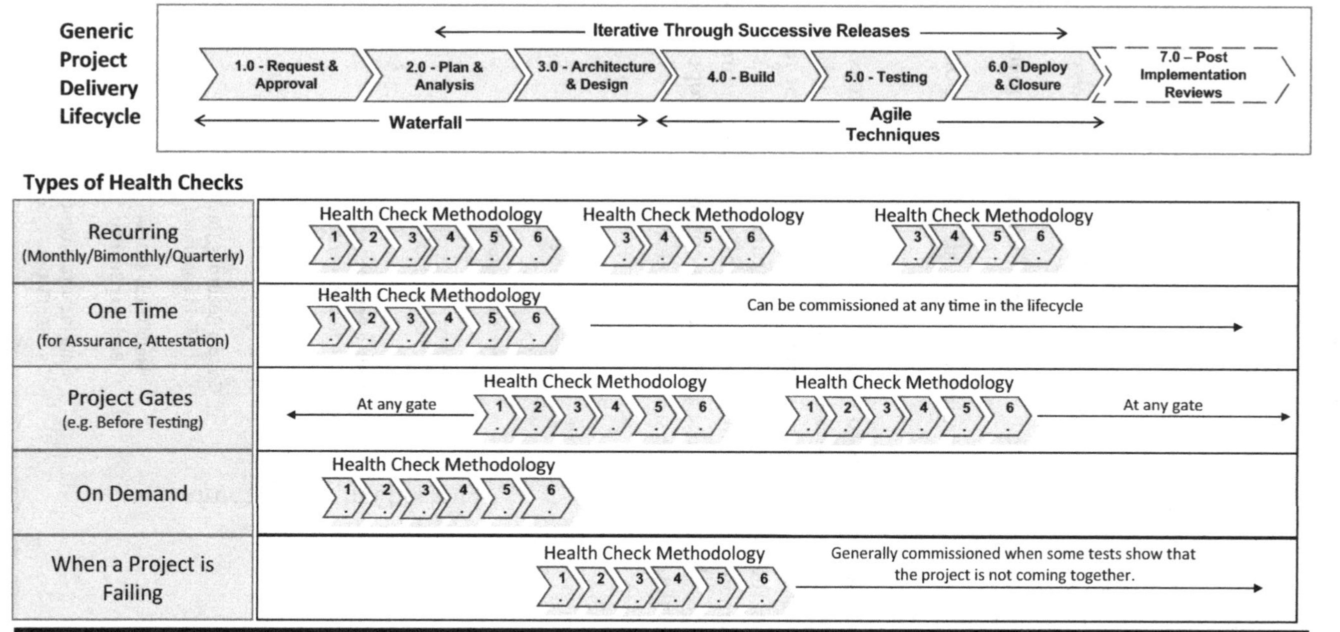

Figure 16.2 Timing of the health check.

These could have been addressed in the original scoping of the assessment, but as usually happens, the assessment activities drive more perspective into what needs to happen after the assessment report is delivered and so the questions may still be unanswered. Here are the items to consider:

1. Who is going to implement the recommendations contained in the assessment report?
2. How is progress against the recommendation adoption going to be measured?
3. How is the outcome of the recommendations themselves going to be measured?
4. How are new facts going to be incorporated into the recommendations as they emerge?
5. Who will ensure that the project does not fall back into the original state over a period of time?

There are several key questions to consider here, and the health assessment leader should discuss these with the assessment sponsors at some point in the lifecycle. It's rare that a final assessment report is delivered and the assessment team just leaves, however, that is the prerogative of the health check sponsors. It's recommended that the requirements in the monitoring role for the assessment team be clarified in writing. Some possibilities that the assessment sponsors could propose are shown in Figure 16.3 and described in the sections that follow.

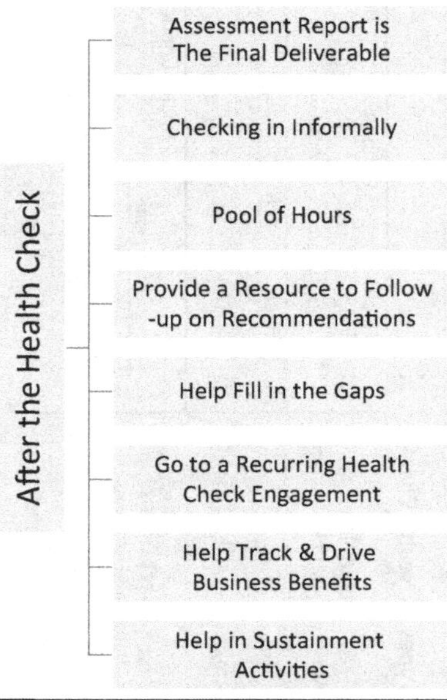

Figure 16.3 Options after the assessment report is delivered.

Assessment Report Is the Final Deliverable

In this option, the project team just requested a one-time report. They want to take full responsibility for the follow-up activities including implementing a full or partial set of the recommendations and tracking business value. The success of this approach depends on several factors. For example, is the project team really prepared to take full responsibility and objectively follow the recommendations in the health check report, or is the objective to put it on the back burner? Another possibility is that the project team is, in fact, focused on implementing the appropriate recommendations in the report and are going to dedicate their time to getting this done.

Checking in Informally

A small departure from the previous option where the project team feels they can get the job done, but extend an invitation for the health check assessment leadership to check in from time to time. If the assessment team was composed from internal resources, as shown in Figure 16.4, they can provide this service seamlessly. If needed, this informal activity can even be "formalized" at limited incremental cost to the project or organization.

If the health check team was sourced from an external vendor, this may be more problematic. The assessment lead could call in from time to time, take someone on the team out to diner, and informally ask about the state of the key dimensions. Any time spent could be viewed as a pre-sales activity or an investment in the client relationship. For external vendors the following option might be the better one for both the organization and for the health check team to plan their time.

Pool of Hours

Another approach that is actually a good compromise between a formal set of responsibilities and the informal checkpoints is to negotiate a pool of hours for the assessment team members to use from time to time for any of the following

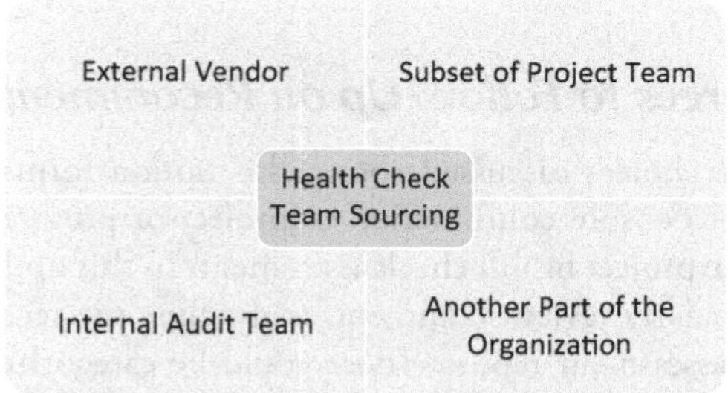

Figure 16.4 Sources for the health check team.

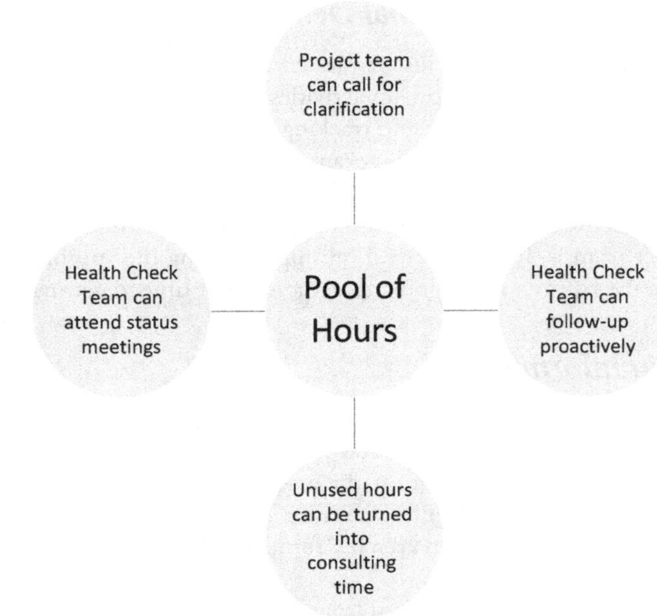

Figure 16.5 Pool of health check team hours.

activities, and as shown in Figure 16.5. The pool of hours can be used for any authorized activity, and there can be an agreement to replenish the hours in the pool if the business sponsors feel the money is being well used. This is a reasonable compromise to give responsibility to the project team, while providing them with an option to continue benefiting from external expertise.

Another advantage of allocating a general pool of hours to draw upon is the team's ability to use the hours surgically across the entire project lifecycle. The health check could have been completed in an early phase of the project, while the team may need assistance in evaluating their user acceptance testing results much later in the process. The pool of hours approach supports this requirement.

Provide Resources to Follow-Up on Recommendations

From the self-serve choices discussed above, this option formalizes a role for the health check team to ensure continuation of project or program adjustments that were initiated by the project health check assessment. In this option, resource (s) can be dedicated to regularly review, comment, and adjust the recommendations that were made in the assessment report. Those could be categorized in 30-, 60-, and 90-day targets. The team would comment but not do any of the activities related to implementing the recommendations.

Help Fill in the Gaps

This option begins to incorporate members of the assessment team or those under their guidance to take responsibility to implement specific recommendations. This approach offers advantages in the following instances:

- The core project team does not have the capacity to do the work themselves.
- The core project team does not have the skills to do the work themselves (e.g. project lead, solution architecture).
- The business sponsors want to see skin in the game from the health check team so that the success becomes shared (and same with the opposite situation).
- The project team dynamics are better with the continued and regular involvement of the health check assessment team.

Go to a Recurring Health Check Arrangement

The assessment sponsors may feel the assessment team did a great job and want to turn their involvement into a recurring health check model, with a frequency tied to milestones, project gates, or even something like monthly, bimonthly or quarterly.

This approach offers the advantage of providing continuity from members of the health check team who are more likely to remain on the initiative if this option is selected quickly, otherwise they may end up working on other projects for other clients.

Conversion from the single health check to a recurring frequency would not be very challenging. The scope parameters should be updated, but, as shown in Figure 16.6, the startup activities do not have to be repeated—for example, the assessment team already has access to the documentation and have created templates to track feedback. Most of the time where "create" is used in an activity in the health check methodology, the word can be changed to "update". This is a tremendous time savings. Most monthly recurring health checks require about five days of effort per month, versus the 3–6 weeks of effort for a one-time health check. The economies of scale apply by reducing the effort of the initiative at the unit level while providing more volume of the product.

Help Track and Drive Business Benefits

Another option that can be combined with some of the previous ones is to mandate the health check team to set up the tracking and measurement vehicles to measure and report on specific business benefits. There is a level of higher persuasion if the benefit reports are coming from an independent or quasi-independent source. They would use the handful of CSFs and KPIs, along with the baselines and thresholds established in the business case, and track these after the project goes live. While the health check team can do some setup activities, the measurement activities are done

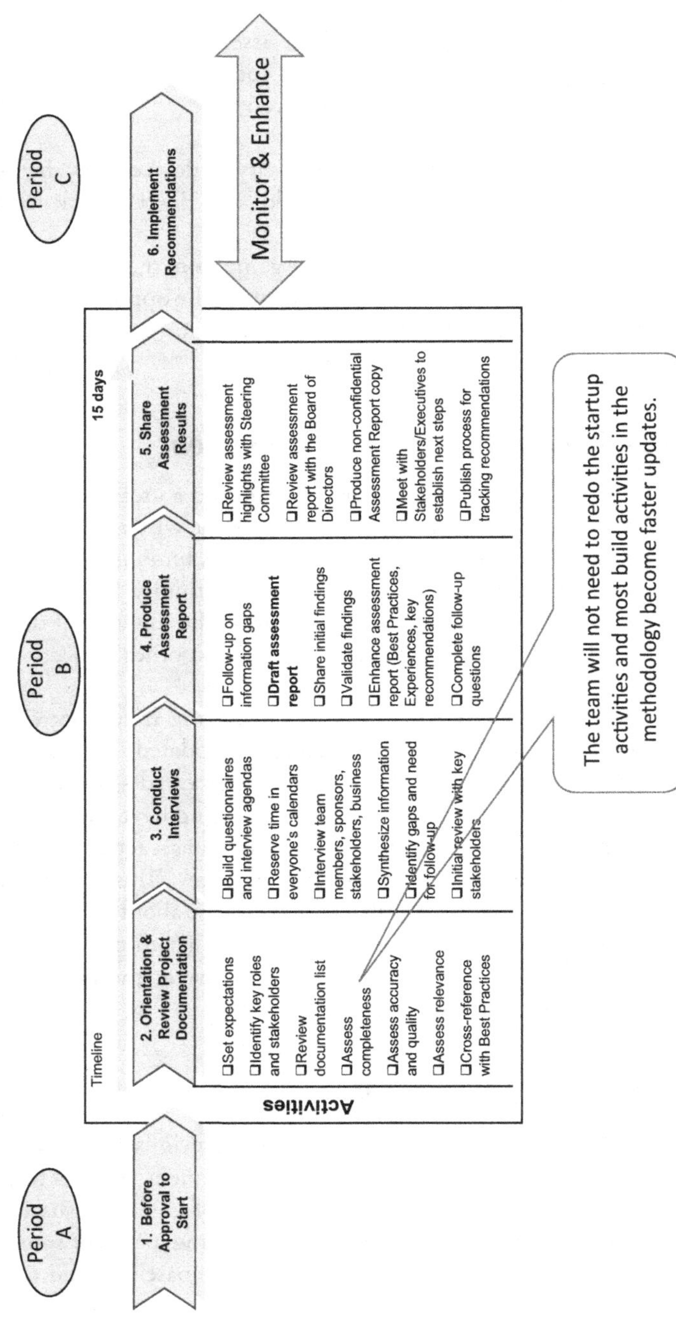

Figure 16.6 Recurring health checks streamline activities.

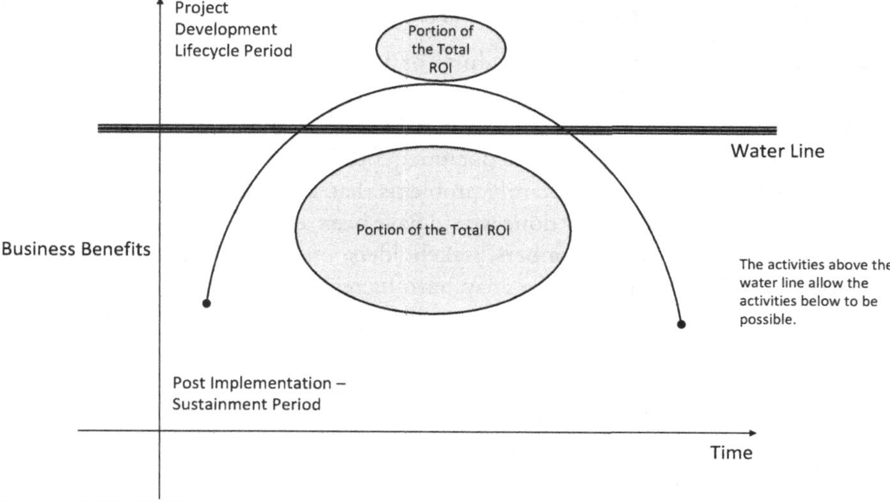

Figure 16.7 Below the waterline.

after go live and during the sustainment period. The health check team can also provide comparatives from industry to serve as additional data points to demonstrate what can be achievable by the organization.

Help in Sustainment Activities

As shown in Figure 16.7, all the activities prior to implementation represent the tip of the iceberg or curve of the total Return on Investment (ROI) of the value of the program. The rest of the curve below the waterline is the lion's share of ROI. While activities above the waterline enable the activities below to even be possible, it's all the work that happens in sustainment which will ultimately drive the ROI through the realization of business value. Hiring the assessment team to drive activities at this time, even if the health check was completed early in the project lifecycle, is a good approach to bringing expertise to the project sustainment team in a surgical way to focus on critical items.

Driving the Health Check Action Items to Multiply Business Value

There are many benefits accruing from the IT health check. These can be classified as procedural or incidental benefits and action benefits which require additional work to be realized.

Procedural or Incidental Benefits

These are being referred to as procedural or incidental benefits because they are accruing as a consequence of simply executing the health check methodology. For example, the project team needed to share deliverables. This might have caused the team to scramble to assemble these documents to meet the health check request. This might have helped them identify problems that were otherwise sliding by. The mere act of getting this activity done would have been a benefit to the project initiative. Similarly, giving team members, stakeholders, business owners, and others an opportunity to express their views may have increased morale. In fact, there may have been many more incidental benefits accruing from the health check, as follows:

- Improved deliverable quality
- Categorization of deliverables
- Confirmation of regular management meetings
- Team members felt they were being heard, maybe for the first time since the project was started
- Improved understanding of roles and responsibilities
- Definition of the governance processes
- Dry run to respond to requests from groups such as internal audit or external regulators
- Communication within the team through the interviews and then when the final report was presented

The actualization of the benefits will vary from project to project and organization to organization. This is a partial list of the benefits already accrued, there are many others. Consider the following example:

> In one past project, an external regulator was performing a health check on a core retail ERP system. They sent a list of requests to review specific deliverables. There was not much lead time for the external review. Their point was that the documents should already exist if the project was being well managed. In this instance, there were teeth to the review because the request was from a regulator. A failure to produce the deliverables or if the deliverables were not acceptable to the regulator could cause the project to be delayed until they were convinced it was safe for it to continue. As a health check had been completed on the initiative only four months earlier, the team already had the deliverables that were requested. These included: Project Charter (including evidence of executive signoff), Disaster Recovery Plan, Proof that the Disaster Recovery Plan had been tested, Contingency Plan, Business Requirements (including evidence of business signoff), Security Plan and User Permissions, Risk Log and Mitigation Strategy, all status reports, status reports shared with the board of directors, minutes of management

meetings, decision log, testing plan, OCM plan, methodology review, and the testing results. Had the team not been through the health check and updated these based on the recommendations the results of the regulatory review could have ended badly. Instead, the review went smoothly and passed the regulator.

Health Check Action Items: Driving the Assessment Recommendations

As discussed in the previous section, there are many incidental benefits that derive from a health check that in themselves have already likely improved the quality and direction of the project. However, depending on the state of the project (e.g. it needs a rescue intervention or simply incremental adjustments) and the phase of development, specific action items can translate into even more spectacular returns. The first of these is to determine how the recommendations in the final assessment report are going to be adopted.

Assuming that the project management team has opted to implement some or all of the recommendations from the health check assessment, there must be some type of monitoring in place as well as designated resources to implement the recommendations, as shown in Figure 16.8 and described below:

- Prioritize the recommendations for implementation: Divide into the next 30, 60, 90, 90+ day categories
- Identify ownership, timelines, and acceptance criteria
- Identify monitoring team
- Update Governance Approach to include progress updates

The approach shown in Figure 16.8 categorizes all the key recommendations and ensures that each is prioritized by the steering committee. This increases the likelihood that they will have the full support of the project team as well. The example suggests a breakdown of 30, 60, 90 days—roughly one month apart. This has worked well on initiatives in the past, however, the intervals are only suggestions and could be changed to smaller or larger gaps. The process flow in Figure 16.8 involves key resources from the project team who are assigned ownership over each recommendation to be implemented. They must then identify work effort and acceptance criteria. This would be shared with the project manager and updated in the project plan. The health check team is also retained in advance to provide oversight or monitoring for the entire recommendation management process. Their involvement is shown in Figure 16.9 and could be any or some combination of the following:

- Observers: This may be the least valuable role. The health check team members attend status meetings and, for the most part observe progress. They may be called upon to provide best practices and information. For the most part they are reacting and not being proactive.

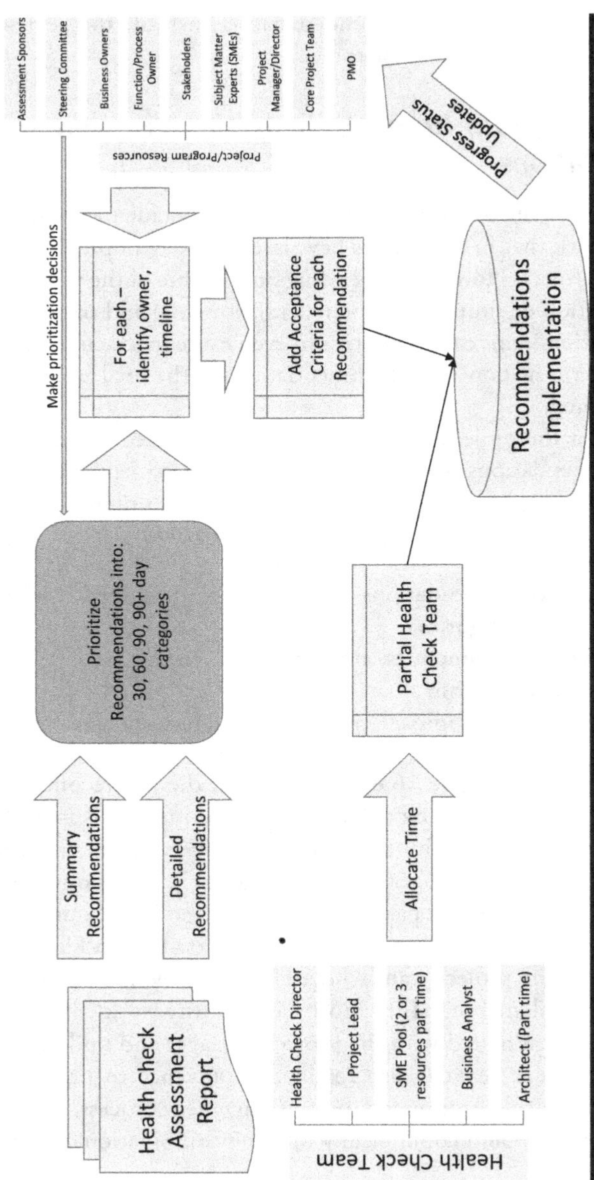

Figure 16.8 Managing implementation of assessment recommendations

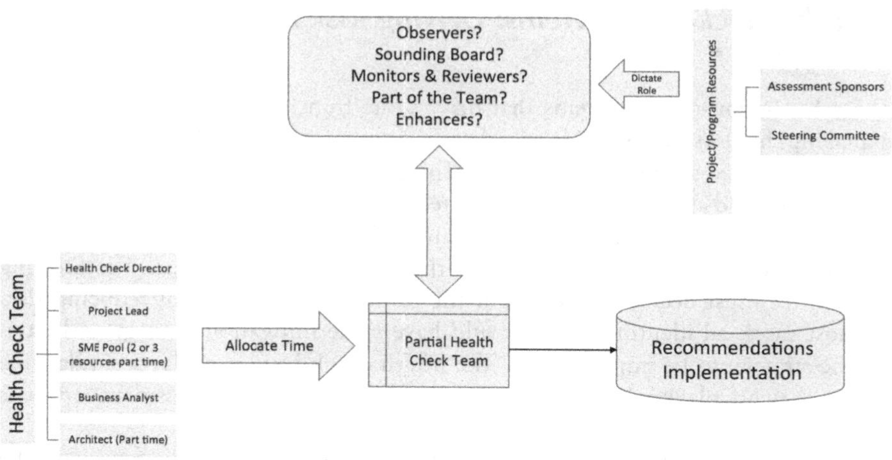

Figure 16.9 Action oriented roles of the health check team.

- Sounding board: In this role, designated members of the health check team attend status meetings and are actively used as a sounding board in the planning and execution of the recommendations.
- Monitors and Reviewers: The health check team members take on a review role again. This is the most natural extension from the health check role. They would attend status meetings, ask questions, be inquisitive, provide comparable information and best practices, and provide status updates to management on progress or lack thereof. In one sense, they are continuing in the role of health check assessment for the implementation of the recommendations.
- Part of the Team: Members of the health check team could even be seconded to the recommendation implementation team. As such, they would become accountable for implementing the recommendations they are allotted perhaps in conjunction with other members of the project team. This is a decision that must be made between the management of both groups as the reviewer has become a reviewee in a sense. However, as stated in the early parts of this book, there are several ways to view this. While there is benefit in keeping the health check team entirely independent. It may be efficient to have certain members of the health check team start in an independent capacity but then use their knowledge to accelerate development of key solutions in the project itself. This is a business and logistics decision to be made at the executive management level.
- Enhancers: In this role, the health check team will continue the recommendations portion of the health check by looking for opportunities to enhance the value, content, and number of recommendations related to the health check. The assessment sponsors will need to put parameters on the depth and reach of enhancement that is appropriate and responsible.

Health Check Action Items: Driving Risk Mitigation Strategies

The other action-oriented items that drive value from the health check is that of managing the risks that were identified at the Summary Report Dashboard level and in all the detailed sections of the report. This process is shown in Figure 16.10. The risk items should also be reviewed by the Steering Committee and prioritized. Unlike recommendations, risks are about probabilities, likelihoods, estimated impacts, and severity. They may never materialize, or they could be catastrophic. The Steering Committee must decide where to put the team's focus in terms of reducing risk. In most cases, all identified risks should have some mitigation strategy and dates for the strategy to be implemented. The health check team can play a similar role to that they are playing in driving recommendations from the assessment report as discussed in the previous section.

An update on risk management should be included in all status reports to the team and those shared with executives and the board of directors.

Sustainment Period Opportunities

Regardless of when the IT health check was done or repeatedly done in the project lifecycle, the sustainment period, as was shown in Figure 16.7, represents the largest portion of the ROI that can be realized in the solution timeline. Recall that, as shown in Figure 16.11, the full solution timeline is more than that typically described as the project lifecycle. It contains the phases that follow 6.0 Deploy and Closure. The length of each chevron is not proportional to the duration of time it actually represents. For example, the sustainment period can last for many years, while the development lifecycle could have been twelve months. Here are some key considerations for each of the phases shown in Figure 16.11:

- Phase 8.0 Stabilization Period: This is all hands-on deck and typically lasts between 10 and 60 days. Service Level Agreements are negotiated in advance to ensure that critical defects get immediate attention and users are given the support they need to use the system. The focus is on usage and getting staff on the system rather than on measuring business benefits. The exception to this could be the need to produce business reports to prove that the system is working correctly.
- Phase 9.0 Sustainment Period: This is the larger period where operational efficiencies are gained through the full utilization of the system's functionality. The system must also be maintained, patches applied, and new functionality must be added to continue to support the business. This period of time is discussed below.

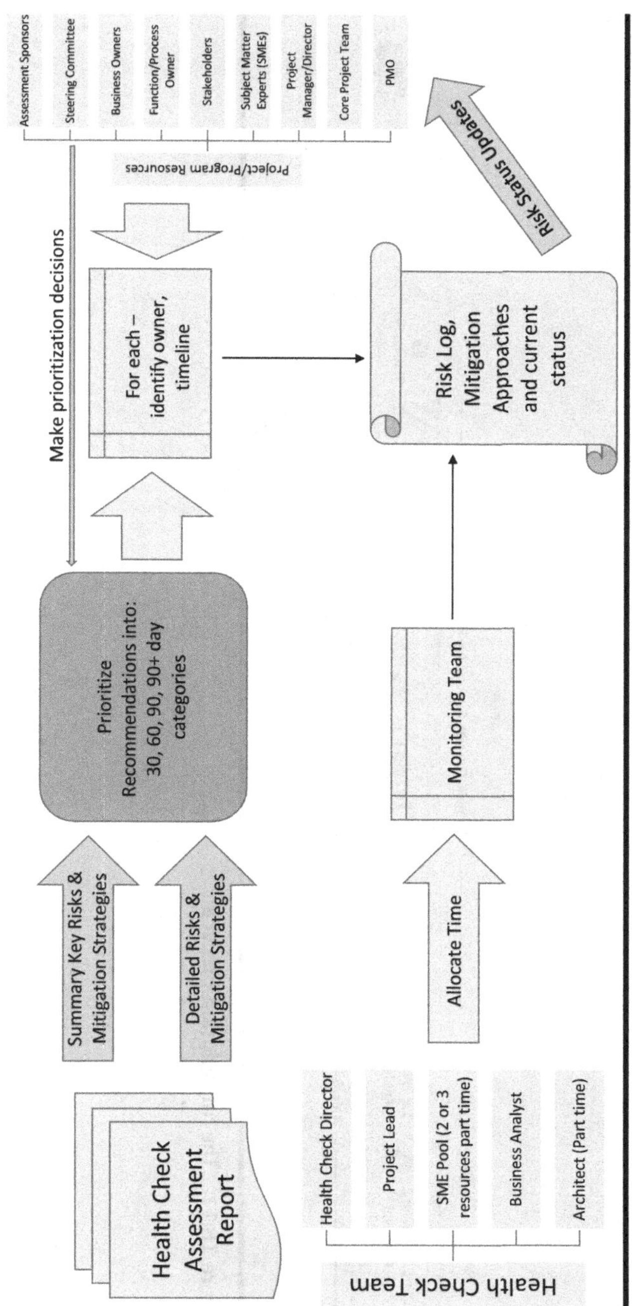

Figure 16.10 Managing risks and mitigation strategies.

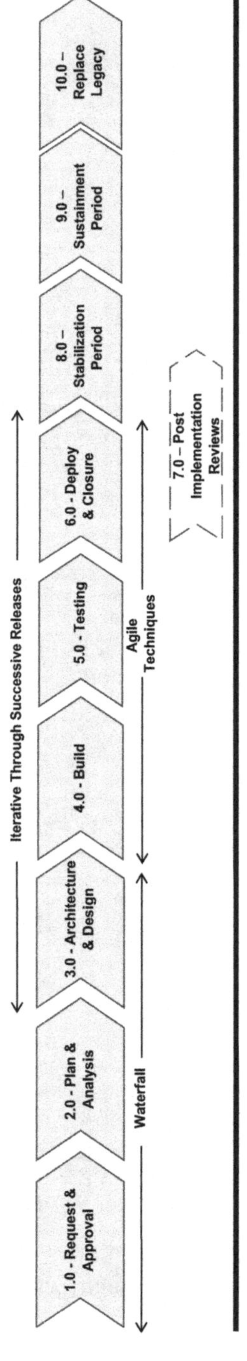

Figure 16.11 The full solution lifecycle.

- Phase 10.0 Replace Legacy: At some point, even the most modern systems become legacy-like. Also new components and tangential systems become available. For some, the cycle begins again but with a better handle on the "As Is" architecture, processes, and standards.

Regardless of the phase the project health check was completed, there must be consideration for post-implementation activities as shown in Figure 16.12. These can be included as recommendations in the final assessment report, or more ideally involve the health check team as the project is launching. Some common forms this can take are as follows:

- Prepare for sustainment: This period tends to be very hectic on most projects. There are lots of "to do" check lists and detailed schedules to ensure nothing was overlooked or forgotten. Have the users been trained? Are the super users ready? Are the URLs in the communication emails easy to spot? Do they work? Are the security profiles set up so users can log in after go-live? There would be hundreds of these questions at this time and a knowledgeable source of resources from the health check team can provide great value to the effort at this time.
- Business Readiness Health Check: This can be an independent assessment of the business capability to support the system in production and for the organization's ability to use it. This check can also include the KPIs and the CSFs that were identified at the beginning of the project or identified during the health check discovery activities.
- Post Mortem Review: The health check team can conduct a post-mortem review with all the stakeholders to determine what went well, what could be improved, and any other suggestions that can be rolled up as lessons learned for other initiatives. This exercise may also identify additional opportunities to capture and drive more business value.
- After Implementation Health Checks: The health check team can be commissioned to continue doing health checks in the sustainment period to provide a view on how the project is performing against metrics.

Some of the key considerations that drive higher business value in the post-implementation phase are shown in Figure 16.13 and described below. As discussed previously, these activities must be part of the overall project plan or they should be flagged in the health check assessment report. Based on the decision of the steering committee, the health check team may have a role to play during the sustainment period.

Sustainment Team

After a project is implemented, there is a period in which all hands are on deck for a warranty period (say 30 to 60 days). After that, the resources begin to drop off

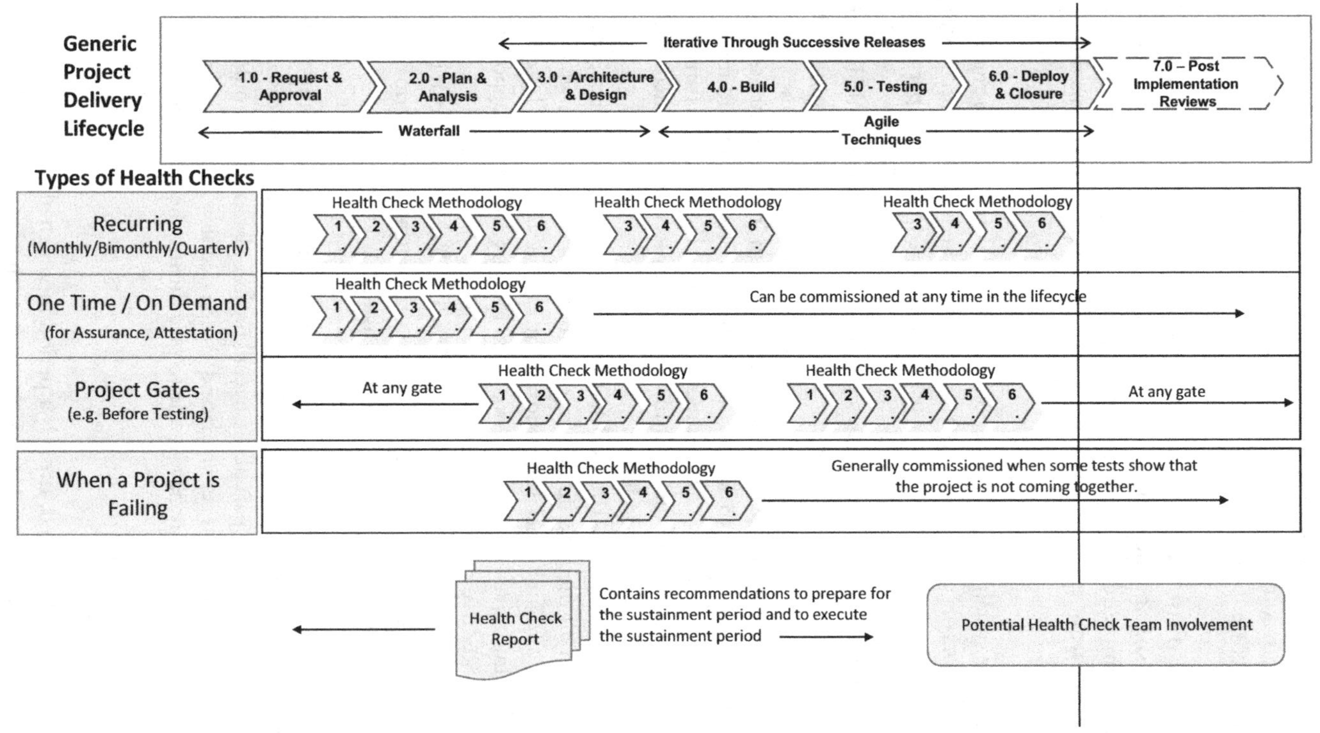

Figure 16.12 Health check focus on sustainment.

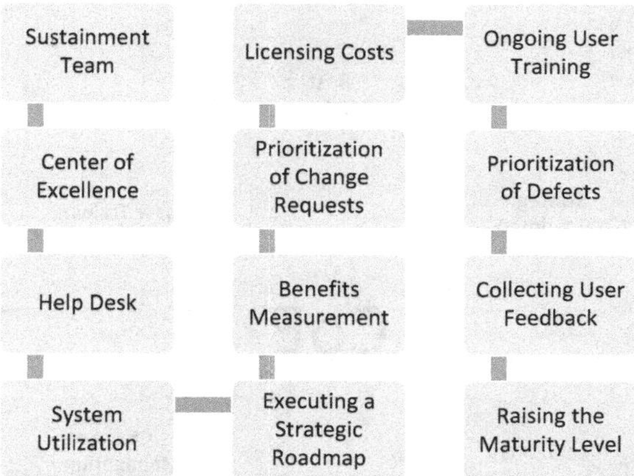

Figure 16.13 Sustainment period activities.

and control passes to a Sustainment Team. Members of this team should have been identified, trained, and staffed while the development project itself was still running. In fact, an assessment finding would have pointed this out if a sustainment team was not in the plan and there was no evidence that one was being staffed, trained, and prepared to take over once the project was live and past the warranty "all hands-on deck" period.

Typically, members of the sustainment team would have been selected from members of the core project team. There will also need to be a steering committee staffed by business and technology leaders. This group will own the following:

- Business value that was originally described in the business case
- All prioritization of changes and defects
- All new changes
- Budget

Strategic plan for the solution

Center of Excellence

The sustainment team can be part of the Center of Excellence (CoE). There may be one or more Center's of Excellence supporting the solution set that was implemented. The mandate for each CoE includes the following:

- Be the repository of best practices. This could involve investigating, documenting or creating them. Work with the PMO if it exists to maintain and distribute these.

Figure 16.14 Center of excellence components.

- Work with the sustainment team, if it is separate from the CoE to manage the software platforms. This includes managing new releases, applying patches, and ensuring security.
- Coordinate upgrades to the software platforms.
- Track and share benefits from the system.
- Ensure that the system is maximizing benefits to the organization.
- Coordinate with other Steering Committees.
- Work across the organization to ensure that the software solution is being used effectively.
- Support the PMO and project teams.
- Follow-on user training.
- Solution Roadmap.
- Budget controls

Help Desk

The help desk must be either setup, or if there is already a help desk, it needs to be enhanced to support the system. The help desk can make a big difference to the benefits a system is providing an organization. Users who are unable to perform a function on the system are directly impacting productivity. The help desk must have the technical ability to support and track tickets. Help desk operators must also be trained to support the system or escalate to the next line of support. These additional lines must have contracts in place to start support at system go-live or following the initial all hands-on deck sustainment period.

The help desk should provide a regular report that is shared with the sustainment team and the Center of Excellence related to the system shows tickets, resolutions, and work that remains to be addressed by priority.

System Utilization

Most large software systems, like ERP/CRM/HRIS, have built tools or there are third parties that have built these tools to measure the performance of a system once it has gone live. The diagnostic tools will measure which transactions are the most common, how efficiently transactions are performing, transactions that are never called, and provide other diagnostics. This information can be used to tune the system, improve business processes, and find savings. If a transaction is never used, why pay for it in any way? If a handful of transactions are handling 80% of the business, they should be the focus of improvement attempts to drive the most business value and ROI.

Licensing Costs

The costs of the software licenses are a big component of the relatively fixed component of the overall IT spend. Negotiating to make these as low as possible during sustainment can be enabled while looking at new solutions with the software vendors. They are likely to be accommodating if new deals are on the way. Here are some considerations:

- Ensure you are not paying for licenses you are not using.
- Ensure that you are compliant with the licensing requirements. If the system is licensed for 1,000 named users, ensure there are never any more.
- Get advice on the licensing agreements and contracts to optimize the value your organization is getting.
- Negotiate deals with vendors at times they are most incented to close business

Prioritization of Change Requests

After go-live, there will be several buckets of work. One of these is a list of change requests, some of which can be considered to be projects in themselves. The sustainment team must work with a Steering Committee to prioritize each of these based on business value and other considerations. The Steering Committee must have representation from the business units that are impacted by the system either directly or indirectly. The Information Technology (IT) group should also be represented on this committee.

Prioritization of Defects

Defects are another bucket of work that the sustainment team must manage after go-live. Defects will be stored with a priority. The sustainment team needs to understand how the defects are being prioritized. Is a critical defect really critical to the business or is it just important to the person who entered it into the ticketing system? The sustainment team also must ensure that change requests are not being added as defects to either get more attention (higher priority) or to hide the fact that they were missed in the business requirements in the first place.

Benefits Measurement

This is one of the most important activities in sustainment from a reporting perspective. The KPIs and CSFs should be turned into tables and tracked as a function of time. Figure 16.15 shows a subset of target dimensions. The true value from the system should be recorded against these types of dimensions. Adjustments can then be made to catchup or changes initiated to over perform.

Executing a Strategic Roadmap

Part of the mandate for the CoE is to maintain a strategic roadmap that includes evolution of the implemented solutions. A two to five-year window is fairly standard, with a lot of detail in the first two years, and major milestones in the remaining years. This would, of course, be a rolling deliverable and should be updated perhaps yearly or even every six months.

Dimension	Benefit Criteria	KPI Subset
Customer	Improve Customer Satisfaction on call centre	No More than 10% Call-backs (current Baseline is 20%)
Operational	Improve Operating Efficiency	Reduce Operational Costs by 1% every quarter Increase inventory turns to 3 per year
Financial	Margin	Improve Margin up to 50% (current baseline is 20%)

Figure 16.15 Measuring benefits.

Ongoing User Training

The user base would have been trained prior to go-live on most projects. The sustainment team and the Center of Excellence must work with HR to provide refresher training courses, training courses for new employees, and upgraded curriculum to reflect changes to the functionality of the system through change requests. There should also be productivity aids that assist users to quickly get instructions for the majority of the work they need to do on the system.

Collecting Feedback

Users will have feedback on a system after using it for a period of time. Some parts of the system will garner positive feedback, while other parts may be slow or lacking in functional richness. There will also be feedback on the business processes. Some will be deemed unnecessary or a waste of time.

For example, when systems go live, a lot of controls are usually put in place. Trying to pay an invoice? It may require three levels of approval and one of them is on vacation for four weeks with no delegation. On one initiative in the past, invoices were getting backed up by months over the summer, as one signer took vacation, then another, and another. Some invoices were not being paid for months on end. A process that seemed great on paper and which was approved by internal audit was not effective in real life. Similarly on another project, a CxO started to complain that she needed to sign in to the system every day to approve items that she should be able to delegate to her assistant.

While some of these could have been foreseen in advance, there will be many examples of users finding ways to do things faster, better, and cheaper. It's prudent to either speak directly to a subset of users on their experience or to send out surveys every few months to capture this feedback and assess it at the Steering Committee level in the CoE.

Executive Reporting

The CoE should meet with the Executive Team to identify the reports and information they want to see about the new system after implementation. Some common examples include the following:

- Business Metrics Report
- Business Benefits Tracking
- Control Reports
- System Usage and Availability
- Defects
- Change Requests
- Risk log
- Security Issues

	Level	Description	Timeline Targets
	Level 6: Center of Excellence Best Practices	Ability of the Centre of Excellence to offer best practices to the industry.	Not needed
	Level 5: Center of Excellence Mature	Business/IT partnership – strategy, anticipating and aggressive.	Not needed
Desired Target	Level 4: Center of Excellence Working	Forward looking, leveraging IT for new business innovations.	**3 Years**
	Level 3: Center of Excellence Started	Strong alignment between business/IT. Measurable payback periods. Measure against the business case.	**1 Year**
	Level 2: Stabilized ERP and Business Value Driven	Functional End-Users, strong infrastructure, complete interfaces, and increased automation.	**6 months**
Today	Level 1: Core Implementation	Core system implemented, users trained. KPIs are defined.	**Go live**

Figure 16.16 Setting the maturity level target.

Raising the Maturity Level

Every system experience offers an opportunity to raise the majority level of the organization including IT. It is not necessary or even recommended to reach the highest level of majority as the expense associated with this may not provide a sufficient payback to the organization. Figure 16.16 shows an example where the CoE members would have worked with the Steering Committee to set a target of maturity level 4 to be reached within three years of go-live. The higher majority levels were removed from scope as they would not provide value for the additional cost investment.

Closing Perspective

This chapter examined approaches for the health check team to provide value to the initiative once the health check was completed. This included passive to proactive involvement. As the health check team has built up extensive knowledge through their review of the documentation and conducting individual interviews, it is prudent for an organization to keep them involved, even after the formal health check is done.

Figure 16.17 shows the benefits that the organization derives in the period after the health checks are normally done. Everything comes together in the Sustainment Period, and as shown by what's below the waterline in the figure, it's imperative that organizations use the learnings and possibly the resources of the health check initiative to drive success during the sustainment phase.

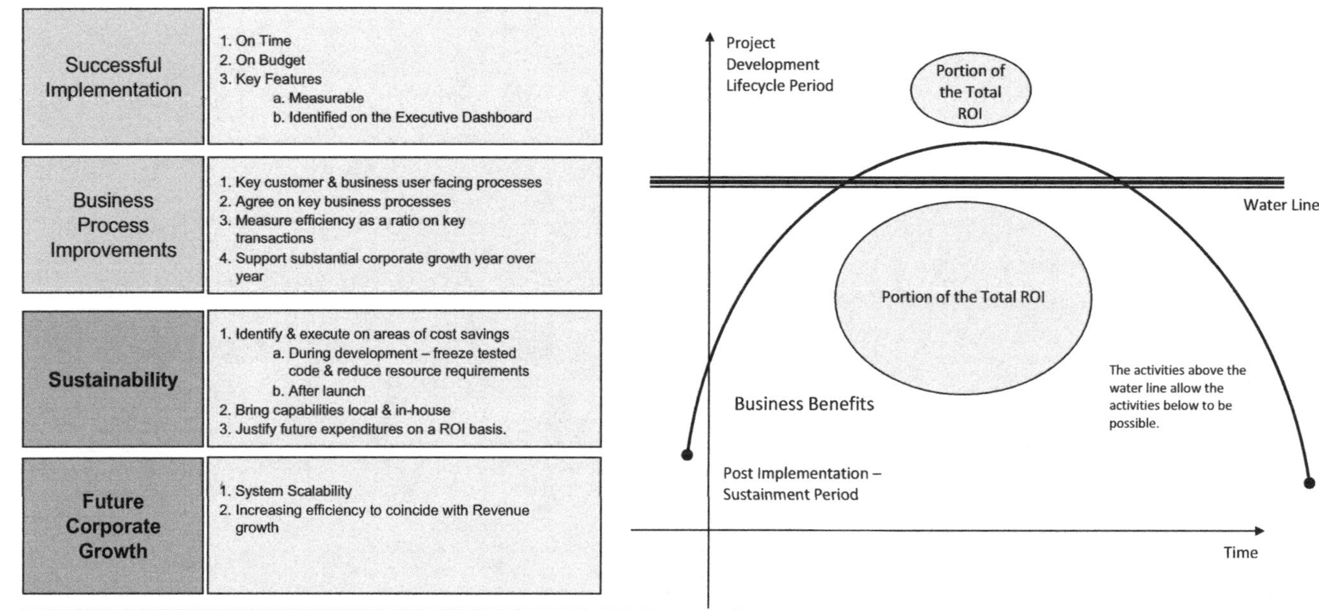

Figure 16.17 Program benefits.

Chapter 17

Case Studies

This chapter focuses on a set of case studies of projects or programs where a health check assessment was formally commissioned at various times during their project development and delivery lifecycle. Figure 17.1 shows a template of the basic information that is discussed in this chapter for each project or program that is included as a case study.

The fields included in the case study template provide the following information:

- Case Study Name: A name to distinguish the case study.
- Statement of the Problem: An overall description of the problem that the project or program was experiencing.
- Phase When Health Check Commissioned: This information is provided for analysis purposes to understand the impacts of when a health check is commissioned in the project development and delivery lifecycle.
- Technology: The core technology, without getting too specific, to protect identities of the organizations involved. Cases included in this chapter are essentially based on the most popular software packages in the marketplace.
- Geography: The number of users and the geography impacted by the initiative.
- Key Findings: The key observations made by the health check assessment team.
- Key Recommendations: The key recommendations made by the health check assessment team.
- Recommendations Adopted: Identification of the recommendations that were adopted by the organization and an explanation of why some of the recommendations were held in reserve or not taken up.
- Impact of Health Check on the Organization: The impact of the health check on the initiative in terms of business benefits and project/program metrics.

DOI: 10.1201/9781003269786-21

Case Study Name:	______________________
Statement of the Problem:	______________________
Phase When Health Check Commissioned:	______________________
Technology:	______________________
Geography:	______________________
Key Findings:	______________________
Key Recommendations:	______________________
Recommendations Adopted:	______________________
Impact of Health Check:	______________________

Figure 17.1 Case study template.

Project/Program Case Studies

Figure 17.2 shows the case studies that are discussed in more detail in this chapter. These are introduced below. Out of the six case studies included in this chapter, all accepted some of the recommendations made in the Health Check Assessment Report. Roughly half were spectacularly improved in terms of project implementation and business value realization. In one case, some of the recommendations were accepted, while the majority were not for corporate culture reasons. The remaining initiatives benefited greatly from incremental adjustments and enjoyed benefit paybacks that exceeded over 10,000% return:

Case Study	Project Name and Short Description	Point Where Health Check Commissioned
1	Financial ERP Implementation	After testing started with poor results
2	HRIS/GL Implementation	As testing phases were being pushed out
3	Mid Market ERP/Financials Implementation	After design phase and several missed deadlines
4	Retail Implementation	Proactively from the start as an assurance item
5	Global ERP/CRM Implementation	After North American launch
6	Content Management System	After several missed implementation deadlines for phase 1

Figure 17.2 Health check case studies.

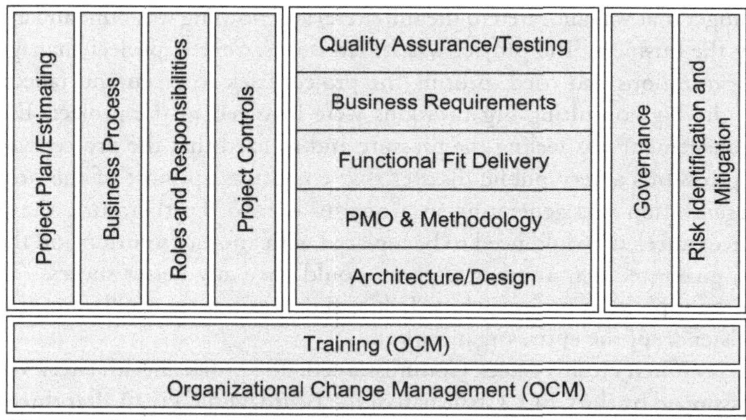

Figure 17.3 Health check evaluation framework.

Here are a list of case studies that are discussed in this chapter, as well as the type of project intervention that the health check assessment team recommended for each initiative.

Case Study 1: Financial ERP Implementation—Full project rescue.
Case Study 2: HRIS/GL Implementation—Incremental adjustment and increased benefits focus.
Case Study 3: Mid-Market ERP/Financials Implementation—Full project rescue.
Case Study 4: Retail Implementation—Recurring proactive assurance.
Case Study 5: Global ERP/CRM Implementation—Incremental adjustment.
Case Study 6: Content Management System—Incremental adjustment

Slight variations of the evaluation criteria shown in Figure 17.3 were used to evaluate each of these projects, based on the specific interests of the assessment sponsors.

Case Study 1: Financial ERP Implementation

The first example was a health check, commissioned by the CEO and Chairman of a mid-sized Financial Services (FSI) organization that was doing an end-to-end digital transformation that included the implementation of a new CRM and ERP system that had been underway but was experiencing many issues and was on the verge of being canceled.

- Case Study Name: Financial ERP Implementation (1000 users).
- Statement of the Problem: The project had been running for about 12 months and roughly $24 million had been consumed (roughly 40% of the original

budget that was allocated to the initiative) and nothing was built and approved by the business. The project was in red status. Several project managers and organizations had tried to bring the project back to green and failed. Many of the big consulting organizations were involved in the project. Executive management was feeling the pressure and realized that the project was heading towards a very public disaster that could use up most of the profits the organization was generating in a quarter or two. Furthermore, the project, once canceled, would need to be replaced with another solution and there was no guarantee that another attempt would have any better success. This was an example of a project where failure did threaten the wellbeing, if not the existence, of the entire organization.

- Phase When Health Check Commissioned: The project health check was commissioned by the CEO, Chairman of the Board, and CHRO after three missed deadlines and continued delays in the first system integration test cycle.
- Technology: One of the top ERP solutions in the world. Several modules, a data warehousing system, a risk management solution, a compliance solution, and a content management solution were also included in the architecture.
- Geography: The solution was going to cover the breadth of a single country—coast to coast. About 1000 employees and several thousand vendors would be using some functionality offered by the solution.
- Key Findings: The project was well on the way to failure and cancellation. There was no realistic project plan, roles and responsibilities were unclear, lots of destructive politics were being played, and no meaningful scope management was being enforced. It was interesting that the Board of Directors wanted a firm project plan baselined, yet an examination of the activities revealed dozens of examples that were intended to "discover additional detail or tasks to complete an objective". By definition, these would spawn additional activities, changing the baseline of the project implementation schedule.
- Key Recommendations: There were several key recommendations coming out of the health check. Chief among these was the need to have one central executive in charge of the program and to find a streamlined set of activities for a critical path through the project. See other recommendations in the discussion of the summary dashboard below.
- Recommendations Adopted: All the recommendations included in the health check summary dashboard were adopted by the Board of Directors and Executive Management.
- Impact of Health Check: The health check led to a full project rescue intervention. Three implementation dates were proposed based on a complete project reset and a newly defined critical path. The three dates represented optimistic estimating, pessimistic estimating, and a realistic viewpoint. The project was managed as an intervention and was implemented within the parameters of success accepted by the board of directors.

Summary Dashboard

Figure 17.4 shows the summary dashboard that the health check team created. From the scores allocated to each dimension in the evaluation criteria, it is clear that most dimensions were not up to par—they needed work to be functioning at an acceptable score (75% or higher, even 50% with a plan to get to 75%+ would be acceptable). The health check revealed that the following areas needed to improve:

- There were too many risks to even allow the April 30 deadline to be feasible. This health check was done about 11 months before that deadline.
- There were single points of failure, e.g. if the solution architect had left, there would be a huge gap in the resource base and this would push out the timeline.
- End-to-End Process Validation was not Complete. Transactions were being processed as standalone items. There were no process strings defined, which is what would need to implemented in a "to be world".
- Needed a clear well-communicated Definition of Project Success that was understood by all the stakeholders.
- There were some Resourcing Gaps. For example, there was no one at an Executive level who was responsible on a day-to-day basis for the project. There were also too few Business Analysts to work with the technical team to build out the solutions. This was also slowing the project down.
- Needed a process to control costs. The burn rate was approaching $3 million a month and climbing. Vendors were bringing resources onto the project with minimal supervision and responsibilities.
- There were at least four different consulting vendors/Sis, small boutiques, and employees involved in the initiative. They were not acting as one unified team.
- Lack of buy-in to project management principles (e.g. PMI and common methodologies)
- Missing a sustainability plan for after go-live
- There were clearly destructive political behaviors on the program with resources constantly pointing fingers at someone else, and being too timid to make decisions.

Health Check Recommendations

The following recommendations were considered to be key for recovering the large project:

- Hire an interim executive leader to have ownership over the program
- Find a critical path for the project plan

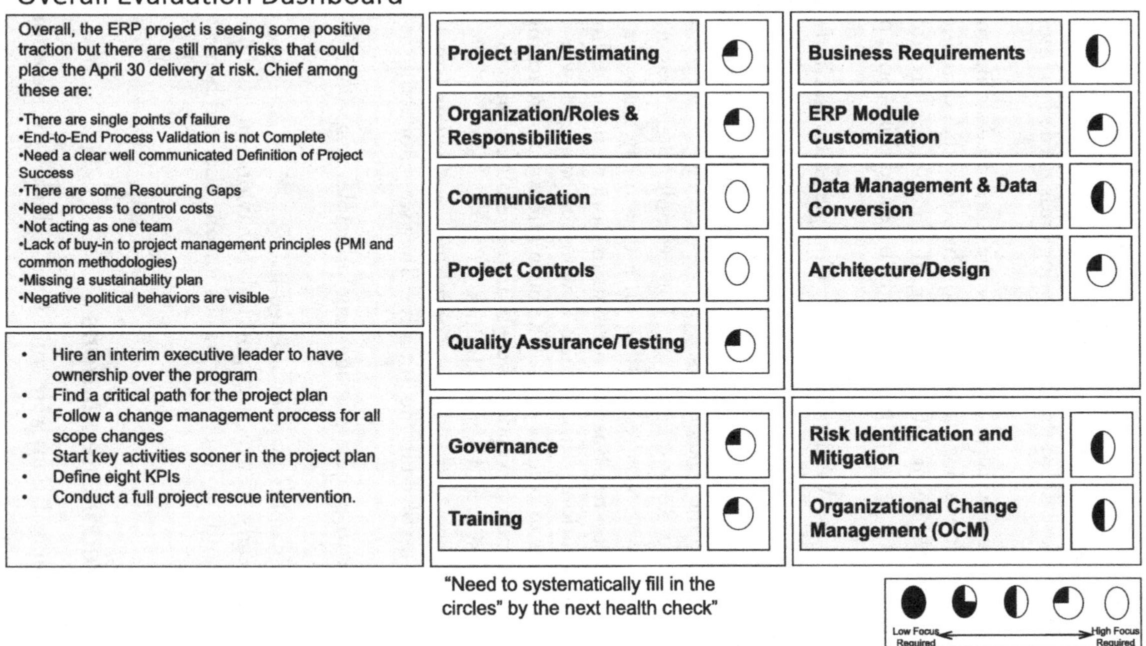

Figure 17.4 Financial ERP implementation summary dashboard.

- Follow a change management process for all scope changes
- Start key activities sooner in the project plan
- Define eight KPIs to define and manage the business benefits that would justify the project expenditure
- Conduct a full project rescue intervention and a project reset once the new leader was onboarded

Lessons Learned from This Example

1. Find a leader who is experienced in implementing large, complex projects or programs with a traceable history of success.
2. Establish a streamlined definition of success from the executive team.
3. Define the KPIs reflecting the highest business value

Case Study 2: HRIS/GL Implementation

This case study is about a Human Resources Information System and General Ledger solution that was rolled out in several countries. Overall, the project was making progress, but one of the global Chief Human Resources leaders wanted an independent health check by an experienced health check team to be completed.

- Case Study Name: HRIS/GL Implementation (5,000 users).
- Statement of the Problem: The project had been running for about eight months with a monthly burn rate commensurate with the functionality that had been defined for the first six months. The project was considered to be in Green status and seemed to be tracking well. However, deadlines started to be missed, team members started saying they were not fully engaged or did not know what they were supposed to be doing, and week-to-week delays starting setting in. Since this project was going to impact how all the employees, contractors, and vendors were going to be paid, it was very high profile.
- Phase When Health Check Commissioned: Towards the end of the first six sprints that were not in a position to be put into system integration testing.
- Technology: One of the top HRIS solutions and a separate mainstream financial system. A robust reporting solution, 30 APIs, and some regulatory systems.
- Geography: Several countries. Over 5,000 users, some unionized. Over 1,000 subcontractors.

- Key Findings: Most of the workstreams were performing well. But there were some crucial exceptions. For example, scope management was not effective. New requirements were being added with minimal push back from management, which resulted in a lack of buy-in for the project milestone dates. Some detail-oriented governance and management was needed to readjust the project's trajectory and bring it back on ae path to success. Also, some "out of the box thinking" was needed to tightly manage deliverables from some strong SMEs but who were unable to deliver if left alone for too many days. Weekly checklists needed to be produced to ensure that all the team members knew what they were doing, when they were supposed to deliver, and that they could ask for assistance.
- Key Recommendations: These included the following: (1). Hire an interim leader to run the program; (2). Identify a critical path through the project plan; (3). Maintain a tight control on scope through a tight change management process. Only business value items were considered, others were put into a backlog that would be examined after go-live; (4). Micro-management of some resources. Yes, while not desirable, in this case it made all the difference. This may be a good example of "out-of-the-box'" thinking or contrarian thinking that made a positive difference in the project.
- Recommendations Adopted: All the recommendations included in the health check summary dashboard were adopted.
- Impact of Health Check: The health check led to incremental adjustments that allowed the project to be implemented within 15% of the budget. No issues in payroll or other HR activities were reported after go-live and during the initial sustainment period of 60 days. The project was deemed to be very successful.

Summary Dashboard

Figure 17.5 shows the summary dashboard that the health check team created. While some of the dimensions need work, for the most part the scores were around 50% and there is evidence that the team could scale up from there. The health check revealed that the following areas needed to improve:

- Missing APIs for downstream systems. This was very risky because some of the APIs connected to external vendors who would need time to test the APIs once built. Their timelines would impact the HRIS implementation.
- Scope had not been baselined and there was no rigorous change control process. Users said something was important and the requirement was just added to the backlog with a high priority.
- Interim deadlines were being missed and there was no plan to make up the lost time.

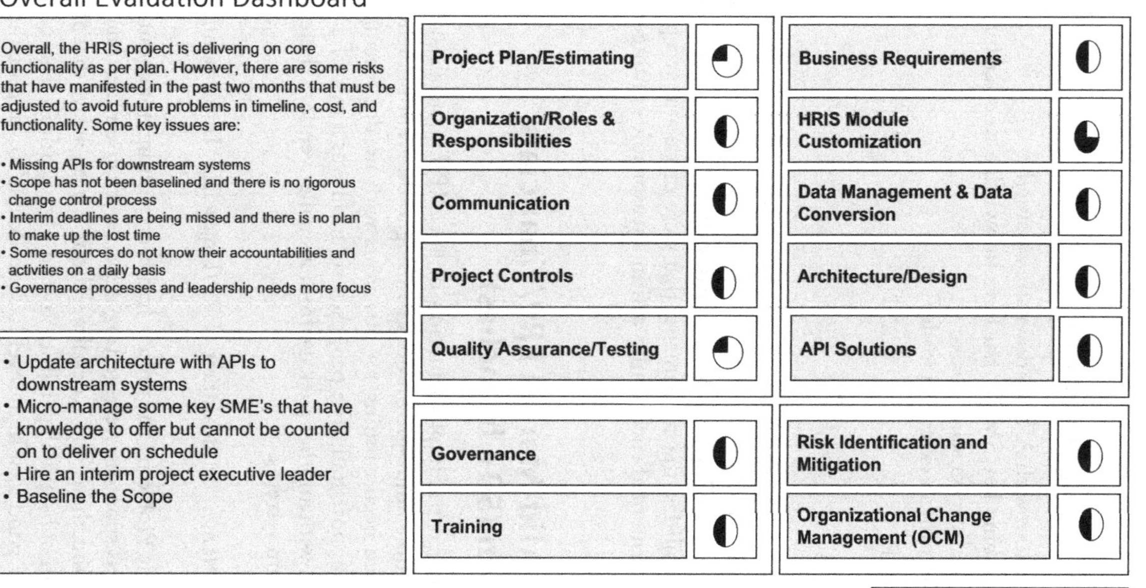

Figure 17.5 HRIS/GL implementation summary dashboard.

- Some resources did not know their accountabilities and activities on a daily basis.
- Governance processes and leadership needed more attention and support.

Health Check Recommendations

- Update architecture with APIs to downstream systems
- Micro-manage some key SME's that have knowledge to offer but cannot be counted on to deliver on schedule
- Hire an interim project executive leader
- Baseline the Scope

Lessons Learned

Many good things were happening on this project, but it was still drifting towards failure. This was because of a lack of a focused experienced leader who was not insisting on tight scope control with the relevant justification. With the relevant experience and leadership abilities, the adjustments that were made and accepted allowed the project to be implemented successfully within a reasonable contingency.

Case Study 3: Mid-Market ERP/Financials Implementation (50+ branches)

This case study involved the implementation of an ERP/Financials system in the cloud to replace multiple home-grown ones running at different branches. Some of the legacy systems had been running for 30+ years with no documentation and a few knowledgeable support staff. The proposed solution was a mix of a major ERP Azure-based solution with another package from a smaller vendor. There were also a few dozen downstream systems.

- Case Study Name: Mid-Market ERP/Financials Implementation (50+ branches).
- Statement of the Problem: The project had been running for about 14 months and the business sponsors were getting nervous because milestone dates were being missed and there was a deadline about a year away, that if breached, would result in substantial penalties to the organization. The project plan, while it looked good at a high level had no details to support the milestone dates. Some parts of the proposed solution was highly customized and was still being built when testing cycles were supposed to be starting. With 50 branches to be trained across the country, it was mandatory to have implementation dates that people would believe and plan around.

- Phase When Health Check Commissioned: The project health check was commissioned by the Business Sponsor—a COO-level executive.
- Technology: Cloud-based ERP solution to be integrated with a smaller package.
- Geography: Single country, 50 branches, about 1,000 users.
- Key Findings: The project was well on the way to failure and a catastrophic outcome. Risks were not even being acknowledged at some senior levels of the organization. The project plan was not being tracked, commitments were being made and not met. Morale was dropping as few team members believed the implementation dates were real and felt frustrated that management was not being transparent with options. There was also a lot destructive politics, but unlike in other situations, this was at the top of the organization and difficult to resolve. The very people who commissioned the health check were big contributors to the runaway project heading towards failure. Their response was to be bewildered that a "simple" project could get so out of control. It had to be someone else's fault they would repeat in interviews. Instead of making the tough scoping decisions, and realizing that they had underestimated the effort from the beginning, they kept procrastinating and looking the other way.
- Key Recommendations: These included setting direction for the project team to build a realistic project plan, acknowledge the risks so that they could be mitigated, and to find a critical path through the project plan that could be delivered in time to avoid the impending penalties.
- Recommendations Adopted: Unlike the other cases studies, most of the recommendations that were shared were, in fact, NOT adopted. Every time an interim deadline was missed, optimistic thinking was used to suggest that somehow the next once was achievable until it was not.
- Impact of Health Check: The health check explained some of the risks, but most of the recommendations were not adopted due to the politics at the top. They were able to get more funding, pay the penalties for missing the implementation dates, and stretch the project lifecycle by two years before the initiative was implemented.

Summary Dashboard

Figure 17.6 shows the summary dashboard that the health check team created. From the scores allocated to each dimension in the evaluation criteria, it is clear that most dimensions were faring very poorly. Many dimensions do not even rate a score. The health check revealed that the following areas needed to improve:

- There was no single point of accountability, responsibility & authority. Governance was shared between three vendors.

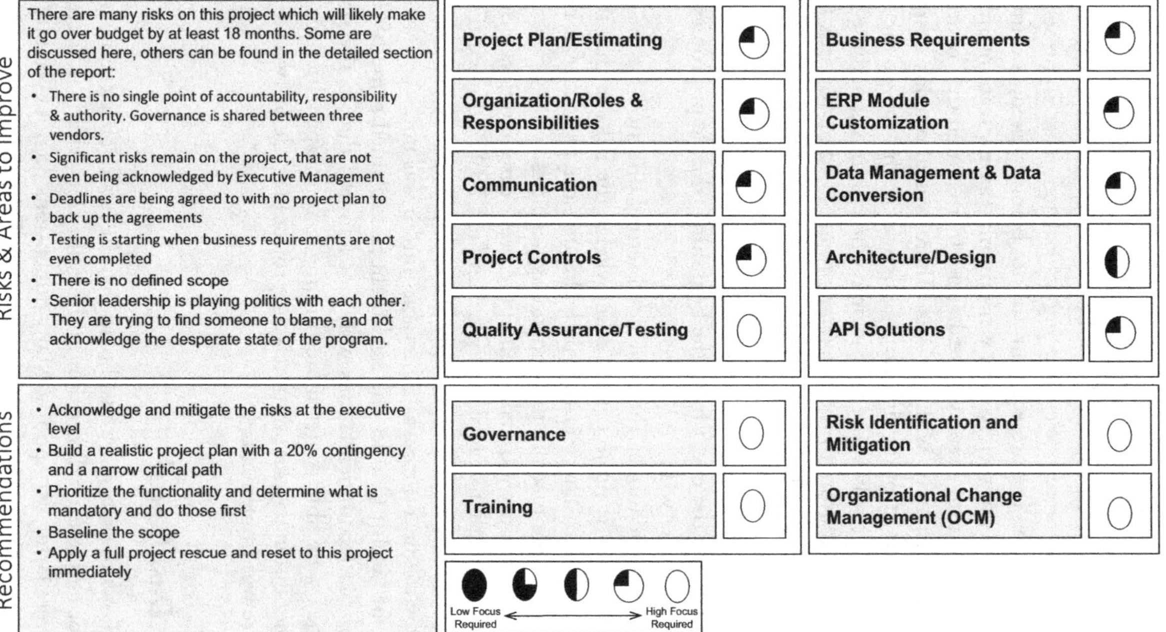

Overall Evaluation Dashboard
Risks & Areas to Improve
There are many risks on this project which will likely make it go over budget by at least 18 months. Some are discussed here, others can be found in the detailed section of the report:
• There is no single point of accountability, responsibility & authority. Governance is shared between three vendors.
• Significant risks remain on the project, that are not even being acknowledged by Executive Management
• Deadlines are being agreed to with no project plan to back up the agreements
• Testing is starting when business requirements are not even completed
• There is no defined scope
• Senior leadership is playing politics with each other. They are trying to find someone to blame, and not acknowledge the desperate state of the program.
Project Plan/Estimating
Organization/Roles & Responsibilities
Communication
Project Controls
Quality Assurance/Testing
Business Requirements
ERP Module Customization
Data Management & Data Conversion
Architecture/Design
API Solutions
Recommendations
• Acknowledge and mitigate the risks at the executive level
• Build a realistic project plan with a 20% contingency and a narrow critical path
• Prioritize the functionality and determine what is mandatory and do those first
• Baseline the scope
• Apply a full project rescue and reset to this project immediately
Governance
Training
Risk Identification and Mitigation
Organizational Change Management (OCM)
Low Focus Required
High Focus Required

Figure 17.6 Mid-market ERP/financials implementation (50+ branches) summary dashboard.

- Significant risks remained on the project, that were not even being acknowledged by the Executive Management. This frustrated any attempts to make difficult decisions and to initiate the required tradeoffs in functionality and designs.
- Deadlines were being agreed to with no project plan to back up the agreements.
- Testing started when business requirements were not even completed let alone signed off by the business owners.
- There was no defined scope let alone a baseline to work with. As use cases were defined, the scope just increased to include the new ideas from the business team.
- Senior leadership was playing politics with each other. They were trying to find someone to blame, and not acknowledge the desperate state of the program.
- Negative political behaviors were visible.

In addition to the summary key observations and risks, the assessment team also included additional details in the detailed sections of the health check report. Figures 17.7 and 17.8 show additional comments for each dimension in the evaluation criteria. Based on all this evidence, it was clear to the assessment team that the project was not going to be implemented successfully based on the original metrics. Only a full rescue would save it, not incremental adjustments or even a stop-gap solution that worked in other projects.

Health Check Recommendations

- Acknowledge and mitigate the risks at an executive level
- Build a realistic project plan with a 20% contingency and a narrow critical path
- Prioritize the functionality and determine what is mandatory and do those first
- Baseline the scope and apply strict change control based on specific business value
- Apply a full project rescue and reset to this project immediately

Lessons Learned

A project can only be successful with support from the top of the house. Destructive politics at that level did not allow the health check recommendations to be fully adopted. The health check did provide a roadmap to eventual implementation of the solution, but the cost was still higher than it needed to be if the full recommendations had been implemented.

Governance	Governance is shared between a large SI, a software vendor, and the client PMO. Who's in charge?
Risk Identification & Mitigation	Significant risks remain on the project. Eg, delivery of the base system to meet the Pilots is a key risk as user stories were still being finalized in Jan/Feb timeframe. The ones that are delivered have NOT been signed off by all of the organizations. Senior management is not in agreement on the nature and impact of the risks.
Architecture/Design	The architecture is changing and relies on interfaces that are being developed.
User Training (OCM)	User training materials rely on functionality & configuration that is not yet built and 'To Be' business processes that are still being defined. Training has to be rolled out to 50 branches.
Organizational Change Management (OCM)	The Organization design has started in Dec/Jan by all accounts, but is not yet supported by agreed to 'To Be' processes. Once done, these will need to be accepted at the branch level and then rolled out.
PMO & Methodology	The development team is using an agile methodology. The client is expecting a turnkey solution, with proven tasks and activities. Such a plan was not available in early Dec & requires months of effort to drive out. **There is no critical path defined.**

Figure 17.7 Additional details around project risks (Part A).

Project Plan/Estimating	There was no end-to-end project plan. The new version is relying on updates from an iterative process, which, by definition, contradicts the expectation of a waterfall implementation approach. There is no reasonable contingency in the estimates.
Business Requirements	Business requirements were still being signed off in January. In some cases, the user stories (600+) were being defined for the first time. These will need to be localized for the different branches.
Business Process	The 'To Be' business process has not been designed yet. The objective appears to be to drive it out as the sprints are done. This leaves little time for user training, refinement, or testing. The "As Is" version has not been signed off by the business.
Quality Assurance/Testing	User Acceptance Test cases are not yet defined. They will be built by a user team that has never done a project of this magnitude. Every branch office will have the ability to UAT their own localized version of the implementation. There is very little time available to deal with defects that will inevitably rise.
Functional Fit Delivery	Functional fit will be required for each branch. This means we may have up to 50 unique configurations that will have to be managed before a rollout wave.
Project Controls	Major scope changes are discussed and time is spent without a detailed cost/benefit analysis and a risk assessment. This can have a devastating impact on project delivery. Segregation of user duties is not defined.
Roles & Responsibilities	It is not clear who the single point of overall management is for the program or its projects. It is also unclear who owns the solution architecture, data architecture, and the business architecture.

Figure 17.8 Additional details around project risks (Part B).

Case Study 4: Retail Implementation

In this case study, the project was just beginning. The project charter had been built, and the core project team was being assembled. As the proposed system was going to replace all the existing legacy systems including warehouse management, store operations, financial systems, reporting systems, and other ERP functions, executive management felt that a parallel, recurring health check would provide good assurance and even find ways to reduce the spend, drive higher business value, and help identify and mitigate risks before they damaged the project.

- Case Study Name: Retail Implementation
- Statement of the Problem: This program did not start with a problem, but rather the CFO and CEO wanted to be proactive and drive the best business value from the program.
- Phase When Health Check Commissioned: The project health check was commissioned by the CFO with support from the CEO.
- Technology: End-to-End retail, warehousing, store operations, and financial systems needed to be integrated together.
- Geography: The solution was going to cover several states. About 900 employees and several hundred vendors would be using some functionality in the solution.
- Key Findings: As the health checks were done monthly, issues and risks could be identified before they become problems. Some of the key findings and recommendations for the 24-month lifecycle, made at different times are summarized below.
- Key Recommendations: The key recommendation was to add contingency to the project plan, create a critical path, and to identify a small set of important KPIs. A pilot store was identified to validate the initial rollout before risking the entire enterprise.
- Recommendations Adopted: All the recommendations included in the health check summary dashboard were adopted.
- Impact of Health Check: With each recommendation being adopted, the project was implemented successfully. The CEO was very satisfied to add up to 6 months to the original timeline—which he acknowledged was the right thing to do to ensure the project was sized correctly. He agreed that the original estimates were too optimistic. This avoided creating problems that could have led to an 18-month overage that the health check team warned about in their report.

Summary Dashboard

Figure 17.9 shows a point-in-time summary dashboard that the health check team created for the initiative. These would change from month to month, but any

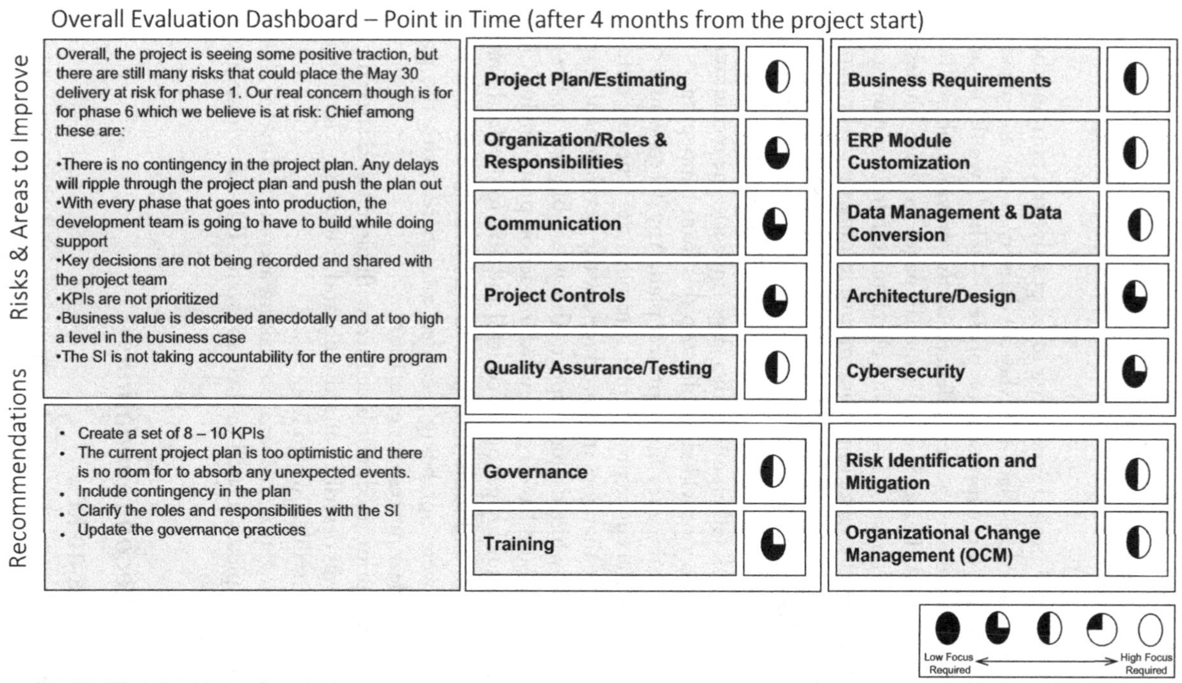

Overall Evaluation Dashboard – Point in Time (after 4 months from the project start)

Risks & Areas to Improve

Overall, the project is seeing some positive traction, but there are still many risks that could place the May 30 delivery at risk for phase 1. Our real concern though is for for phase 6 which we believe is at risk: Chief among these are:

•There is no contingency in the project plan. Any delays will ripple through the project plan and push the plan out
•With every phase that goes into production, the development team is going to have to build while doing support
•Key decisions are not being recorded and shared with the project team
•KPIs are not prioritized
•Business value is described anecdotally and at too high a level in the business case
•The SI is not taking accountability for the entire program

Recommendations

- Create a set of 8 – 10 KPIs
- The current project plan is too optimistic and there is no room for to absorb any unexpected events.
- Include contingency in the plan
- Clarify the roles and responsibilities with the SI
- Update the governance practices

Project Plan/Estimating
Organization/Roles & Responsibilities
Communication
Project Controls
Quality Assurance/Testing
Business Requirements
ERP Module Customization
Data Management & Data Conversion
Architecture/Design
Cybersecurity
Governance
Training
Risk Identification and Mitigation
Organizational Change Management (OCM)

Low Focus Required ↔ High Focus Required

Figure 17.9 Retail implementation summary dashboard.

issues that were identified would generally be addressed in the subsequent month or two after the news was delivered in a steering committee chaired by the CEO, CIO, COO, CFO, and attended by members of senior management. As shown in Figure 17.9, the project scores suggested the project was tracking well, but there was room for improvement to resolve issues that would lead to problems in the future. The health check revealed that the following areas needed to improve:

- Overall, the ERP project was seeing some positive traction but there were still many risks that could place the May 30 delivery at risk for phase 1. The real concern though was expressed for phase 6—which would be at the receiving end of all the overages experienced in the previous phases (e.g. Phase 2, Phase 3, Phase 4, Phase 5). Any time slippages in those phases would pass right through to Phase 6. The health check team felt, if unmanaged, problems would start to materialize in the one month leading up to the implementation date of Phase 1, and then compound with each phase, conceivably adding 18 months to the project timeline if all the risks they identified started to materialize. That event would be catastrophic, but at the point in time of the review, this was only a risk (albeit one with a large impact). The recommendations the health check report provided would stop this from happening.
- There was no contingency in the project plan. Any delays would consequently ripple through the entire project plan and push the schedule out.
- With every phase that goes into production, the development team was going to have to build while doing support. This was a big risk to the project, and once unleased would have a downward impact on productivity. Once this spiral starts, it can quickly get out of control and lead to the death march projects we all hear about and sometimes have to deal with.
- Key decisions were not being recorded and shared with the project team. There was no clear process for escalation.
- KPIs were not prioritized, nor baselined with targets and stretch goals.
- Business value was described anecdotally and at too high a level in the business case to be measurable after go live.
- The System Integrator (SI) was not taking accountability for the entire program, only the pieces related to their software. This left a huge gap in end-to-end planning.

Health Check Recommendations

- Create a set of 8–10 KPIs
- The current project plan was too optimistic and there was no room for to absorb any unexpected events. Include contingency in the plan
- Clarify the roles and responsibilities with the SI and get them to take end-to-end ownership over the program
- Update the governance practices

Lessons Learned

Planning with reasonable estimates is far better than being optimistic about events. That situation only results in creating issues that make situations worse and more expensive to correct over the duration of a project.

Case Study 5: Global ERP/CRM Implementation

In this case study, the organization had implemented an ERP/CRM solution in one country and wanted to roll it out globally. A health check was commissioned to determine how to learn lessons from the first implementation and to implement a global rollout that would be efficient and well received. The health check was completed over a period of six weeks about five months after the ERP system went live in a handful of countries. While the ERP implementation was running the business, there was a feeling that processes were inefficient and that there were problems building up with the solution.

- Case Study Name: Global ERP/CRM Implementation (1,200 users).
- Statement of the Problem: After the system was implemented, the business users felt they did not know how to use it efficiently. Previous processes, like month-end were taking longer to complete. Change requests were not being proceeded to add requested functionality. A large number of defects were being identified and added to the back log on a consistent basis.

  A global rollout needed to be done sooner than later to standardize the organization onto one system. Specifically, the organization was running multiple financial systems that required extensive financial consolidations every month. Many processes were being manually completed. This caused additional work effort and introduced more errors into the data. The situation was clearly unsustainable.
- Phase When Health Check Commissioned: The project health check was commissioned by the CEO after the first major phase was completed.
- Technology: Core modules of a well know ERP including manufacturing, distribution, financials, quality control and executive reporting.
- Geography: The solution from one country was going to be rolled out globally, in multiple currencies and languages.
- Key Findings: While the first phase did implement an ERP solution that was being used to manage the business in one country, many complaints were heard from the business users and technology team during the health check interviews. Different groups were working overtime to get their work done on a regular basis. This work load grew with the increased volume of transactions going through the system. This suggested that the more work put through the system, the greater the work load on the users. This goes counter to the

objectives of implementing an ERP solution in the first place and the situation was not sustainable.

- Key Recommendations: The health check review recommended that the current implementation be stabilized before creating a global template. They also recommended revamping the user training and then to determine whether efficiencies could be gained. The global launch would only work when the new metric was met.
- Recommendations Adopted: All the recommendations included in the health check summary dashboard were adopted at the CEO level and mandated to the organization as a whole.
- Impact of Health Check: The approach recommended by the health check was effective and let to a global rollout that did not experience the same issues as the first implementation. The organization was effective in getting and implementing lessons learned.

Summary Dashboard

Figure 17.10 shows the summary dashboard that the health check team created. They used the grades given to each dimension as a baseline to signal when the global launch should be executed. The left column was the current grade, while the right column was the target grade. Positioning the review in this format shows that organizations do not necessarily have to be at 75% or higher in every dimension. It takes time, money, and experience to achieve the higher evaluation scores. Figure 17.11 shows a view of the maturity levels that organizations implementing

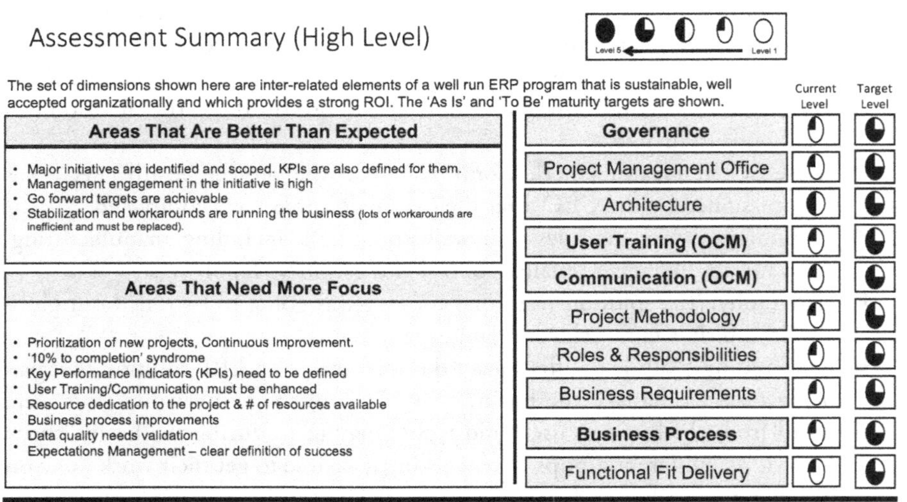

Figure 17.10 Global ERP/CRM summary dashboard.

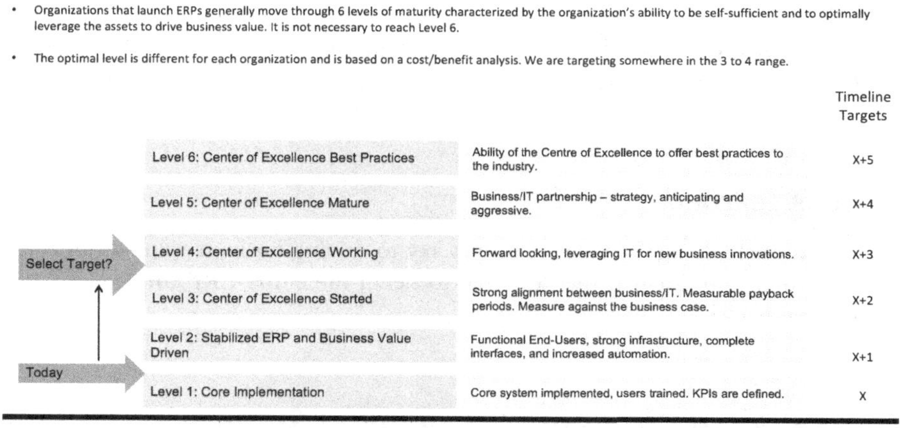

- Organizations that launch ERPs generally move through 6 levels of maturity characterized by the organization's ability to be self-sufficient and to optimally leverage the assets to drive business value. It is not necessary to reach Level 6.
- The optimal level is different for each organization and is based on a cost/benefit analysis. We are targeting somewhere in the 3 to 4 range.

	Level	Description	Timeline Targets
	Level 6: Center of Excellence Best Practices	Ability of the Centre of Excellence to offer best practices to the industry.	X+5
	Level 5: Center of Excellence Mature	Business/IT partnership – strategy, anticipating and aggressive.	X+4
Select Target?	Level 4: Center of Excellence Working	Forward looking, leveraging IT for new business innovations.	X+3
	Level 3: Center of Excellence Started	Strong alignment between business/IT. Measurable payback periods. Measure against the business case.	X+2
	Level 2: Stabilized ERP and Business Value Driven	Functional End-Users, strong infrastructure, complete interfaces, and increased automation.	X+1
Today	Level 1: Core Implementation	Core system implemented, users trained. KPIs are defined.	X

Figure 17.11 Program maturity levels.

ERP solutions generally experience. Depending on their past experience, many will start at Maturity Level 1. They use external vendors and consultants to bring in the experience related to the higher levels of maturity and then over time transfer that into an inhouse Center of Excellence. A timeline can also be set as a target for when the organization is expected to transition to the next level. Here were the major observations from the review:

- Major initiatives are identified and scoped. KPIs are also defined for them.
- Management engagement in the initiative is high
- Go forward targets are achievable
- Stabilization and workarounds are running the business (lots of workarounds are inefficient and must be replaced).
- Many initiatives are experiencing the "10% to completion" syndrome. They seem to be stuck at 90% done and can't get to the finish line.

Health Check Recommendations

- Prioritization of new projects, Continuous Improvement.
- Focus on one initiative stuck at the "10% to completion" syndrome and find a way to get it over the finish line before consuming resources on all the stuck projects.
- Key Performance Indicators (KPIs) need to be defined.
- User Training/Communication must be enhanced.
- Resource dedication to the project & # of resources available have to be increased to meet the project plan requirements.

- Business process improvements need to be documented.
- Data quality needs validation and a threshold that is acceptable to the business.
- Expectations Management—clear definition of success required by the Executive Leadership Team.

Lessons Learned

Organizational Change Management was key to driving business value on this initiative. Going too fast had the potential to derail the entire ERP implementation on a global basis.

Case Study 6: Content Management System

In this case study, a global organization headquartered in Europe was under competitive pressure to launch an online content management system. The implementation date was a hard stop—determined by when their competitors were expected to launch their rival content management systems and consumer products.

- Case Study Name: Content Management System (1 million+ users).
- Statement of the Problem: The project had been running for about 8 months. During weekly status reports, most of the news was expressed in a positive light. However, some key pieces of the architecture kept getting postponed—with optimism that it would not be a problem. One of the senior IT sponsors saw red warning flags and called for a health check to be done.
- Phase When Health Check Commissioned: The project health check was commissioned by VP Technology and Delivery during the testing cycle of one of the development sprints.
- Technology: Content Management Tool, Website Development Tools, eCommerce Engine.
- Geography: The solution was going to be localized for Europe but could be accessed globally.
- Key Findings: The status reporting was found to be too optimistic. The architectural components that kept slipping past their deadlines were, in fact, showstoppers. The team members who should have been focused on getting those done were allocated to other projects. The business owners were feeling the pressure and felt the project was not going to succeed. There were also major communication gaps on the project development team. With developers in different time zones, they were not communicating in a timely manner so requests would take over a day to even get a response.
- Key Recommendations: The assessment recommended that the technical lead stay in the same physical location as the business sponsors so that they could

collectively agree on ways to streamline the functionality to meet the mandatory implementation date. Key technical resources were to be focused on completing the critical architectural components that were in the critical path. A daily check was recommended and attendance was mandatory regardless of time zone.

- Recommendations Adopted: All the recommendations included in the health check summary dashboard were adopted.
- Impact of Health Check: The health check led to some key adjustments to resourcing, priorities, and inter-team communication. The project was implemented on the original implementation date.

Summary Dashboard

Figure 17.12 shows the summary dashboard that the health check team created. At first glance the project seemed to be doing well with a few areas that needed focus. However, on deeper inspection of the impacts of these pieces, the project was in fact on the way to failure. Here were the observations from the project team:

- The Content Components were well behind schedule and were on the critical path.
- Too much functionality was defined to be included in the mandatory implementation timeframe.
- The development team, being in different time zones, was not working well together. There was too much delay in communicating back and forth.

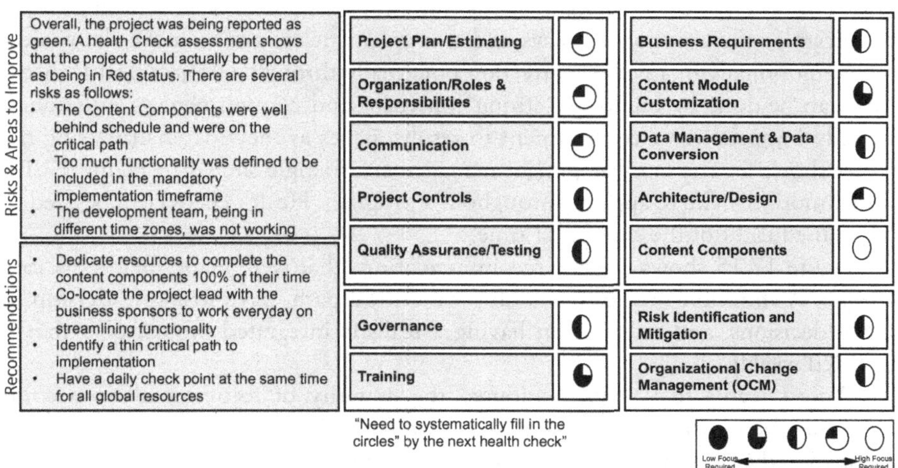

Figure 17.12 Content management system summary dashboard.

Health Check Recommendations

- Dedicate resources to complete the content components 100% of their time.
- Co-locate the project lead with the business sponsors to work every day on streamlining functionality.
- Identify a thin critical path to implementation.
- Have a daily checkpoint at the same time for all global resources to increase communication and awareness.

Lessons Learned

Project management needs to be wary of optimistic reporting. Had the health check not been commissioned when it was, this project would have failed with global ramifications to the organization. It would have been front-page news. The relatively short duration of the health check still provided significant recommendations that were able to put the project back on a path to success.

Closing Perspective

This chapter provided a set of case studies for health check assessments that followed the health check methodology shown in Figure 17.13. The health checks were commissioned at different points in their respective development lifecycles. All of the assessments provided value, but the magnitude of this was entirely determined by the number of recommendations adopted by management.

Every large program follows a curve of emotion that includes optimism, despair, anger, disbelief, and then hope that the initiative would do better. It is imperative to recognize the emotional valleys and to implement actions to move the project team emotionally in a positive direction potentially through a project health check. This can be done by building a strong consensus and commitment to milestones. Equally important is a commitment to resolve issues as they materialize using the levers shown in the familiar project management triangle shown in Figure 17.14. This Emotional Curve appears throughout a program. Health checks can be used to lower the height of the curve over time.

Figure 17.15 shows the key recommendations that were made for the six case studies. A common theme is to look for a critical path, have strong leadership to make decisions, and to insist on having a realistic integrated project plan that is updated weekly.

Project teams that actively adopted the majority of recommendations coming from the health check experienced a strong turnaround, project success, and attained higher business value. This is shown in Figure 17.16. There is also a correlation between the magnitude of business value received by completing health checks earlier in the project lifecycle, and to retain them over the lifecycle of the project.

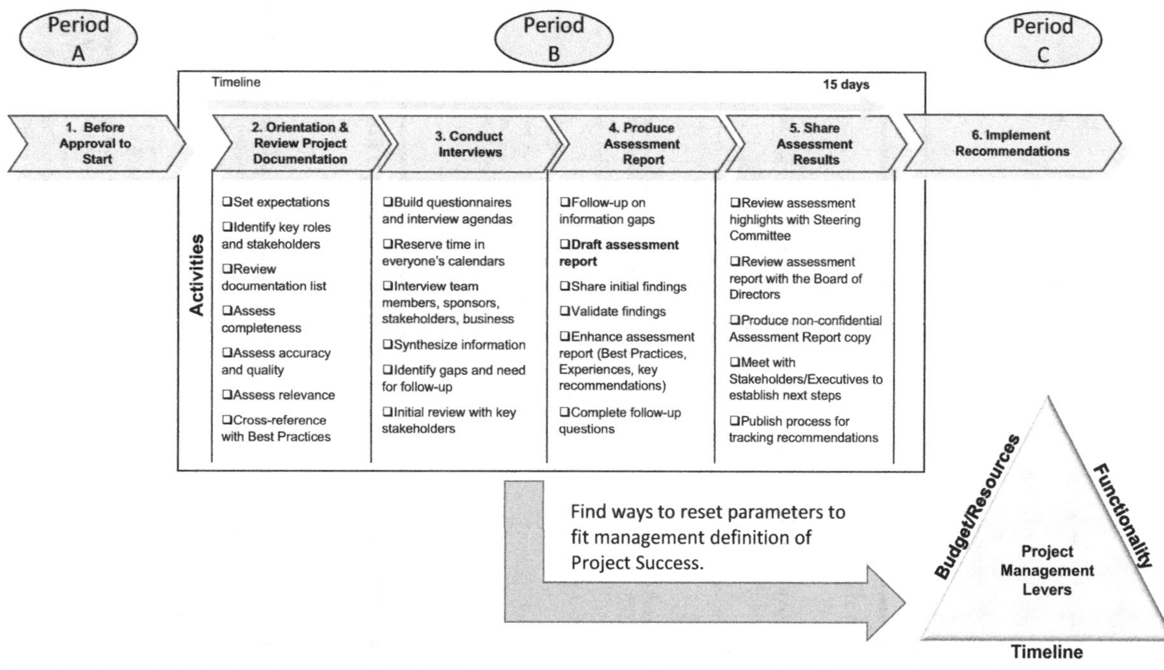

Figure 17.13 Health check methodology.

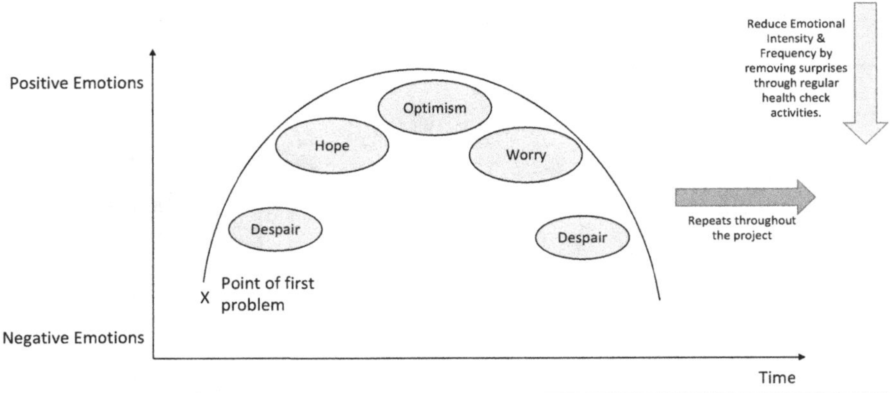

Figure 17.14 Emotional curve.

Case Study	Project Name and Short Description	Key Recommendations (up to three)
1	Financial ERP Implementation	• Complete Project Reset and rescue • Hire an interim Project Executive
2	HRIS/GL Implementation	• Identify a critical path through the project plan; • Maintain tight control on scope through a tight change management process. • Streamline the project plan
3	Mid Market ERP/Financials Implementation (50 Branches)	• Acknowledge and mitigate the risks at an executive level • Build a realistic project plan with a 20% contingency and a narrow critical path • Apply a full project rescue and reset to this project immediately
4	Retail Implementation	• Create a set of 8 – 10 KPIs • The current project plan is too optimistic and there is no room to absorb unexpected events. • Include contingency in the project plan
5	Global ERP/CRM Implementation	• Complete the Organization Change Management activities • Re-take the user training to gain efficiencies
6	Content Management System	• Dedicate users to work on the critical path • Co-locate the decision makers to keep finding a critical path

Figure 17.15 Health check case studies with the top 1, 2, 3 key recommendation (that make the difference).

Case Study	Project Name and Short Description	Impact of the Health Check Recommendations
1	Financial ERP Implementation	The project was rescued and delivered within the revised budget and timeline that was acceptable to executive management.
2	HRIS/GL Implementation	The project required some adjustment and met the parameters of project success.
3	Mid Market ERP/Financials Implementation	Only some recommendations were adopted. The project was very late but eventually went live.
4	Retail Implementation	The recurring health check drove strong business value and mitigated strong risks that would have been vey problematic.
5	Global ERP/CRM Implementation	The global implementation met the parameters set by executive management based on learnings from the first country wide implementation. This was an OCM solution.
6	Content Management System	This project was successfully implemented on time and budget.

Figure 17.16 Health check case studies with impact of adopted recommendations.

Chapter 18

Conclusion

This book has looked at every aspect of conducting and benefitting from a Health Check. As was shown in previous chapters, health checks pay for themselves and provide many multiples of business value almost every single time they are employed. Generally, a single recommendation that is adopted, even if it saves the project as little as one month, provides multiples of financial benefits that far outweigh the cost of the Health Check. Figure 18.1 shows a sample calculation which demonstrates the multiples of business value generated by health checks from a highly conservative perspective. The figure calculates the value of a health check to an organization over a five-year period. Based on a projected 25% benefit of a health check, an investment of $250,000 would yield a benefit of $25 million. This is the experience on some projects that organizations using health checks have enjoyed in the past. On most projects, there would be enough of a benefit through the identification of risks or meaningful recommendations to accelerate development making the investment in the health check pay for itself many times over.

According to one study, most organizations that used a health check during an ERP/CRM/HRIS system implementation later said: (1) They should have used the health check team from the start of the project; (2) The Health Check paid for itself many times over. (3) They believe this process would have saved them a lot of time and money, and would have produced better results the sooner they started; (3) They would recommend the use of Health Checks on other future programs and to their colleagues in other organizations at any point in the project development lifecycle.

Several chapters in this book discussed how to draw maximum value from Health Checks for the organization. In the rarer instances where a commissioned health check is itself not working well, the assessment sponsors should be direct with the health check leaders and reiterate the expectations in the engagement letter, recast the health check team, or reduce the scope of the health check. Some examples of drivers that could cause this include a clash between personalities, lack

DOI: 10.1201/9781003269786-22

•	Cost to Develop and Implement IT program:	$50 Million
•	Cost of running the program over 5 years (20%) or $10million/yr x 5	$50 Million
•	Benefits from implementation after year 1: $50million/yr x 4	$200 Million
•	Net Benefits after 5 Years: $200 million - $50 million - $50 million	$100 Million
•	Cost of Health Check: $50k /yr	$250,000
•	Reduce Benefit Leakage due to recommendations from Health Check: 25%	$25 Million

Figure 18.1 Calculating health check benefits.

of relevant experience in the health check team, political struggles, and others. This does not happen very often, but the sponsors should remain vigilant in order to drive maximum value for the organization.

The Health Check Components

This book examined all aspects of a health check process and supporting components aligned to a proven health check methodology. Figure 18.2 shows a list of the topics covered in this book.

- Driving Business Value
- Health Check Methodology
- Roles and Responsibilities
- Types of Health Checks
- Health Check Evaluation Criteria
- Project or Program Deliverables
- Health Check Questionnaire
- Health Check Interviews
- Health Check Assessment Report
- Project Intervention & Rescue Techniques
- Completing the Health Check
- Health Check Support in Sustainment

Figure 18.2 IT project or program health check components.

Driving Business Value

There can be several drivers to justify a project or program, including those listed in the following categories:

- Regulatory: The project or program may be required by the regulator (usually by specific dates). This requirement is the cost of doing business and the initiative can be considered to be mandatory.
- Deal with Reputational Risk: This could be any initiative being undertaken to protect the reputation of the organization without a direct expectation of any other financial reward, although there may be indirect benefits.
- Competitors offer it (table stakes): If the competition is providing services, the driver may be to scale to their offerings. There should be direct benefits of doing this, but the business case will partly be driven by having no choice to advance or lose marketshare to the competition and potentially go out of business.
- Legacy Systems are Archaic: The systems can no longer be modified to serve new business requirements, or are becoming too expensive to maintain and operate. At some point, legacy systems become risky and expensive to maintain and must be replaced, and in some cases, vendors no longer support the older systems so there is no choice but to upgrade. Similarly, custom developed solutions are also difficult to support as the technical skillsets become more difficult to find over time for the older technologies. The choice of how much to spend on a new system can be determined by a business value case after accounting for a baseline that must be supported to keep the older platforms running in the first place.
- Need Access to New Markets: Modifications are needed for the system to enter new markets, perhaps with new currencies, languages, and new customer channels.
- Cost Savings: The system is expected to result in measurable savings in operating costs or by keeping costs level while increasing customer transactions and volumes dramatically.
- Increased Market Share: This should translate into increased revenues, but the success of the implementation will determine the impact on the financial bottom line. A bad implementation might open up market share, but still be more costly than it needs to be.
- Organizational Restructuring: This could be a drive for operational efficiencies or a positioning in the marketplace.
- Increased Revenue: The IT systems might require more functionality, with specific robustness, to drive increased revenues into the organization.

Aside from the regulatory category which is mandated to stay in business, the others at some level drive business value. Even Reputational Risk can be measured against impact on sales through increased customer satisfaction. Organizational restructuring would also have an impact on business value through more efficiency (e.g. through cost savings).

As we discussed in previous chapters, business benefits breakdown into several periods of time and the largest potential impacts comes from a generally underserved period of time after the initiative is implemented into production. Figure 18.3 shows the tip of the iceberg of driving business value. Most of the business value is realized during the sustainment period which is typically 5 to 20 times the duration of the implementation phase. The work clearly doesn't stop at implementation, though everything done during those phases enables the achievements that can be enjoyed subsequently in the sustainment phase.

Figure 18.4 offered a view of this relationship where the traditional view of a successful project is too limited. From a health check perspective, the assessment team needs to review the future sustainment plans and ensure that CSFs and KPIs are included throughout the project development lifecycle and then measured and reported during sustainment to executive management and the Center of Excellence.

Health Check Methodology

The health check methodology described in this book is a proven framework that has been used on many projects and programs around the world and delivered assessment results that drove higher business value and rescued projects that were at various stages of potential failure. Figure 18.5 shows the three periods of the methodology, which has five leading phases. As shown in an altered cube view, these phases are somewhat iterative in terms of how they interact with the deliverables, interviews, presentations, and then the implementation of recommendations. There will be some back and forth between these outcomes until the health check is officially completed.

Key Roles and Responsibilities

Several levels of roles and responsibilities were discussed in this book. Figure 18.6 shows two sets of resources. The left side of the figure shows the roles related to a project or program. Usually someone at the senior levels of the organization will commission a health check on a proactive or reactive basis, for reasons as follows:

- Drive business value
- Get another independent opinion
- Get assurance that the project is heading towards a successful conclusion
- Use it as insurance to show that due diligence was done, but problems still emerged
- Perform due diligence on the program for another party such as the Board of Directors or for a corporate merger

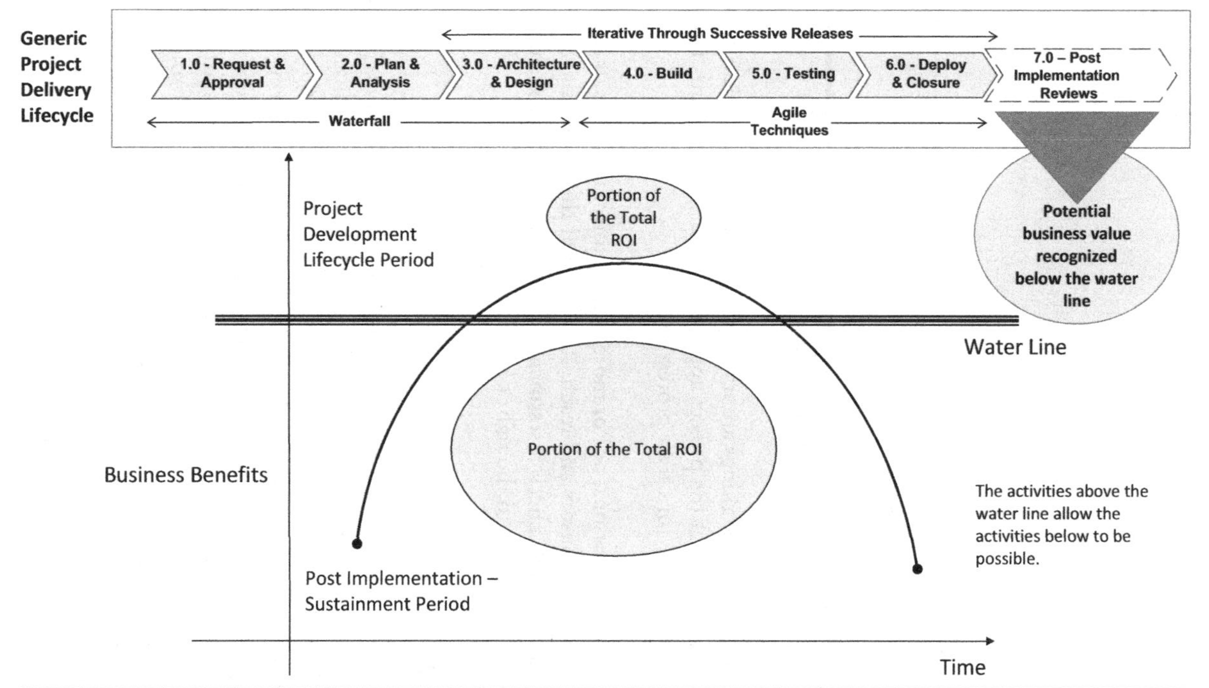

Figure 18.3 Business benefits below the waterline.

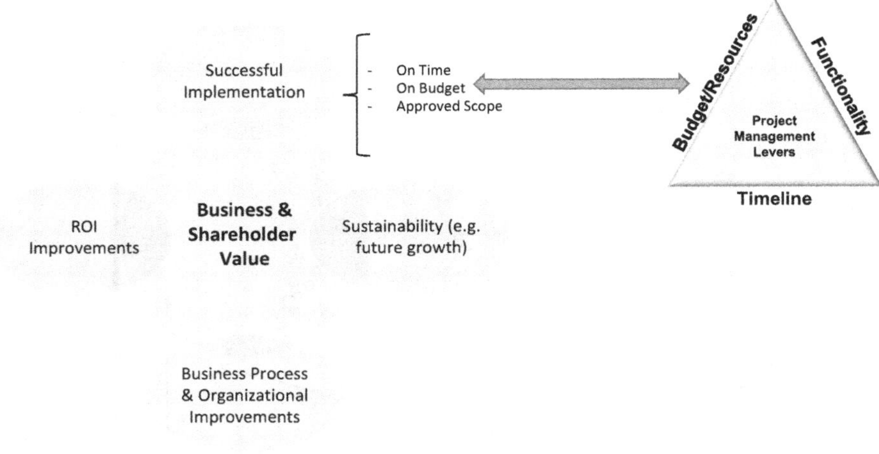

Figure 18.4 Driving business and shareholder value phases.

- Reaction to news that things are starting to go badly on a project or program
- Starting to worry that the project appears to be heading towards failure
- Get some insurance for career protection

Based on these or other reasons, one or more senior project resources or stakeholders will act as assessment sponsors and reach out to one of the parties shown in Figure 18.7 to conduct a health check assessment of the initiative. The members of the assessment team are shown to the right of Figure 18.6.

Types of Health Checks

The impetus that drove the assessment sponsors might also dictate the type of health check that they would like to commission. Figure 18.8 shows the different types of common health checks used in the industry. In some cases, a one time health check can be commissioned and then turned into one of the other recurring ones, either monthly, at specific methodology gates, or at some other major events.

The expression of interest from members of the project team starts a dialogue with the health check team. This team can come from a variety of sources, as was shown in Figure 18.7. Each of the sources offers pros and cons discussed in several chapters of this book.

The dialogue starts between the two teams to finalize a scope of work and either a project charter (for internally sourced health checks) or a statement of work (for externally sourced health checks) is built and officially signed off. The next section summarizes completion of this document.

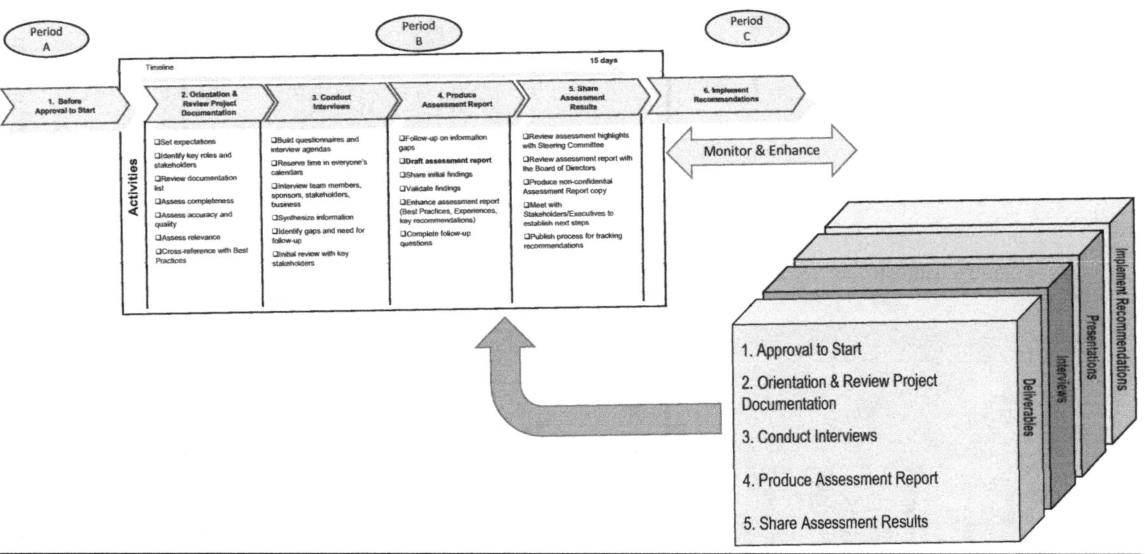

Figure 18.5 Health check methodology.

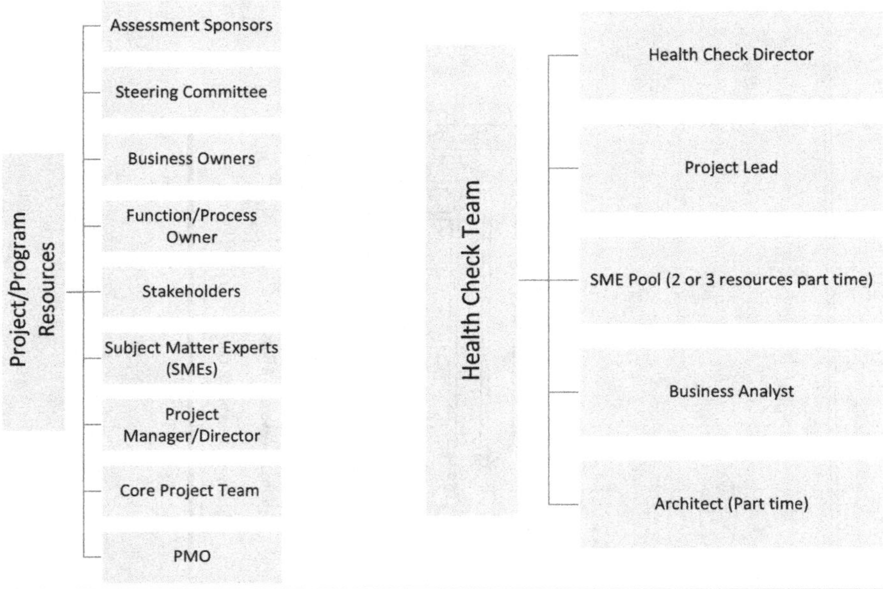

Figure 18.6 Roles and responsibilities.

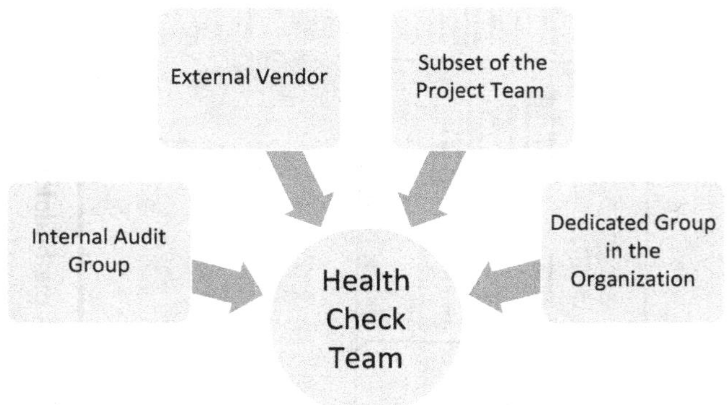

Figure 18.7 Sourcing the health check team.

Health Check Evaluation Criteria

The scope of work includes the areas of the project or program that will be reviewed as part of the health check. A starting point for the conversation is shown in Figure 18.9, which serves as a starting point for the evaluation criteria. Each rectangle or bar represents a dimension that is included in the health check. This can

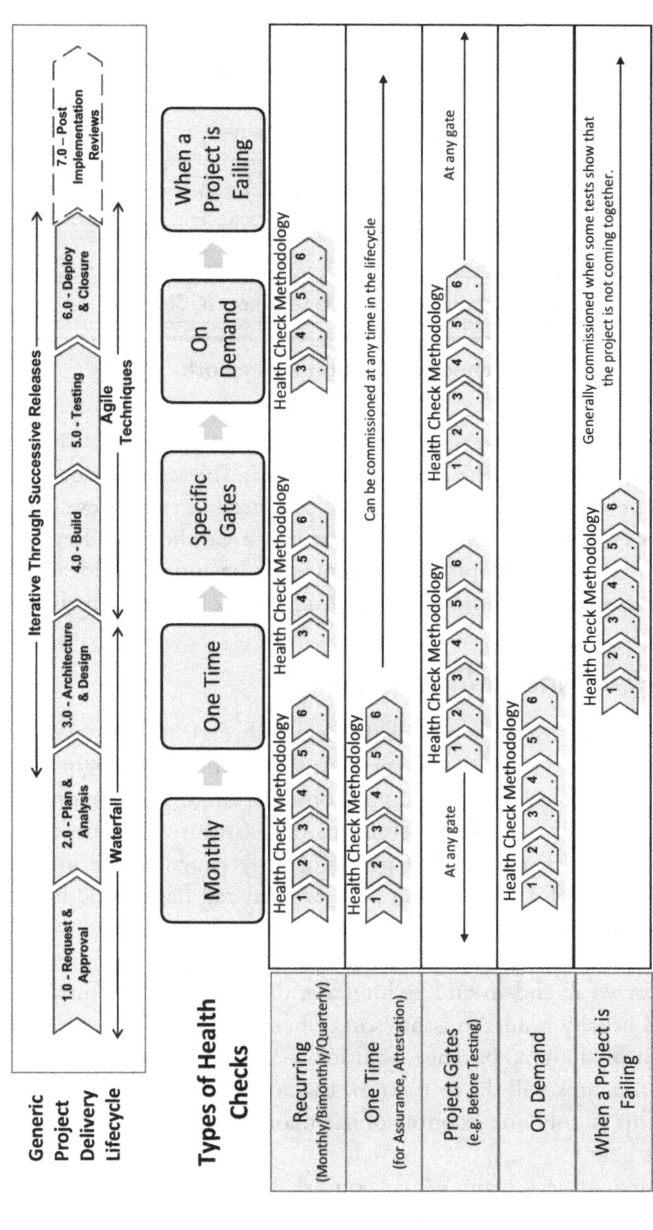

Figure 18.8 Types and timing of health checks.

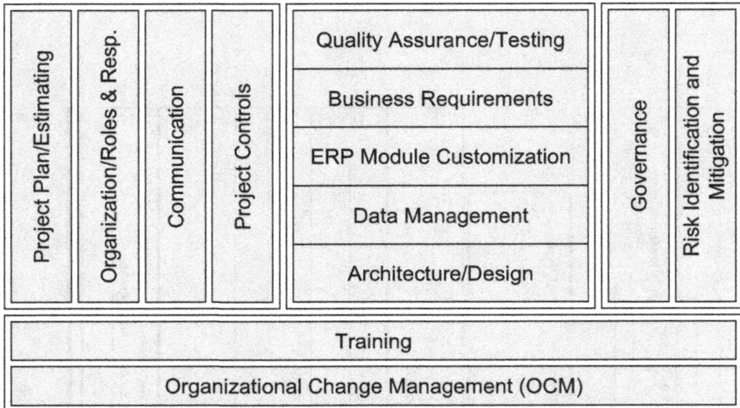

Figure 18.9 Sample health check evaluation framework.

be customized for the specific scope that is being commissioned. The customized figure should be included in the scoping document. The scoping document can be finalized with the deliverables expected to be produced in the review. These include a Health Check Assessment Report and Potentially a Confidential Report for a limited reading audience. The scoping document must be approved, ideally in writing, from both the assessment sponsors and the leadership of the health check team.

Project or Program Deliverables

As part of the early stages of the review, the health check team must get access to the project or program deliverables. They need to review these and begin to keep notes that include observations, comments, questions, warnings, and other meta information that will eventually make its way into the final assessment report in some form.

The state of the deliverables is a powerful early gauge of the initiative's well-being. There are lots of early warning flags or even red flags to be found in these deliverables. Some examples include the following:

- Missing or weak end-to-end architecture diagrams: This is surprisingly common and usually results in issues somewhere down the line, even when delivering out-of-the-box package solutions. Without a documented solution architecture, how will the team know that all the integration points have been tested? This is only one example of the many issues that will arise if there is a weakness here.
- Fragmented project plan: When you ask for a project plan to review, very often you are sent one, but upon closer inspection, what you're really getting are a collection of project plans from different parts of the organization typically one or two per vendor that is engaged. Not only is this a warning flag,

but a red flag that suggests the team is not working together, that there are integration gaps, and communication gaps. This suggests that someone needs to take charge of the integration activities. Look to see if there is a missing role in the roles and responsibilities documentation and flag this as a major warning in the assessment report.

- No roles and responsibilities document: There is nothing to rely on here except written roles and responsibilities. Do not assume that a job title is enough. What are the project managers responsible for? Who is setting baseline activities? Who is in charge of making decisions for the project? What is being tested? Who is involved in project escalation? Is someone looking after the risks? A thorough roles and responsibilities document that is broadly shared should be in place and signed off by management
- Lack of requirements: Regardless of the methodology that is being built, there have to be business requirements, nonfunctional requirements, and use cases. These deliverables should be captured and transferred from the business to the business analysts to the technical teams. There must be evidence of a process that is thorough, understood, and repeated - with signoffs. If the team does not have the time to get the requirements right, how are they going to find the time to get the solution right when there is ambiguity in what is being built.
- Lack of signoffs: It's common to find that signoffs are missing or anecdotal on important deliverables in many organizations. This is a red warning flag (not orange, not yellow, but red) and the assessment team should look deeper to see if there are missing signatures on other key deliverables that were prerequisites to deliverables currently being developed. This could result in confusion and rework later in the project timeline.
- No Review Mandates: Is an architecture review board mandate documented? If not, how are architecture decisions being made? How many other boards and committees have missing mandates and unclear authority? What is the difference between the Steering Committee and the Operating Committee?

The review team needs to examine the full list of deliverables that are applicable to the methodologies being used and ask key questions, such as the following:

- Are there any missing deliverables?
- Are the deliverables that are being shared incomplete?
- How do we know the content is correct?
- What is the process for review and signoff?
- Are the future deliverables accounted for?
- What are the risks? Are they being mitigated?
- Is the team making assumptions that are wrong, inconsistent, or incomplete?
- Are there too many unknowns in the documentation?
- Are key decisions being made and documented?

A review of the deliverables produces a list of questions and areas to dig into deeper during the next part of the health check methodology.

Health Check Questionnaire

Using the information gleaned from the deliverables and the scoping document, the health check team needs to produce a a set of customized questionnaires for 1–1 or 1–many meetings with team members. Aside from common questions about the state of the project, there should be specific questions matched to the role of the attendee (e.g. questions on Devops for an operations director). This is an excellent opportunity to get more information directly from those closest to the project. This is part of the discovery cycle to get as much information about the project as possible.

Health Check Interviews

The health check team organizes a set of interviews with team members to go through the questionnaires. Earlier chapters of the book described the type of emotions team members would be experiencing at this stage of the project whose management has commissioned a project review. The interviews offer one of the best opportunities to build trusted relationships with members of the team that are open to them and looking for assistance. The health check interviews end the formal discovery activities. There may be several rounds of interviews and some informal interactions between the teams as more questions and answers are shared.

Given the diverse opinions and attitudes that are generally encountered during these project team-health check team interviews, it is necessary to confirm information that was gathered through other sources that could include documentation or other team members. It's important to offer and honor confidentiality during the sessions, and to include information in an aggregated format on the final reports.

Health Check Assessment Report

The process of completing the assessment health check report is iterative and takes about a 1/3 of the time allotted for the health check lifecycle. As shown in Figure 18.10, there is a sample Table of Contents that can be customized to specific initiatives. The report goes through several states from interim to final. The main part of the report that executive members spend the most time on are the Overall Executive Review Dashboard and the Summary Dashboard. These contain the scores for each the dimensions in the review criteria.

Figure 18.11 shows a variation of the dashboards already seen in this book. This was an example of a follow-on health check after an initial assessment was done about eight to nine months earlier. At that first assessment, the health check team recommended targets for each evaluation criteria. Figure 18.11 shows the progress

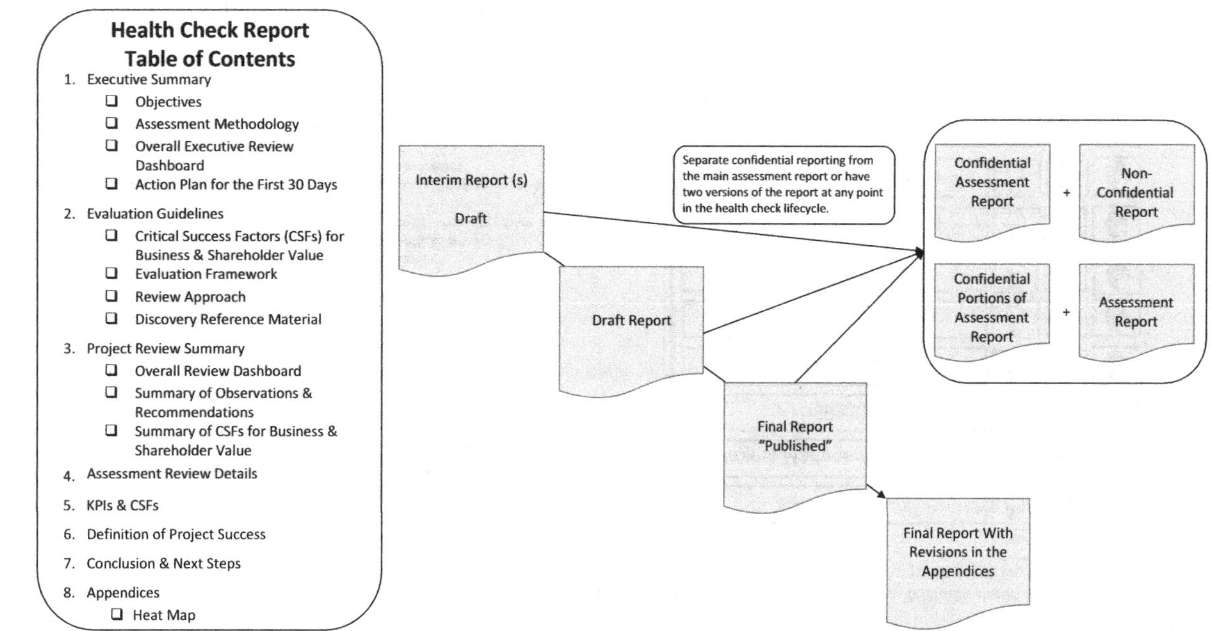

Figure 18.10 Health check assessment report states & table of contents.

State of the ERP & BI Program (Jan -> Sept)
Well done
Needs Work
When we met in Jan we discussed the results of a detailed assessment of the ERP program & end-user survey. We have made improvements in key areas that drive the ERP program & the IT Team's ability to deliver it. These are reflected in the Sept column. As you can see we have observed steady progress in the program in the past nine months.
Updates
1. We are making progress on the key tent pole priorities
• Sales Management
• Budget Planning and Forecasting
• China ERP Implementation
• Germany ERP Implementation
• Continuous Improvement Priorities
2. We have removed/reduced risks we were facing from the ERP implementation
• Appropriate staffing
• Methodologies
• Improved business requirements
• Better communication with offices & team
3. We are seeing some reduction in IT costs relative to where they would have been (Rightsizing costs)
4. We are identifying potential savings and efficiencies in other areas
• Documentation of business processes
• Identification of efficiencies
3. We have improved the overall IT infrastructure (e.g. Disaster Recovery Planning)
Jan
Sept
Target
Governance
Project Management Office
Architecture
User Training (OCM)
Communication (OCM)
Project Methodology
Roles & Responsibilities
Business Requirements
Business Process
Functional Fit Delivery

Figure 18.11 Summary dashboard showing progress.

the team made in each of the dimensions that were reviewed first in January and then again in September of the same year. The first column of scores represents the target for the subsequent review.

Project Intervention and Rescue Techniques

Once the discovery activities in the health check methodology are completed, the team begins to analyze and socialize findings with members of the project team to confirm facts and observations. The project may be tracking well in all the metrics, in which case the assessment team can recommend techniques to drive business value higher and to position the initiative to meet or exceed other stretch goals. It's also very common to discover that some sort of adjustments needs to be initiated to bring the project back on track. Figure 18.12 shows the common types of interventions that the project team might recommend: A small adjustment, Stop-Gap measures, Partial rescue, or a full project rescue. The techniques to do each of these, when properly applied can provide significant success. There have been projects with a global span to small organizations that have been saved with these techniques.

Completing the Health Check

With all the observations and recommendations in place, the health check assessment report can be finalized. The next step in the health check methodology, as shown in Figure 18.13, is to complete one or more presentations to the following groups: the assessment sponsors, project team, operating committee, steering committee, and potentially depending on the size, complexity, and impact of the initiative to the Board of Directors and other groups in the organization. These are important to set the stage for generating buy-in and support across the organization to implement the recommendations so that the initiative and the organization can benefit. The health check team should also clarify any future role on the initiative after the formal part of the engagement is completed. In many instances, the

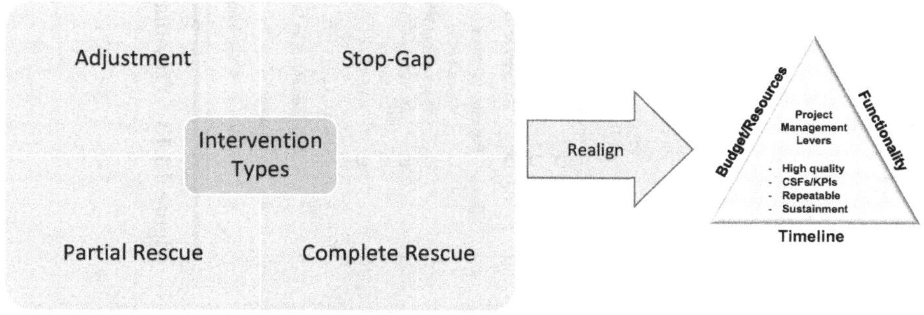

Figure 18.12 Realigning with success metrics.

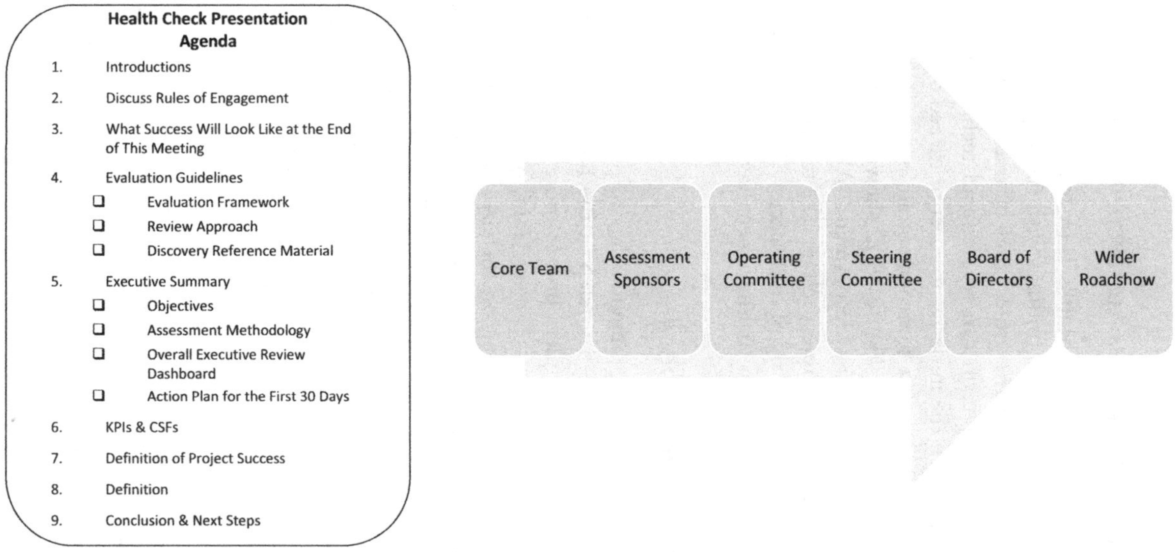

Health Check Presentation Agenda

1. Introductions
2. Discuss Rules of Engagement
3. What Success Will Look Like at the End of This Meeting
4. Evaluation Guidelines
   - ❑ Evaluation Framework
   - ❑ Review Approach
   - ❑ Discovery Reference Material
5. Executive Summary
   - ❑ Objectives
   - ❑ Assessment Methodology
   - ❑ Overall Executive Review Dashboard
   - ❑ Action Plan for the First 30 Days
6. KPIs & CSFs
7. Definition of Project Success
8. Definition
9. Conclusion & Next Steps

Core Team

Assessment Sponsors

Operating Committee

Steering Committee

Board of Directors

Wider Roadshow

Figure 18.13 Presentation roadshow.

conclusion of the health check assessment does not neatly coinside with completion of the project or program. Nonetheless, the recommendations should be looking into the post-implementation period to ensure the organization is set up for success when the system is live.

Diagnostic and Intervention Toolkit

While all the deliverables in the methodology have their importance, the ones shown in Figure 18.14 are integral parts of what could be termed as a diagnostic and intervention toolkit. The contents or lack thereof in these deliverables tells a story or provides clear clues on the weaknesses and strengths of an initiative and where to focus efforts if an intervention is required. Some key considerations are included below:

Project Charter

The project charter sets the parameters for an initiative so it's surprising that many projects or programs either do not have one or is a very skeletal document. The health check team should issue warnings and recommendations in the assessment report under any of the following conditions:

- There is no project charter
- The project charter has not officially been signed off by executive management
- The project charter does not contain a strong business case or point to one
- Business and technology owners have not been identified
- The deadlines are not realistic
- There is missing information or the document is too vague

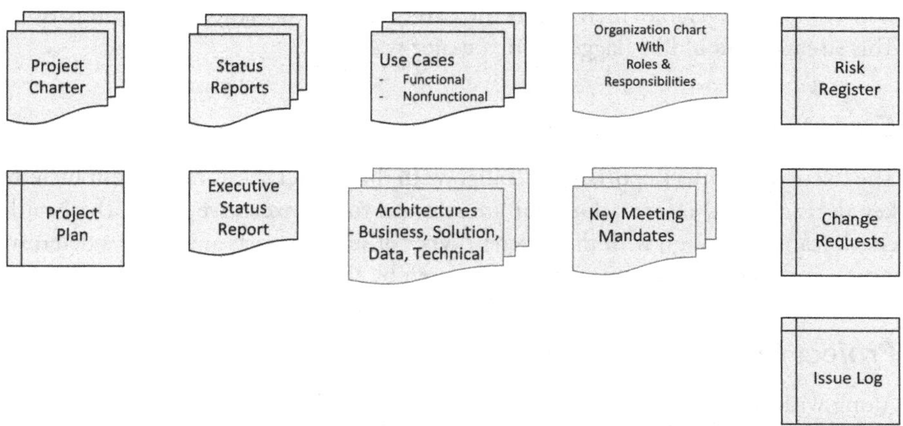

Figure 18.14 A diagnostic and intervention toolkit (top level).

- There is not an approved budget
- There is missing or inconsistent information

Status Reports

The project or program status reports always tell a story about how well a project is being managed. Status reports should be mandated on every program. There is sometimes a tendency to delay them or to skip content. They should be a living and breathing record of how well an initiative is progressing. Here are some key considerations:

- Project status reports are not being done
- There is an insufficient level of detail in the status reports
- Issues and risks are being included but there is no evidence they are being tracked or actively managed
- Status reports are not being completed on a meaningful schedule
- They are not being reviewed in project status meetings
- All the key dimensions of the project are not included in the status reports
- Are executive decisions being recorded in the status reports (and then in a common location)?

Is the status report always in "Green" status? That's a warning flag that the team is not aware of issues that are confronting the project. It may be true that the project is indeed being managed well and the project is well on it's way to a successful conclusion. But a situation where the status is staying "Green" over extended periods of time is worth a deeper look.

The status of the different parts of the status report (Red, Orange, Yellow, Green) should match the information in the rest of the status report. For example, if a status report is saying the project is "Green" and there are extensive risks, pending decisions, or late deliverables then clearly the two types of information are incompatible. This situation should be flagged with a major warning.

Executive Status Reports

The Executive Status Reports should align with the project status reports but include key decisions and information that are relevant to the executive team. The health check team must align with the different types of status reports and make a determination if the correct information is being seen by the executive team.

Project Plan

Along with the status reports, the project plan also tells a story about the program. Ideally there should be a high-level plan that shows the entire initiative on a page or two with key deliverables and milestones clearly marked. There should also be a detailed plan that shows tasks and resources aligned to the high-level plan so that a reviewer can switch between the two and follow the entire story. The word "story" has been used several times intentionally. A story implies a level of completeness, internal logic, and threads that connect different parts of the program together. It's critical to be able to follow the story when all the deliverables in this section are being reviewed. For example, are the resources identified in the project plan included in the organization charts? Some key considerations for the health check review include the following:

- Is there an end-to-end plan or just individual schedules from different members of the team?
- Is the project plan at a level of detail that can be tracked?
- Are resources included at the correct level (e.g. activities)?
- Does the time for activities and tasks seem reasonable for the team that is assigned?
- Are completed tasks being marked accordingly?

Architectures

Architecture is the backbone of the entire solution. Many projects delay documenting the different architectures, which can be problematic. For example, how can the team know what to test in the end-to-end solution if no one can provide the details of what's being implemented. How will the non-functional test scenarios be identified? There are several levels of architecture that should be documented, as shown in Figure 18.15. For the different types of architectures (e.g. Business, Solution, Application, Technical, Data, Network, and others), there should be "As Is" (current state) and "To Be" (Future State) versions. These can also start with a conceptual view

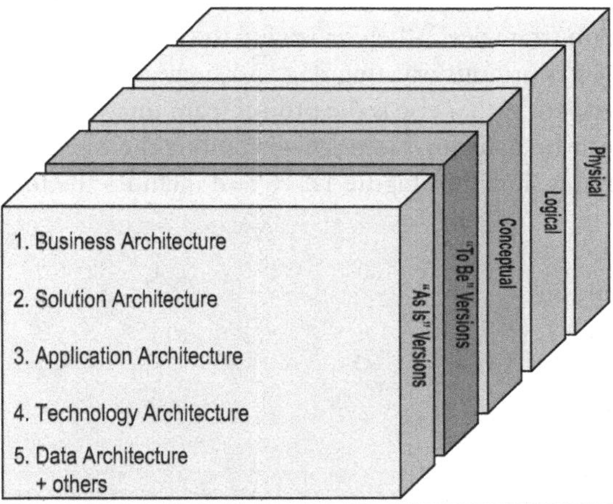

Figure 18.15 Architecture groupings.

with a deeper logical view and then ultimately a physical view of each architecture. There can also be interim "To Be" states reflecting interim release implementations.

Use Cases

The business requirements must be captured in some way. These can be in requirements documents, functional (both functional and non-functional) documents, and/or a series of prioritized use cases.

Organization Chart with Roles and Responsibilities

The organization charts should cover both the project team and other key users in the organization. These documents are important to satisfy a variety of needs during a project health check assessment, an intervention, and a full project rescue. Some considerations are as follows:

- The charts show the level of the resources being assigned to the project
- Reporting structures in a matrix environment are captured
- They offer a checklist to build the training plan
- They offer a checklist to determine who to interview, the knowledge they have, and the functional groups they influence

The organization charts are one of the first documents that should be requested by a health check team.

Risk Register

The risk register should be a very public document containing all the reasonable risks and mitigation strategies. When reviewing the register, if obvious risks are missing, then that is an enormous warning flag and suggests that a deeper dive be done by the assessment team. What else is the project team unaware of? There are a variety of formats that can be used for the risk register, but the essential information that should be captured is shown in Figure 18.16 and includes the following:

- Risk name
- Risk description
- Impact Severity
- Probability of Occurrance
- Risk raised by
- Mitigation Strategy
- Resolution Required Date
- Status
- + other information that is of interest to the organization

Description Key Risks	Raised By	Severity of Impact	Occurrence Probability	Mitigation Strategy	Timeline for Mitigation

LEGEND:

Severity	Impact Severity
High	Impacts all metrics
Medium	There is a possibility of impact on one or more metrics
Low	Although there is some impact, it can be contained.

Figure 18.16 Sample risk log.

Change Requests

The list of change requests is also an important indication of the completeness of the business requirements. If a lot of changes have been identified, the health check team needs to understand the underlying reasons for these. Were requirements missed? Are business users having a difficult time making up their minds? Is there really an end vision for the project?

On one past case, a senior executive asked an interim program director who was moving to a new organization whether the project was going to be implemented on a new schedule after the old one was missed. The program director said that if the business requirements were signed off by a specific date (that he gave) and that the change request log had a low number of items, then the project would likely make the date and that there was a confirmed end vision. The date was missed and the project was eventually canceled after spending a lot of money in capturing, prototyping, and configuring ever changing business requirements

Issue Log

In addition to risks, there should be an active issue log that contains a list of all the issues ever raised on the project. Issues that are closed should be moved out of the active list in some way. The health check team should look for evidence that the list is actively being managed and issues are being owned and resolved. Issues are sometimes used to delay making important decisions and conclusions. The list is an indication about the number of unknowns that are building up on the initiative and how they could impact work already completed at a future date.

Closing Perspective

This chapter provided a brief recap of the health check techniques and principles covered in this book. A large number of health checks completed in the past have shown that they provide enormous benefits to organizations by driving business value higher, identifying problems before they can impact a project's success, and to identify techniques to save projects that are hurtling towards failure.

Health checks generally have a nominal cost, regardless of who is executing them, and the payback can be measured in many multiples of the investment. Figure 18.17 shows the roller coaster of emotions that are generally felt on IT projects and programs. Health Checks can provide a meaningful anchor to get the project team to focus on common objectives.

Applying the Health Check Methodology and producing an assessment report filled with facts and recommendations has been shown to produce outstanding results that any organization can realize. Over time the emotional rollercoaster can begin to flatten and disappear as shown in Figure 18.18.

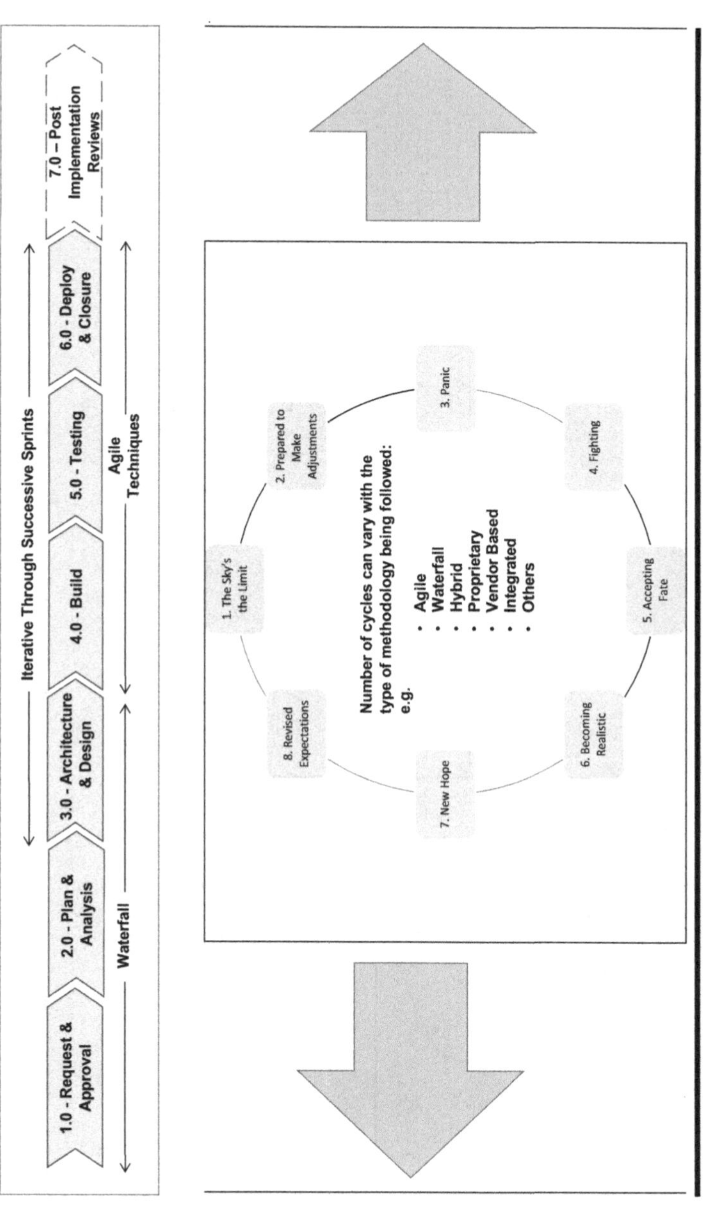

Figure 18.17 Emotional rollercoaster.

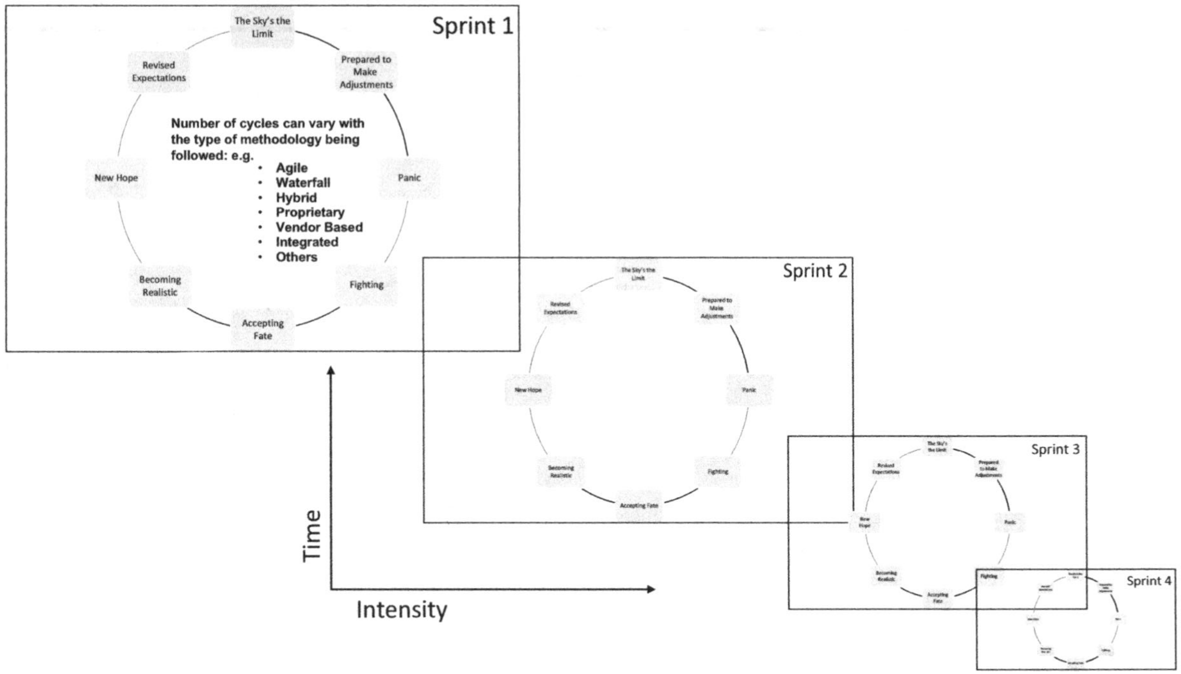

Figure 18.18 Emotional rollercoasters by sprint.

Appendix: IT Project or Program Health Check Questionnaire

The following questionnaire was used to collect executive, business, and technology experiences with IT Project or Program Health Checks.

Key Findings:

- 95% of the participants had been involved in health checks in the past or were in organizations that used them in some way (either through an external vendor or internal staff).
- 95% of the participants confirmed they would use health checks in the future.
- 90% saw more value in the health check in many multiples above the cost.
- 100% of the participants confirmed they would recommend others to use health checks, at least surgically, on projects and programs.

Let's Get Started | **Return completed surveys to:**

Your Full Name: (First Last)	
Title:	
Contact Email:	
Cell Phone (optional);	
Primary Industry of Employment:	
Permission to include your name in the Acknowledgement Section:	

Size of Organization (employees) (check one)	☐ Less than 100	☐ 100 or more but less than 500	☐ 500 or more but less than 1000	☐ 1000 or more but less than 10000	☐ 10000+
Organization Revenue (US$) (check one)	☐ Less $10 Mil	☐ $10 mil or more but less than $100 mil	☐ $100 mil or more but less than a $Bill	☐ $Bill or more but less than $10 Bil	☐ $10 Bill+

Figure A.1a Health Check Survey Page 1.

IT Health-Checks | **Return completed surveys to:**

Have you used Project Health Checks on IT programs/Projects?	☐ Yes
How often & when do you use them?	
Scope & Expectations of the Health Check Program?	
Contracted Deliverables:	

Figure A.1b Health Check Survey Page 2.

Overview **Return completed surveys to:**

Did they provide value?	☐ Yes	Explain	
Describe the Value	Budget Timeline	Business Functionality Quality	Business Value Other
Comments:			

Suggest Areas of Improvement:

Would you consider IT Health Checks in the future? Explain?

Figure A.1c Health Check Survey Page 3.

Business Value Levers **Return completed surveys to:**

Please check all the items in the following list that apply when identifying anticipated business benefits from a project or program:

New Opportunities	☐ Yes	☐ No	Reason (if known)	☐ Don't Know/NA
Cost Savings	☐ Yes	☐ No	Reason (if known)	☐ Don't Know/NA
Revenue Generation	☐ Yes	☐ No	Reason (if known)	☐ Don't Know/NA
Omni Channel	☐ Yes	☐ No	Reason (if known)	☐ Don't Know/NA
Table Stakes?	☐ Yes	☐ No	Reason (if known)	☐ Don't Know/NA
Market Share ?	☐ Yes	☐ No	Reason (if known)	☐ Don't Know/NA

Figure A.1d Health Check Survey Page 4.

Business Value Levers				**Return completed surveys to:**
Organization Restructuring	☐ Yes	☐ No	____ Reason (if known)	☐ Don't Know/NA
Other	____ Explain			
Other	____ Explain			
Other	____ Explain			

Figure A.1e Health Check Survey Page 5.

Bibliography

Alter, Stephen. 1999. *Information Systems: A Management Perspective*. 3rd ed. Boston, MA: Addison-Wesley.

Band, Williams A. 1991. *Creating Value for Customers*. New York: John Wiley & Sons.

Bender, Paul S. 1983. *Resource Management*. New York: John Wiley & Sons.

Booch, Grady. 1996. *Object Solutions. Managing the Object-Oriented Project*. Boston, MA: Addison-Wesley.

Brooks, Frederick P. 1995. *The Mythical Man-Month*. Anniversary ed. Boston, MA: Addison-Wesley.

Carson, Willian M. Spring 1994. "Strategic Planning and the Anatomy of Change." *Journal of Management Consulting*, 1, 30–39.

Champy, James. 1995. *Reengineering Management: The Mandate for New Leadership*. New York: Harper Collins.

Connell, John and Linda Shafer. 1994. *Object-Oriented Rapid Prototyping*. Englewood Cliffs, NJ: Prentice-Hall.

Cummings, Thomas and Christopher Worley. 1997. *Organizational Development and Change*. 6th ed. Mason, OH: International Thompson.

Cusumano, Michael and Richard Shelby. 1995. *How the World's Most Powerful Software Company Creates Technology, Shapes Markets, and Manages People*. New York: Free Press.

Frohnhoefer, Ray R. 2019. *Risk Assessment Framework: Successfully Navigating Uncertainty*. Los Angeles: PPC Group, LLC.

Kerzner, Harold. 2017. *Project Management: A Systems Approach to Planning, Scheduling, and Controlling*. 12th ed. New York: Wiley.

McCarthy, Robert. 2020. *Lean Six Sigma: A Practical Guide for Getting Started with Lean Six Sigma along with How It Can Be Integrated with Agile and Scrum*. Independently published.

Purba, Sanjiv and Bob Delaney. 2003. *High Value IT Consulting*. New York: McGraw-Hill Osborne.

Purba, Sanjiv and Joseph Zucchero. 2004. *Project Rescue: Avoiding a Project Management Disaster*. New York: McGraw-Hill Osborne.

Wysocki, Robert 2019. *Effective Project Management: Traditional, Agile, Extreme, Hybrid*. Indianapolis, IN: Wiley.

Index

Page numbers in *italics* refers figures and **bold** refers tables.

C

D

E

Printed in the United States
by Baker & Taylor Publisher Services